Voltairine de Cleyre

Poems, Essays, Sketches and Stories, 1885–1911

edited by
ALEXANDER BERKMAN

Biographical sketch by Hippolyte Havel

The Selected Works of Voltairine de Cleyre

Edited by Alexander Berkman
This edition © 2016 AK Press (Chico, Oakland, Edinburgh, Baltimore)

ISBN: 978-1-84935-256-7
Library of Congress Control Number: 2016941999

AK Press	AK Press
370 Ryan Ave. #100	33 Tower St.
Chico, CA 95973	Edinburgh EH6 7BN
USA	Scotland
www.akpress.org	www.akuk.com
akpress@akpress.org	ak@akedin.demon.co.uk

The above addresses would be delighted to provide you with the latest AK Press distribution catalog, which features books, pamphlets, zines, and stylish apparel published and/or distributed by AK Press. Alternatively, visit our websites for the complete catalog, latest news, and secure ordering.

Cover design by Margaret Killjoy | birdsbeforethestorm.net

Printed in the USA

This edition is a facsimile reprint of the original, by Mother Earth Publishing Association, 1914.

Contents

Poems

4

CONTENTS

Essays

Sketches and Stories

Introduction

"**N**ATURE has the habit of now and then producing a type of human being far in advance of the times; an ideal for us to emulate; a being devoid of sham, uncompromising, and to whom the truth is sacred; a being whose selfishness is so large that it takes in the whole human race and treats self only as one of the great mass; a being keen to sense all forms of wrong, and powerful in denunciation of it; one who can reach into the future and draw it nearer. Such a being was VOLTAIRINE DE CLEYRE."

What could be added to this splendid tribute by Jay Fox to the memory of VOLTAIRINE DE CLEYRE? These admirable words express the sentiments of all the friends and comrades of that remarkable woman whose whole life was dedicated to a dominant idea.

Like many other women in public life, VOLTAIRINE DE CLEYRE was a voluminous letter writer. Those letters addressed to her comrades, friends, and admirers would form her real biography; in them we trace her heroic struggles, her activity, her beliefs, her doubts, her mental changes—in short, her whole life, mirrored in a manner no biographer will ever be able to equal. To collect and publish this correspondence as a part of VOLTAIRINE DE CLEYRE's works is impossible; the task is too big for the present undertaking. But let us hope that we will find time and means to publish at least a part of this correspondence in the near future.

The average American still holds to the belief that Anarchism is a foreign poison imported into the States from decadent Europe by criminal paranoiacs. Hence the ridiculous attempt of our lawmakers to stamp out Anarchy, by passing a statute which forbids Anarchists from other lands to enter the country. Those wise Solons are ignorant of the fact that Anarchist theories and ideas were propounded in our Commonwealth ere Proudhon or Bakunin entered the arena of intellectual struggle and formulated their thesis of perfect freedom and economic independence in Anarchy. Neither are they acquainted with the writings of Lysander Spooner, Josiah Warren, Stephen Pearl Andrews, William B. Greene, or Benjamin Tucker, nor familiar with the propagandistic work of Albert R. Parsons, Dyer D. Lum, C. L. James, Moses Harman, Ross Winn, and a host of other Anarchists who sprang from the native stock and soil. To call their attention to these facts is quite as futile as to point out that the tocsin of revolt resounds in the writings of Emerson, Thoreau, Hawthorne, Whitman, Garrison, Wendell Phillips, and other seers of America; just as futile as to prove to them that the pioneers in the movement for woman's emancipation in America were permeated with Anarchist thoughts and feelings. Hardened by a fierce struggle and strengthened by a vicious persecution, those brave champions of sex-freedom defied the respectable mob by proclaiming their independence from prevailing cant and hypocrisy. They inaugurated the tremendous sex revolt among the American women— a purely native movement which has yet to find its historian.

VOLTAIRINE DE CLEYRE belongs to this gallant array of rebels who swore allegiance to the cause of universal liberty, thus forfeiting the respect of all "honorable citizens," and bringing upon their heads the persecution of the ruling class. In the real history of the struggle for human emancipation, her name will be found among the

foremost of her time. Born shortly after the close of
the Civil War, she witnessed during her life the most
momentous transformation of the nation; she saw the
change from an agricultural community into an industrial
empire; the tremendous development of capital in this
country, with the accompanying misery and degradation
of labor. Her life path was sketched ere she reached the
age of womanhood: she had to become a rebel! To stand
outside of the struggle would have meant intellectual
death. She chose the only way.

VOLTAIRINE DE CLEYRE was born on November 17,
1866, in the town of Leslie, Michigan. She died on
June 6, 1912, in Chicago. She came from French-Ameri-
can stock, on her mother's side of Puritan descent. Her
father, Auguste de Cleyre, was a native of western Flan-
ders, but his family was of French origin. He emigrated
to America in 1854. Being a freethinker and a great
admirer of Voltaire, he insisted on the birthday of the
child that the new member of the family should be called
Voltairine. Though born in Leslie, the earliest recollec-
tions of Voltairine were of the small town of St. John's,
in Clinton County, her parents having removed to that
place a year after her birth. Voltairine did not have a
happy childhood; her earliest life was embittered by want
of the common necessities, which her parents, hard as
they tried, could not provide. A vein of sadness can be
traced in her earliest poems—the songs of a child of
talent and great fantasy. A deep sorrow fell into her
heart at the age of four, when the teacher of the primary
school refused to admit her because she was too young.
But she soon succeeded in forcing her entrance into the
temple of knowledge. An earnest student, she was gra-
duated from the grammar school at the age of twelve.

Strength of mind does not seem to have been a characteristic of Auguste de Cleyre, for he recanted his libertarian ideas, returned to the fold of the church, and became obsessed with the idea that the highest vocation for a woman was the life of a nun. He determined to put the child into a convent. Thus began the great tragedy of VOLTAIRINE's *early life*. Her beloved mother, a member of the Presbyterian Church, opposed this idea with all her strength, but in vain: the will of the lord of the household prevailed, and the child was sent to the Convent of Our Lady of Lake Huron, at Sarnia, in the Province of Ontario, Canada. Here she experienced four years of terrible ordeal; only after much repression, insubordination, and atonement, she forced her way back into the living world. In the sketch, "The Making of an Anarchist," she tells us of the strain she underwent in that living tomb:

"How I pity myself now, when I remember it, poor lonesome little soul, battling solitary in the murk of religious superstition, unable to believe and yet in hourly fear of damnation, hot, savage, and eternal, if I do not instantly confess and profess! How well I recall the bitter energy with which I repelled my teacher's enjoinder, when I told her I did not wish to apologize for an adjudged fault as I could not see that I had been wrong and would not feel my words. 'It is not necessary,' said she, 'that we should feel what we say, but it is always necessary that we obey our superiors.' 'I will not lie,' I answered hotly, and at the same time trembled lest my disobedience had finally consigned me to torment! I struggled my way out at last, and was a freethinker when I left the institution, three years later, though I had never seen a book or heard a word to help me in my loneliness. It had been like the Valley of the Shadow of Death, and there are white scars on my soul yet, where

Ignorance and Superstition burnt me with their hell-fire in those stifling days. Am I blasphemous? It is their word, not mine. Beside that battle of my young days all others have been easy, for whatever was without, within my own Will was supreme. It has owed no allegiance, and never shall; it has moved steadily in one direction, the knowledge and assertion of its own liberty, with all the responsibility falling thereon."

During her stay at the convent there was little communication between her and her parents. In a letter from Mrs. Eliza de Cleyre, the mother of VOLTAIRINE, we are informed that she decided to run away from the convent after she had been there a few weeks. She escaped before breakfast, and crossed the river to Port Huron; but, as she had no money, she started to walk home. After covering seventeen miles, she realized that she never could do it; so she turned around and walked back, and entering the house of an acquaintance in Port Huron asked for something to eat. They sent for her father, who afterwards took her back to the convent. What penance they inflicted she never told, but at sixteen her health was so bad that the convent authorities let her come home for a vacation, telling her, however, that she would find her every movement watched, and that everything she said would be reported to them. The result was that she started at every sound, her hands shaking and her face as pale as death. She was about five weeks from graduating at that time. When her vacation was over, she went back and finished her studies. And then she started for home again, but this time she had money enough for her fare, and she got home to stay, never to go back to the place that had been a prison to her. She had seen enough of the convent to decide for herself that she could not be a nun.

The child who had sung:

"There's a love supreme in the Great Hereafter,
    The buds of Earth are bloom in Heaven,
The smiles of the world are ripples of laughter
    When back to its Aidenn the soul is given,
And the tears of the world, though long in flowing,
    Water the fields of the bye-and-bye;
They fall as dews on the sweet grass growing,
    When the fountains of sorrow and grief run dry.
Though clouds hang over the furrows now sowing
    There's a harvest sun-wreath in the After-sky.

"No love is wasted, no heart beats vainly,
    There's a vast perfection beyond the grave;
Up the bays of heaven the stars shine plainly—
    The stars lying dim on the brow of the wave.
And the lights of our loves, though they flicker and wane, they
    Shall shine all undimmed in the ether nave.
For the altars of God are lit with souls
    Fanned to flaming with love where the star-wind
        rolls."

returned from the convent a strong-minded freethinker.
She was received with open arms by her mother, almost
as one returned from the grave. With the exception of
the education derived from books, she knew no more
than a child, having almost no knowledge of practical
things.

Already in the convent she had succeeded in impress-
ing her strong personality upon her surroundings. Her
teachers could not break her; they were therefore forced
to respect her. In a polemic with the editor of the
Catholic *Buffalo Union* and *Times,* a few years ago,
Voltairine wrote: "If you think that I, as your op-
ponent, deserve the benefit of truth, but as a stranger
you doubt my veracity, I respectfully request you to
submit this letter to Sister Mary Medard, my former
teacher, now Superioress at Windsor, or to my revered
friend, Father Siegfried, Overbrook Seminary, Over-

brook, Pa., who will tell you whether, in their opinion, my disposition to tell the truth may be trusted."

Reaction from the repression and the cruel discipline of the Catholic Church helped to develop VOLTAIRINE'S inherent tendency toward free-thought; the five-fold murder of the labor leaders in Chicago, in 1887, shocked her mind so deeply that from that moment dates her development toward Anarchism. When in 1886 the bomb fell on the Haymarket Square, and the Anarchists were arrested, VOLTAIRINE DE CLEYRE, who at that time was a free-thought lecturer, shouted: "They ought to be hanged!" They were hanged, and now her body rests in Waldheim Cemetery, near the grave of those martyrs. Speaking at a memorial meeting in honor of those comrades, in 1901, she said: "For that ignorant, outrageous, bloodthirsty sentence I shall never forgive myself, though I know the dead men would have forgiven me, though I know those who loved them forgive me. But my own voice, as it sounded that night, will sound so in my ears till I die—a bitter reproach and a shame. I have only one word of extenuation for myself and the millions of others who did as I did that night— ignorance."

She did not remain long in ignorance. In "The Making of an Anarchist" she describes why she became a convert to the idea and why she entered the movement. "Til! then," she writes, "I believed in the essential justice of the American law and trial by jury. After that I never could. The infamy of that trial has passed into history, and the question it awakened as to the possibility of justice under law has passed into clamorous crying across the world."

At the age of nineteen VOLTAIRINE had consecrated herself to the service of humanity. In her poem, "The

Burial of My Past Self," she thus bids farewell to her youthful life:

"And now, Humanity, I turn to you;
    I consecrate my service to the world!
Perish the old love, welcome to the new—
    Broad as the space-aisles where the stars are whirled!"

Yet the pure and simple free-thought agitation in its narrow circle could not suffice her. The spirit of rebellion, the spirit of Anarchy, took hold of her soul. The idea of universal rebellion saved her; otherwise she might have stagnated like so many of her contemporaries, suffocated in the narrow surroundings of their intellectual life. A lecture of Clarence Darrow, which she heard in 1887, led her to the study of Socialism, and then there was for her but one step to Anarchism. Dyer D. Lum, the fellow worker of the Chicago martyrs, had undoubtedly the greatest influence in shaping her development; he was her teacher, her confidant, and comrade; his death in 1893 was a terrible blow to VOLTAIRINE.

VOLTAIRINE spent the greater part of her life in Philadelphia. Here, among congenial friends, and later among the Jewish emigrants, she did her best work. In 1897 she went on a lecture tour to England and Scotland, and in 1902, after an insane youth had tried to take her life, she went for a short trip to Norway to recuperate from her wounds. Hers was a life of bitter economic struggle and an unceasing fight with physical weakness, partly resulting from this very economic struggle. One wonders how, under such circumstances, she could have produced such an amount of work. Her poems, sketches, propagandistic articles and essays may be found in the *Open Court, Twentieth Century, Magazine of Poetry, Truth, Lucifer, Boston Investigator, Rights of Labor, Truth Seeker, Liberty, Chicago Liberal,*

Free Society, Mother Earth, and in *The Independent.*
She translated Jean Grave's "Moribund Society and
Anarchy" from the French, and left an unfinished trans-
lation of Louise Michel's work on the Paris Commune.
In *Mother Earth* appeared her translations from the
Jewish of Libin and Peretz. In collaboration with Dyer
D. Lum she wrote a novel on social questions, which
has unfortunately remained unfinished.

VOLTAIRINE DE CLEYRE's views on the sex-question,
on agnosticism and free-thought, on individualism and
communism, on non-resistance and direct action, underwent many changes. In the year 1902 she wrote: "The
spread of Tolstoy's 'War and Peace' and 'The Slavery
of Our Times,' and the growth of the numerous Tolstoy
clubs having for their purpose the dissemination of the
literature of non-resistance, is an evidence that many receive the idea that it is easier to conquer war with peace.
I am one of these. I can see no end of retaliation, unless
some one ceases to retaliate." She adds, however: "But
let no one mistake this for servile submission or meek
abnegation; my right shall be asserted no matter at what
cost to me, and none shall trench upon it without my
protest." But as she used to quote her comrade, Dyer
D. Lum: "Events proved to be the true schoolmasters."
The last years of her life were filled with the spirit of
direct action, and especially with the social importance
of the Mexican Revolution. The splendid propaganda
work of Wm. C. Owen in behalf of this tremendous
upheaval inspired her to great effort. She, too, had
found out by experience that only action counts, that
only a direct participation in the struggle makes life
worth while.

VOLTAIRINE DE CLEYRE was one of the most remarkable personalities of our time. She was a born iconoclast;

her spirit was too free, her taste too refined, to accept any idea that has the slightest degree of limitation. A great sadness, a knowledge that there is a universal pain, filled her heart. Through her own suffering and through the suffering of others she reached the highest exaltation of mind; she was conscious of all the vanities of life. In the service of the poor and oppressed she found her life mission. In an exquisite tribute to her memory, Leonard D. Abbott calls VOLTAIRINE DE CLEYRE a priestess of Pity and of Vengeance, whose voice has a vibrant quality that is unique in literature. We are convinced that her writings will live as long as humanity exists.

HIPPOLYTE HAVEL.

POEMS

Poems

THE BURIAL OF MY PAST SELF

Poor Heart, so weary with thy bitter grief!
  So thou art dead at last, silent and chill!
The longed-for death-dart came to thy relief,
  And there thou liest, Heart, forever still.

Dead eyes, pain-pressed beneath their black-fringed pall!
  Dead cheeks, dark-furrowed with so many tears!
So thou art passed far, far beyond recall,
  And all thy hopes are past, and all thy fears.

Thy lips are closed at length in the long peace!
  Pale lips! so long they have thy woe repressed,
They seem even now when life has run its lease
  All dumbly pitiful in their mournful rest.

And now I lay thee in thy silent tomb,
  Printing thy brow with one last solemn kiss;
Laying upon thee one fair lily bloom,
  A symbol of thy rest;—oh, rest is bliss.

No, Heart, I would not call thee back again;
  No, no; too much of suffering hast thou known;
But yet, but yet, it was not all in vain—
  Thy unseen tears, thy solitary moan!

For out of sorrow joy comes uppermost;
  Where breaks the thunder soon the sky smiles blue;
A better love replaces what is lost,
  And phantom sunlight pales before the true!

The seed must burst before the germ unfolds,
  The stars must fade before the morning wakes;
Down in her depths the mine the diamond holds;
  A new heart pulses when the old heart breaks.

And now, Humanity, I turn to you;
  I consecrate my service to the world!
Perish the old love, welcome to the new—
  Broad as the space-aisles where the stars are whirled!

GREENVILLE, MICH., 1885.

NIGHT ON THE GRAVES

O'er the sweet, quiet homes in the silent grave-city,
Softly the dewdrops, the night-tears, fall;
Broadly about, like the wide arms of pity,
The silver-shot darkness lies over all.
Heroes, asleep 'neath the red-hearted rose-wreaths,
Leaf-crowned with honor, flower-crowned with rest,
Gently above you each moon-dripping bough breathes
A far-echoed whisper, "Sleep well; ye are blest."

Oh! never, as long as the heart pulses quicker
At the dear name of Country may yours be forgot;
Nor may we, till the last puny life spark shall flicker,
Your deeds from the tablets of Memory blot!
Spirits afloat in the night-shrouds that bound us,
Souls of the "Has-Been" and of the "To-Be"
Keep the fair light of Liberty shining around us,
Till our souls may go back to the mighty SOUL-SEA.

ST. JOHNS, MICH., 1886 (Decoration Day).

THE CHRISTIAN'S FAITH

(The two following poems were written at that period of my life when the questions of the existence of God and the divinity of Jesus had but recently been settled, and they present the pros and cons which had been repeating themselves over and over again in my brain for some years.)

We contrast light and darkness,—light of God,
And darkness from the Stygian shades of hell;
Fumes of the pit infernal rising up
Have clouded o'er the brain, laid reason low;—
For when the eye looks on fair Nature's face
And sees not God, then is she blind indeed!
No night so starless, even in its gloom,
As his who wanders on without a hope
In that great, just Hereafter all must meet!—
No heart so dull, so heavy, and so void,
As that which lives for this chill world alone!
No soul so groveling, unaspiring, base,
As that which, here, forgets the afterhere!

And still through all the darkness and the gloom
Its voice will not be stilled, its hopes be quenched;
It cries, it screams, it struggles in its chains,
And bleeds upon the altar of the mind,—
Unwilling sacrifice to thought misled.
The soul that knows no God can know no peace.
Thus speaketh light, the herald of our God!
In that far dawn where shone each rolling world
First lit with shadowed splendor of the stars,
In that fair morning when Creation sang
Its praise of God, e'er yet it dreamed of sin,
Pure and untainted as the source of life
Man dwelt in Eden. There no shadows came,
No question of the goodness of our Lord,
Until the prince of darkness tempted man,
And, yielding to the newly born desire,
He fell! Sank in the mire of ignorance!
And Man, who put himself in Satan's power,
Since then has wandered far in devious ways,
Seeing but now and then a glimpse of light,
Till Christ is come, the living Son of God!
Far in his heavenly home he viewed the world,
Saw all her sadness and her sufferings,
Saw all her woes, her struggles, and her search
For some path leading up from out the Night.
Within his breast the fount of tears was touched;
His great heart swelled with pity, and he said:
"Father, I go to save the world from sin."
Ah! What power but a soul divinely clad
In purity, in holiness and love,
Could leave a home of happiness and light
For this lost World of suffering and death?
He came: the World tossed groaning in her sleep;
He touched her brow: the nightmare passed away;
He soothed her heart, red with the stain of sin;
And she forgot her guilt in penitence;
She washed the ruby out with pearls of tears.
He came, he suffered, and he died for us;
He felt the bitterest woes a soul can feel;
He probed the darkest depths of human grief;
He sounded all the deeps and shoals of pain;
Was cursed for all his love; thanked with the cross,

Whereon he hung nailed, bleeding, glorified,
As the last smoke of holocaust divine.
"Ah! This was all two thousand years ago!"
Two thousand years ago, and still he cries,
With voice sweet calling through the distant dark:
"O souls that labor, struggling in your pain,
Come unto me, and I will give you rest!
For every woe of yours, and every smart,
I, too, have felt:—the mockery, the shame,
The sneer, the scoffing lip, the hate, the lust,
The greed of gain, the jealousy of man,
Unstinted have been measured out to me.
I know them all, I feel them all with you!
And I have known the pangs of poverty,
The cry of hunger and the weary heart
Of childhood burdened with the weight of age!
O sufferers, ye all are mine to love!
The pulse-beats of my heart go out with you,
And every drop of agony that drips
From my nailed hands adown this bitter cross,
Cries out, 'O God! accept the sacrifice,
And ope the gates of heaven to the world!'
Ye vermin of the garret, who do creep
Your weary lives away within its walls;
Ye children of the cellar, who behold
The sweet, pale light, strained through the lothsome air
And doled to you in tid-bits, as a thing
Too precious for your use; ye rats in mines,
Who knaw within the black and somber pits
To seek poor living for your little ones;
Ye women who stitch out your lonely lives,
Unmindful whether sun or stars keep watch;
Ye slaves of wheels; ye worms that bite the dust
Where pride and scorn have ground you 'neath the heel;
Ye Toilers of the earth, ye weary ones,—
I know your sufferings, I feel your woes;
My peace I give you; in a little while
The pain will all be over, and the grave
Will sweetly close above your folded hands!
And then?—Ah, Death, no conqueror art thou!
For I have loosed thy chains; I have unbarred
The gates of heaven! In my Father's house

Of many mansions I prepare a place;
And rest is there for every heart that toils!
Oh, all ye sick and wounded ones who grieve
For the lost health that ne'er may come again;
Ye who do toss upon a couch of pain,
Upon whose brow disease has laid his hand,
Within whose eyes the dull and heavy sight
Burns like a taper burning very low,
Upon whose lips the purple fever-kiss
Rests his hot breath, and dries the sickened palms,
Scorches the flesh and e'en the very air;
Ye who do grope along without the light;
Ye who do stumble, halting on your way;
Ye whom the world despises as unclean;
Know that the death-free soul has none of these:
The unbound spirit goes unto its God,
Pure, whole, and beauteous as newly born!
Oh, all ye mourners, weeping for the dead;
Your tears I gather as the grateful rain
Which rises from the sea and falls again,
To nurse the withering flowers from its touch;
No drop is ever lost! They fall again
To nurse the blossoms of some other heart!
I would not dry one single dew of grief:
The sorrow-freighted lashes which bespeak
The broken heart and soul are dear to me;
I mourn with them, and mourning so I find
The grief-bowed soul with weeping oft grows light!
But yet ye mourn for them not without hope:
Beyond the woes and sorrows of the earth,
As stars still shine though clouds obscure the sight,
The friends ye mourn as lost immortal live;
And ye shall meet and know their souls again,
Through death transfigured, through love glorified!
Oh, all ye patient waiters for reward,
Scorned and despised by those who know not worth,
I know your merit and I give you hope;
For in my Father's law is justice found.
See how the seed-germ, toiling underground,
Waits patiently for time to burst its shell;
And by and by the golden sunlight warms
The dark, cold earth; the germ begins to shoot.

And upward trends until two small green leaves
Unfold and wave and drink the pure, fresh air.
The blossoms come and go with Summer's breath,
And Autumn brings the fruit-time in her hand.
So ye, who patient watch and wait and hope,
Trusting the sun may bring the blossoms out,
Shall reap the fruited labor by and by.
I am your friend; I wait and hope with you,
Rejoice with you when the hard vict'ry's won!
And still for you, O prisoners in cells,
I hold the dearest gifts of penitence,
Forgiveness and charity and hope!
I stretch the hands of mercy through the bars;
White hands,—like doves they bring the branch of peace!
Repent, believe,—and I will expiate
Upon this bitter cross all your deep guilt!
Oh, take my gift, accept my sacrifice!
I ask no other thing but only—trust!
Oh, all ye martyrs, bleeding in your chains;
Oh, all ye souls that live for others' good;
Oh, all ye mourners, all ye guilty ones,
And all ye suffering ones, come unto me!
Ye are all my brothers, all my sisters, all!
And as I love one, so I love you all.
Accept my love, accept my sacrifice;
Make not my cross ·more bitter than it is
By shrinking from the peace I bring to you!"

St. Johns, Mich., April, 1887.

THE FREETHINKER'S PLEA

Grand eye of Liberty, light up my page!
Like promised morning after night of age
Thy dawning youth breaks in the distant east!
Thy cloudy robes like silken curtains creased
And swung in folds are floating fair and free!
The shadows of the cycles turn and flee;
The budding stars, bright minds that gemmed the night,
Are bursting into broad, bright-petaled light!
Sweet Liberty, how pure thy very breath!
How dear in life, how doubly dear in death!

Ah, slaves that suffer in your self-forged chains,
Praying your Christ to touch and heal your pains,
Tear off your shackling irons, unbind your eyes,
Seize the grand hopes that burn along the skiees!
Worship not God in temples built of gloom;
Far sweeter incense is the flower-bloom
Than all the fires that Sacrifice may light;
And grander is the star-dome gleaming bright
With glowing worlds, than all your altar lamps
Pale flickering in your clammy, vaulted damps;
And richer is the broad, full, fair sun sheen,
Dripping its orient light in streams between
The fretted shafting of the forest trees,
Throwing its golden kisses to the breeze,
Lifting the grasses with its finger-tips,
And pressing the young blossoms with warm lips,
Show'ring its glory over plain and hill,
Wreathing the storm and dancing in the rill;
Far richer in wild freedom falling there,
Shaking the tresses of its yellow hair,
Than all subdued within the dim half-light
Of stained glass windows, drooping into night.
Oh, grander far the massive mountain walls
Which bound the vista of the forest halls,
Than all the sculptured forms which guard the piles
That arch your tall, dim, gray, cathedral aisles!
And gladder is the carol of a bird
Than all the anthems that were ever heard
To steal in somber chanting from the tone
Of master voices praising the Unknown.
In the great wild, where foot of man ne'er trod,
There find we Nature's church and Nature's God!
Here are no fetters! though is free as air;
Its flight may spread far as its wings may dare;
And through it all one voice criees, "God is love,
And love is God!" Around, within, above,
Behold the working of the perfect law,—
The law immutable in which no flaw
Exists, and from which no appeal is made;
Ev'n as the sunlight chases far the shade
And shadows chase the light in turn again,
So every life is fraught with joy and pain;

The stinging thorn lies hid beside the rose;
The bud is blighted ere its leave unclose;
So pleasure born of Hope may oft-time yield
A stinging smart of thorns, a barren field!
But let it be: the buds will bloom again,
The fields will freshen in the summer rain;
And never storm scowls dark but still, somewhere,
A bow is bending in the upper air.
Then learn the law if thou wouldst live aright;
And know no unseen power, no hand of might,
Can set aside the law which wheels the stars;
No incompleteness its perfection mars;
The buds will wake in season, and the rain
will fall when clouds hang heavy, and again
The snows will tremble when the winter's breath
Congeals the cloud-tears, as the touch of Death
Congeals the last drop on the sufferer's cheek.
Thus do all Nature's tongues in chorus speak:
"Think not, O man, that thou canst e'er escape
One jot of Justice's law, nor turn thy fate
By yielding sacrifice to the Unseen!
Purged by thyself alone canst thou be clean.
One guide to happiness thou mayst learn:
Love toward the world begets love in return.
And if to others you the measure mete
Of love, be sure your harvest will be sweet;
But if ye sow broadcast the seed of hate,
Ye'll reap again, albeit ye reap it late.
Then let your life-work swell the great flood-tide
Of love towards all the world; the world is wide,
The sea of life is broad; its waves stretch far;
No range, no barrier, its sweep may bar;
The world is filled, is trodden down with pain;
The sea of life is gathered up of rain,—
A throat, a bed, a sink, for human tears,
A burial of hopes, a miasm of fears!
But see! the sun of love shines softly out,
Flinging its golden fingers all about,
Pressing its lips in loving, soft caress,
Upon the world's pale cheek; the pain grows less,
The tears are dried upon the quivering lashes,
An answering sunbeam 'neath the white lids flashes!

The sea of life is dimpled o'er with smiles,
The sun of love the cloud of woe beguiles,
And turns its heavy brow to forehead fair,
Framed in the glory of its sun-gilt hair.
Be thine the warming touch, the kiss of love;
Vainly ye seek for comfort from above,
Vainly ye pray the Gods to ease your pain;
The heavy words fall back on you again!
Vainly ye cry for Christ to smooth your way;
The thorns sting sharper while ye kneeling pray!
Vainly ye look upon the world of woe,
And cry, "O God, avert the bitter blow!"
Ye cannot turn the lightning from its track,
Nor call one single little instant back;
The law swerves not, and with unerring aim
The shaft of justice falls; he bears the blame
Who violates the rule: do well your task,
For justice overtakes you all at last.
Vainly ye patient ones await reward,
Trusting th' Almighty's angel to record
Each bitter tear, each disappointed sigh;
Reward descends not, gifted from on high,
But is the outgrowth of the eternal law:
As from the earth the toiling seed-germs draw
The food which gives them life and strength to bear
The storms and suns which sweep the upper air,
So ye must draw from out the pregnant earth
The metal true wherewith to build your worth;
So shall ye brave the howling of the blast,
And smile triumphant o'er the storm at last.
Nor dream these trials are without their use;
Between your joys and griefs ye cannot choose,
And say your life with either is complete:
Ever the bitter mingles with the sweet.
The dews must press the petals down at night,
If in the dawning they would glisten bright;
If sunbeams needs must ripen out the grain
Not less the early blades must woo the rain:
If now your eyes be wet with weary tears,
Ye'll gather them as gems in after years;
And if the rains now sodden down your path,
Ye'll reap rich harvest in the aftermath.

Ye idle mourners, crying in your grief,
The souls ye weep have found the long relief:
Why grieve for those who fold their hands in peace?
Their sore-tried hearts have found a glad release;
Their spirits sink into the solemn sea!
Mourn ye the prisoner from his chains let free?
Nay, ope your ears unto the living cry
That pleads for living comfort! Hark, the sigh
Of million heartaches rising in your ears!
Kiss back the living woes, the living tears!
Go down into the felon's gloomy cell;
Send there the ray of love: as tree-buds swell
When spring's warm breath bids the cold winter cease,
So will his heart swell with the hope of peace.
Be filled with love, for love is Nature's God;
The God which trembles in the tender sod,
The God which tints the sunset, lights the dew,
Sprinkles with stars the firmament's broad blue,
And draws all hearts together in a free
Wide sweep of love, broad as the ether-sea.
No other law or guidance do we need;
The world's our church, to do good is our creed.

St. Johns, Mich., 1887.

TO MY MOTHER

Some souls there are which never live their life;
Some suns there are which never pierce their cloud;
Some hearts there are which cup their perfume in,
And yield no incense to the outer air.
Cloud-shrouded, flower-cupped heart: such is thine own:
So dost thou live with all thy brightness hid;
So dost thou dwell with all thy perfume close;
Rich in thy treasured wealth, aye, rich indeed—
And they are wrong who say thou "dost not feel."
But I—I need blue air and opened bloom;
To keep my music means that it must die;
And when the thrill, the joy, the love of life is gone,
I, too, am dead—a corpse, though not entombed.

Let me live then—but a while—the gloom soon comes,
The flower closes and the petals shut;
Through them the perfume slips out, like a soul—
The long, still sleep of death—and then the Grave.

CLEVELAND, OHIO, March, 1889.

BETRAYED

So, you're the chaplain!   You needn't say what you have come
    for; I can guess.
You've come to talk about Jesus' love, and repentance and rest
    and forgiveness!
You've come to say that my sin is great, yet greater the mercy
    Heaven will mete,
If I, like Magdalen, bend my head, and pour my tears at your
    Saviour's feet.
Your promise is fair, but I've little faith: I relied on promises
    once before;
They brought me to this—this prison cell, with its iron-barred
    window, its grated door!
Yet he, too, was fair who promised me, with his tender mouth
    and his Christ-like eyes;
And his voice was as sweet as the summer wind that sighs
    through the arbors of Paradise.
And he seemed to me all that was good and pure, and noble and
    strong, and true and brave!
I had given the pulse of my heart for him, and deemed it a
    precious boon to crave.

You say that Jesus so loved the world he died to redeem it
    from its sin:
It isn't redeemed, or no one could be so fair without, and so
    black within.
I trusted his promise, I gave my life;—the truth of my love is
    known on high,
If there is a God who knows all things;—his promise was false,
    his *love* was a lie!

It was over soon, Oh! soon, the dream,—and me, he had called
"his life," "his light,"

He drove me away with a sneering word, and you Christians
said that "it served me right."

I was proud, Mr. Chaplain, even then; I set my face in the
teeth of Fate,

And resolved to live honestly, come what might, and sink beneath neither scorn nor hate.

Yes, and I prayed that the Christ above would help to bear the
bitter cross,

And put something here, where my heart had been, to fill up the
aching void of loss.

It's easy for you to say what I should do, but none of you ever
dream how hard

Is the way that you Christians make for us, with your "sin no
more," "trust the Lord."

When for days and days you are turned from work with cold
politeness, or open sneer,

You get so you don't trust a far-off God, whose creatures are
cold, and they, so near.

You hold your virtuous lives aloof, and refuse us your human
help and hand,

And set us apart as accursèd things, marked with a burning,
Cain-like brand.

But I didn't bend, though many days I was weary and hungry,
and worn and weak,

And for many a starless night I watched, through tears that
grooved down my pallid cheek.

They are all dry now! They say I'm hard, because I never weep
or moan!

You can't draw blood when the heart's bled out! you can't find
tears or sound in a stone!

And I don't know why *I* should be mild and meek: no one has
been very mild to me.

You say that Jesus would be—perhaps! but Heaven's a *long* way
off, you see.

That will do; I know what you're going to say: "I can have it
right here in this narrow cell."

The *soul* is slow to accept Christ's heav'n when his followers chain the body in hell.

Not but I'm just as well off here,—better, perhaps, than I was outside.

The world was a prison-house to me, where I dwelt, defying and defied.

I don't know but I'd think more of what you say, if they'd given us both a common lot;

If justice to me had been justice to him, and covered our names with an equal blot;

But they took him into the social court, and pitied, and said he'd been "led astray";

In a month the stain on *his* name had passed, as a cloud that crosses the face of day!

He joined the Church, and he's preaching now, just as you are, the love of God,

And the duty of sinners to kneel and pray, and humbly to kiss the chastening rod.

If they'd dealt with me as they dealt by him, may be I'd credit your Christian love;

If they'd dealt with him as they dealt by me, I'd have more faith in a just Above.

I don't know, but sometimes I used to think that she, who was told there was no room

In the inn at Bethlehem, might look down with softened eyes thro' the starless gloom.

Christ wasn't a woman—he couldn't know the pain and endurance of it; but *she*,

The mother who bore him, she might know, and Mary in Heaven might pity me.

Still that was useless: it didn't bring a single mouthful for me to eat,

Nor work to get it, nor sheltering from the dreary wind and the howling street.

Heavenly pity won't pass as coin, and earthly shame brings a higher pay.

Sometimes I was tempted to give it up, and go, like others, the easier way;

But I didn't; no, sir, I kept my oath, though my baby lay in my arms and cried,

And at last, to spare it—I poisoned it; and kissed its murdered
    lips when it died.

I'd never seen *him* since it was born (he'd said that it wasn't
    his, you know);

But I took its body and laid it down at the steps of his door, in
    the pallid glow

Of the winter morning; and when he came, with a love-tune
    hummed on those lips of lies,

It lay at his feet, with its pinched white face staring up at him
    from its dead, blue eyes;

I hadn't closed them; they were like his, and so was the mouth
    and the curled gold hair,

And every feature so like his own,—for I am dark, sir, and he
    is fair.

'Twas a moment of triumph, that showed me yet there was a
    passion I could feel,

When I saw him bend o'er its meagre form, and, starting back-
    wards, cry out and reel!

If there *is* a time when all souls shall meet the reward of the
    deeds that are done in the clay,

When accused and accuser stand face to face, he will cry out
    so in the Judgment Day!

The rest? Oh, nothing. They hunted me, and with virtuous
    lawyers' virtuous tears

To a virtuous jury, convicted me; and I'm sentenced to stay here
    for twenty years.

Do I repent? Yes, I do; but wait till I tell you of what I repent,
    and why.

I repent that I ever believed a man could be anything but a
    living lie!

I repent because every noble thought, or hope, or ambition, or
    earthly trust,

Is as dead as dungeon-bleached bones in me,—as dead as my
    child in its murdered dust!

Do I repent that I killed the babe? Am I repentant for that,
    you ask?

I'll answer the truth as I feel it, sir; I leave to others the pious
    mask.

Am I repentant because I saved its starving body from Famine's
    teeth?

Because I hastened what time would do, to spare it pain and
    relieve its death?
Am I repentant because I held it were better a *grave* should
    have no name
Than a *living being*, whose only care must come from a mother
    weighed with shame?
Am I repentant because I thought it were better the tiny form
    lay hid
From the heartless stings of a brutal world, unknown, unnamed,
    'neath a coffin lid?
Am I repentant for the act, the last on earth in my power, to save
From the long-drawn misery of life, in the early death and the
    painless grave?
I'm *glad* that I did it! Start if you will! I'll repeat it over; I
    say I'm *glad!*
No, I'm neither a fiend, nor a maniac—don't look as if I were
    going mad!

Did I not love it? Yes, I loved with a strength that you, sir, can
    never feel;
It's only a strong love can kill to save, tho' itself be torn where
    time cannot heal.
You see my hands—they are red with its blood! Yet I would
    have cut them, bit by bit,
And fed them, and smiled to see it eat, if that would have
    saved and nourished it!
"Beg!" I *did* beg,—and "pray!" I *did* pray! God was as stony
    and hard as Earth,
And Christ was as deaf as the stars that watched, or the night
    that darkened above his birth!
And I—I feel stony now, too, like them; deaf to sorrow and
    mute to grief!
Am I heartless?—yes:—it-is-*all*-CUT-OUT! Torn! Gone! All
    gone! Like my dead belief.

Do I not fear for the judgment hour? So unrepentant, so hard
    and cold?
Wait! It is little I trust in that; but if ever the scrolled sky
    shall be uprolled,
And the lives of men shall be read and known, and their acts be
    judged by their very worth,
And the Christ you speak of shall come again, and the thunders
    of Justice shake the earth,

You will hear the cry, "Who murdered here? Come forth to
    the judgment, false heart and eyes,
That pulsed with accurséd strength of lust, and loaded faith
    with envenomed lies!
Come forth to the judgment, haughty dames, who scathed the
    mother with your scorn,
And answer here, to the poisoned child, *who* decreed its murder
    ere it was born?
Come forth to the judgment ye who heaped the gold of earth
    in your treasured hoard,
And answer, 'guilty,' to those who stood all naked and starving,
    beneath your board.
Depart, accurséd! I know you not! Ye heeded not the com-
    mand of Heaven,
'Unto the least of these ye give, it is even unto the Master given.' "

Judgment! Ah, sir, to see that day, I'd willingly pass thro' a
    hundred hells!
I'd believe, then, the Justice that hears each voice buried alive
    in these prison cells!
But, no—it's not that; that will never be! I trusted too long,
    and He answered not.
There *is* no avenging God on high!—we live, we struggle, and—
    we rot.

Yet does Justice come! and, O Future Years! sorely ye'll reap,
    and in weary pain,
When ye garner the sheaves that are sown to-day, when the
    clouds that are gathering fall in rain!
The time will come, aye! the time *will* come, when the child
    ye conceive in lust and shame,
Quickened, will mow you like swaths of grass, with a sickle
    born of Steel and Flame.
Aye, tremble, shrink, in your drunken den, coward, traitor, and
    Child of Lie!
The unerring avenger stands close to you, and the dread hour
    of parturition's nigh!
Aye! wring your hands, for the air is black! thickly the cloud-
    troops whirl and swarm!
See! yonder, on the horizon's verge, play the lightning-shafts of
    the coming storm!

ADRIAN, MICH., July, 1889.

OPTIMISM

There's a love supreme in the great hereafter,
  The buds of earth are blooms in heaven;
The smiles of the world are ripples of laughter
  When back to its Aidenn the soul is given:
And the tears of the world, though long in flowing,
  Water the fields of the bye-and-bye;
They fall as dews on the sweet grass growing
  When the fountains of sorrow and grief run dry.
Though clouds hang over the furrows now sowing
  There's a harvest sun-wreath in the After-sky!

No love is wasted, no heart beats vainly,
  There's a vast perfection beyond the grave;
Up the bays of heaven the stars shine plainly,
  The stars lying dim on the brow of the wave.
And the lights of our loves, though they flicker and wane, they
  Shall shine all undimmed in the ether-nave.
For the altars of God are lit with souls
  Fanned to flaming with love where the star-wind rolls.

St. Johns, Michigan, 1889.

AT THE GRAVE IN WALDHEIM

Quiet they lie in their shrouds of rest,
  Their lids kissed close 'neath the lips of peace;
Over each pulseless and painless breast
The hands lie folded and softly pressed,
As a dead dove presses a broken nest;
  Ah, broken hearts were the price of these!

The lips of their anguish are cold and still,
  For them are the clouds and the gloom all past;
No longer the woe of the world can thrill
The chords of those tender hearts, or fill
The silent dead-house! The "people's will"
  Has snapped asunder the strings at last.

"The people's will!"   Ah, in years to come,
  Dearly ye'll weep that ye did not save!
Do ye not hear now the muffled drum,
The tramping feet and the ceaseless hum,
Of the million marchers,—trembling, dumb,
  In their tread to a yawning, giant grave?

And yet, ah! yet there's a rift of white!
  'Tis breaking over the martyrs' shrine!
Halt there, ye doomed ones,—it scathes the **night,**
As lightning darts from its scabbard bright
And sweeps the face of the sky with light!
  "No more shall be spilled out the blood-**red wine!"**

These are the words it has written there,
  Keen as the lance of the northern morn;
The sword of Justice gleams in its glare,
And the arm of Justice, upraised and **bare,**
Is true to strike, aye, 'tis strong to dare;
  It will fall where the curse of our land **is born.**

No more shall the necks of the nations be **crushed,**
  No more to dark Tyranny's throne bend **the knee;**
No more in abjection be ground to the dust!
By their widows, their orphans, our dead **comrades' trust,**
By the brave heart-beats stilled, by the brave **voices hushed,**
  We swear that humanity yet shall be **free!**

PITTSBURG, 1889.

THE HURRICANE

("We are the birds of the coming storm."—**August Spies.**)

  The tide is out, the wind blows off the shore;
  Bare burn the white sands in the scorching **sun;**
  The sea complains, but its great voice is low.

      Bitter thy woes, O People,
        And the burden
      Hardly to be borne!
      Wearily grows, O People,
        All the aching
      Of thy pierced heart, bruised **and torn!**

But yet thy time is not,
   And low thy moaning.
Desert thy sands!
Not yet is thy breath hot,
   Vengefully blowing;
It wafts o'er lifted hands.

The tide has turned; the vane veers slowly round;
Slow clouds are sweeping o'er the blinding light;
White crests curl on the sea,—its voice grows deep.

Angry thy heart, O People,
   And its bleeding
Fire-tipped with rising hate!
Thy clasped hands part, O People,
   For thy praying
Warmed not the desolate!
God did not hear thy moan:
   Now it is swelling
To a great drowning cry;
A dark wind-cloud, a groan,
   Now backward veering
From that deaf sky!

The tide flows in, the wind roars from the depths,
The whirled-white sand heaps with the foam-white waves;
Thundering the sea rolls o'er its shell-crunched wall!

Strong is thy rage, O People,
   In its fury
Hurling thy tyrants down!
Thou metest wage, O People.
   Very swiftly,
Now that thy hate is grown:
Thy time at last is come;
   Thou heapest anguish,
Where thou thyself wert bare!
No longer to thy dumb
   God clasped and kneeling,
Thou answerest thine own prayer.

SEA ISLE CITY, N. J., August, 1889.

  * Since the death of the author this poem has been put to music
by the young American composer, George Edwards.

UT SEMENTEM FECERIS, ITA METES

(To the Czar, on a woman, a political prisoner, being flogged to
death in Siberia.)

How many drops must gather to the skies
Before the cloud-burst comes, we may not know;
How hot the fires in under hells must glow
Ere the volcano's scalding lavas rise,
Can none say; but all wot the hour is sure!
Who dreams of vengeance has but to endure!
He may not say how many blows must fall,
How many lives be broken on the wheel,
How many corpses stiffen 'neath the pall,
How many martyrs fix the blood-red seal;
But certain is the harvest time of Hate!
And when weak moans, by an indignant world
Re-echoed, to a throne are backward hurled,
Who listens, hears the mutterings of Fate!

PHILADELPHIA, February, 1890.

BASTARD BORN

Why do you clothe me with scarlet of shame?
  Why do you point with your finger of scorn?
What is the crime that you hissingly name
  When you sneer in my ears, "Thou bastard born?"

Am I not as the rest of you,
  With a hope to reach, and a dream to live?
With a soul to suffer, a heart to know
  The pangs that the thrusts of the heartless give?

I am no monster! Look at me—
  Straight in my eyes, that they do not shrink!
Is there aught in them you can see
  To merit this hemlock you make me drink?

This poison that scorches my soul like fire,
  That burns and burns until love is dry,
And I shrivel with hate, as hot as a pyre,
  A corpse, while its smoke curls up to the sky?

Will you touch my hand? It is flesh like yours;
  Perhaps a little more brown and grimed,
For it could not be white while the drawers' and hewers',
  My brothers, were calloused and darkened and slimed.

Yet touch it! It is no criminal's hand!
  No children are toiling to keep it fair!
It is free from the curse of the stolen land,
  It is clean of the theft of the sea and air!

It has set no seals to a murderous law,
  To sign a bitter, black league with death!
No covenants false do these fingers draw
  In the name of "The State" to barter Faith!

It bears no stain of the yellow gold
  That earth's wretches give as the cost of heaven!
No priestly garment of silken fold
  I wear as the price of their "sins forgiven"!

Still do you shrink! Still I hear the hiss
  Between your teeth, and I feel the scorn
That flames in your gaze! Well, what is this,
  This crime I commit, being "bastard born"?

What! You whisper my "eyes are gray,"
  The "color of hers," up there on the hill,
Where the white stone gleams, and the willow spray
  Falls over her grave in the starlight still!

My "hands are shaped like" those quiet hands,
  Folded away from their life, their care;
And the sheen that lies on my short, fair strands
  Gleams darkly down on her buried hair!

My voice is toned like that silent tone
  That might, if it could, break up through the sod
With such rebuke as would shame your stone,
  Stirring the grass-roots in their clod!

And my heart-beats thrill to the same strong chords;
  And the blood that was hers is mine to-day;

And the thoughts she loved, I love; and the words
  That meant most to her, to me most say!

She was my mother—I her child!
  Could ten thousand priests have made us more?
Do you curse the bloom of the heather wild?
  Do you trample the flowers and cry "impure"?

Do you shun the bird-songs' silver shower?
  Does their music arouse your curling scorn
That none but God blessed them?   The whitest flower,
  The purest song, were but "bastard born"!

This is my sin,—I was born of her!
  This is my crime,—that I reverence deep!
God, that her pale corpse may not stir,
  Press closer down on her lids—the sleep!

Would you have me hate her?   Me, who knew
  That the gentlest soul in the world looked there,
Out of the gray eyes that pitied you
  E'en while you cursed her?   The long brown hair

That waved from her forehead, has brushed my cheek,
  When her soft lips have drunk up my salt of grief;
And the voice, whose echo you hate, would speak
  The hush of pity and love's relief!

And those still hands that are folded now
  Have touched my sorrows for years away!
Would you have me question her whence and how
  The love-light streamed from her heart's deep ray?

Do you question the sun that it gives its gold?
  Do you scowl at the cloud when it pours its rain
Till the fields that were withered and burnt and old
  Are fresh and tender and young again?

Do you search the source of the breeze that sweeps
  The rush of the fever from tortured brain?
Do you ask whence the perfume that round you creeps
  When your soul is wrought to the quick with pain?

She was my Sun, my Dew, my Air,
  The highest, the purest, the holiest;
PEACE—was the shade of her beautiful hair,
  LOVE—was all that I knew on her breast!

Would you have me forget? Or remembering
  Say that her love had bloomed from Hell?
Then BLESSED BE HELL! And let Heaven sing
  "*Te Deum laudamus*," until it swell

And ring and roll to the utterest earth,
  That the damned are free,—since out of sin
Came the whiteness that shamed all ransomed worth
  Till God opened the gates, saying "Enter in!"

          *   *   *   *

What! In the face of the witness I bear
  To her measureless love and her purity,
Still of your hate would you make me to share,
  Despising that she gave life to me?

You would have me stand at her helpless grave,
  To dig through its earth with a venomed dart!
This is Honor! and Right! and Brave!
  To fling a stone at her pulseless heart!

This is Virtue! To blast the lips
  Speechless beneath the Silence dread!
To lash with Slander's scorpion whips
  The voiceless, defenseless, helpless dead!

          *   *   *   *

God! I turn to an adder now!
  Back upon you I hurl your scorn!
Bind the scarlet upon your brow!
  Ye it is, who are "bastard born"!

Touch me not! These hands of mine
  Despise your fairness—the leper's white!
Tanned and hardened and black with grime,
  They are clean beside your souls to-night!

Basely born! 'Tis ye are base!
  Ye who would guerdon holy trust

With slavish law to a tyrant race,
  To sow the earth with the seed of lust.

Base! By Heaven! Prate of peace,
  When your garments are red with the stain of wars.
Reeling with passion's mad release
  By your sickly gaslight damn the stars!

Blurred with wine ye behold the snow
  Smirched with the foulness that blots within!
What of purity can ye know,
  Ye ten-fold children of Hell and Sin?

Ye to judge her! Ye to cast
  The stone of wrath from your house of glass!
Know ye the Law, that ye dare to blast
  The bell of gold with your clanging brass?

Know ye the harvest the reapers reap
  Who drop in the furrow the seed of scorn?
Out of this anguish ye harrow deep,
  Ripens the sentence: "*Ye,* bastard born!"

Ay, sin-begotten, hear the curse;
  Not mine—not hers—but the fatal Law!
"Who bids one suffer, shall suffer worse;
  Who scourges, himself shall be scourgèd raw!

"For the thoughts ye think, and the deeds ye do,
  Move on, and on, till the flood is high,
And the dread dam bursts, and the waves roar through,
  Hurling a cataract dirge to the sky!

"To-night ye are deaf to the beggar's prayer;
  To-morrow the thieves shall batter your wall!
Ye shall feel the weight of a starved child's care
  When your warders under the Mob's feet fall!

"'Tis the roar of the whirlwind ye invoke
  When ye scatter the wind of your brother's moans;
'Tis the red of your hate on your own head broke,
  When the blood of the murdered spatters the stones!

"Hark ye! Out of the reeking slums,
  Thick with the fetid stench of crime,
Boiling up through their sickening scums,
  Bubbles that burst through the crimson wine,

"Voices burst—with terrible sound,
  Crying the truth your dull souls ne'er saw!
We are *your* sentence! The wheel turns round!
  The bastard spawn of your bastard law!"

This is bastard: That Man should say
  How Love shall love, and how Life shall live!
Setting a tablet to groove God's way,
  Measuring how the divine shall give!

             *   *   *   *

O, Evil Hearts! Ye have maddened me,
  That I should interpret the voice of God!
Quiet! Quiet! O angered Sea!
  Quiet! I go to her blessed sod!

             *   *   *   *

Mother, Mother, I come to you!
  Down in your grasses I press my face!
Under the kiss of their cold, pure dew,
  I may dream that I lie in the dear old place!

Mother, sweet Mother, take me back,
  Into the bosom from whence I came!
Take me away from the cruel rack,
  Take me out of the parching flame!

Fold me again with your beautiful hair,
  Speak to this terrible heaving Sea!
Over me pour the soothing of prayer,
  The words of the Love-child of Galilee:

"Peace—be still!" Still,—could I but hear!
  Softly,—I listen.—O fierce heart, cease!
Softly,—I breathe not,—low,—in my ear,—
  Mother, Mother—I heard you!—Peace!

Enterprise, Kansas, January, 1891.

HYMN

(This hymn was written at the request of a Christian Science friend who proposed to set it to music. It did not represent my beliefs either then or since, but rather what I wish might be my beliefs, had I not an inexorable capacity for seeing things as they are.—a vast scheme of mutual murder, with no justice anywhere, and no God in the soul or out of it.)

I am at peace—no storm can ever touch me;
  On my clear heights the sunshine only falls;
Far, far below glides the phantom voice of sorrows,
  In peace-lifted light the Silence only calls.
Ah, Soul, ascend! The mountain way, up-leading,
  Bears to the heights whereon the Blest have trod!
Lay down the burden;—stanch the heart's sad bleeding;
  BE YE AT PEACE, for know that Ye are God!

Not long the way, not far in a dim heaven;
  In the locked Self seek ye the guiding star:
Clear shine its rays, illumining the shadow;
  There, where God is, there, too, O Souls ye are.
Ye are at one, and bound in Him forever,
  Ev'n as the wave is bound in the great sea;
Never to drift beyond, below Him, never!
  Whole as God is, so, even so, are ye.

PHILADELPHIA, 1892.

YOU AND I

(A reply to "You and I in the Golden Weather," by Dyer D. Lum.)

You and I, in the sere, brown weather,
  When clouds hang thick in the frowning sky,
When rain-tears drip on the bloomless heather,
Unheeding the storm-blasts will walk together,
  And look to each other—You and I.

You and I, when the clouds are shriven
  To show the cliff-broods of lightnings high;
When over the ramparts, swift, thunder-driven,
Rush the bolts of Hate from a Hell-lit Heaven,
  Will smile at each other—You and I.

You and I, when the bolts are falling,
  The hot air torn with the earth's wild cries,
Will lean through the darkness where Death is calling,
Will search through the shadows where Night is palling,
  And find the light in each other's eyes.

You and I, when black sheets of water
  Drench and tear us and drown our breath,
Below this laughter of Hell's own daughter,
Above the smoke of the storm-girt slaughter,
  Will hear each other and gleam at Death.

You and I, in the gray night dying,
  When over the east-land the dawn-beams fly,
Down in the groans, in the low, faint crying,
Down where the thick blood is blackly lying,
  Will reach out our weak arms, You and I.

You and I, in the cold, white weather,
  When over our corpses the pale lights lie,
Will rest at last from the dread endeavor,
Pressed to each other, for parting—never!
  Our dead lips together, You and I.

You and I, when the years in flowing
  Have left us behind with all things that die,
With the rot of our bones shall give soil for growing
The loves of the Future, made sweet for blowing
  By the dew of the kiss of a last good-bye!

PHILADELPHIA, 1892.

THE TOAST OF DESPAIR

We have cried,—and the Gods are silent;
  We have trusted,—and been betrayed;
We have loved,—and the fruit was ashes;
  We have given,—the gift was weighed.

We know that the heavens are empty,
  That friendship and love are names;
That truth is an ashen cinder,
  The end of life's burnt-out flames.

Vainly and long have we waited,
  Through the night of the human roar,
For a single song on the harp of Hope,
  Or a ray from a day-lit shore.

Songs aye come floating, marvelous sweet,
  And bow-dyed flashes gleam;
But the sweets are Lies, and the weary feet
  Run after a marsh-light beam.

In the hour of our need the song departs,
  And the sea-moans of sorrow swell;
The siren mocks with a gurgling laugh
  That is drowned in the deep death-knell.

The light we chased with our stumbling feet
  As the goal of happier years,
Swings high and low and vanishes,—
  The bow-dyes were of our tears.

God is a lie, and Faith is a lie,
  And a tenfold lie is Love;
Life is a problem without a why,
  And never a thing to prove.

It adds, and subtracts, and multiplies,
  And divides without aim or end;
Its answers all false, though false-named true,—
  Wife, husband, lover, friend.

We know it now, and we care no more;
  What matters life or death?
We tiny insects emerge from earth,
  Suffer, and yield our breath.

Like ants we crawl on our brief sand-hill,
  Dreaming of "mighty things,"—
Lo, they crunch, like shells in the ocean's wrath,
  In the rush of Time's awful wings.

The sun smiles gold, and the planets white,
  And a billion stars smile, still;
Yet, fierce as we, each wheels towards death,
  And cannot stay his will.

Then build, ye fools, your mighty things,
  That Time shall set at naught;
Grow warm with the song the sweet Lie sings,
  And the false bow your tears have wrought.

For us, a truce to Gods, loves, and hopes,
  And a pledge to fire and wave;
A swifter whirl to the dance of death,
  And a loud huzza for the Grave!

PHILADELPHIA, 1892.

IN MEMORIAM

(To Dyer D. Lum, my friend and teacher, who died April 6, 1893.)

Great silent heart! These barren drops of grief
  Are not for you, attained unto your rest;
This sterile salt upon the withered leaf
  Of love, is mine—mine the dark burial guest.

Far, far within that deep, untroubled sea
  We watched together, walking on the sands,
Your soul has melted,—painless, silent, free;
  Mine the wrung heart, mine the clasped, useless hands.

Into the whirl of life, where none remember,
  I bear your image, ever unforgot;
The "Whip-poor-will," still "wailing in December,"
  Cries the same cry—cries, cries, and ceases not.

The future years with all their waves of faces
  Roll shoreward singing the great undertone;
Yours is not there;—in the old, well-loved places
  I look, and pass, and watch the sea alone.

Alone along the gleaming, white sea-shore,
  The sea-spume spraying thick around my head,
Through all the beat of waves and winds that roar,
  I go, remembering that you are dead.

That you are dead, and nowhere is there one
  Like unto you;—and nowhere Love leaps Death;—
And nowhere may the broken race be run;—
  Nowhere unsealed the seal that none gainsaith.

Yet in my ear that deep, sweet undertone
  Grows deeper, sweeter, solemner to me,—
Dreaming your dreams, watching the light that shone
  So whitely to you, yonder, on the sea.

Your voice is there, there in the great life-sound—
  Your eyes are there, out there, within the light;
Your heart, within the pulsing Race-heart drowned,
  Beats in the immortality of Right.

O Life, I love you for the love of him
  Who showed me all your glory and your pain!
"Unto Nirvana"—so the deep tones sing—
  And there—and there—we—shall—be—one—again.

GREENSBURG, PA., April 9th, 1893.

OUT OF THE DARKNESS

Who am I? Only one of the commonest common people,
Only a worked-out body, a shriveled and withered soul,
What right have I to sing then? None; and I do not, I cannot.
Why ruin the rhythm and rhyme of the great world's songs with
    moaning?
I know not—nor why whistles must shriek, wheels ceaselessly
    mutter;
Nor why all I touch turns to clanging and clashing and discord;
I know not;—I know only this,—I was born to this, live in it
    hourly,
Go round with it, hum with it, curse with it, would laugh with
    it, had it laughter;
It is my breath—and that breath goes outward from me in
    moaning.

O you, up there, I have heard you; I am "God's image defaced,"
"In heaven reward awaits me," "hereafter I shall be perfect";
Ages you've sung that song, but what is it to me, think you?
If you heard down here in the smoke and the smut, in the smear
    and the offal,
In the dust, in the mire, in the grime and in the slime, in the
    hideous darkness,
How the wheels turn your song into sounds of horror and
    loathing and cursing,
The offer of lust, the sneer of contempt and acceptance, thieves'
    whispers,
The laugh of the gambler, the suicide's gasp, the yell of the
    drunkard,
If you heard them down here you would cry, "The reward of
    such is damnation,"
If you heard them, I say, your song of "rewarded hereafter"
    would fail.

You, too, with your science, your titles, your books, and your
    long explanations
That tell me how I am come up out of the dust of the cycles,
Out of the sands of the sea, out of the unknown primeval
    forests,—
Out of the growth of the world have become the bud and the
    promise,—

Out of the race of the beasts have arisen, proud and triumphant,—
You, if you knew how your words rumble round in the wheels
   of labor!
If you knew how my hammering heart beats, "Liar, liar, you lie!
Out of all buds of the earth we are most blasted and blighted!
What beast of all the beasts is not prouder and freer than we?"
You, too, who sing in high words of the glory of Man universal,
The beauty of sacrifice, debt of the future, the present immortal,
The glory of use, absorption by Death of the being in Being,
You, if you knew what jargon it makes, down here, would be
   quiet.

Oh, is there no one to find or to speak a meaning to *me*,
To me as I am,—the hard, the ignorant, withered-souled worker?
To me upon whom God and Science alike have stamped "failure,"
To me who know nothing but labor, nothing but sweat, dirt, and
   sorrow,
To me whom you scorn and despise, you up there who sing while
   I moan?
To me as I am,—for me as I am—not dying but living;
Not my future, my present! my body, my needs, my desires! Is
   there no one,
In the midst of this rushing of phantoms—of Gods, of Science,
   of Logic,
Of Philosophy, Morals, Religion, Economy,—all this that helps
   not,
All these ghosts at whose altars you worship, these ponderous,
   marrowless Fictions,
Is there no one who thinks, is there nothing to help this dull
   moaning me?

PHILADELPHIA, April, 1893.

MARY WOLLSTONECRAFT

The dust of a hundred years
  Is on thy breast,
And thy day and thy night of tears
  Are centurine rest.
Thou to whom joy was dumb,
  Life a broken rhyme,
Lo, thy smiling time is come,
  And our weeping time.
Thou who hadst sponge and myrrh
  And a bitter cross,
Smile, for the day is here
  That we know our loss;—
Loss of thine undone deed,
  Thy unfinished song,
Th' unspoken word for our need,
  Th' unrighted wrong;
Smile, for we weep, we weep,
  For the unsoothed pain,
The unbound wound burned deep,
  That we might gain.
Mother of sorrowful eyes
  In the dead old days,
Mother of many sighs,
  Of pain-shod ways;
Mother of resolute feet
  Through all the thorns,
Mother soul-strong, soul-sweet,—
  Lo, after storms
Have broken and beat thy dust
  For a hundred years,
Thy memory is made just,
  And the just man hears.
Thy children kneel and repeat:
  "Though dust be dust,
Though sod and coffin and sheet
  And moth and rust
Have folded and molded and pressed,
  Yet they cannot kill;
In the heart of the world at rest
  She liveth still."

PHILADELPHIA, April 27th, 1893.

THE GODS AND THE PEOPLE

What have you done, O skies,
That the millions should kneel to you?
Why should they lift wet eyes,
Grateful with human dew?

Why should they clasp their hands,
And bow at thy shrines, O heaven,
Thanking thy high commands
For the mercies that thou hast given?

What have those mercies been,
O thou, who art called the Good,
Who trod through a world of sin,
And stood where the felon stood?

What is that wondrous peace
Vouchsafed to the child of dust,
For whom all doubt shall cease
In the light of thy perfect trust?

How hast Thou heard their prayers
Smoking up from the bleeding sod,
Who, crushed by their weight of cares,
Cried up to Thee, Most High God?

  * * * *

Where the swamps of Humanity sicken,
Read the answer, in dumb, white scars!
You, Skies, gave the sore and the stricken
The light of your far-off stars!

The children who plead are driven,
Shelterless, through the street,
Receiving the mercy of Heaven
Hard-frozen in glittering sleet!

The women who prayed for pity,
Who called on the saving Name,
Through the walks of your merciless city
Are crying the rent of shame.

The starving, who gazed on the plenty
In which they might not share,
Have died in their hunger, rent by
The anguish of unheard prayer!

The weary who plead for remission,
For a moment, only, release,
Have sunk, with unheeded petition:
This is the Christ-pledged Peace.

These are the mercies of Heaven,
These are the answers of God
To the prayers of the agony-shriven,
From the paths where the millions plod!

The silent scorn of the sightless!
The callous ear of the deaf!
The wrath of might to the mightless!
The shroud, and the mourning sheaf!

Light—to behold their squalor!
Breath—to draw in life's pain!
Voices to plead and call for
Heaven's help!—hearts to bleed—in vain!

    *   *   *   *

What have you done, O Church,
That the weary should bless your name?
Should come with faith's holy torch
To light up your altar'd fane?

Why should they kiss the folds
Of the garment of your High Priest?
Or bow to the chalice that holds
The wine of your Sacred Feast?

Have you blown out the breath of their sighs?
Have you strengthened the weak, the ill?
Have you wiped the dark tears from their eyes,
And bade their sobbings be still?

Have you touched, have you known, have you felt,
Have you bent and softly smiled

In the face of the woman, who dwelt
In lewdness—to feed her child?

Have you heard the cry in the night
Going up from the outraged heart,
Masked from the social sight
By the cloak that but angered the smart?

Have you heard the children's moan,
By the light of the skies denied?
Answer, O Walls of Stone,
In the name of your Crucified!

      *   *   *   *

Out of the clay of their heart-break,
From the red dew of its sod,
You have mortar'd your brick, for Christ's sake,
And reared a palace to God!

Your painters have dipped their brushes
In the tears and the blood of the race,
Whom, LIVING, your dark frown crushes—
And limned—a DEAD Savior's face!

You have seized, in the name of God, the
Child's crust from famine's dole;
You have taken the price of its body
And sung a mass for its soul!

You have smiled on the man, who, deceiving,
Paid exemption to ease your wrath!
You have cursed the poor fool who believed him,
Though her body lay prone in your path!

You have laid the seal on the lip!
You have bid us to be content!
To bow 'neath our master's whip,
And give thanks for the scourge—"heav'n sent."

These, O Church, are your thanks;
These are the fruits without flaw,
That flow from the chosen ranks
Who keep in your perfect law;

Doors hard-locked on the homeless!
Stained glass windows for bread!
On the living, the law of dumbness,
And the law of need, for—the *dead!*

Better the dead, who, not needing,
Go down to the vaults of the Earth,
Than the living whose hearts lie bleeding,
Crushed by you at their very birth.

      *   *   *   *

What have you done, O State,
That the toilers should shout your ways;
Should light up the fires of their hate
If a "traitor" should dare dispraise?

How do you guard the trust
That the people repose in you?
Do you keep to the law of the just,
And hold to the changeless true?

What do you mean when you say
"The home of the free and brave"?
How free are your people, pray?
Have you no such thing as a slave?

What are the lauded "rights,"
Broad-sealed, by your Sovereign Grace?
What are the love-feeding sights
You yield to your subject race?

      *   *   *   *

The rights!—Ah! the right to toil,
That another, idle, may reap;
The right to make fruitful the soil
And a meagre pittance to keep!

The right of a woman to own
Her body, spotlessly pure,
And starve in the street—alone!
The right of the wronged—to endure!

The right of the slave—to his yoke!
The right of the hungry—to pray!
The right of the toiler—to vote
For the master who buys his day!

You have sold the sun and the air!
You have dealt in the price of blood!
You have taken the lion's share
While the lion is fierce for food!

You have laid the load of the strong
On the helpless, the young, the weak!
You have trod out the purple of wrong;—
Beware where its wrath shall wreak!

"Let the Voice of the People be heard!
O——" You strangled it with your rope!
Denied the last dying word,
While your Trap and your Gallows spoke!

But a thousand voices rise
Where the words of the martyr fell;
The seed springs fast to the Skies
Watered deep from that bloody well!"

*   *   *   *

Hark! Low down you will hear
The storm in the underground!
Listen, Tyrants, and fear!
Quake at that muffled sound!

"Heavens, that mocked our dust,
Smile on, in your pitiless blue!
Silent as you are to us,
So silent are we to you!

"Churches that scourged our brains!
Priests that locked fast our hands!
We planted the torch in your chains
Now gather the burning brands!

"States that have given us LAW,
When we asked for THE RIGHT TO EARN BREAD!
The Sword that Damocles saw
By a hair swings over your head!

"What ye have sown ye shall reap:
Teardrops, and Blood, and Hate,
Gaunt gather before your Seat,
And knock at your palace gate!

"There are murderers on your Thrones!
There are thieves in your Justice-halls!
White Leprosy cancers their stones,
And gnaws at their worm-eaten walls!

"And the Hand of Belshazzar's Feast
Writes over, in flaming light:
THOUGHT'S KINGDOM NO MORE TO THE PRIEST;
NOR THE LAW OF RIGHT UNTO MIGHT."

JOHN P. ALTGELD

(After an incarceration of six long years in Joliet state prison
for an act of which they were entirely innocent, namely, the throwing of the Haymarket bomb, in Chicago, May 4th, 1886, Oscar Neebe,
Michael Schwab, and Samuel Fielden, were liberated by Gov. Altgeld,
who thus sacrificed his political career to an act of justice.)

There was a tableau! Liberty's clear light
   Shone never on a braver scene than that.
   Here was a prison, there a Man who sat
High in the Halls of state! Beyond, the might
   Of ignorance and Mobs, whose hireling press
Yells at their bidding like the slaver's hounds,
   Ready with coarse caprice to curse or bless,
To make or unmake rulers!—Lo, there sounds
   A grating of the doors! And three poor men,
Helpless and hated, having naught to give,
Come from their long-sealed tomb, look up, and live,
   And thank this Man that they are free again.
And He—to all the world this Man dares say,
   "Curse as you will! I have been just this day."

PHILADELPHIA, June, 1893.

THE CRY OF THE UNFIT

The gods have left us, the creeds have crumbled;
   There are none to pity and none to care:
Our fellows have crushed us where we have stumbled;
   They have made of our bodies a bleeding stair.

Loud rang the bells in the Christmas steeples;
   We heard them ring through the bitter morn:
The promise of old to the weary peoples
   Came floating sweetly,—"Christ is born."

But the words were mocking, sorely mocking,
   As we sought the sky through our freezing tears,
We children, who've hung the Christmas stocking,
   And found it empty two thousand years.

No, there is naught in the old creed for us;
 Love and peace are to those who win;
To them the delight of the golden chorus,
 To us the hunger and shame and sin.

Why then live on since our lives are fruitless,
 Since peace is certain and death is rest;
Since our masters tell us the strife is bootless,
 And Nature scorns her unwelcome guest?

You who have climbed on our aching bodies,
 You who have thought because we have toiled,
Priests of the creed of a newer goddess,
 Searchers in depths where the Past was foiled.

Speak in the name of the faith that you cherish!
 Give us the truth! We have bought it with woe!
Must we forever thus worthlessly perish,
 Burned in the desert and lost in the snow?

Trampled, forsaken, foredoomed, and forgotten,—
 Helplessly tossed like the leaf in the storm?
Bred for the shambles, with curses begotten,
 Useless to all save the rotting grave-worm?

Give us some anchor to stay our mad drifting!
 Give, for your own sakes! for lo, where our blood,
A red tide to drown you, is steadily lifting!
 Help! or you die in the terrible flood!

PHILADELPHIA, 1893.

IN MEMORIAM

To Gen. M. M. Trumbull.

(No man better than Gen. Trumbull defended my martyred comrades in Chicago.)

Back to thy breast, O Mother, turns thy child,
  He whom thou garmentedst in steel of truth,
  And sent forth, strong in the glad heart of youth,
To sing the wakening song in ears beguiled
By tyrants' promises and flatterers' smiles;
These searched his eyes, and knew nor threats nor wiles
  Might shake the steady stars within their blue,
Nor win one truckling word from off those lips,—
  No—not for gold nor praise, nor aught men do
To dash the Sun of Honor with eclipse,
O Mother Liberty, those eyes are dark,
  And the brave lips are white and cold and dumb;
  But fair in other souls, through time to come,
Fanned by thy breath glows the Immortal Spark.

PHILADELPHIA, May, 1894.

THE WANDERING JEW

(The above poem was suggested by the reading of an article describing an interview with the "wandering Jew," in which he was represented as an incorrigible grumbler. The Jew has been, and will continue to be, the grumbler of earth,—until the prophetic ideal of justice shall be realized: "BLESSED BE HE.")

"Go on."—"THOU shalt go on till I come."

Pale, ghostly Vision from the coffined years,
  Planting the cross with thy world-wandering feet,
  Stern Watcher through the centuries' storm and beat,
In those sad eyes, between those grooves of tears,—
  Those eyes like caves where sunlight never dwells
  And stars but dimly shine—stand sentinels
That watch with patient hope, through weary days,
  That somewhere, sometime, He indeed may "come,"
And thou at last find thee a resting place,
  Blast-driven leaf of Man, within the tomb.

Aye, they have cursed thee with the bitter curse,
  And driven thee with scourges o'er the world;
  Tyrants have crushed thee, Ignorance has hurled
Its black anathema;—but Death's pale hearse,
  That bore them graveward, passed them silently;
  And vainly didst thou stretch thy hands and cry,
"Take me instead";—not yet for thee the time,
  Not yet—not yet: thy bruised and mangled limbs
Must still drag on, still feed the Vulture, Crime,
  With bleeding flesh, till rust its steel beak dims.

Aye, "till He come,"—He,—FREEDOM, JUSTICE, PEACE—
  Till then shalt thou cry warning through the earth,
  Unheeding pain, untouched by death and birth,
Proclaiming "Woe, woe, woe," till men shall cease
  To seek for Christ within the senseless skies,
  And, joyous, find him in each other's eyes.
Then shall be builded such a tomb for thee
  Shall beggar kings' as diamonds outshine dew!
The Universal Heart of Man shall be
  The sacred urn of "the accursed Jew."

PHILADELPHIA, 1894.

THE FEAST OF VULTURES

(As the three Anarchists, Vaillant, Henry and Caserio, were led
to their several executions, a voice from the prison cried loudly, "Vive
l'anarchie!" Through watch and ward the cry escaped, and no man
owned the voice; but the cry is still resounding through the world.)

A moan in the gloam in the air-peaks heard—
The Bird of Omen—the wild, fierce Bird,
  Aflight
    In the night,
      Like a whizz of light,
Arrowy winging before the storm,
    Far away flinging,
    The whistling, singing,
White-curdled drops, wind-blown and warm,
    From its beating, flapping,
      Thunderous wings;
    Crashing and clapping
      The split night swings,
And rocks and totters,

Bled of its levin,
And reels and mutters
A curse to Heaven!
Reels and mutters and rolls and dies,
With a wild light streaking its black, blind eyes.

Far, far, far,
Through the red, mad morn,
Like a hurtling star,
Through the air upborne,
The Herald-Singer,
The Terror-Bringer,
Speeds—and behind, through the cloud-rags torn,
Gather and wheel a million wings,
Clanging as iron where the hammer rings;
The whipped sky shivers,
The White Gate shakes,
The ripped throne quivers,
The dumb God wakes,
And feels in his heart the talon-stings—
The dead bodies hurled from beaks for slings.
"Ruin! Ruin!" the Whirlwind cries,
And it leaps at his throat and tears his eyes;
"Death for death, as ye long have dealt;
The heads of your victims your heads shall pelt;
The blood ye wrung to get drunk upon,
Drink, and be poisoned! On, Herald, on!"

Behold, behold,
How a moan is grown!
A cry hurled high 'gainst a scaffold's joist!
The Voice of Defiance—the loud, wild Voice!
Whirled
Through the world,
A smoke-wreath curled
(Breath 'round hot kisses) around a fire!
See! the ground hisses
With curses, and glisses
With red-streaming blood-clots of long-frozen ire,
Waked by the flying
Wild voice as it passes;
Groaning and crying,
The surge of the masses
Rolls and flashes

With thunderous roar—
Seams and lashes
The livid shore—
Seams and lashes and crunches and beats,
And drags a ragged wall to its howling retreats!

Swift, swift, swift,
'Thwart the blood-rain's fall,
Through the fire-shot rift
Of the broken wall,
The prophet-crying
The storm-strong sighing,
Flies—and from under Night's lifted pall,
Swarming, menace ten million darts,
Uplifting fragments of human shards!

Ah, white teeth chatter,
And dumb jaws fall,
While winged fires scatter
Till gloom gulfs all
Save the boom of the cannon that storm the forts
That the people bombard with their comrades' hearts;
"Vengeance! Vengeance!" the voices scream,
And the vulture pinions whirl and stream!
"Knife for knife, as ye long have dealt;
The edge ye whetted for us be felt,
Ye chopper of necks, on your own, your own!
Bare it, Coward! On, Prophet, on!"

Behold how high
Rolls a prison cry!

PHILADELPHIA, August, 1894.

THE SUICIDE'S DEFENSE

(Of all the stupidities wherewith the law-making powe⋅ has signaled its own incapacity for dealing with the disorders of society, none appears so utterly stupid as the law which punishei an attempted suicide. To the question "What have you to say in your defense?" I conceive the poor wretch might reply as follows:)

To say in my defense? Defense of what?
Defense to whom? And why defense at all?
Have I wronged any? Let that one accuse!
Some priest there mutters I "have outraged God"!
Let God then try me, and let none dare judge
Himself as fit to put Heaven's ermine on!
Again I say, let the wronged one accuse.
Aye, silence! There is none to answer me.
And whom could I, a homeless, friendless tramp,
To whom all doors are shut, all hearts are locked,
All hands withheld—whom could I wrong, indeed
By taking that which benefited none
And menaced all?
          Aye, since ye will' it so,
Know then your risk. But mark, 'tis not defense,
'Tis accusation that I hurl at you.
See to't that ye prepare your own defense.
My life, I say, is an eternal threat
To you and yours; and therefore it were well
To have foreborne your unasked services.
And why? Because I hate you! Every drop
Of blood that circles in your plethoric veins
Was wrung from out the gaunt and sapless trunks
Of men like me, who in your cursed mills
Were crushed like grapes within the wine-press ground.
To us ye leave the empty skin of life;
The heart of it, the sweet of it, ye pour
To fete your dogs and mistresses withal!
Your mistresses! Our daughters! Bought, for bread,
To grace the flesh that once was father's arms!

Yes, I accuse you that ye murdered me!
Ye killed the Man—and this that speaks to you
Is but the beast that ye have made of me!
What! Is it life to creep and crawl and beg,
And slink for shelter where rats congregate?

And for one's ideal dream of a fat meal?
Is it, then, life, to group like pigs in sties,
And bury decency in common filth,
Because, forsooth, your income must be made,
Though human flesh rot in your plague-rid dens?
Is it, then, life, to wait another's nod,
For leave to turn yourself to gold for him?
Would it be life to you? And was I less
Than you? Was I not born with hopes and dreams
And pains and passions even as were you?

But these ye have denied. Ye seized the earth,
Though it was none of yours, and said: "Hereon
Shall none rest, walk or work, till first to me
Ye render tribute!" Every art of man,
Born to make light of the burdens of the world,
Ye also seized, and made a tenfold curse
To crush the man beneath the thing he made.
Houses, machines, and lands—all, all are yours;
And us you do not need. When we ask work
Ye shake your heads. Homes?—Ye evict us. Bread?—
"Here, officer, this fellow's begging. Jail's
The place for him!" After the stripes, what next?—
Poison!—I took it!—Now you say 'twas sin
To take this life which troubled you so much.
Sin to escape insult, starvation, brands
Of felony, inflicted for the crime
Of asking food! Ye hypocrites! Within
Your secret hearts the sin is that I *failed!*
Because I failed ye judge me to the stripes,
And the hard toil denied when I was free.
So be it. But beware!—A prison cell's
An evil bed to grow morality!
Black swamps breed black miasms; sickly soils
Yield poison fruit; snakes warmed to life will sting.
This time I was content to go alone;
Perchance the next I shall not be so kind.

PHILADELPHIA, September, 1894.

A NOVEL OF COLOR

(The following is a true and particular account of what happened on the night of December 11, 1895; but it is likely to be unintelligible to all save the Chipmunks and the Elephant, who, however, will no doubt recognize themselves.)

Chapter I.

Chipmunks three sat on a tree,
And they were as green as green could be;
They cracked nuts early, they cracked nuts late,
And chirruped and chirruped, and ate and ate;
"'Tis a pity of chipmunks without nuts,
And a gnawing hunger in their guts;
But they should be wise like you and me,
And color themselves to suit the tree.
Ah chee, ah chee, ah chee, ah chee!
Gay chaps are we, we chipmunks three!"

An elephant white in sorry plight,
Hungry and dirty and sad bedight,
Straggled one day on the nutting ground;
"Lo," chattered the chipmunks, "our chance is found!
Behold the beast's color; were he as we,
Green and sleek and nut-full were he!
But the beast is big, and the beast is white,
And his skin full of emptiness serves him right!
Ah chee, ah chee, ah chee, ah chee!
Let us 'sit on him, sit on him,' chipmunks three."

Chapter II.

Three chipmunks green right gay were seen
To leap on the beast his brows between;
They munched at his ears and chiffered his chin,
And sat and sat and sat on him!
Not a single available spot of hide
Where a well-sleeked chipmunk could sit with pride,
But was chipped and chipped and chip-chip-munked,
Till aught but an elephant must have flunked.
Ah chee, ah chee, ah chee, ah chee!
What a ride we're having, we chipmunks three!"

Chapter III.

Br-r-r-r-r-r-r-r-f-f-f-f-f! ! !

Chapter IV.

"What was it blew? Ah whew, ah whew!"
Three green chipmunks have all turned blue!
The elephant smiles a peaceful smile,
And lifts off a tree-trunk sans haste or guile.
"Seize him, seize him! He's stealing our tree!
We're undone, undone," shriek the chipmunks three.
The elephant calmly upraised his trunk,
And said, "Did I hear a green chipmunk?"

*   *   *   *   *

"Ah chee, ah chee, ah chee, ah choo!"
"Chippy, you're blue!" "So're you!"   "So're you!"

Philadelphia, December, 1895.

GERMINAL

(The last word of Angiolillo.)

Germinal!—The Field of Mars is plowing,
And hard the steel that cuts, and hot the breath
Of the great Oxen, straining flanks and bowing
Beneath his goad, who guides the share of Death.

Germinal!—The Dragon's teeth are sowing,
And stern and white the sower flings the seed
He shall not gather, though full swift the growing;
Straight down Death's furrow treads, and does not heed.

Germinal!—The Helmet Heads are springing
Far up the Field of Mars in gleaming files;
With wild war notes the bursting earth is ringing.

*   *   *   *   *

Within his grave the sower sleeps, and smiles.

London, October, 1897.

"LIGHT UPON WALDHEIM"

(The figure on the monument over the grave of the Chicago martyrs in Waldheim Cemetery is a warrior woman, dropping with her left hand a crown upon the forehead of a fallen man just past his agony, and with her right drawing a dagger from her bosom.)

Light upon Waldheim! And the earth is gray;
　A bitter wind is driving from the north;
The stone is cold, and strange cold whispers say:
　"What do ye here with Death? Go forth! Go forth!"

Is this thy word, O Mother, with stern eyes,
　Crowning thy dead with stone-caressing touch?
May we not weep o'er him that martyred lies,
　Slain in our name, for that he loved us much?

May we not linger till the day is broad?
　Nay, none are stirring in this stinging dawn—
None but poor wretches that make no moan to God:
　What use are these, O thou with dagger drawn?

"Go forth, go forth! Stand not to weep for these,
　Till, weakened with your weeping, like the snow
Ye melt, dissolving in a coward peace!"
　Light upon Waldheim! Brother, let us go!

London, October, 1897.

LOVE'S COMPENSATION

I went before God, and he said,
　"What fruit of the life I gave?"
"Father," I said, "It is dead,
　And nothing grows on the grave."

Wroth was the Lord and stern:
　"Hadst thou not to answer me?
Shall the fruitless root not burn,
　And be wasted utterly?"

"Father," I said, "forgive!
  For thou knowest what I have done;
That another's life might live
  Mine turned to a barren stone."

But the Father of Life sent fire
  And burned the root in the grave;
And the pain in my heart is dire
  For the thing that I could not save.

For the thing it was laid on me
  By the Lord of Life to bring;
Fruit of the ungrown tree
  That died for no watering.

Another has gone to God,
  And his fruit has pleased Him well;
For he sitteth high, while I—plod
  The dry ways down towards hell.

Though thou knowest, thou knowest, Lord,
  Whose tears made that fruit's root wet;
Yet thou drivest me forth with a sword,
  And thy Guards by the Gate are set.

Thou wilt give me up to the fire,
  And none shall deliver me;
For I followed my heart's desire,
  And I labored not for thee:

I labored for him thou hast set
  On thy right hand, high and fair;
Thou lovest him, Lord; and yet
  'Twas my love won Him there.

But this is the thing that hath been,
  Hath been since the world began,—
That love against self must sin,
  And a woman die for a man.

And this is the thing that shall be,
  Shall be till the whole world die,
Kismet:—My doom is on me!
  Why murmur since I am I?

PHILADELPHIA, August, 1898.

THE ROAD BUILDERS

("Who built the beautiful roads?" queried a friend of the present order, as we walked one day along the macadamized driveway of Fairmount Park.)

I saw them toiling in the blistering sun,
Their dull, dark faces leaning toward the stone,
Their knotted fingers grasping the rude tools,
Their rounded shoulders narrowing in their chest,
The sweat drops dripping in great painful beads.
I saw one fall, his forehead on the rock,
The helpless hand still clutching at the spade,
The slack mouth full of earth.

                    And he was dead.
His comrades gently turned his face, until
The fierce sun glittered hard upon his eyes,
Wide open, staring at the cruel sky.
The blood yet ran upon the jagged stone;
But it was ended. He was quite, quite dead:
Driven to death beneath the burning sun,
Driven to death upon the road he built.

He was no "hero," he; a poor, black man,
Taking "the will of God" and asking naught;
Think of him thus, when next your horse's feet
Strike out the flint spark from the gleaming road;
Think that for this, this common thing, The Road,
A human creature died; 'tis a blood gift,
To an o'erreaching world that does not thank.
Ignorant, mean and soulless was he? Well,—
Still human; and you drive upon his corpse.

PHILADELPHIA, July 24, 1900.

ANGIOLILLO

We are the souls that crept and cried in the days when they
    tortured men;
His was the spirit that walked erect, and met the beast in its den.

Ours are the eyes that were dim with tears for the thing they
    shrunk to see;
His was the glance that was crystal keen with the light that
    makes men free.

Ours are the hands that were wrung in pain, in helpless pain
    and shame;
His was the resolute hand that struck, steady and keen to its aim.

Ours are the lips that quivered with rage, that cursed and prayed
    in a breath:
His was the mouth that opened but once to speak from the
    throat of Death.

"Assassin, Assassin!" the World cries out, with a shake of its
    dotard head;
"Germinal!" rings back the grave where lies the Dead that is
    not dead.

"Germinal, Germinal," sings the Wind that is driving before
    the Storm;
"Few are the drops that have fallen yet,—scattered, but red and
    warm."

"Germinal, Germinal," sing the Fields, where furrows of men
    are plowed;
"Ye shall gather a harvest over-rich, when the ear at the full
    is bowed."

Springing, springing, at every breath, the Word of invincible
    strife,
The word of the Dead, that is calling loud down the battle ranks
    of Life!

For these are the Dead that live, though the earth upon them lie:
But the doers of deeds of the Night of the Dead, they are the
    Live that die.

TORRESDALE, PA., August 1, 1900.

AVE ET VALE

Comrades, what matter the watch-night **tells**
  That a New Year comes or goes?
What to us are the crashing bells
  That clang out the Century's close?

What to us is the gala dress?
  The whirl of the dancing feet?
The glitter and blare in the laughing **press,**
  And din of the merry street?

Do we not know that our brothers **die**
  In the cold and the dark to-night?
Shelterless faces turned toward the **sky**
  Will not see the New Year's light!

Wandering children, lonely, lost,
  Drift away on the human sea,
While the price of their lives in a glass **is tossed**
  And drunk in a revelry!

Ah, know we not in their feasting **halls**
  Where the loud laugh echoes again,
That brick and stone in the mortared **walls**
  Are the bones of murdered men?

Slowly murdered! By day and day,
  The beauty and strength are reft,
Till the Man is sapped and sucked **away,**
  And a Human Rind is left!

A Human Rind, with old, thin hair,
  And old, thin voice to pray
For alms in the bitter winter air,—
  A knife at his heart alway.

And the pure in heart are impure **in flesh**
  For the cost of a little food:
Lo, when the Gleaner of Time shall **thresh,**
  Let these be accounted good.

For these are they who in bitter blame
  Eat the bread whose salt is sin;
Whose bosoms are burned with the scarlet shame,
  Till their hearts are seared within.

The cowardly jests of a hundred years
  Will be thrown where they pass to-night,
Too callous for hate, and too dry for tears,
  The saddest of human blight.

Do we forget them, these broken ones,
  That our watch to-night is set?
Nay, we smile in the face of the year that comes
  Because we do not forget.

We do not forget the tramp on the track,
  Thrust out in the wind-swept waste,
The curses of Man upon his back,
  And the curse of God in his face.

The stare in the eyes of the buried man
  Face down in the fallen mine;
The despair of the child whose bare feet ran
  To tread out the rich man's wine;

The solemn light in the dying gaze
  Of the babe at the empty breast,
The wax accusation, the sombre glaze
  Of its frozen and rigid rest;

They are all in the smile that we turn to the east
  To welcome the Century's dawn;
They are all in our greeting to Night's high priest,
  As we bid the Old Year begone.

Begone and have done, and go down and be dead
  Deep drowned in your sea of tears!
We smile as you die, for we wait the red
  Morn-gleam of a hundred-years

That shall see the end of the age-old wrong,—
  The reapers that have not sown,—
The reapers of men with their sickles strong
  Who gather, but have not strown.

For the earth shall be his and the fruits thereof
  And to him the corn and wine,
Who labors the hills with an even love
  And knows not "thine and mine."

And the silk shall be to the hand that weaves,
  The pearl to him who dives,
The home to the builder; and all life's sheaves
  To the builder of human lives.

And none go blind that another see,
  Or die that another live;
And none insult with a charity
  That is not theirs to give.

For each of his plenty shall freely share
  And take at another's hand:
Equals breathing the Common Air
  And toiling the Common Land.

A dream? A vision? Aye, what you will;
  Let it be to you as it seems:
Of this Nightmare Real we have our fill;
  To-night is for "pleasant dreams."

Dreams that shall waken the hope that sleeps
  And knock at each torpid Heart
Till it beat drum taps, and the blood that creeps
  With a lion's spring upstart!

For who are we to be bound and drowned
  In this river of human blood?
Who are we to lie in a swound,
  Half sunk in the river mud?

Are we not they who delve and blast
    And hammer and build and burn?
Without us not a nail made fast!
    Not a wheel in the world should turn!

Must we, the Giant, await the grace
    That is dealt by the puny hand
Of him who sits in the feasting place,
    While we, his Blind Jest, stand

Between the pillars? Nay, not so:
    Aye, if such thing were true,
Better were Gaza again, to show
    What the giant's rage may do!

But yet not this: it were wiser far
    To enter the feasting hall
And say to the Masters, "These things are
    Not for you alone, but all."

And this shall be in the Century
    That opes on our eyes to-night;
So here's to the struggle, if it must be,
    And to him who fights the fight.

And here's to the dauntless, jubilant throat
    That loud to its Comrade sings,
Till over the earth shrills the mustering note,
    And the World Strike's signal rings.

PHILADELPHIA, January 1, 1901.

MARSH-BLOOM

(To Gaetano Bresci.)

Requiem, requiem, requiem,
Blood-red blossom of poison stem
   Broken for Man,
Swamp-sunk leafage and dungeon bloom,
Seeded bearer of royal doom,
   What now is the ban?

What to thee is the island grave?
With desert wind and desolate wave
   Will they silence Death?
Can they weight thee now with the heaviest stone?
Can they lay aught on thee with "Be alone,"
   That hast conquered breath?

Lo, "it is finished"—a man for a king!
Mark you well who have done this thing:
   The flower has roots;
Bitter and rank grow the things of the sea;
Ye shall know what sap ran thick in the tree
   When ye pluck its fruits.

Requiem, requiem, requiem,
Sleep on, sleep on, accursed of them
   Who work our pain;
A wild Marsh-blossom shall blow again
From a buried root in the slime of men,
   On the day of the Great Red Rain.

PHILADELPHIA, July, 1901.

WRITTEN—IN—RED*

(To Our Living Dead in Mexico's Struggle.)

Written in red their protest stands,
For the Gods of the World to see;
On the dooming wall their bodiless hands
Have blazoned "Upharsin," and flaring brands
Illumine the message: "Seize the lands!
Open the prisons and make men free!"
Flame out the living words of the dead
    Written—in—red.

Gods of the World! Their mouths are dumb!
Your guns have spoken and they are dust.
But the shrouded Living, whose hearts were numb,
Have felt the beat of a wakening drum
Within them sounding—the Dead Men's tongue—
Calling: "Smite off the ancient rust!"
Have beheld "Resurrexit," the word of the Dead,
    Written—in—red.

Bear it aloft, O roaring flame!
Skyward aloft, where all may see.
Slaves of the World! Our cause is the same;
One is the immemorial shame;
One is the struggle, and in One name—
MANHOOD—we battle to set men free.
"Uncurse us the Land!" burn the words of the Dead,
    Written—in—red.

* Voltairine de Cleyre's last poem.

ESSAYS

The Dominant Idea

IN everything that lives, if one looks searchingly, is limned the shadow line of an idea—an idea, dead or living, sometimes stronger when dead, with rigid, unswerving lines that mark the living embodiment with the stern, immobile cast of the non-living. Daily we move among these unyielding shadows, less pierceable, more enduring than granite, with the blackness of ages in them, dominating living, changing bodies, with dead, unchanging souls. And we meet, also, living souls dominating dying bodies—living ideas regnant over decay and death. Do not imagine that I speak of human life alone. The stamp of persistent or of shifting Will is visible in the grass-blade rooted in its clod of earth, as in the gossamer web of being that floats and swims far over our heads in the free world of air.

Regnant ideas, everywhere! Did you ever see a dead vine bloom? I have seen it. Last summer I trained some morning-glory vines up over a second-story balcony; and every day they blew and curled in the wind, their white, purple-dashed faces winking at the sun, radiant with climbing life. Higher every day the green heads crept, carrying their train of spreading fans waving before the sun-seeking blossoms. Then all at once some mischance happened, — some cut-worm or some mischievous child tore one vine off below, the finest and most ambitious one, of course. In a few hours the leaves hung limp, the sappy stem wilted and began to wither;

in a day it was dead,—all but the top, which still clung longingly to its support, with bright head lifted. I mourned a little for the buds that could never open now, and pitied that proud vine whose work in the world was lost. But the next night there was a storm, a heavy, driving storm, with beating rain and blinding lightning. I rose to watch the flashes, and lo! the wonder of the world! In the blackness of the mid-Night, in the fury of wind and rain, the dead vine had flowered. Five white, moon-faced blossoms blew gaily round the skeleton vine, shining back triumphant at the red lightning. I gazed at them in dumb wonder. Dear, dead vine, whose will had been so strong to bloom that in the hour of its sudden cut-off from the feeding earth it sent the last sap to its blossoms; and, not waiting for the morning, brought them forth in storm and flash, as white night-glories, which should have been the children of the sun.

In the daylight we all came to look at the wonder, marveling much, and saying, "Surely these must be the last." But every day for three days the dead vine bloomed; and even a week after, when every leaf was dry and brown, and so thin you could see through it, one last bud, dwarfed, weak, a very baby of a blossom, but still white and delicate, with five purple flecks, like those on the live vine beside it, opened and waved at the stars, and waited for the early sun. Over death and decay the Dominant Idea smiled: the vine was in the world to bloom, to bear white trumpet blossoms dashed with purple; and it held its will beyond death.

Our modern teaching is that ideas are but attendant phenomena, impotent to determine the actions or relations of life, as the image in the glass which should say to the body it reflects: "*I* shall shape *thee*." In truth we know that directly the body goes from before the mirror, the transient image is nothingness; but the real body has its being to live, and will live it, heedless of vanished phantoms of itself, in response to the ever-shifting pressure of things without it.

It is thus that the so-called Materialist Conception of History, the modern Socialists, and a positive majority of Anarchists would have us look upon the world of ideas,—shifting, unreal reflections, having naught to do in the determination of Man's life, but so many mirror appearances of certain material relations, wholly powerless to act upon the course of material things. Mind to them is in itself a blank mirror, though in fact never wholly blank, because always facing the reality of the material and bound to reflect some shadow. To-day I am somebody, to-morrow somebody else, if the scenes have shifted; my Ego is a gibbering phantom, pirouetting in the glass, gesticulating, transforming, hourly or momentarily, gleaming with the phosphor light of a deceptive unreality, melting like the mist upon the hills. Rocks, fields, woods, streams, houses, goods, flesh, blood, bone, sinew,—these are realities, with definite parts to play, with essential characters that abide under all changes; but my Ego does not abide; it is manufactured afresh with every change of these.

I think this unqualified determinism of the material is a great and lamentable error in our modern progressive movement; and while I believe it was a wholesome antidote to the long-continued blunder of Middle Age theology, viz.: that Mind was an utterly irresponsible entity making laws of its own after the manner of an Absolute Emperor, without logic, sequence, or relation, ruler over matter, and its own supreme determinant, not excepting God (who was himself the same sort of a mind writ large)—while I do believe that the modern reconception of Materialism has done a wholesome thing in pricking the bubble of such conceit and restoring man and his "soul" to its "place in nature," I nevertheless believe that to this also there is a limit; and that the absolute sway of Matter is quite as mischievous an error as the unrelated nature of Mind; even that in its direct action upon personal conduct, it has the more ill effect of the two. For if the doctrine of free-will has raised up fanatics and persecutors, who, assuming that men may be good under all conditions if they merely wish to be so, have sought to persuade other men's wills with threats, fines, imprisonments, torture, the spike, the wheel, the axe, the fagot, in order to make them good and save them against their obdurate wills; if the doctrine of Spiritualism, the soul supreme, has done this, the doctrine of Materialistic Determinism has produced shifting, self-excusing, worthless, parasitical characters, who are *this* now and *that* at some other time, and anything and nothing upon principle. "My conditions have made me so," they cry, and there is no more to be said; poor mirror-ghosts! how could they help it! To be sure, the influence of such a character rarely reaches so far as that of the principled persecutor; but for every one of the latter, there are a hundred of these easy, doughy characters, who will fit any baking tin, to whom determinist self-excusing appeals; so the balance of evil between the two doctrines is *about* maintained.

What we need is a true appraisement of the power and rôle of the Idea. I do not think I am able to give such a true appraisement; I do not think that any one— even *much* greater intellects than mine—will be able to do it for a long time to come. But I am at least able to suggest it, to show its necessity, to give a rude approximation of it.

And first, against the accepted formula of modern Materialism, "Men are what circumstances make them,"

I set the opposing declaration, "Circumstances are what men make them"; and I contend that both these things are true up to the point where the combating powers are equalized, or one is overthrown. In other words, my conception of mind, or character, is not that it is a powerless reflection of a momentary condition of stuff and form, but an active modifying agent, reacting on its environment and transforming circumstances, sometimes greatly, sometimes, though not often, entirely.

All over the kingdom of life, I have said, one may see dominant ideas working, if one but trains his eyes to look for them and recognize them. In the human world there have been many dominant ideas. I cannot conceive that ever, at any time, the struggle of the body before dissolution can have been aught but agony. If the reasoning that insecurity of conditions, the expectation of suffering, are circumstances which make the soul of man uneasy, shrinking, timid, what answer will you give to the challenge of old Ragnar Lodbrog, to that triumphant death-song hurled out, not by one cast to his death in the heat of battle, but under slow prison torture, bitten by serpents, and yet singing: "The goddesses of death invite me away—now end I my song. The hours of my life are run out. I shall smile when I die"? Nor can it be said that this is an exceptional instance, not to be accounted for by the usual operation of general law, for old King Lodbrog the Skalder did only what his fathers did, and his sons and his friends and his enemies, through long generations; they set the force of a dominant idea, the idea of the superascendant ego, against the force of torture and of death, ending life as they wished to end it, with a smile on their lips. But a few years ago, did we not read how the helpless Kaffirs, victimized by the English for the contumacy of the Boers, having been forced to dig the trenches wherein

for pleasant sport they were to be shot, were lined up
on the edge, and seeing death facing them, began to
chant barbaric strains of triumph, smiling as they fell?
Let us admit that such exultant defiance was owing to
ignorance, to primitive beliefs in gods and hereafters;
but let us admit also that it shows the power of an idea
dominant.

Everywhere in the shells of dead societies, as in the
shells of the sea-slime, we shall see the force of purposive
action, of intent *within* holding its purpose against ob-
stacles *without.*

I think there is no one in the world who can look upon
the steadfast, far-staring face of an Egyptian carving,
or read a description of Egypt's monuments, or gaze
upon the mummied clay of its old dead men, without
feeling that the dominant idea of that people in that age
was to be enduring and to work enduring things, with
the immobility of their great still sky upon them and the
stare of the desert in them. One must feel that whatever other ideas animated them, and expressed themselves in their lives, this was the dominant idea. *That
which was* must remain, no matter at what cost, even if
it were to break the everlasting hills: an idea which
made the live humanity beneath it, born and nurtured
in the coffins of caste, groan and writhe and gnaw its
bandages, till in the fullness of time it passed away: and
still the granite mould of it stares with empty eyes out
across the world, the stern old memory of the *Thing-
that-was.*

I think no one can look upon the marbles wherein
Greek genius wrought the figuring of its soul, without
feeling an apprehension that the things are going to
leap and fly; that in a moment one is like to be set upon
by heroes with spears in their hands, by serpents that
will coil around him; to be trodden by horses that may

trample and flee; to be smitten by these gods that have as little of the idea of stone in them as a dragon-fly, one instant poised upon a wind-swayed petal edge. I think no one can look upon them without realizing at once that those figures came out of the boil of life; they seem like rising bubbles about to float into the air, but beneath them other bubbles rising, and others, and others,—there will be no end of it. When one's eyes are upon one group, one feels that behind one, perhaps, a figure is uptoeing to seize the darts of the air and hurl them on one's head; one must keep whirling to face the miracle that appears about to be wrought—stone leaping! And this though nearly every one is minus some of the glory the old Greek wrought into it so long ago; even the broken stumps of arms and legs live. And the dominant idea is Activity, and the beauty and strength of it. Change, swift, ever-circling Change! The making of things and the casting of them away, as children cast away their toys, not interested that these shall endure, so that they themselves realize incessant activity. Full of creative power, what matter if the creature perished. So there was an endless procession of changing shapes in their schools, their philosophies, their dramas, their poems, till at last it wore itself to death. And the marvel passed away from the world. But still their marbles live to show what manner of thoughts dominated them.

And if we wish to know what master-thought ruled the lives of men when the mediæval period had had time to ripen it, one has only at this day to stray into some quaint, out-of-the-way English village, where a strong old towered Church yet stands in the midst of little straw-thatched cottages, like a brooding mother-hen surrounded by her chickens. Everywhere the greatening of God, and the lessening of Man: the Church so looming, the home so little. The search for the spirit, for the *enduring* thing (not the poor endurance of granite which in the ages crumbles, but the eternal), the eternal,— and contempt for the body which perishes, manifest in studied uncleanliness, in mortifications of the flesh, as if the spirit should have spat its scorn upon it.

Such was the dominant idea of that middle age which has been too much cursed by modernists. For the men who built the castles and the cathedrals were men of mighty works, though they made no books, and though their souls spread crippled wings, because of their very endeavors to soar too high. The spirit of voluntary subordination for the accomplishment of a great work, which proclaimed the aspiration of the common soul,—that was the spirit wrought into the cathedral stones; and it is not wholly to be condemned.

In waking dream, when the shadow-shapes of world-ideas swim before the vision, one sees the Middle-Age Soul an ill-contorted, half-formless thing, with dragon wings and a great, dark, tense face, strained sunward with blind eyes.

If now we look around us to see what idea dominates our own civilization, I do not know that it is even as attractive as this piteous monster of the old darkness. The relativity of things has altered: Man has risen and God has descended. The modern village has better homes and less pretentious churches. Also the conception of dirt and disease as much-sought afflictions, the patient suffering of which is a meet offering to win God's pardon, has given place to the emphatic promulgation of cleanliness. We have Public School nurses notifying parents that "pediculosis capitis" is a very contagious and unpleasant disease; we have cancer associations gathering up such cancers as have attached themselves to impecunious persons, and carefully experimenting with a view to cleaning them out of the human race; we have tuberculosis societies attempting the Herculean labor of clearing the Augean stables of our modern factories of the deadly bacillus, and they have got as far as spittoons with water in them in some factories; and others, and others, and others, which, while not yet overwhelmingly successful in their avowed purposes, are evidence sufficient that humanity no longer seeks dirt as a means of grace. We laugh at those old superstitions, and talk much about exact experimental knowledge. We endeavor to galvanize the Greek corpse, and pretend that we enjoy physical culture. We dabble in many things; but the one great real idea of our age, not copied from any other, not pretended, not raised to life by any conjuration, is the Much Making of Things,—not the making of beautiful things, not the joy of spending living energy in creative work; rather the shameless, merciless driving and over-driving, wasting and draining of the last bit of energy, only to produce heaps and heaps of things,—things ugly, things harmful, things useless, and at the best largely unnecessary. To what end are they produced? Mostly the producer does not know; still less does he care. But he is possessed with the idea that he *must* do it, every one is doing it, and every year the making of things goes on more and faster; there are mountain ranges of things made and making, and still men go about desperately seeking to increase the list of created things, to start fresh heaps and to add to the existing heaps. And with what agony of body, under what stress and strain of danger and fear of danger, with what mutilations and maimings and lamings they struggle on, dashing themselves out against these rocks of wealth! Verily, if the vision of the Mediæval Soul is painful in its blind staring and pathetic striving, grotesque in its senseless tortures, the Soul of the

Modern is most amazing with its restless, nervous eyes, ever searching the corners of the universe, its restless, nervous hands ever reaching and grasping for some useless toil.

And certainly the presence of things in abundance, things empty and things vulgar and things absurd, as well as things convenient and useful, has produced the desire for the possession of things, the exaltation of the possession of things. Go through the business street of any city, where the tilted edges of the strata of things are exposed to gaze, and look at the faces of the people as they pass,—not at the hungry and smitten ones who fringe the sidewalks and plaint dolefully for alms, but at the crowd,—and see what idea is written on their faces. On those of the women, from the ladies of the horse-shows to the shop girls out of the factory, there is a sickening vanity, a consciousness of their clothes, as of some jackdaw in borrowed feathers. Look for the pride and glory of the free, strong, beautiful body, lithe-moving and powerful. You will not see it. You will see mincing steps, bodies tilted to show the cut of a skirt, simpering, smirking faces, with eyes cast about seeking admiration for the gigantic bow of ribbon in the over-dressed hair. In the caustic words of an acquaintance, to whom I once said, as we walked, "Look at the amount of vanity on all these women's faces," "No: look at the little bit of womanhood showing out of all that vanity!"

And on the faces of the men, coarseness! Coarse desires for coarse things, and lots of them: the stamp is set so unmistakably that "the wayfarer though a fool need not err therein." Even the frightful anxiety and restlessness begotten of the creation of all this, is less distasteful than the abominable expression of lust for the things created.

Such is the dominant idea of the western world, at

least in these our days. You may see it wherever you look, impressed plainly on things and on men; very likely, if you look in the glass, you will see it there. And if some archæologist of a long future shall some day unbury the bones of our civilization, where ashes or flood shall have entombed it, he will see this frightful idea stamped on the factory walls he shall uncover, with their rows and rows of square lightholes, their tons upon tons of toothed steel, grinning out of the skull of this our life; its acres of silk and velvet, its square miles of tinsel and shoddy. No glorious marbles of nymphs and fawns, whose dead images are yet so sweet that one might wish to kiss them still; no majestic figures of winged horses, with men's faces and lions' paws casting their colossal symbolism in a mighty spell forward upon Time, as those old stone chimeras of Babylon yet do; but meaningless iron giants, of wheels and teeth, whose secret is forgotten, but whose business was to grind men up, and spit them out as housefuls of woven stuffs, bazaars of trash, wherethrough other men might wade. The statues he shall find will bear no trace of mythic dream or mystic symbol; they will be statues of merchants and ironmasters and militiamen, in tailored coats and pantaloons and proper hats and shoes.

But the dominant idea of the age and land does not necessarily mean the dominant idea of any single life. I doubt not that in those long gone days, far away by the banks of the still Nile, in the abiding shadow of the pyramids, under the heavy burden of other men's stolidity, there went to and fro restless, active, rebel souls who hated all that the ancient society stood for, and with burning hearts sought to overthrow it.

I am sure that in the midst of all the agile Greek intellect created, there were those who went about with downbent eyes, caring nothing for it all, seeking some higher revelation, willing to abandon the joys of life, so that they drew near to some distant, unknown perfection their fellows knew not of. I am certain that in the dark ages, when most men prayed and cowered, and beat and bruised themselves, and sought afflictions, like that St. Teresa who said, "Let me suffer, or die," there were some, many, who looked on the world as a chance jest, who despised or pitied their ignorant comrades, and tried to compel the answers of the universe to their questionings, by the patient, quiet searching which came to be Modern Science. I am sure there were hundreds, thousands of them, of whom we have never heard.

And now, to-day, though the Society about us is dominated by Thing-Worship, and will stand so marked for all time, that is no reason any single soul should be. Because the one thing seemingly worth doing to my neighbor, to all my neighbors, is to pursue dollars, that is no reason I should pursue dollars. Because my neighbors conceive they need an inordinate heap of carpets, furniture, clocks, china, glass, tapestries, mirrors, clothes, jewels—and servants to care for them, and detectives to keep an eye on the servants, judges to try the thieves, and politicians to appoint the judges, jails to punish the culprits, and wardens to watch in the jails, and tax collectors to gather support for the wardens, and fees for the tax collectors, and strong houses to hold the fees, so that none but the guardians thereof can make off with them,— and therefore, to keep this host of parasites, need other men to work for them, and make the fees; because my neighbors want all this, is that any reason I should devote myself to such a barren folly? and bow my neck to serve to keep up the gaudy show?

Must we, because the Middle Age was dark and blind and brutal, throw away the one good thing it wrought into the fibre of Man, that the inside of a human being was worth more than the outside? that to conceive a higher thing than oneself and live toward that is the only way of living worthily? The goal strived for should, and must, be a very different one from that which led the mediæval fanatics to despise the body and belabor it with hourly crucifixions. But one can recognize the claims and the importance of the body without therefore sacrificing truth, honor, simplicity, and faith, to the vulgar gauds of body-service, whose very decorations debase the thing they might be supposed to exalt.

I have said before that the doctrine that men are nothing and circumstances all, has been, and is, the bane of our modern social reform movements.

Our youth, themselves animated by the spirit of the old teachers who believed in the supremacy of ideas, even in the very hour of throwing away that teaching, look with burning eyes to the social East, and believe that wonders of revolution are soon to be accomplished. In their enthusiasm they foreread the gospel of Circumstances to mean that very soon the pressure of material development must break down the social system—they give the rotten thing but a few years to last; and then, they themselves shall witness the transformation, partake in its joys. The few years pass away and nothing happens; enthusiasm cools. Behold these same idealists then, successful business men, professionals, property owners, money lenders, creeping into the social ranks they once despised, pitifully, contemptibly, at the skirts of some impecunious personage to whom they have lent money, or done some professional service gratis; behold them lying, cheating, tricking, flattering, buying and selling themselves for any frippery, any cheap little pretense. The Dominant Social Idea has seized them, their lives are swallowed up in it; and when you ask the reason why, they tell you that Circumstances compelled them so to do. If you quote their lies to them, they smile with calm complacency, assure you that when Circumstances demand lies, lies are a great deal better than truth; that tricks are sometimes more effective than honest dealing; that flattering and duping do not matter, if the end to be attained is desirable; and that under existing "Circumstances" life isn't possible without all this; that it is going to be possible whenever Circumstances have made truth-telling easier than lying, but till then a man must look out for himself, by all means. And so the cancer goes on rotting away the moral fibre, and the man becomes a lump, a squash, a piece of slippery slime, taking all shapes and losing all shapes, according to what particular hole or corner he wishes to glide into, a disgusting embodiment of the moral bankruptcy begotten by Thing-Worship.

Had he been dominated by a less material conception of life, had his will not been rotted by the intellectual reasoning of it out of its existence, by its acceptance of its own nothingness, the unselfish aspirations of his earlier years would have grown and strengthened by exercise and habit; and his protest against the time might have been enduringly written, and to some purpose.

Will it be said that the Pilgrim fathers did not hew, out of the New England ice and granite, the idea which gathered them together out of their scattered and obscure English villages, and drove them in their frail ships over the Atlantic in midwinter, to cut their way against all opposing forces? Were they not common men, subject to the operation of common law? Will it be said that Circumstances aided them? When death, disease, hunger, and cold had done their worst, not one of those remaining was willing by an *easy lie* to return to material comfort and the possibility of long days.

Had our modern social revolutionists the vigorous and undaunted conception of their own powers that these had, our social movements would not be such pitiful abortions,—core-rotten even before the outward flecks appear.

"Give a labor leader a political job, and the system becomes all right," laugh our enemies; and they point mockingly to Terence Powderly and his like; and they quote John Burns, who as soon as *he* went into Parliament declared: "The time of the agitator is past; the time of the legislator has come." "Let an Anarchist marry an heiress, and the country is safe," they sneer:—and they have the right to sneer. But would they have that right, could they have it, if our lives were not in the first instance dominated by more insistent desires than those we would fain have others think we hold most dear?

It is the old story: "Aim at the stars, and you may hit the top of the gatepost; but aim at the ground, and you will hit the ground."

It is not to be supposed that any one will attain to the full realization of what he purposes, even when those purposes do not involve united action with others; he *will* fall short; he will in some measure be overcome by contending or inert opposition. But something he will attain, if he continues to aim high.

What, then, would I have? you ask. I would have men invest themselves with the dignity of an aim higher than the chase for wealth; choose a thing to do in life outside of the making of things, and keep it in mind,—not for a day, nor a year, but for a lifetime. And then keep faith with themselves! Not be a light-o'-love, to-day professing this and to-morrow that, and easily reading oneself out of both whenever it becomes convenient; not advocating a thing to-day, and to-morrow kissing its enemies' sleeve, with that weak, coward cry in the mouth, "Circumstances make me." Take a good look into yourself, and if you love Things and the power and the plenitude of Things better than you love your own dignity, human dignity, Oh, say so, say so! Say it to yourself, and abide by it. But do not blow hot and cold in one breath. Do not try to be a social reformer and a respected possessor of Things at the same time. Do not preach the straight and narrow way while going joyously upon the wide one. *Preach the wide one,* or do not preach at all; but do not fool yourself by saying you would like to help usher in a free society, but you cannot sacrifice an armchair for it. Say honestly, "I love armchairs better than free men, and pursue them because I choose; not because circumstances make me. I love hats, large, large hats, with many feathers and great bows; and I would rather have those hats than trouble myself about social dreams that will never be accomplished in my day. The world worships hats, and I wish to worship with them."

But if you choose the liberty and pride and strength of the single soul, and the free fraternization of men, as the purpose which your life is to make manifest, then do not sell it for tinsel. Think that your soul is strong and will hold its way; and slowly, through bitter struggle perhaps, the strength will grow. And the foregoing of possessions for which others barter the last possibility of freedom, will become easy.

At the end of life you may close your eyes, saying: "I have not been dominated by the Dominant Idea of my Age; I have chosen mine own allegiance, and served it. I have proved by a lifetime that there is that in man which saves him from the absolute tyranny of Circumstance, which in the end conquers and remoulds Circumstance, —the immortal fire of Individual Will, which is the salvation of the Future."

Let us have Men, Men who will say a word to their souls and keep it—keep it not when it is easy, but keep it when it is hard—keep it when the storm roars and there

is a white-streaked sky and blue thunder before, and
one's eyes are blinded and one's ears deafened with the
war of opposing things; and keep it under the long leaden
sky and the gray dreariness that never lifts. Hold unto
the last: that is what it means to have a Dominant Idea,
where the same idea has been worked out by a whole
and unmake Circumstance.

Anarchism

THERE are two spirits abroad in the world,—the spirit of Caution, the spirit of Dare, the spirit of Quiescence, the spirit of Unrest; the spirit of Immobility, the spirit of Change; the spirit of Hold-fast-to-that-which-you-have, the spirit of Let-go-and-fly-to-that-which-you-have-not; the spirit of the slow and steady builder, careful of its labors, loath to part with any of its achievements, wishful to keep, and unable to discriminate between what is worth keeping and what is better cast aside, and the spirit of the inspirational destroyer, fertile in creative fancies, volatile, careless in its luxuriance of effort, inclined to cast away the good together with the bad.

Society is a quivering balance, eternally struck afresh, between these two. Those who look upon Man, as most Anarchists do, as a link in the chain of evolution, see in these two social tendencies the sum of the tendencies of individual men, which in common with the tendencies of all organic life are the result of the action and counteraction of inheritance and adaptation. Inheritance, continually tending to repeat what has been, long, long after it is outgrown; adaptation continually tending to break down forms. The same tendencies under other names are observed in the inorganic world as well, and anyone who is possessed by the modern scientific mania for

Monism can easily follow out the line to the vanishing point of human knowledge.

There has been, in fact, a strong inclination to do this among a portion of the more educated Anarchists, who having been working men first and Anarchists by reason of their instinctive hatred to the boss, later became students and, swept away by their undigested science, immediately conceived that it was necessary to fit their Anarchism to the revelations of the microscope, else the theory might as well be given up. I remember with considerable amusement a heated discussion some five or six years since, wherein doctors and embryo doctors sought for a justification of Anarchism in the development of the amoeba, while a fledgling engineer searched for it in mathematical quantities.

Myself at one time asserted very stoutly that no one could be an Anarchist and believe in God at the same time. Others assert as stoutly that one cannot accept the spiritualist philosophy and be an Anarchist.

At present I hold with C. L. James, the most learned of American Anarchists, that one's metaphysical system has very little to do with the matter. The chain of reasoning which once appeared so conclusive to me, namely, that Anarchism being a denial of authority over the individual could not co-exist with a belief in a Supreme Ruler of the universe, is contradicted in the case of Leo Tolstoy, who comes to the conclusion that none has a right to rule another just because of his belief in God, just because he believes that all are equal children of one father, and therefore none has a right to rule the other. I speak of him because he is a familiar and notable personage, but there have frequently been instances where the same idea has been worked out by a whole sect of believers, especially in the earlier (and persecuted) stages of their development.

It no longer seems necessary to me, therefore, that one should base his Anarchism upon any particular world conception; it is a theory of the relations due to man and comes as an offered solution to the societary problems arising from the existence of these two tendencies of which I have spoken.   No matter where those tendencies come from, all alike recognize them as existent; and however interesting the speculation, however fascinating to lose oneself back, back in the molecular storm-whirl wherein the figure of man is seen merely as a denser, fiercer group, a livelier storm centre, moving among others, impinging upon others, but nowhere separate, nowhere exempt from the same necessity that acts upon all other centers of force,—it is by no means necessary in order to reason oneself into Anarchism.

Sufficient are a good observant eye and a reasonably reflecting brain, for anyone, lettered or unlettered, to recognize the desirability of Anarchistic aims.   This is not to say that increased knowledge will not confirm and expand one's application of this fundamental concept; (the beauty of truth is that at every new discovery of fact we find how much wider and deeper it is than we at first thought it).   But it means that first of all Anarchism is concerned with present conditions, and with the very plain and common people; and is by no means a complex or difficult proposition.

Anarchism, alone, apart from any proposed economic reform, is just the latest reply out of many the past has given, to that daring, breakaway, volatile, changeful spirit which is never content.   The society of which we are part puts certain oppressions upon us,—oppressions which have arisen out of the very changes accomplished by this same spirit, combined with the hard and fast lines of old habits acquired and fixed before the changes were thought of. Machinery, which as our Socialistic comrades continually emphasize, has wrought a revolution in Industry, is the creation of the Dare Spirit; it has fought its way against ancient customs, privilege, and cowardice at every step, as the history of any invention would show if traced backward through all its transformations. And what is the result of it? That a system of working, altogether appropriate to hand production and capable of generating no great oppressions while industry remained in that state, has been stretched, strained to fit production in mass, till we are reaching the bursting point; once more the spirit of Dare must assert itself—claim new freedoms, since the old ones are rendered null and void by the present methods of production.

To speak in detail: in the old days of Master and Man—not so old but what many of the older workingmen can recall the conditions, the workshop was a fairly easy-going place where employer and employed worked together, knew no class feelings, chummed it out of hours, as a rule were not obliged to rush, and when they were, relied upon the principle of common interest and friendship (not upon a slave-owner's power) for overtime assistance. The proportional profit on each man's labor may even have been in general higher, but the total amount possible to be undertaken by one employer was relatively so small that no tremendous aggregations of wealth could arise. To be an employer gave no man power over another's incomings and outgoings, neither upon his speech while at work, nor to force him beyond endurance when busy, nor to subject him to fines and tributes for undesired things, such as ice-water, dirty spittoons, cups of undrinkable tea and the like; nor to the unmentionable indecencies of the large factory. The individuality of the workman was a plainly recognized quantity: his life was his own; he could not be locked in and driven to death, like a street-car horse, for the good of the general public and the paramount importance of Society.

With the application of steam-power and the development of Machinery, came these large groupings of workers, this subdivision of work, which has made of the employer a man apart, having interests hostile to those of his employes, living in another circle altogether, knowing nothing of them but as so many units of power, to be reckoned with as he does his machines, for the most part despising them, at his very best regarding them as dependents whom he is bound in some respects to care for, as a humane man cares for an old horse he cannot use. Such is his relation to his employes; while to the general public he becomes simply an immense cuttle-fish with tentacles reaching everywhere,—each tiny profit-sucking mouth producing no great effect, but in aggregate drawing up such a body of wealth as makes any declaration of equality or freedom between him and the worker a thing to laugh at.

The time is come therefore when the spirit of Dare calls loud through every factory and work-shop for a change in the relations of master and man. There must be some arrangement possible which will preserve the benefits of the new production and at the same time restore the individual dignity of the worker,—give back the bold independence of the old master of his trade, together with such added freedoms as may properly accrue to him as his special advantage from society's material developments.

This is the particular message of Anarchism to the worker. It is not an economic system; it does not come to you with detailed plans of how you, the workers, are to conduct industry; nor systemized methods of exchange; nor careful paper organizations of "the administration of things." It simply calls upon the spirit of individuality to rise up from its abasement, and hold itself paramount in no matter what economic reorganization shall come about. Be men first of all, not held in slavery by the things you make; let your gospel be, "Things for men, not men for things."

Socialism, economically considered, is a positive proposition for such reorganization. It is an attempt, in the main, to grasp at those great new material gains which have been the special creation of the last forty or fifty years. It has not so much in view the reclamation and further assertion of the personality of the worker as it has a just distribution of products.

Now it is perfectly apparent that Anarchy, having to do almost entirely with the relations of men in their thoughts and feelings, and not with the positive organization of production and distribution, an Anarchist needs to supplement his Anarchism by some economic propositions, which may enable him to put in practical shape to himself and others this possibility of independent manhood. That will be his test in choosing any such proposition,—the measure in which individuality is secured. It is not enough for him that a comfortable ease, a pleasant and well-ordered routine, shall be secured; free play for the spirit of change—that is his first demand.

Every Anarchist has this in common with every other Anarchist, that the economic system must be subservient to this end; no system recommends itself to him by the mere beauty and smoothness of its working; jealous of the encroachments of the machine, he looks with fierce suspicion upon an arithmetic with men for units, a society running in slots and grooves, with the precision so beautiful to one in whom the love of order is first, but which only makes him sniff—"Pfaugh! it smells of machine oil."

There are, accordingly, several economic schools among Anarchists; there are Anarchist Individualists, Anarchist Mutualists, Anarchist Communists and Anarchist Socialists. In times past these several schools have bitterly denounced each other and mutually refused to recognize each other as Anarchists at all. The more narrow-minded on both sides still do so; true, they do not consider it is narrow-mindedness, but simply a firm and solid grasp of the truth, which does not permit of tolerance towards error. This has been the attitude of the bigot in all ages, and Anarchism no more than any other new doctrine has escaped its bigots. Each of these fanatical adherents of either collectivism or individualism believes that no Anarchism is possible without that particular economic system as its guarantee, and is of course thoroughly justified from his own standpoint. With the extension of what Comrade Brown calls the New Spirit, however, this old narrowness is yielding to the broader, kindlier and far more reasonable idea, that all these economic conceptions may be experimented with, and there is nothing un-Anarchistic about any of them until the element of compulsion enters and obliges unwilling persons to remain in a community whose economic arrangements they do not agree to. (When I say "do not agree to" I do not mean that they have a mere distaste for, or that they think might well be altered for some other preferable arrangement, but with which, nevertheless, they quite easily put up, as two persons each living in the same house and having different tastes in decoration, will submit to some color of window shade or bit of bric-a-brac which he does not like so well, but which nevertheless, he cheerfully puts up with for the satisfac-

tion of being with his friend. I mean serious differences
which in their opinion threaten their essential liberties.
I make this explanation about trifles, because the objections which are raised to the doctrine that men may
live in society freely, almost always degenerate into trivi-
alities,—such as, "what would you do if two ladies
wanted the same hat?" etc. We do not advocate the
abolition of common sense, and every person of sense is
willing to surrender his preferences at times, provided
he is not *compelled* to at all costs.)

Therefore I say that each group of persons acting
socially in freedom may choose any of the proposed
systems, and be just as thorough-going Anarchists as
those who select another. If this standpoint be accepted,
we are rid of those outrageous excommunications which
belong properly to the Church of Rome, and which serve
no purpose but to bring us into deserved contempt with
outsiders.

Furthermore, having accepted it from a purely theoretical process of reasoning, I believe one is then in an
attitude of mind to perceive certain material factors in
the problem which account for these differences in proposed systems, and which even demand such differences,
so long as production is in its present state.

I shall now dwell briefly upon these various propositions, and explain, as I go along, what the material factors are to which I have just alluded. Taking the last
first, namely, Anarchist Socialism,—its economic program
is the same as that of political Socialism, in its entirety;
—I mean before the working of practical politics has
frittered the Socialism away into a mere list of governmental ameliorations. Such Anarchist Socialists hold
that the State, the Centralized Government, has been and
ever will be the business agent of the property-owning
class; that it is an expression of a certain material condi-

tion purely, and with the passing of that condition the
State must also pass; that Socialism, meaning the complete taking over of all forms of property from the hands
of men as the indivisible possession of Man, brings with
it as a logical, inevitable result the dissolution of the
State. They believe that every individual having an
equal claim upon the social production, the incentive to
grabbing and holding being gone, crimes (which are in
nearly all cases the instinctive answer to some antecedent
denial of that claim to one's share) will vanish, and with
them the last excuse for the existence of the State. They
do not, as a rule, look forward to any such transformations in the material aspect of society, as some of the
rest of us do. A Londoner once said to me that he believed London would keep on growing, the flux and re-
flux of nations keep on pouring through its serpentine
streets, its hundred thousand buses keep on jaunting just
the same, and all that tremendous traffic which fascinates
and horrifies continue rolling like a great flood up and
down, up and down, like the sea-sweep,—after the realization of Anarchism, as it does now. That Londoner's
name was John Turner; he said, on the same occasion,
that he believed thoroughly in the economics of Socialism.

Now this branch of the Anarchist party came out of
the old Socialist party, and originally represented the
revolutionary wing of that party, as opposed to those
who took up the notion of using politics. And I believe
the material reason which accounts for their acceptance
of that particular economic scheme is this (of course it
applies to all European Socialists) that the social development of Europe is a thing of long-continued history; that almost from time immemorial there has been
a recognized class struggle; that no workman living, nor
yet his father, nor his grandfather, nor his great-grand-
father has seen the land of Europe pass in vast blocks

from an unclaimed public inheritance into the hands of an ordinary individual like himself, without a title or any distinguishing mark above himself, as we in America have seen. The land and the land-holder have been to him always unapproachable quantities,—a recognized source of oppression, class, and class-possession.

Again, the industrial development in town and city—coming as a means of escape from feudal oppression, but again bringing with it its own oppressions, also with a long history of warfare behind it, has served to bind the sense of class fealty upon the common people of the manufacturing towns; so that blind, stupid, and Church-ridden as they no doubt are, there is a vague, dull, but very certainly existing feeling that they must look for help in association together, and regard with suspicion or indifference any proposition which proposes to help them by helping their employers. Moreover, Socialism has been an ever recurring dream through the long story of revolt in Europe; Anarchists, like others, are born into it. It is not until they pass over seas, and come in contact with other conditions, breathe the atmosphere of other thoughts, that they are able to see other possibilities as well.

If I may venture, at this point, a criticism of this position of the Anarchist Socialist, I would say that the great flaw in this conception of the State is in supposing it to be of *simple* origin; the State is not merely the tool of the governing classes; it has its root far down in the religious development of human nature; and will not fall apart merely through the abolition of classes and property. There is other work to be done. As to the economic program, I shall criticise that, together with all the other propositions, when I sum up.

Anarchist Communism is a modification, rather an evolution, of Anarchist Socialism. Most Anarchist Communists, I believe, do look forward to great changes in the distribution of people upon the earth's surface through the realization of Anarchism. Most of them agree that the opening up of the land together with the free use of tools would lead to a breaking up of these vast communities called cities, and the formation of smaller groups or communes which shall be held together by a free recognition of common interests only.

While Socialism looks forward to a further extension of the modern triumph of Commerce—which is that it has brought the products of the entire earth to your door-step—free Communism looks upon such a fever of exportation and importation as an unhealthy development, and expects rather a more self-reliant development of home resources, doing away with the mass of supervision required for the systematic conduct of such world exchange. It appeals to the plain sense of the workers, by proposing that they who now consider themselves helpless dependents upon the boss's ability to give them a job, shall constitute themselves independent producing groups, take the materials, do the work (they do that now), deposit the products in the warehouses, taking what they want for themselves, and letting others take the balance. To do this no government, no employer, no money system is necessary. There is only necessary a decent regard for one's own and one's fellow-worker's self-hood. It is not likely, indeed it is devoutly to be hoped, that no such large aggregations of men as now assemble daily in mills and factories, will ever come together by mutual desire. (A factory is a hot-bed for all that is vicious in human nature, and largely because of its crowding only.)

The notion that men cannot work together unless they have a driving-master to take a percentage of their product, is contrary both to good sense and observed fact.

As a rule bosses simply make confusion worse confounded when they attempt to mix in a workman's snarls, as every mechanic has had practical demonstration of; and as to social effort, why men worked in common while they were monkeys yet; if you don't believe it, go and watch the monkeys. They don't surrender their individual freedom, either.

In short, the real workmen will make their own regulations, decide when and where and how things shall be done. It is not necessary that the projector of an Anarchist Communist society shall say in what manner separate industries shall be conducted, nor do they presume to. He simply conjures the spirit of Dare and Do in the plainest workmen—says to them: "It is you who know how to mine, how to dig, how to cut; you will know how to organize your work without a dictator; we cannot tell you, but we have full faith that you will find the way yourselves. You will never be free men until you acquire that same self-faith."

As to the problem of the exact exchange of equivalents which so frets the reformers of other schools, to him it does not exist. So there is enough, who cares? The sources of wealth remain indivisible forever; who cares if one has a little more or less, so all have enough? Who cares if something goes to waste? Let it waste. The rotted apple fertilizes the ground as well as if it had comforted the animal economy first. And, indeed, you who worry so much about system and order and adjustment of production to consumption, you waste more human energy in making your account than the precious calculation is worth. Hence money with all its retinue of complications and trickeries is abolished.

Small, independent, self-resourceful, freely cooperating communes—this is the economic ideal which is accepted by most of the Anarchists of the Old World to-day.

As to the material factor which developed this ideal among Europeans, it is the recollection and even some still remaining vestiges of the mediæval village commune —those oases in the great Sahara of human degradation presented in the history of the Middle Ages, when the Catholic Church stood triumphant upon Man in the dust. Such is the ideal glamored with the dead gold of a sun which has set, which gleams through the pages of Morris and Kropotkin. We in America never knew the village commune. White Civilization struck our shores in a broad tide-sheet and swept over the country inclusively; among us was never seen the little commune growing up from a state of barbarism independently, out of primary industries, and maintaining itself within itself. There was no gradual change from the mode of life of the native people to our own; there was a wiping out and a complete transplantation of the latest form of European civilization. The idea of the little commune, therefore, comes instinctively to the Anarchists of Europe,—particularly the continental ones; with them it is merely the conscious development of a submerged instinct. With Americans it is an importation.

I believe that most Anarchist Communists avoid the blunder of the Socialists in regarding the State as the offspring of material conditions purely, though they lay great stress upon its being the tool of Property, and contend that in one form or another the State will exist so long as there is property at all.

I pass to the extreme Individualists,—those who hold to the tradition of political economy, and are firm in the idea that the system of employer and employed, buying and selling, banking, and all the other essential institutions of Commercialism, centering upon private property, are in themselves good, and are rendered vicious merely by the interference of the State. Their chief economic propositions are: land to be held by individuals or companies for such time and in such allotments as they use only; redistribution to take place as often as the members of the community shall agree; what constitutes use to be decided by each community, presumably in town meeting assembled; disputed cases to be settled by a so-called free jury to be chosen by lot out of the entire group; members not coinciding in the decisions of the group to betake themselves to outlying lands not occupied, without let or hindrance from any one.

Money to represent all staple commodities, to be issued by whomsoever pleases; naturally, it would come to individuals depositing their securities with banks and accepting bank notes in return; such bank notes representing the labor expended in production and being issued in sufficient quantity, (there being no limit upon any one's starting in the business, whenever interest began to rise more banks would be organized, and thus the rate per cent would be constantly checked by competition), exchange would take place freely, commodities would circulate, business of all kinds would be stimulated, and, the government privilege being taken away from inventions, industries would spring up at every turn, bosses would be hunting men rather than men bosses, wages would rise to the full measure of the individual production, and forever remain there. Property, real property, would at last exist, which it does not at the present day, because no man gets what he makes.

The charm in this program is that it proposes no sweeping changes in our daily retinue; it does not bewilder us as more revolutionary propositions do. Its remedies are self-acting ones; they do not depend upon conscious efforts of individuals to establish justice and build harmony; competition in freedom is the great automatic valve which opens or closes as demands increase or diminish, and all that is necessary is to let well enough alone and not attempt to assist it.

It is sure that nine Americans in ten who have never heard of any of these programs before, will listen with far more interest and approval to this than to the others. The material reason which explains this attitude of mind is very evident. In this country outside of the Negro question we have never had the historic division of classes; we are just making that history now; we have never felt the need of the associative spirit of workman with workman, because in our society it has been the individual that did things; the workman of to-day was the employer to-morrow; vast opportunities lying open to him in the undeveloped territory, he shouldered his tools and struck out single-handed for himself. Even now, fiercer and fiercer though the struggle is growing, tighter and tighter though the workman is getting cornered, the line of division between class and class is constantly being broken, and the first motto of the American is "the Lord helps him who helps himself." Consequently this economic program, whose key-note is "let alone", appeals strongly to the traditional sympathies and life habits of a people who have themselves seen an almost unbounded patrimony swept up, as a gambler sweeps his stakes, by men who played with them at school or worked with them in one shop a year or ten years before.

This particular branch of the Anarchist party does not accept the Communist position that Government arises from Property; on the contrary, they hold Government responsible for the denial of real property (viz.: to the producer the exclusive possession of what he has produced). They lay more stress upon its metaphysical origin in the authority-creating Fear in human nature. Their attack is directed centrally upon the idea of

Authority; thus the material wrongs seem to flow from the spiritual error (if I may venture the word without fear of misconstruction), which is precisely the reverse of the Socialistic view.

Truth lies not *"between* the two," but in a synthesis of the two opinions.

Anarchist Mutualism is a modification of the program of Individualism, laying more emphasis upon organization, co-operation and free federation of the workers. To these the trade union is the nucleus of the free co-operative group, which will obviate the necessity of an employer, issue time-checks to its members, take charge of the finished product, exchange with different trade groups for their mutual advantage through the central federation, enable its members to utilize their credit, and likewise insure them against loss. The mutualist position on the land question is identical with that of the Individualists, as well as their understanding of the State.

The material factor which accounts for such differences as there are between Individualists and Mutualists, is, I think, the fact that the first originated in the brains of those who, whether workmen or business men, lived by so-called independent exertion. Josiah Warren, though a poor man, lived in an Individualist way, and made his free-life social experiment in small country settlements, far removed from the great organized industries. Tucker also, though a city man, has never had personal association with such industries. They had never known directly the oppressions of the large factory, nor mingled with workers' associations. The Mutualists had; consequently their leaning towards a greater Communism. Dyer D. Lum spent the greater part of his life in building up workmen's unions, himself being a hand worker, a book-binder by trade.

I have now presented the rough skeleton of four different economic schemes entertained by Anarchists. Re·member that the point of agreement in all is: *no compulsion*. Those who favor one method have no intention of forcing it upon those who favor another, so long as equal tolerance is exercised toward themselves.

Remember, also, that none of these schemes is proposed for its own sake, but because through it, its projectors believe, liberty may be best secured. Every Anarchist, *as* an Anarchist, would be perfectly willing to surrender his own scheme directly, if he saw that another worked better.

For myself, I believe that all these and many more could be advantageously tried in different localities; I would see the instincts and habits of the people express themselves in a free choice in every community; and I am sure that distinct environments would call out distinct adaptations.

Personally, while I recognize that liberty would be greatly extended under any of these economies, I frankly confess that none of them satisfies me.

Socialism and Communism both demand a degree of joint effort and administration which would beget more regulation than is wholly consistent with ideal Anarchism; Individualism and Mutualism, resting upon property, involve a development of the private policeman not at all compatible with my notions of freedom.

My ideal would be a condition in which all natural resources would be forever free to all, and the worker individually able to produce for himself sufficient for all his vital needs, if he so chose, so that he need not govern his working or not working by the times and seasons of his fellows. I think that time may come; but it will only be through the development of the modes of production and the taste of the people. Meanwhile we all cry with one voice for the freedom *to try*.

Are these all the aims of Anarchism? They are just the beginning. They are an outline of what is demanded for the material producer. If as a worker, you think no further than how to free yourself from the horrible bondage of capitalism, then that is the measure of Anarchism for you. But you yourself put the limit there, if there it is put. Immeasurably deeper, immeasurably higher, dips and soars the soul which has come out of its casement of custom and cowardice, and dared to claim its Self.

Ah, once to stand unflinchingly on the brink of that dark gulf of passions and desires, once at last to send a bold, straight-driven gaze down into the volcanic Me, *once*, and in that once, and in that once *forever*, to throw off the command to cover and flee from the knowledge of that abyss,—nay, to dare it to hiss and seethe if it will, and make us writhe and shiver with its force! Once and forever to realize that one is not a bundle of well-regulated little reasons bound up in the front room of the brain to be sermonized and held in order with copy-book maxims or moved and stopped by a syllogism, but a bottomless, bottomless depth of all strange sensations, a rocking sea of feeling wherever sweep strong storms of unaccountable hate and rage, invisible contortions of disappointment, low ebbs of meanness, quakings and shudderings of love that drives to madness and will not be controlled, hungerings and moanings and sobbing that smite upon the inner ear, now first bent to listen, as if all the sadness of the sea and the wailing of the great pine forests of the North had met to weep together there in that silence audible to you alone. To look down into that, to know the blackness, the midnight, the dead ages in oneself, to feel the jungle and

the beast within,—and the swamp and the slime, and
the desolate desert of the heart's despair—to see, to
know, to feel to the uttermost,—and then to look at one's
fellow, sitting across from one in the street-car, so deco-
rous, so well got up, so nicely combed and brushed and
oiled and to wonder what lies beneath that commonplace
exterior,—to picture the cavern in him which somewhere far below has a narrow gallery running into your
own—to imagine the pain that racks him to the finger-tips
perhaps while he wears that placid ironed-shirt-front
countenance—to conceive how he too shudders at himself and writhes and flees from the lava of his heart and
aches in his prison-house not daring to see himself—to
draw back respectfully from the Self-gate of the plainest,
most unpromising creature, even from the most debased
criminal, because one knows the nonentity and the criminal in oneself—to spare all condemnation (how much
more trial and sentence) because one knows the stuff
of which man is made and recoils at nothing since all
is in himself,—this is what Anarchism may mean to you.
It means that to me.

And then, to turn cloudward, starward, skyward, and
let the dreams rush over one—no longer awed by outside powers of any order—recognizing nothing superior
to oneself—painting, painting endless pictures, creating
unheard symphonies that sing dream sounds to you alone,
extending sympathies to the dumb brutes as equal
brothers, kissing the flowers as one did when a child,
letting oneself go free, go free beyond the bounds of
what *fear* and *custom* call the "possible,"—this too Anarchism may mean to you, if you dare to apply it so.
And if you do some day,—if sitting at your work-bench,
you see a vision of surpassing glory, some picture of
that golden time when there shall be no prisons on the
earth, nor hunger, nor houselessness, nor accusation, nor

judgment, and hearts open as printed leaves, and candid as fearlessness, if then you look across at your low-browed neighbor, who sweats and smells and curses at his toil,—remember that as you do not know his depth neither do you know his height. He too might dream if the yoke of custom and law and dogma were broken from him. Even now you know not what blind, bound, motionless chrysalis is working there to prepare its winged thing.

Anarchism means freedom to the soul as to the body,—in every aspiration, every growth.

A few words as to the methods. In times past Anarchists have excluded each other on these grounds also; revolutionists contemptuously said "Quaker" of peace men; "savage Communists" anathematized the Quakers in return.

This too is passing. I say this: all methods are to the individual capacity and decision.

There is Tolstoy,—Christian, non-resistant, artist. His method is to paint pictures of society as it is, to show the brutality of force and the uselessness of it; to preach the end of government through the repudiation of all military force. Good! I accept it in its entirety. It fits his character, it fits his ability. Let us be glad that he works so.

There is John Most—old, work-worn, with the weight of prison years upon him,—yet fiercer, fiercer, bitterer in his denunciations of the ruling class than would require the energy of a dozen younger men to utter—going down the last hills of life, rousing the consciousness of wrong among his fellows as he goes. Good! That consciousness must be awakened. Long may that fiery tongue yet speak.

There is Benjamin Tucker—cool, self-contained, critical,—sending his fine hard shafts among foes and friends with icy impartiality, hitting swift and cutting keen,—and ever ready to nail a traitor. Holding to passive resistance as most effective, ready to change it whenever he deems it wise. That suits him; in his field he is alone, invaluable.

And there is Peter Kropotkin appealing to the young, and looking with sweet, warm, eager eyes into every colonizing effort, and hailing with a child's enthusiasm the uprisings of the workers, and believing in revolution with his whole soul. Him too we thank.

And there is George Brown preaching peaceable expropriation through the federated unions of the workers; and this is good. It is his best place; he is at home there; he can accomplish most in his own chosen field.

And over there in his coffin cell in Italy, lies the man whose method was to kill a king, and shock the nations into a sudden consciousness of the hollowness of their law and order. Him too, him and his act, without reserve I accept, and bend in silent acknowledgement of the strength of the man.

For there are some whose nature it is to think and plead, and yield and yet return to the address, and so make headway in the minds of their fellowmen; and there are others who are stern and still, resolute, implacable as Judah's dream of God;—and those men strike —strike once and have ended. But the blow resounds across the world. And as on a night when the sky is heavy with storm, some sudden great white flare sheets across it, and every object starts sharply out, so in the flash of Bresci's pistol shot the whole world for a moment saw the tragic figure of the Italian people, starved, stunted, crippled, huddled, degraded, murdered; and at the same moment that their teeth chattered with fear, they came and asked the Anarchists to explain themselves. And hundreds of thousands of people read more in those few days than they had ever read of the idea before.

Ask a method? Do you ask Spring her method? Which is more necessary, the sunshine or the rain? They are contradictory—yes; they destroy each other—yes, but from this destruction the flowers result.

Each choose that method which expresses your self-hood best, and condemn no other man because he expresses his Self otherwise.

Anarchism and American Traditions

A MERICAN traditions, begotten of religious rebellion, small self-sustaining communities, isolated conditions, and hard pioneer life, grew during the colonization period of one hundred and seventy years from the settling of Jamestown to the outburst of the Revolution. This was in fact the great constitution-making epoch, the period of charters guaranteeing more or less of liberty, the general tendency of which is well described by Wm. Penn in speaking of the charter for Pennsylvania: "I want to put it out of my power, or that of my successors, to do mischief."

The revolution is the sudden and unified consciousness of these traditions, their loud assertion, the blow dealt by their indomitable will against the counter force of tyranny, which has never entirely recovered from the blow, but which from then till now has gone on remolding and regrappling the instruments of governmental power, that the Revolution sought to shape and hold as defenses of liberty.

To the average American of to-day, the Revolution means the series of battles fought by the patriot army with the armies of England. The millions of school children who attend our public schools are taught to draw maps of the siege of Boston and the siege of Yorktown, to know the general plan of the several campaigns, to quote the number of prisoners of war surrendered with Burgoyne; they are required to remember the date when Washington crossed the Delaware on the ice; they are told to "Remember Paoli," to repeat "Molly Stark's a widow," to call General Wayne "Mad Anthony Wayne," and to execrate Benedict Arnold; they know that the Declaration of Independence was signed on the Fourth of July, 1776, and the Treaty of Paris in 1783; and then they think they have learned the Revolution—blessed be George Washington! They have no idea why it should have been called a "revolution" instead of the "English war," or any similar title: it's the name of it, that's all. And name-worship, both in child and man, has acquired such mastery of them, that the name "American Revolution" is held sacred, though it means to them nothing more than successful force, while the name "Revolution" applied to a further possibility, is a spectre detested and abhorred. In neither case have they any idea of the content of the word, save that of armed force. That has already happened, and long happened, which Jefferson foresaw when he wrote:

"The spirit of the times may alter, will alter. Our rulers will become corrupt, our people careless. A single zealot may become persecutor, and better men be his victims. It can never be too often repeated that the time for fixing every essential right, on a legal basis, is while our rulers are honest, ourselves united. *From the conclusion of this war we shall be going down hill.* It will not then be necessary to resort every moment to the people for support. They will be forgotten, therefore, and their rights disregarded. They will forget themselves in the sole faculty of making money, and will never think of uniting to effect a due respect for their rights. The shackles, therefore, which shall not be knocked off at the

conclusion of this war, will be heavier and heavier, till
our rights shall revive or expire in a convulsion."

To the men of that time, who voiced the spirit of that
time, the battles that they fought were the least of the
Revolution; they were the incidents of the hour, the
things they met and faced as part of the game they were
playing; but the stake they had in view, before, during,
and after the war, the real Revolution, was a change in
political institutions which should make of government
not a thing apart, a superior power to stand over the
people with a whip, but a serviceable agent, responsible,
economical, and trustworthy (but never so much trusted
as not to be continually watched), for the transaction of
such business as was the common concern, and to set the
limits of the common concern at the line where one man's
liberty would encroach upon another's.

They thus took their starting point for deriving a min-
imum of government upon the same sociological ground
that the modern Anarchist derives the no-government
theory; viz., that equal liberty is the political ideal. The
difference lies in the belief, on the one hand, that the clos-
est approximation to equal liberty might be best secured
by the rule of the majority in those matters involving
united action of any kind (which rule of the majority
they thought it possible to secure by a few simple arrangements for election), and, on the other hand, the
belief that majority rule is both impossible and undesirable; that any government, no matter what its forms, will
be manipulated by a very small minority, as the development of the State and United States governments has
strikingly proved; that candidates will loudly profess
allegiance to platforms before elections, which as officials
in power they will openly disregard, to do as they please;
and that even if the majority will could be imposed, it
would also be subversive of equal liberty, which may be

best secured by leaving to the voluntary association of those interested in the management of matters of common concern, without coercion of the uninterested or the opposed.

Among the fundamental likenesses between the Revolutionary Republicans and the Anarchists is the recognition that the little must precede the great; that the local must be the basis of the general; that there can be a free federation only when there are free communities to federate; that the spirit of the latter is carried into the councils of the former, and a local tyranny may thus become an instrument for general enslavement. Convinced of the supreme importance of ridding the municipalities of the institutions of tyranny, the most strenuous advocates of independence, instead of spending their efforts mainly in the general Congress, devoted themselves to their home localities, endeavoring to work out of the minds of their neighbors and fellow-colonists the institutions of entailed property, of a State-Church, of a class-divided people, even the institution of African slavery itself. Though largely unsuccessful, it is to the measure of success they did achieve that we are indebted for such liberties as we do retain, and not to the general government. They tried to inculcate local initiative and independent action. The author of the Declaration of Independence, who in the fall of '76 declined a re-election to Congress in order to return to Virginia and do his work in his own local assembly, in arranging there for public education which he justly considered a matter of "common concern," said his advocacy of public schools was not with any "view to take its ordinary branches out of the hands of private enterprise, which manages *so much better* the concerns to which it is equal"; and in endeavoring to make clear the restrictions of the Constitution upon the functions of the general government, he likewise said: "Let the general government be reduced to foreign concerns only, and let our affairs be disentangled from those of all other nations, except as to commerce, *which the merchants will manage the better the more they are left free to manage for themselves,* and the general government may be reduced to a very simple organization, and a very inexpensive one; a few plain duties to be performed by a few servants." This then was the American tradition, that private enterprise manages better all that to which it is equal. Anarchism declares that private enterprise, whether individual or co-operative, is equal to all the undertakings of society. And it quotes the particular two instances, Education and Commerce, which the governments of the States and of the United States have undertaken to manage and regulate, as the very two which in operation have done more to destroy American freedom and equality, to warp and distort American tradition, to make of government a mighty engine of tyranny, than any other cause, save the unforeseen developments of Manufacture.

It was the intention of the Revolutionists to establish a system of common education, which should make the teaching of history one of its principal branches; not with the intent of burdening the memories of our youth with the dates of battles or the speeches of generals, nor to make of the Boston Tea Party Indians the one sacrosanct mob in all history, to be revered but never on any account to be imitated, but with the intent that every American should know to what conditions the masses of people had been brought by the operation of certain institutions, by what means they had wrung out their liberties, and how those liberties had again and again been filched from them by the use of governmental force, fraud, and privilege. Not to breed security, laudation, complacent indolence, passive acquiescence in the acts of a government protected by the label "home-made," but to beget a wakeful jealousy, a never-ending watchfulness of rulers, a determination to squelch every attempt of those entrusted with power to encroach upon the sphere of individual action—this was the prime motive of the revolutionists in endeavoring to provide for common education.

"Confidence," said the revolutionists who adopted the Kentucky Resolutions, "is everywhere the parent of despotism; free government is founded in jealousy, not in confidence; it is jealousy, not confidence, which prescribes limited constitutions to bind down those whom we are obliged to trust with power; our Constitution has accordingly fixed the limits to which, and no further, our confidence may go. * * * In questions of power, let no more be heard of confidence in man, but bind him down from mischief by the chains of the Constitution."

These resolutions were especially applied to the passage of the Alien laws by the monarchist party during John Adams' administration, and were an indignant call from the State of Kentucky to repudiate the right of the general government to assume undelegated powers, for, said they, to accept these laws would be "to be bound by laws made, not with our consent, but by others against our consent—that is, to surrender the form of government we have chosen, and to live under one deriving its powers from its own will, and not from our authority." Resolutions identical in spirit were also passed by Virginia, the following month; in those days the States still considered themselves supreme, the general government subordinate.

To inculcate this proud spirit of the supremacy of the people over their governors was to be the purpose of public education! Pick up to-day any common school history, and see how much of this spirit you will find therein. On the contrary, from cover to cover you will find nothing but the cheapest sort of patriotism, the inculcation of the most unquestioning acquiescence in the deeds of government, a lullaby of rest, security, confidence,—the doctrine that the Law can do no wrong, a Te Deum in praise of the continuous encroachments of the powers of the general government upon the reserved rights of the States, shameless falsification of all acts of rebellion, to put the government in the right and the rebels in the wrong, pyrotechnic glorifications of union, power, and force, and a complete ignoring of the essential liberties to maintain which was the purpose of the revolutionists. The anti-Anarchist law of post-McKinley passage, a much worse law than the Alien and Sedition acts which roused the wrath of Kentucky and Virginia to the point of threatened rebellion, is exalted as a wise provision of our All-Seeing Father in Washington.

Such is the spirit of government-provided schools. Ask any child what he knows about Shays's rebellion, and he will answer, "Oh, some of the farmers couldn't pay their taxes, and Shays led a rebellion against the court-house at Worcester, so they could burn up the deeds; and when Washington heard of it he sent over an army quick and taught 'em a good lesson"—"And what was the result of it?" "The result? Why—why—the result was—Oh yes, I remember—the result was they saw the need of a strong federal government to collect the taxes and pay the debts." Ask if he knows what was said on the other side of the story, ask if he knows that the men who had given their goods and their health and their strength for the freeing of the country now found themselves cast into prison for debt, sick, disabled, and poor, facing a new tyranny for the old; that their demand was that the land should become the free communal possession of those who wished to work it, not subject to tribute, and the child will answer "No." Ask him if he ever read Jefferson's letter to Madison about it, in which he says:

"Societies exist under three forms, sufficiently distinguishable. 1. Without government, as among our Indians. 2. Under government wherein the will of every one has a just influence; as is the case in England in a slight degree, and in our States in a great one. 3. Under government of force, as is the case in all other monarchies, and in most of the other republics. To have an idea of the curse of existence in these last, they must be seen. It is a government of wolves over sheep. It is a problem not clear in my mind that the first condition is not the best. But I believe it to be inconsistent with any great degree of population. The second state has a great deal of good in it. . . . It has its evils, too, the principal of which is the turbulence to which it is subject. . . . But even this evil is productive of good. It prevents the degeneracy of government, and nourishes a general attention to public affairs. I hold that a little rebellion now and then is a good thing."

Or to another correspondent: "God forbid that we should ever be twenty years without such a rebellion! . . . What country can preserve its liberties if its rulers are not warned from time to time that the people preserve the spirit of resistance? Let them take up arms. . . . The tree of liberty must be refreshed from time to time with the blood of patriots and tyrants. It is its natural manure." Ask any school child if he was ever taught that the author of the Declaration of Independence, one of the great founders of the common school, said these things, and he will look at you with open mouth and unbelieving eyes. Ask him if he ever heard that the man who sounded the bugle note in the darkest hour of the Crisis, who roused the courage of the soldiers when Washington saw only mutiny and despair ahead, ask him if he knows that this man also wrote, "Government at best is a necessary evil, at worst an intolerable one," and if he is a little better informed than the average he will answer, "Oh well, *he* was an infidel!" Catechize him about the merits of the Constitution which he has learned to repeat like a poll-parrot, and you will find his chief conception is not of the powers withheld from Congress, but of the powers granted.

Such are the fruits of government schools. We, the Anarchists, point to them and say: If the believers in liberty wish the principles of liberty taught, let them never intrust that instruction to any government; for the nature of government is to become a thing apart, an institution existing for its own sake, preying upon the people, and teaching whatever will tend to keep it secure in its seat. As the fathers said of the governments of Europe, so say we of this government also after a century and a quarter of independence: "The blood of the people has become its inheritance, and those who fatten on it will not relinquish it easily."

Public education, having to do with the intellect and spirit of a people, is probably the most subtle and far-reaching engine for molding the course of a nation; but commerce, dealing as it does with material things and producing immediate effects, was the force that bore down soonest upon the paper barriers of constitutional restriction, and shaped the government to its requirements. Here, indeed, we arrive at the point where we, looking over the hundred and twenty-five years of independence, can see that the simple government conceived by the revolutionary republicans was a foredoomed failure. It was so because of (1) the essence of government itself; (2) the essence of human nature; (3) the essence of Commerce and Manufacture.

Of the essence of government, I have already said, it is

a thing apart, developing its own interests at the expense of what opposes it; all attempts to make it anything else fail. In this Anarchists agree with the traditional enemies of the Revolution, the monarchists, federalists, strong government believers, the Roosevelts of to-day, the Jays, Marshalls, and Hamiltons of then,—that Hamilton, who, as Secretary of the Treasury, devised a financial system of which we are the unlucky heritors, and whose objects were twofold: To puzzle the people and make public finance obscure to those that paid for it; to serve as a machine for corrupting the legislatures; "for he avowed the opinion that man could be governed by two motives only, force or interest;" force being then out of the question, he laid hold of interest, the greed of the legislators, to set going an association of persons having an entirely separate welfare from the welfare of their electors, bound together by mutual corruption and mutual desire for plunder. The Anarchist agrees that Hamilton was logical, and understood the core of government; the difference is, that while strong governmentalists believe this is necessary and desirable, we choose the opposite conclusion, NO GOVERNMENT WHATEVER.

As to the essence of human nature, what our national experience has made plain is this, that to remain in a continually exalted moral condition is not human nature. That has happened which was prophesied: we have gone down hill from the Revolution until now; we are absorbed in "mere money-getting." The desire for material ease long ago vanquished the spirit of '76. What was that spirit? The spirit that animated the people of Virginia, of the Carolinas, of Massachusetts, of New York, when they refused to import goods from England; when they preferred (and stood by it) to wear coarse homespun cloth, to drink the brew of their own growths, to fit their appetites to the home supply, rather

than submit to the taxation of the imperial ministry.
Even within the lifetime of the revolutionists the spirit
decayed, The love of material ease has been, in the mass
of men and permanently speaking, always greater than
the love of liberty.   Nine hundred and ninety-nine
women out of a thousand are more interested in the cut
of a dress than in the independence of their sex; nine
hundred and nine-nine men out of a thousand are more
interested in drinking a glass of beer than in questioning
the tax that is laid on it; how many children are not
willing to trade the liberty to play for the promise of a
new cap or a new dress?   This it is which begets the
complicated mechanism of society; this it is which, by
multiplying the concerns of government, multiplies the
strength of government and the corresponding weakness
of the people; this it is which begets indifference to public
concern, thus making the corruption of government easy.

As to the essence of Commerce and Manufacture, it
is this: to establish bonds between every corner of the
earth's surface and every other corner, to multiply the
needs of mankind, and the desire for material possession
and enjoyment.

The American tradition was the isolation of the States
as far as possible.   Said they: We have won our liberties
by hard sacrifice and struggle unto death.   We wish
now to be let alone and to let others alone, that our principles may have time for trial; that we may become accustomed to the exercise of our rights; that we may be
kept free from the contaminating influence of European
gauds, pagents, distinctions.   So richly did they esteem
the absence of these that they could in all fervor write:
"We shall see multiplied instances of Europeans coming
to America, but no man living will ever see an instance
of an American removing to settle in Europe, and con-
tinuing there."   Alas! In less than a hundred years the

highest aim of a "Daughter of the Revolution" was, and is, to buy a castle, a title, and a rotten lord, with the money wrung from American servitude! And the commencial interests of America are seeking a world-empire!

In the earlier days of the revolt and subsequent independence, it appeared that the "manifest destiny" of America was to be an agricultural people, exchanging food stuffs and raw materials for manufactured articles. And in those days it was written: "We shall by virtuous as long as agriculture is our principal object, which will be the case as long as there remain vacant lands in any part of America. When we get piled upon one another in large cities, as in Europe, we shall become corrupt as in Europe, and go to eating one another as they do there." Which we are doing, because of the inevitable development of Commerce and Manufacture, and the concomitant development of strong government. And the parallel prophecy is likewise fulfilled· "If ever this vast country is brought under a single government, it will be one of the most extensive corruption, indifferent and incapable of a wholesome care over so wide a spread of surface." There is not upon the face of the earth to-day a government so utterly and shamelessly corrupt as that of the United States of America. There are others more cruel, more tyrannical, more devastating; there is none so utterly venal.

And yet even in the very days of the prophets, even with their own consent, the first concession to this later tyranny was made. It was made when the Constitution was made; and the Constitution was made chiefly because of the demands of Commerce. Thus it was at the outset a merchant's machine, which the other interests of the country, the land and labor interests, even then foreboded would destroy their liberties. In vain their jealousy of its central power made them enact the first twelve amendments. In vain they endeavored to set bounds over which the federal power dare not trench. In vain they enacted into general law the freedom of speech, of the press, of assemblage and petition. All of these things we see ridden rough-shod upon every day, and have so seen with more or less intermission since the beginning of the nineteenth century. At this day, every police lieutenant considers himself, and rightly so, as more powerful than the General Law of the Union; and that one who told Robert Hunter that he held in his fist something stronger than the Constitution, was perfectly correct. The right of assemblage is an American tradition which has gone out of fashion; the police club is now the mode. And it is so in virtue of the people's indifference to liberty, and the steady progress of constitutional interpretation towards the substance of imperial government.

It is an American tradition that a standing army is a standing menace to liberty; in Jefferson's presidency the army was reduced to 3,000 men. It is American tradition that we keep out of the affairs of other nations. It is American practice that we meddle with the affairs of everybody else from the West to the East Indies, from Russia to Japan; and to do it we have a standing army of 83,251 men.

It is American tradition that the financial affairs of a nation should be transacted on the same principles of simple honesty that an individual conducts his own business; viz., that debt is a bad thing, and a man's first surplus earnings should be applied to his debts; that offices and office-holders should be few. It is American practice that the general government should always have millions of debt, even if a panic or a war has to be forced to prevent its being paid off; and as to the application of its income, office-holders come first. And within the last administration it is reported that 99,000 offices have been

created at an annual expense of $63,000,000. Shades of
Jefferson! "How are vacancies to be obtained? Those
by deaths are few; by resignation none." Roosevelt cuts
the knot by making 99,000 new ones! And few will die,
—and none resign. They will beget sons and daughters,
and Taft will have to create 99,000 more! Verily, a simple and a serviceable thing is our general government.

It is American tradition that the Judiciary shall act
as a check upon the impetuosity of Legislatures, should
these attempt to pass the bounds of constitutional limitation. It is American practice that the Judiciary justifies
every law which trenches on the liberties of the people
and nullifies every act of the Legislature by which the
people seek to regain some measure of their freedom.
Again, in the words of Jefferson: "The Constitution is a
mere thing of wax in the hands of the Judiciary, which
they may twist and shape in any form they please."
Truly, if the men who fought the good fight for the
triumph of simple, honest, free life in that day, were now
to look upon the scene of their labors, they would cry out
together with him who said: "I regret that I am now
to die in the belief that the useless sacrifice of themselves
by the generation of '76 to acquire self-government and
happiness to their country, is to be thrown away by the
unwise and unworthy passions of their sons, and that
my only consolation is to be that I shall not live to see
it."

And now, what has Anarchism to say to all this, this
bankruptcy of republicanism, this modern empire that has
grown up on the ruins of our early freedom? We say
this, that the sin our fathers sinned was that they did not
trust liberty wholly. They thought it possible to compromise between liberty and government, believing the
latter to be "a necessary evil", and the moment the compromise was made, the whole misbegotten monster of our

present tyranny began to grow. Instruments which are set up to safeguard rights become the very whip with which the free are struck.

Anarchism says, 'Make no laws whatever concerning speech, and speech will be free; so soon as you make a declaration on paper that speech shall be free, you will have a hundred lawyers proving that "freedom does not mean abuse, nor liberty license"; and they will define and define freedom out of existence. Let the guarantee of free speech be in every man's determination to use it, and we shall have no need of paper declarations. On the other hand, so long as the people do not care to exercise their freedom, those who wish to tyrannize will do so; for tyrants are active and ardent, and will devote themselves in the name of any number of gods, religious and otherwise, to put shackles upon sleeping men.

The problem then becomes, Is it possible to stir men from their indifference? We have said that the spirit of liberty was nurtured by colonial life; that the elements of colonial life were the desire for sectarian independence, and the jealous watchfulness incident thereto; the isolation of pioneer communities which threw each individual strongly on his own resources, and thus developed all-around men, yet at the same time made very strong such social bonds as did exist; and, lastly, the comparative simplicity of small communities.

All this has mostly disappeared. As to sectarianism, it is only by dint of an occasional idiotic persecution that a sect becomes interesting; in the absence of this, out-landish sects play the fool's role, are anything but heroic, and have little to do with either the name or the substance of liberty. The old colonial religious parties have gradually become the "pillars of society," their animosities have died out their offensive peculiarities have been effaced, they are as like one another as beans in a pod, they build churches and—sleep in them.

As to our communities, they are hopelessly and helplessly interdependent, as we ourselves are, save that continuously diminishing proportion engaged in all around farming; and even these are slaves to mortgages. For our cities, probably there is not one that is provisioned to last a week, and certainly there is none which would not be bankrupt with despair at the proposition that it produce its own food. In response to this condition and its correlative political tyranny, Anarchism affirms the economy of self-sustenance, the disintegration of the great communities, the use of the earth.

I am not ready to say that I see clearly that this *will* take place; but I see clearly that this *must* take place if ever again men are to be free. I am so well satisfied that the mass of mankind prefer material possessions to liberty, that I have no hope that they will ever, by means of intellectual or moral stirrings merely, throw off the yoke of oppression fastened on them by the present economic system, to institute free societies. My only hope is in the blind development of the economic system and political oppression itself. The great characteristic looming factor in this gigantic power is Manufacture. The tendency of each nation is to become more and more a manufacturing one, an exporter of fabrics, not an importer. If this tendency follows its own logic, is must eventually circle round to each community producing for itself. What then will become of the surplus product when the manufacturer shall have no foreign market? Why, then mankind must face the dilemma of sitting down and dying in the midst of it, or confiscating the goods.

Indeed, we are partially facing this problem even now; and so far we are sitting down and dying. I opine, however, that men will not do it forever: and when once by an act of general expropriation they have overcome the reverence and fear of property, and their awe of government, they may waken to the consciousness that things are to be used, and therefore men are greater than things. This may rouse the spirit of liberty.

If, on the other hand, the tendency of invention to simplify, enabling the advantages of machinery to be combined with smaller aggregations of workers, shall also follow its own logic, the great manufacturing plants will break up, population will go after the fragments, and there will be seen not indeed the hard, self-sustaining, isolated pioneer communities of early America, but thousands of small communities stretching along the lines of transportation, each producing very largely for its own needs, able to rely upon itself, and therefore able to be independent. For the same rule holds good for societies as for individuals,—those may be free who are able to make their own living.

In regard to the breaking up of that vilest creation of tyranny, the standing army and navy, it is clear that so long as men desire to fight, they will have armed force in one form or another. Our fathers thought they had guarded against a standing army by providing for the voluntary militia. In our day we have lived to see this militia declared part of the regular military force of the United States, and subject to the same demands as the regulars. Within another generation we shall probably see its members in the regular pay of the general government. Since any embodiment of the fighting spirit, any military organization, inevitably follows the same line of centralization, the logic of Anarchism is that the least objectionable form of armed force is that which springs up voluntarily, like the minute-men of Massachusetts, and disbands as soon as the occasion which called it into existence is past: that the really desirable thing is that all men—not Americans only—should be at peace; and that to reach this, all peaceful persons should withdraw their support from the army, and require that all who make war shall do so at their own cost and risk; that neither pay nor pensions are to be provided for those who choose to make man-killing a trade.

As to the American tradition of non-meddling, Anarchism asks that it be carried down to the individual himself. It demands no jealous barrier of isolation; it knows that such isolation is undesirable and impossible; but it teaches that by all men's strictly minding their own business, a fluid society, freely adapting itself to mutual needs, wherein all the world shall belong to all men, as much as each has need or desire, will result.

And when Modern Revolution has thus been carried to the heart of the whole world—if it ever shall be, as I hope it will,—then may we hope to see a resurrection of that proud spirit of our fathers which put the simple dignity of Man above the gauds of wealth and class, and held that to be an American was greater than to be a king.

In that day there shall be neither kings nor Americans, —only Men; over the whole earth, MEN.

Anarchism In Literature

IN the long sweep of seventeen hundred years which witnessed the engulfment of a moribund Roman civilization, together with its borrowed Greek ideals, under the red tide of a passionate barbarism that leaped to embrace the idea of Triumph over Death, and spat upon the Grecian Joys of Life with the superb contempt of the Norse savage, there was, for Europe and America, but one great animating Word in Art and Literature—Christianity. It boots not here to inquire how close or how remote the Christian ideal as it developed was in comparison with the teachings of the Nazarene. Distorted, blackened, almost effaced, it was yet some faint echo from the hillsides of Olivet, some indistinct vision of the Cross, some dull perception of the white glory of renunciation, that shaped the dreams of the evolving barbarian, and moulded all his work, whether of stone or clay, upon canvas or parchment. Wherever we turn we find a general fixup or caste, an immovable solidity of orders built upon orders, an unquestioning subordination of the individual, ruling every effort of genius. Ascetic shadow upon all; nowhere does a sun-ray of self-expression creep, save as through water, thin and perturbed. The theologic pessimism which appealed to the fighting man as a proper extension of his own superstition—perhaps hardly that, for Heaven was but a change of name for Valhalla,—fell heavily upon the man of dreams, whose creations must come forth, lifeless, after the uniform model, who must bless and ban not as he saw before his eyes but as the one eternal purpose demanded.

At last the barbarian is civilized; he has accomplished his own refinement—and his own rottenness. Still he preaches (and practices) contempt of death—when others do the dying! Still he preaches submission to the will of God—but that others may submit to him! Still he proclaims the Cross—but that others may bear it. Where Rome was in the glut of her vanity and her blood-drunkenness—limbs wound in cloth of gold suppurating with crime, head boastfully nodding as Jove and feet rocking upon slipping slime—there stand the Empires and Republics of those whose forefathers slew Rome.

And now for these three hundred years the Men of Dreams have been watching the Christian Ideal go bankrupt. One by one as they have dared, and each according to his mood, they have spoken their minds; some have reasoned, and some have laughed, and some have appealed, logician, satirist, and exhorter all feeling in their several ways that humanity stood in need of a new moral ideal. Consciously or unconsciously, within the pale of the Church or without, this has been "the spirit moving upon the face of the waters" within them, and at last the creation is come forth, the dream that is to touch the heart-strings of the World anew, and make it sing a stronger song than any it has sung of old. Mark you, it must be stronger, wider, deeper, or it cannot be at all. It must sing all that has been sung, and something more. Its mission is not to deny the past but to reaffirm it and explain it, all of it; and to-day too, and to-morrow too.

And this Ideal, the only one that has power to stir the moral pulses of the world, the only Word that can quicken "Dead Souls" who wait this moral resurrection, the only Word which can animate the dreamer, poet, sculptor, painter, musician, artist of chisel or pen, with power to fashion forth his dream, is ANARCHISM. For Anarchism means fulness of being. It means the return of Greek radiance of life, Greek love of beauty, without Greek indifference to the common man; it means Christian earnestness and Christian Communism, without Christian fanaticism and Christian gloom and tyranny. It means this because it means perfect freedom, material and spiritual freedom.

The light of Greek idealism failed because with all its love of life and the infinite diversity of beauty, and all the glory of its free intellect, it never conceived of material freedom; to it the Helot was as eternal as the Gods. Therefore the Gods passed away, and their eternity was as a little wave of time.

The Christian ideal has failed because with all its sublime Communism, its doctrine of universal equality, it was bound up with a spiritual tyranny seeking to mould into one pattern the thoughts of all humanity, stamping all men with the stamp of submission, throwing upon all the dark umber of *life lived for the purpose of death*, and fruitful of all other tyrannies.

Anarchism will succeed because its message of freedom comes down the rising wind of social revolt first of all to the common man, the material slave, and bids him know that he, too, should have an independent will, and the free exercise thereof; that no philosophy, and no achievement, and no civilization is worth considering or achieving, if it does not mean that he shall be free to labor at what he likes and when he likes, and freely share all that free men choose to produce; that he, the drudge of all the ages, is the corner-stone of the building without whose sure and safe position no structure can nor should endure. And likewise it comes to him who sits in fear of himself, and says: "Fear no more, neither what is without or within. Search fully and freely your Self; hearken to all the voices that rise from that abyss from which you have been commanded to shrink. Learn for yourself what these things are. Belike what they have told you is good, is bad; and this cast mould of goodness, a vile prison-house. Learn to decide your own measure of restraint. Value for yourself the merits of selfishness and unselfishness; and strike you the balance between these two: for if the first be all accredited you make slaves of others, and if the second, your own abasement raises tyrants over you; and none can decide the matter for you so well as you for yourself; for even if you err you learn by it, while if he errs the blame is his, and if he advises well the credit is his, and you are nothing. *Be yourself;* and by self-expression learn self-restraint. The wisdom of the ages lies in the reassertion of all past positivisms, and the denial of all negations, that is, all that has been claimed by the individual for himself is good, but every denial of the freedom of another is bad; whereby it will be seen that many things supposed to be claimed for oneself involve the freedom of others and must be surrendered because they do not come within the sovereign limit, while many things supposed to be evil, since they in nowise infringe upon the liberty of others are wholly good, bringing to dwarfed bodies and narrow souls the vigor and full growth of healthy exercise, and giving a rich glow to life that had else paled out like a lamp in a grave-vault."

To the sybarite it says, Learn to do your own share of hard work; you will gain by it; to the "Man with the Hoe," Think for yourself and boldly take your time for it. The division of labor which makes of one man a Brain and of another a Hand is evil. Away with it.

This is the ethical gospel of Anarchism to which these three hundred years of intellectual ferment have been leading. He who will trace the course of literature for three hundred years will find innumerable bits of drift here and there, indicative of the moral and intellectual revolt. Protestantism itself, in asserting the supremacy of the individual conscience, fired the long train of thought which inevitably leads to the explosion of all forms of authority. The great political writers of the eighteenth century, in asserting the right of self-government, carried the line of advance one step further. America had her Jefferson declaring:

"Societies exist under three forms: 1. Without government as among the Indians. 2. Under governments wherein every one has a just influence. 3. Under governments of force. It is a problem not clear in my mind that the first condition is not the best."

She had, or she and England together had, her Paine, more mildly asserting:

"Governments are, at best, a necessary evil."

And England had also Godwin, who, though still milder in manner and consequently less effective during the troublous period in which he lived, was nevertheless more deeply radical than either, presaging that application of the political ideal to economic concerns so distinctive of modern Anarchism.

"My neighbor," says he, "has just as much right to put an end to my existence with dagger or poison as to deny me that pecuniary assistance without which I must starve."

Nor did he stop here: he carried the logic of individual sovereignty into the chiefest of social institutions, and declared that the sex relation was a matter concerning the individuals sharing it only. Thus he says:

"The institution of marriage is a system of fraud . . . Marriage is law and the worst of all laws. . . . Marriage is an affair of property and the worst of all properties. So long as two human beings are forbidden by positive institution to follow the dictates of their own mind prejudice is alive and vigorous. . . . The abolition of marriage will be attended with no evils. We are apt to consider it to ourselves as the harbinger of brutal lust and depravity; but it really happens in this, as in other cases, that the positive laws which are made to restrain our vices, irritate and multiply them."

The grave and judicial style of "Political Justice" prevented its attaining the great popularity of "The Rights of Man," but the indirect influence of its author bloomed in the rich profusion of Shelleyan fancy, and in all that coterie of young litterateurs who gathered about Godwin as their revered teacher.

Nor was the principle of no-government without its vindication from one who moved actively in official centers, and whose name has been alternately quoted by conservatives and radicals, now with veneration, now with execration. In his essay "On Government," Edmund Burke, the great political weathercock, aligned himself with the germinating movement towards Anarchism when he exclaimed: "They talk of the abuse of government; the thing, the thing itself is the abuse!" This aphoristic utterance will go down in history on its own merits, as the sayings of great men often do, stripped of its accompanying explanations. Men have already forgotten to inquire how and why he said it; the words stand, and will continue a living message, long after the thousands of sheets of rhetoric which won him the epithet of "the Dinner-bell of the House" have been relegated to the dust of museums.

In later days an essayist whose brilliancy of style and capacity for getting on all sides of a question connect him with Burke in some manner as his spiritual offspring, has furnished the Anarchists with one of their most frequent quotations. In his essay on "John Milton," Macaulay declares, "The only cure for the evils of newly acquired liberty is—more liberty." That he nevertheless possessed a strong vein of conservatism, sat in parliament, and took part in legal measures, simply proves that he had his tether and could not go the length of his own logic; that is no reason others should not. The Anarchists accept this fundamental declaration and proceed to its consequence.

But the world-thought was making way, not only in England, where, indeed, constitutional phlegmatism, though stirred beyond its wont by the events of the close of the last century, acted frigidly upon it, but throughout Europe. In France, Rabelais drew the idyllic picture of the Abbey of Thelemes, a community of persons agreeing to practise complete individual freedom among themselves.

Rousseau, however erroneous his basis for the "Social Contract," moved all he touched with his belief that humanity was innately good, and capable of so manifesting itself in the absence of restrictions. Furthermore, his "Confessions" appears the most famous forerunner of the tendency now shaping itself in Literature—that of the free expression of a whole man—not in his stage-character only, but in his dressing-room, not in his decent, scrubbed and polished moral clothes alone, but in his vileness and his meanness and his folly, too, these being indisputable factors in his moral life, and no solution but a false one to be obtained by hiding them and playing they are not there. This truth, acknowledged in America, in our own times, by two powerful writers of very different cast, is being approached by all the manifold paths of the soul's travel. "I have in me the capacity for every crime," says Emerson the transcendentalist. And Whitman, the stanch proclaimer of blood and sinew, and the gospel of the holiness of the body, makes himself one with drunken revelers and the creatures of debauchery as well as with the anchorite and the Christ-soul, that fulness of being may be declared. In the genesis of these declarations we shall find the "Confessions."

It is not the "Social Contract" alone that is open to the criticism of having reasoned from false premises; all the early political writers we have named were equally mistaken, all suffering from a like insufficiency of facts. Partly this was the result of the habit of thought fostered by the Church for seventeen hundred years,—which habit was to accept by faith a sweeping generalization and fit all future discoveries of fact into it; but partly also it is in the nature of all idealism to offer itself, however vaguely in the mist of mind-struggle, and allow time to correct and sharpen the detail. Probably initial steps will always be taken with blunders, while those who are not imaginative enough to perceive the half-shapen figure will nevertheless accept it later and set it upon a firm foundation.

This has been the task of the modern historian, who, no less than the political writer, consciously or unconsciously, is swayed by the Anarchistic ideal and bends his services towards it. It is understood that when we speak of history we do not allude to the unspeakable trash contained in public school text-books (which in general resemble a cellar junk-shop of chronologies, epaulettes, bad drawings, and silly tales, and are a striking instance of the corrupting influence of State management of education, by which the mediocre, nay the absolutely empty, is made to survive), history which is undertaken with the purpose of discovering the real course of the development of human society. Among such efforts, the broken but splendid fragment of his stupendous project, is Buckle's "History of Civilization," —a work in which the author breaks away utterly from the old method of history writing, viz. that of recording court intrigues, the doings of individuals in power as a matter of personal interest, the processions of military pageant, to inquire into the real lives and conditions of the people, to trace their great upheavals, and in what consisted their progress. Gervinus in Germany, who. within only recent years, drew upon himself a prosecution for treason, took a like method, and declared that progress consists in a steady decline of centralized power and the development of local autonomy and the free federation.

Supplementing the work of the historian proper, there has arisen a new class of literature, itself the creation of the spirit of free inquiry, since, up till that had asserted itself, such writings were impossible; it embraces a wide range of studies into the conditions and psychology of prehistoric Man, of which Sir John Lubbock's works will serve as the type. From these, dark as the subject yet is, we are learning the true sources of all authority, and the agencies which are rendering it obsolete; moreover, a curious cycle of development reveals itself; namely, that starting from the point of no authority unconsciously accepted, Man, in the several manifestations of his activity, evolves through stages of belief in many authorities to one authority, and finally to *no authority* again, but this time conscious and reasoned.

Crowning the work of historian and prehistorian, comes the labor of the sociologist. Herbert Spencer, with infinite patience for detail and marvelous power of classification and generalization, takes up the facts of the others, and deduces from them the great Law of Equal Freedom: "A man should have the freedom to do whatsoever he wills, provided that in the doing thereof he infringes not the equal freedom of every other man." The early edition of "Social Statics" is a logical, scientific, and bold statement of the great fundamental freedoms which Anarchists demand.

From the rather taxing study of authors like these, it is a relief to turn to those intermediate writers who dwell between them and the pure fictionists, whose writings are occupied with the facts of life as related to the affections and aspirations of humanity, among whom, "representative men," we immediately select Emerson, Thoreau, Edward Carpenter. Now, indeed, we cease to reason upon the past evolution of liberty, and begin to feel it; begin to reach out after what it *shall* mean. None who are familiar with the thought of Emerson can fail to recognize that it is spiritual Anarchism; from the serene heights of self-possession, the Ego looks out upon its possibilities, unawed by aught without. And he who has dwelt in dream by Walden, charmed by that pure life he has not himself led but wished that, like Thoreau, he might lead, has felt that call of the Anarchistic Ideal which pleads with men to renounce the worthless luxuries which enslave them and those woh work for them, that the buried soul which is doomed to mummy cloths by the rush and jangle of the chase for wealth, may answer the still small voice of the Resurrection, there, in the silence, the solitude, the simplicity of the free life.

A similar note is sounded in Carpenter's "Civilization: Its Cause and Cure," a work which is likely to make the "Civilizer" see himself in a very different light than that in which he usually beholds himself. And again the same vibration shudders through "The City of Dreadful Night," the masterpiece of an obscure genius who was at once essayist and poet of too high and rare a quality to catch the ear stunned by strident commonplaces, but loved by all who seek the violets of the soul, one Thomson, known to literature as "B. V." Similarly obscure, and similarly sympathetic is the "English Peasant," by Richard Heath, a collection of essays so redolent of abounding love, so overflowing with understanding for characters utterly contradictory, painted so tenderly and yet so strongly, that none can read them without realizing that here is a man, who, whatever he *believes* he believes, in reality desires freedom of expression for the whole human spirit, which implies for every separate unit of it.

Something of the Emersonian striving after individual attainment plus the passionate sympathy of Heath is found in a remarkable book, which is too good to have obtained a popular hearing, entitled "The Story of My Heart." No more daring utterance was ever given voice than this: "I pray to find the Highest Soul,—greater than deity, better than God." In the concluding pages of the tenth chapter of this wonderful little book occur the following lines:

"That any human being should dare to apply to another the epithet of 'pauper' is to me the greatest, the vilest, the most unpardonable crime that could be committed. Each human being, by mere birth, has a birthright in this earth and all its productions; and if they do not receive it, then it is they who are injured; and it is not the 'pauper'—oh! inexpressibly wicked world!— it is the well-to-do who are the criminals. It matters not in the least if the poor be improvident, drunken, or evil in any way. Food and drink, roof and clothes, are the inalienable right of every child born into the light. If the world does not provide it freely—not as a grudging gift, but as a right, as the son of the house sits down to breakfast,—then is the world mad. But the world is not mad, only in ignorance."

In catholic sympathy like this, in heart-hunger after a wider righteousness, a higher idea than God, does the Anarchistic ideal come to those who have lived through old phases of religious and social beliefs and "found them wanting." It is the Shelleyan outburst:

"More life and fuller life we want."

He was the Prometheus of the movement, he, the wild bird of song, who flew down into the heart of storm and night, singing unutterably sweet the song of the free man and woman as he passed. Poor Shelley! Happy Shelley! He died not knowing the triumph of his genius; but also he died while the white glow within was yet shining higher, higher! In the light of it, he smiled above the world; had he lived, he might have died alive, as Swinburne and as Tennyson whose old days belie their early strength. Yet men will remember

"Slowly comes a hungry people as a lion drawing nigher,
  Glares at one who nods and winks beside a slowly dying fire,"

and

"Let the great World swing forever down the ringing grooves
    of Change,"

and

"Glory to Man in the highest for Man is the Master of Things"

and

> "While three men hold together,
> The kingdoms are less by three"

until the end "of kingdoms and of kings," though their authors "take refuge in the kingdom" and quaver palsied hymns to royalty with their cracked voices and broken lutes. For this is the glory of the living ideal, that all that is in accord with it lives, whether the mouthpiece through which it spoke would recall it or not. The manifold voice which is one speaks out through all the tongues of genius in its greatest moments, whether it be a Heine writing, in supreme contempt,

> "For the Law has got long arms,
> Priests and Parsons have long tongues
> And the People have long ears,"

a Nekrassoff cursing the railroad built of men, a Hugo painting the battle of the individual man "with Nature, with the Law, with Society," a Lowell crying:

"Law is holy ay, but what law? Is there nothing more divine
  Than the patched up broils of Congress,—venal, full of meat
    and wine?
Is there, say you, nothing higher—naught, God save us, that
    transcends
Laws of cotton texture wove by vulgar men for vulgar ends?
Law is holy: but not your law, ye who keep the tablets whole
While ye dash the Law in pieces, shatter it in life and soul."

and again,

> "One faith against a whole world's unbelief,
> One soul against the flesh of all mankind."

Nor do the master dramatists lag behind the lyric writers; they, too, feel the intense pressure within, which is, quoting the deathword of a man of far other stamp, "germinal." Ibsen's drama, intensely real, common, accepting none of the received rules as to the conventional plot, but having to do with serious questions of the lives of the plain people, holds ever before us the supreme duty of truth to one's inner being in defiance of Custom and Law; it is so in Nora, who renounces all notions of family duty to "find herself"; it is so in Dr. Stockman, who maintains the rectitude of his own soul against the authorities and against the mob; it should have been so in Mrs. Alving, who learns too late that her yielding to social custom has brought a fore-ruined life into the world besides wrecking her own; the Master Builder, John Gabriel Borkman, all his characters are created to vindicate the separate soul supreme within its sphere; those that are miserable and in evil condition are so because they have not lived true to themselves but in obedience to some social hypocrisy. Gerhart Hauptmann likewise feels the new pulsation: he has no hero, no heroine, no intrigue; his picture is the image of the headless and tailless body of struggle,—the struggle of the common man. It begins in the middle, it ends in nothing—as yet. To end in defeat would be to premise surrender—a surrender humanity does not intend; to triumph would be to anticipate the future, and paint life other than it is. Hence it ends where it began, in murmurs. Thus his "Weavers." Octave Mirbeau, likewise, offers his criticism on a world of sheep in "The Bad Shepherds," and Sara Bernhardt plays it. In England and America we have another phase of the rebel drama— the drama of the bad woman, as a distinct figure in social creation with a right to be herself. Have we not the "Second Mrs. Tanqueray" who comes to grief through an endeavor to conform to a moral standard that does not fit? And have we not Zaza, who is worth a thousand of her respectable lover and his respectable wife? And does not all the audience go home in love with her? And begin to quest the libraries for literary justifications of their preference?

And these are not hard to find, for it is in the novel particularly, the novel which is the special creation of the last century, that the new ideal is freest. In a recent essay in reply to Walter Besant, Henry James pleads most Anarchistically for his freedom in the novel. All such pleas will always come as justifications, for as to the freedom it is already won, and all the formalists from Besant to the end of days will never tempt the litterateurs into chains again. But the essay is well worth reading as a specimen of right reasoning on art. As in other modes of literary expression this tendency in the novel dates back; and it is strange enough that out of the mouth of a toady like Walter Scott should have spoken the free, devil-may-care, outlaw spirit (read notably "Quentin Durward"), which is, perhaps, the first phase of self-assertion that has the initial strength to declare itself against the tyranny of Custom; this is why it happens that the fore-runners of social change are often shocking in their rudeness and contempt of manners, and, in fact, more or less uncomfortable persons to have to do with. But they have their irresistible charm all the same, and Scott, who was a true genius despite his toadyism, felt it and responded to it, by always making us love his outlaws best no matter how gently he dealt with kings. Another phase of the free man appears in George Borrow's rollicking, full-blooded, out-of-door gypsies who do not take the trouble to despise law, but simply ignore it, live unconscious of it altogether. George Meredith, in another vein, develops the strong soul over-riding social barriers. Our own Hawthorne in his preface to the "Scarlet Letter," and still more in the "Marble Faun," depicts the vacuity of a life sucking a parasitic existence through government organization, and asserts over and over that the only strength is in him or her—and it is noteworthy that the strongest is in "her"—who resolutely chooses and treads an unbeaten path.

From far away Africa, there speaks again the note of soul rebellion in the exquisite "Dreams" of Olive Schreiner, wherethrough *The Hunter walks alone.* Grant Allen, too, in numerous works, especially "The Woman Who Did," voices the demand for self-hood. Morris gives us his idyllic "News from Nowhere." Zola, the fertile creator of dungheaps crowned with lilies, whose pages reek with the stench of bodies, laboring, debauching, rotting, until the words of Christ cry loud in the ears of him who would put the vision away, "Whited sepulchres, full of dead men's bones and all uncleanliness"—Zola was more than an unconscious Anarchist, he is a conscious one, did so proclaim himself. And close beside him, Maxim Gorki, Spokesman of the Tramp, Visionary of the Despised, who whatever his personal political views may be, and notwithstanding the condemnations he has visited upon the Anarchist, is still an Anarchistic voice in literature. And over against these, austere, simple, but oh! so loving, the critic who shows the world its faults but does not condemn, the man who first took the way of renunciation and then *preached* it, the Christian whom the Church casts out, the Anarchist whom the worst government in the world dares not slay, the author of "Resurrection" and "The Slavery of Our Times."

They come together, from the side of passionate hate and limitless love—the volcano and the sea—they come together in one demand, freedom from this wicked and debasing tyranny called Government, which makes indescribable brutes of all who feel its touch, but worse still of all who touch it.

As for contemporaneous light literature, there are magazine articles and papers innumerable displaying here and there the grasp of the idea. Have we not the *Philistine* and its witty editor, boldly proclaiming in Anarchistic spelling, "I am an Anarkist?" By the way, he may now expect a visitation of the Criminal Anarchy law. And a few years since, Julian Hawthorne, writing in the Denver *Post*, inquired, "Did you ever notice that all the interesting people you meet are Anarchists?" Reason why: there is no other living dream to him who has character enough to be interesting. It is the uninteresting, the dull, the ready-made minds who go on accepting "Dead limbs of gibbeted gods," as they accept their dinner and their bed, which someone else prepares. Let two names, standing for strangely opposing appeals yet standing upon common ground, close this sketch,—two strong flashes of the prismatic fires which blent together in the white ray of our Ideal. The first, Nietzsche, he who proclaims "the Overman," the receiver of the mantle of Max Stirner, the scintillant rhetorician, the pride of Young Germany, who would have the individual acknowledge nothing, neither science, nor logic, nor any other creation of his thought, as having authority over him, its creator. The last, Whitman, the great sympathetic, all-inclusive Quaker, whose love knew no limits, who said to Society's most utterly despised outcast,

"Not until the sun excludes you, will I exclude you,"

and who, whether he be called poet, philosopher, or peasant was supremely Anarchist, and in a moment of weariness with human slavery, cried:

"I think I could turn and live with animals, they seem so placid
and self-contained,
I stand and look at them long and long.
They do not sweat and whine about their conditions,
They do not lie awake in the dark and weep for their sins,
They do not make me sick discussing their duty to God;
Not one is dissatisfied, not one is demented with the mania
of owning things;
Not one kneels to another, nor to his kind that lived thousands
of years ago,
Not one is respectable or unhappy over the whole earth."

The Making of an Anarchist

"HERE was one guard, and here was the other at this end; I was here opposite the gate. You know those problems in geometry of the hare and the hounds—they never run straight, but always in a curve, so, see? And the guard was no smarter than the dogs; if he had run straight to the gate he would have caught me."

It was Peter Kropotkin telling of his escape from the Petro-Paulovsky fortress. Three crumbs on the table marked the relative position of the outwitted guards and the fugitive prisoner; the speaker had broken them from the bread on which he was lunching and dropped them on the table with an amused smile. The suggested triangle had been the starting-point of the life-long exile of the greatest man, save Tolstoy alone, that Russia has produced; from that moment began the many foreign wanderings and the taking of the simple, love-given title "Comrade," for which he had abandoned the "Prince," which he despises.

We were three together in the plain little home of a London workingman—Will Wess, a one-time shoemaker—Kropotkin, and I. We had our "tea" in homely English fashion, with thin slices of buttered bread; and we talked of things nearest our hearts, which, whenever two of three Anarchists are gathered together, means present evidences of the growth of liberty and what our comrades are doing in all lands. And as what they do and say often leads them into prisons, the talk had naturally fallen upon Kropotkin's experience and his daring escape, for which the Russian government is chagrined unto this day.

Presently the old man glanced at the time, and jumped briskly to his feet: "I am late. Good-by, Voltairine; good-by, Will. Is this the way to the kitchen? I must say good-by to Mrs. Turner and Lizzie." And out to the kitchen he went, unwilling, late though he was, to leave without a hand-clasp to those who had so much as washed a dish for him. Such is Kropotkin, a man whose personality is felt more than any other in the Anarchist movement—at once the gentlest, the most kindly, and the most invincible of men. Communist as well as Anarchist, his very heart-beats are rhythmic with the great common pulse of work and life.

Communist am not I, though my father was, and his father before him during the stirring times of '48, which is probably the remote reason for my opposition to things as they are: at bottom convictions are mostly temperamental. And if I sought to explain myself on other grounds, I should be a bewildering error in logic; for by early influences and education I should have been a nun, and spent my life glorifying Authority in its most concentrated form, as some of my schoolmates are doing at this hour within the mission houses of the Order of the Holy Names of Jesus and Mary. But the old ancestral spirit of rebellion asserted itself while I was yet fourteen, a schoolgirl at the Convent of Our Lady of Lake Huron, at Sarnia, Ontario. How I pity myself now, when I remember it, poor lonesome little soul, battling solitary in the murk of religious superstition, unable to believe and yet in hourly fear of damnation, hot, savage, and eternal, if I do not instantly confess and profess! How well I recall the bitter energy with which I repelled my teacher's enjoinder, when I told her that I did not wish to apologize for an adjudged fault, as I could not see that I had been wrong, and would not *feel* my words. "It is not necessary," said she, "that we should feel what we say, but it is always necessary that we obey our superiors." "I will not lie," I answered hotly, and at the same time trembled lest my disobedience had finally consigned me to torment!

I struggled my way out at last, and was a freethinker when I left the institution, three years later, though I had never seen a book or heard a word to help me in my loneliness. It had been like the Valley of the Shadow of Death, and there are white scars on my soul yet, where Ignorance and Superstition burnt me with their hell-fire in those stifling days. Am I blasphemous? It is their word, not mine. Beside that battle of my young days all others have been easy, for whatever was without, within my own Will was supreme. It has owed no allegiance, and never shall; it has moved steadily in one direction, the knowledge and the assertion of its own liberty, with all the responsibility falling thereon.

This, I am sure, is the ultimate reason for my acceptance of Anarchism, though the specific occasion which ripened tendencies to definition was the affair of 1886-7, when five innocent men were hanged in Chicago for the act of one guilty who still remains unknown. Till then I believed in the essential justice of the American law and trial by jury. After that I never could. The infamy of that trial has passed into history, and the question it awakened as to the possibility of justice under law has passed into clamorous crying across the world. With this question fighting for a hearing at a time when, young and ardent, all questions were pressing with a force which later life would in vain hear again, I chanced to attend a

Paine Memorial Convention in an out-of-the-way corner
of the earth among the mountains and the snow-drifts
of Pennsylvania. I was a freethought lecturer at this
time, and had spoken in the afternoon on the lifework of
Paine; in the evening I sat in the audience to hear
Clarence Darrow deliver an address on Socialism. It
was my first introduction to any plan for bettering the
condition of the working-classes which furnished some
explanation of the course of economic development, and
I ran to it as one who has been turning about in darkness runs to the light. I smile now at how quickly I
adopted the label "Socialist" and how quickly I cast it
aside. Let no one follow my example; but I was young.
Six weeks later I was punished for my rashness, when I
attempted to argue for my faith with a little Russian Jew,
named Mozersky, at a debating club in Pittsburgh. He
was an Anarchist, and a bit of a Socrates. He questioned
me into all kinds of holes, from which I extricated myself most awkwardly, only to flounder into others he had
smilingly dug while I was getting out of the first ones
The necessity of a better foundation became apparent:
hence began a course of study in the principles of sociol-
ogy and of modern Socialism and Anarchism as presented in their regular journals. It was Benjamin
Tucker's *Liberty*, the exponent of Individualist Anarchism, which finally convinced me that "Liberty is not
the Daughter but the Mother of Order." And though
I no longer hold the particular economic gospel advocated
by Tucker, the doctrine of Anarchism itself, as then conceived, has but broadened, deepened, and intensified itself
with years.

To those unfamiliar with the movement, the various
terms are confusing. Anarchism is, in truth, a sort of
Protestantism, whose adherents are a unit in the great
essential belief that all forms of external authority must

disappear to be replaced by self-control only, but variously divided in our conception of the form of future society. Individualism supposes private property to be the cornerstone of personal freedom; asserts that such property should consist in the absolute possession of one's own product and of such share of the natural heritage of all as one may actually use. Communist-Anarchism, on the other hand, declares that such property is both unrealizable and undesirable; that the common possession and use of all the natural sources and means of social production can alone guarantee the individual against a recurrence of inequality, and its attendants, government and slavery. My personal conviction is that both forms of society, as well as many intermediations, would, in the absence of government, be tried in various localities, according to the instincts and material condition of the people, but that well founded objections may be offered to both. Liberty and experiment alone can determine the best forms of society. Therefore I no longer label myself otherwise than as "Anarchist" simply.

I would not, however, have the world think that I am an "Anarchist by trade." Outsiders have some very curious notions about us, one of them being that Anarchists never work. On the contrary, Anarchists are nearly always poor, and it is only the rich who live without work. Not only this, but it is our belief that every healthy human being will, by the laws of his own activity, choose to work, though certainly not as now, for at present there is little opportunity for one to find his true vocation. Thus I, who in freedom would have selected otherwise, am a teacher of language. Some twelve years since, being in Philadelphia and without employment, I accepted the proposition of a small group of Russian Jewish factory workers to form an evening class in the common English branches. I know well enough that behind the desire to help me to make a living lay the wish that I might thus take part in the propaganda of our common cause. But the incidental became once more the principal, and a teacher of working men and women I have remained from that day. In those twelve years that I have lived and loved and worked with foreign Jews I have taught over a thousand, and found them, as a rule, the brightest, the most persistent and sacrificing students, and in youth dreamers of social ideals. While the "intelligent American" has been cursing him as the "ignorant foreigner," while the short-sighted workingman has been making life for the "sheeny" as intolerable as possible, silent and patient the despised man has worked his way against it all. I have myself seen such genuine heroism in the cause of education practiced by girls and boys, and even by men and women with families, as would pass the limits of belief to the ordinary mind. Cold, starvation, self-isolation, all endured for years in order to obtain the means for study; and, worse than all, exhaustion of body even to emaciation—this is common. Yet in the midst of all this, so fervent is the social imagination of the young that most of them find time besides to visit the various clubs and societies where radical thought is discussed, and sooner or later ally themselves either with the Socialist Sections, the Liberal Leagues, the Single Tax Clubs, or the Anarchist Groups. The greatest Socialist daily in America is the Jewish *Vorwaerts,* and the most active and competent practical workers are Jews. So they are among the Anarchists.

I am no propagandist at all costs, or I would leave the story here; but the truth compels me to add that as the years pass and the gradual filtration and absorption of American commercial life goes on, my students become successful professionals, the golden mist of enthusiasm vanishes, and the old teacher must turn for comradeship to the new youth, who still press forward with burning eyes, seeing what is lost forever to those whom common success has satisfied and stupified. It brings tears sometimes, but as Kropotkin says, "Let them go; we have had the best of them." After all, who are the really old? Those who wear out in faith and energy, and take to easy chairs and soft living; not Kropotkin, with his sixty years upon him, who has bright eyes and the eager interest of a little child; not fiery John Most, "the old warhorse of the revolution," unbroken after his ten years of imprisonment in Europe and America; not grey-haired Louise Michel, with the aurora of the morning still shining in her keen look which peers from behind the barred memories of New Caledonia; not Dyer D. Lum, who still smiles in his grave, I think; nor Tucker, nor Turner, nor Theresa Clairmunt, nor Jean Grave—not these. I have met them all, and felt the springing life pulsating through heart and hand, joyous, ardent, leaping into action. Not such are the old, but your young heart that goes bankrupt in social hope, dry-rotting in this stale and purposeless society. Would you be always young? Then be an Anarchist, and live with the faith of hope, though you be old.

I doubt if any other hope has the power to keep the fire alight as I saw it in 1897, when we met the Spanish exiles released from the fortress of Montjuich. Comparatively few persons in America ever knew the story of that torture, though we distributed fifty thousand copies of the letters smuggled from the prison, and some few newspapers did reprint them. They were the letters of men incarcerated on mere suspicion for the crime of an unknown person, and subjected to tortures the bare mention of which makes one shudder. Their nails were torn out, their heads compressed in metal caps, the most

ˉsensitive portions of the body twisted between guitar
strings, their flesh burned with red hot irons; they had
been fed on salt codfish after days of starvation, and
refused water; Juan Ollé, a boy nineteen years old, had
gone mad; another had confessed to something he had
never done and knew nothing of. This is no horrible imagination. I who write have myself shaken some of
those scarred hands. Indiscriminately, four hundred people of all sorts of beliefs—Republicans, trade unionists,
Socialists, Free Masons, as well as Anarchists—had
been cast into dungeons and tortured in the infamous
"zero." Is it a wonder that most of them came out
Anarchists? There were twenty-eight in the first lot that
we met at Euston Station that August afternoon,—homeless wanderers in the whirlpool of London, released without trial after months of imprisonment, and ordered to
leave Spain in forty-eight hours! They had left it, singing their prison songs; and still across their dark and
sorrowful eyes one could see the eternal Maytime bloom.
They drifted away to South America chiefly, where four
or five new Anarchist papers have since arisen, and several colonizing experiments along Anarchist lines are
being tried. So tyranny defeats itself, and the exile becomes the seed-sower of the revolution.

And not only to the heretofore unaroused does he bring
awakening, but the entire character of the world movement is modified by this circulation of the comrades of
all nations among themselves. Originally the American
movement, the native creation which arose with Josiah
Warren in 1829, was purely individualistic; the student
of economy will easily understand the material and historical causes for such development. But within the
last twenty years the communist idea has made great
progress, owing primarily to that concentration in capitalist production which has driven the American work-

ingman to grasp at the idea of solidarity, and, secondly, to the expulsion of active communist propagandists from Europe. Again, another change has come within the last ten years. Till then the application of the idea was chiefly narrowed to industrial matters, and the economic schools mutually denounced each other; to-day a large and genial tolerance is growing. The young generation recognizes the immense sweep of the idea through all the realms of art, science, literature, education, sex relations and personal morality, as well as social economy, and welcomes the accession to the ranks of those who struggle to realize the free life, no matter in what field. For this is what Anarchism finally means, the whole unchaining of life after two thousand years of Christian asceticism and hypocrisy.

Apart from the question of ideals, there is the question of method. "How do you propose to get all this?" is the question most frequently asked us. The same modification has taken place here. Formerly there were "Quakers" and "Revolutionists"; so there are still. But while they neither thought well of the other, now both have learned that each has his own use in the great play of world forces. No man is in himself a unit, and in every soul Jove still makes war on Christ. Nevertheless, the spirit of peace grows; and while it would be idle to say that Anarchists in general believe that any of the great industrial problems will be solved without the use of force, it would be equally idle to suppose that they consider force itself a desirable thing, or that it furnishes a final solution to any problem. From peaceful experiment alone can come final solution, and that the advocates of force know and believe as well as the Tolstoyans. Only they think that the present tyrannies provoke resistance. The spread of Tolstoy's "War and Peace" and "The Slavery of Our Times," and the growth of numerous

Tolstoy clubs having for their purpose the dissemination of the literature of non-resistance, is an evidence that many receive the idea that it is easier to conquer war with peace. I am one of these. I can see no end of retaliations unless someone ceases to retaliate. But let no one mistake this for servile submission or meek abnegation; my right shall be asserted no matter at what cost to me, and none shall trench upon it without my protest.

Good-natured satirists often remark that "the best way to cure an Anarchist is to give him a fortune." Substituting "corrupt" for "cure," I would subscribe to this; and believing myself to be no better than the rest of mortals, I earnestly hope that as so far it has been my lot to work, and work hard, and for no fortune, so I may continue to the end; for let me keep the integrity of my soul, with all the limitations of my material conditions, rather than become the spineless and ideal-less creation of material needs. My reward is that I live with the young; I keep step with my comrades; I shall die in the harness with my face to the east—the East and the Light.

The Eleventh of November, 1887

MEMORIAL ORATION*

L ET me begin my address with a confession. I make it sorrowfully and with self-disgust; but in the presence of great sacrifice we learn humility, and if my comrades could give their lives for their belief, why, let me give my pride. Yet I would not give it, for personal utterance is of trifling importance, were it not that I think at this particular season it will encourage those of our sympathizers whom the recent outburst of savagery may have disheartened, and perhaps lead some who are standing where I once stood to do as I did later.

This is my confession: Fifteen years ago last May when the echoes of the Haymarket bomb rolled through the little Michigan village where I then lived, I, like the rest of the credulous and brutal, read one lying newspaper headline, "Anarchists throw a bomb in a crowd in the Haymarket in Chicago," and immediately cried out, "They ought to be hung."—This, though I had never believed in capital punishment for ordinary criminals. For that ignorant, outrageous, blood-thirsty sentence I shall never forgive myself, though I know the

---

*Delivered on November 11, 1901, in Chicago.

dead men would have forgiven me, though I know those who loved them forgive me. But my own voice, as it sounded that night, will sound so in my ears till I die,— a bitter reproach and shame. What had I done? Credited the first wild rumor of an event of which I knew nothing, and, in my mind, sent men to the gallows without asking one word of defense! In one wild, unbalanced moment threw away the sympathies of a lifetime, and became an executioner at heart. And what I did that night millions did, and what I said millions said. I have only one word of extenuation for myself and all those people—ignorance. I did not know what Anarchism was. I had never seen it used save in histories, and there it was always synonymous with social confusion and murder. I believed the newspapers. I thought these men had thrown that bomb, unprovoked, into a mass of men and women, from a wicked delight in killing. And so thought all those millions of others. But out of those millions there were some few thousand—I am glad I was one of them—who did not let the matter rest there.

I know not what resurrection of human decency first stirred within me after that,—whether it was an intellectual suspicion that may be I did not know all the truth of the case and could not believe the newspapers, or whether it was the old strong undercurrrent of sympathy which often prompts the heart to go out to the accused, without a reason; but this I do know that though I was no Anarchist at the time of the execution, it was long and long before that, that I came to the conclusion that the accusation was false, the trial a farce, that there was no warrant either in justice or in law for their conviction; and that the hanging, if hanging there should be, would be the act of a society composed of people who had said what I said on the first night, and who had kept their eyes and ears fast shut ever since, determined to see nothing and to know nothing but rage and vengeance. Till the very end I hoped that mercy might intervene, though justice did not; and from the hour I knew neither would nor ever could again, I distrusted law and lawyers, judges and governors alike. And my whole being cried out to know what it was these men had stood for, and why they were hanged, seeing it was not proven they knew anything about the throwing of the bomb.

Little by little, here and there, I came to know that what they had stood for was a very high and noble ideal of human life, and what they were hanged for was preaching it to the common people,— the common people who were as ready to hang them, in their ignorance, as the court and the prosecutor were in their malice! Little by little I came to know that these were men who had a clearer vision of human right than most of their fellows; and who, being moved by deep social sympathies, wished to share their vision with their fellows, and so proclaimed it in the market-place. Little by little I realized that the misery, the pathetic submission, the awful degradation of the workers, which from the time I was old enough to begin to think had borne heavily upon my heart, (as they must bear upon all who have hearts to feel at all), had smitten theirs more deeply still,—so deeply that they knew no rest save in seeking a way out,—and that was more than I had ever had the sense to conceive. For me there had never been a hope there should be no more rich and poor; but a vague idea that there might not be so rich and so poor, if the workingmen by combining could exact a little better wages, and make their hours a little shorter. It was the message of these men, (and their death swept that message far out into ears that would never have heard their living voices), that all such little dreams are folly. That not in demanding little, not in striking for an hour

less, not in mountain labor to bring forth mice, can any
lasting alleviation come; but in demanding, much,—all,—
in a bold self-assertion of the worker to toil any hours
he finds sufficient, not that another finds for him,—here
is where the way out lies.   That message, and the
message of others, whose works, associated with theirs,
their death drew to my notice, took me up, as it were,
upon a mighty hill, wherefrom I saw the roofs of the
workshops of the little world.   I saw the machines, the
things that men had made to ease their burden, the
wonderful things, the iron genii, I saw them set their
iron teeth in the living flesh of the men who made them;
I saw the maimed and crippled stumps of men go limping
away into the night that engulfs the poor, perhaps to be
thrown up in the flotsam and jetsam of beggary for a
time, perhaps to suicide in some dim corner where the
black surge throws its slime.

I saw the rose fire of the furnace shining on the
blanched face of the man who tended it, and knew surely
as I knew anything in life, that never would a free man
feed his blood to the fire like that.

I saw swart bodies, all mangled and crushed, borne
from the mouths of the mines to be stowed away in a
grave hardly less narrow and dark than that in which the
living form had crouched ten, twelve, fourteen hours
a day; and I knew that in order that I might be warm—
I, and you, and those others who never do any dirty
work—those men had slaved away in those black graves,
and been crushed to death at last.

I saw beside city streets great heaps of horrible colored
earth, and down at the bottom of the trench from which
it was thrown, so far down that nothing else was visible,
bright gleaming eyes, like a wild animal's hunted into its
hole.   And I knew that free men never chose to labor
there, with pick and shovel in that foul, sewage-soaked

earth, in that narrow trench, in that deadly sewer gas ten, eight, even six hours a day. Only slaves would do it.

I saw deep down in the hull of the ocean liner the men who shoveled the coal—burned and seared like paper before the grate; and I knew that "the record" of the beautiful monster, and the pleasure of the ladies who laughed on the deck, were paid for with these withered bodies and souls.

I saw the scavenger carts go up and down, drawn by sad brutes driven by sadder ones; for never a man, a man in full possession of his self-hood, would freely choose to spend all his days in the nauseating stench that forces him to swill alcohol to neutralize it.

And I saw in the lead works how men were poisoned, and in the sugar refineries how they went insane; and in the factories how they lost their decency; and in the stores how they learned to lie; and I knew it was slavery made them do all this. I knew the Anarchists were right,—the whole thing must be changed, the whole thing was wrong,—the whole system of production and distribution, the whole ideal of life.

And I questioned the government then; they had taught me to question it. What have you done—you the keepers of the Declaration and the Constitution— what have you done about all this? What have you done to preserve the conditions of freedom to the people?

Lied, deceived, fooled, tricked, bought and sold and got gain! You have sold away the land, that you had no right to sell. You have murdered the aboriginal people, that you might seize the land in the name of the white race, and then steal it away from them again, to be again sold by a second and a third robber. And that buying and selling of the land has driven

the people off the healthy earth and away from the
clean air into these rot-heaps of humanity called cities,
where every filthy thing is done, and filthy labor
breeds filthy bodies and filthy souls. Our boys are
decayed with vice before they come to manhood; our
girls—ah, well might John Harvey write:

> "Another begetteth a daughter white and gold,
>   She looks into the meadow land water, and the world
> Knows her no more; they have sought her field and fold
>   But the City, the City hath bought her,
> It hath sold
>   Her piecemeal, to students, rats, and reek of the grave-
>   yard mould."

You have done this thing, gentlemen who engineer
the government; and not only have you caused this
ruin to come upon others; you yourselves are rotten
with this debauchery. You exist for the purpose of
granting privileges to whoever can pay most for you,
and so limiting the freedom of men to employ themselves that they must sell themselves into this frightful slavery or become tramps, beggars, thieves, prostitutes, and murderers. And when you have done all
this, what then do you do to them, these creatures of
your own making? You, who have set them the example in every villainy? Do you then relent, and
remembering the words of the great religious teacher
to whom most of you offer lip service on the officially
religious day, do you go to these poor, broken,
wretched creatures and love them? Love them and
help them, to teach them to be better? No: you build
prisons high and strong, and there you beat, and starve,
and hang, finding by the working of your system
human beings so unutterably degraded that they are

willing to kill whomsoever they are told to kill at so
much monthly salary.

This is what the government is, has always been,
the creator and defender of privilege; the organization
of oppression and revenge. To hope that it can ever
become anything else is the vainest of delusions. They
tell you that Anarchy, the dream of social order without goverment, is a wild fancy. The wildest dream
that ever entered the heart of man is the dream that
mankind can ever help itself through an appeal to law,
or to come to any order that will not result in slavery
wherein there is any excuse for government.

It was for telling the people this that these five men
were killed. For telling the people that the only way
to get out of their misery was first to learn what their
rights upon this earth were;—freedom to use the land
and all within it and all the tools of production—and
then to stand all together and take them, themselves,
and not to appeal to the jugglers of the law. Abolish
the law—that is abolish privilege,—and crime will
abolish itself.

They will tell you these men were hanged for advocating force. What! These creatures who drill men
in the science of killing, who put guns and clubs in
hands they train to shoot and strike, who hail with
delight the latest inventions in explosives, who exult
in the machine that can kill the most with the least
expenditure of energy, who declare a war of extermination upon people who do not want their civilization,
who ravish, and burn, and garotte and guillotine, and
hang, and electrocute, they have the impertinence to
talk about the unrighteousness of force! True, these
men did advocate the right to resist invasion by force.
You will find scarcely one in a thousand who does
not believe in that right. The one will be either a real

Christian or a non-resistant Anarchist. It will not be a believer in the State. No, no; it was not for advocating forcible resistance on principle, but for advocating forcible resistance to their tyrannies, and for advocating a society which would forever make an end of riches and poverty, of governors and governed.

The spirit of revenge, which is always stupid, accomplished its brutal act. Had it lifted its eyes from its work, it might have seen in the background of the scaffold that bleak November morning the dawn-light of Anarchy whiten across the world.

So it came first,—a gleam of hope to the proletaire, a summons to rise and shake off his material bondage. But steadily, steadily the light has grown, as year by year the scientist, the literary genius, the artist, and the moral teacher, have brought to it the tribute of their best work, their unpaid work, the work they did for love. To-day it means not only material emancipation, too; it comes as the summing up of all those lines of thought and action which for three hundred years have been making towards freedom; it means fulness of being, the free life.

And I say it boldly, notwithstanding the recent outburst of condemnation, notwithstanding the cry of lynch, burn, shoot, imprison, deport, and the Scarlet Letter A to be branded low down upon the forehead, and the latest excuse for that fond esthetic decoration "the button," that for two thousand years no idea has so stirred the world as this,—none which had such living power to break down barriers of race and degree, to attract prince and proletaire, poet and mechanic, Quaker and Revolutionist. No other ideal but the free life is strong enough to touch the man whose infinite pity and understanding goes alike to the hypocrite priest and the victim of Siberian whips; the loving rebel who stepped from his title and his wealth to labor with all the laboring earth; the sweet strong singer who sang

> "No Master, high or low";

the lover who does not measure his love nor reckon on return; the self-centered one who "will not rule, but also will not ruled be"; the philosopher who chanted the Over-man; the devoted woman of the people; ay, and these too,—these rebellious flashes from the vast cloud-hung ominous obscurity of the anonymous, these souls whom governmental and capitalistic brutality has whipped and goaded and stung to blind rage and bitterness, these mad young lions of revolt, these Winkelrieds who offer their hearts to the spears.

Crime and Punishment

MEN are of three sorts: the turn backs, the rush-aheads, and the indifferents. The first and second are comparatively few in number. The really conscientious conservative, eternally looking backward for his models and trying hard to preserve that which is, is almost as scarce an article as the genuine radical, who is eternally attacking that which is and looking forward to some indistinct but glowing vision of a purified social life. Between them lies the vast nitrogenous body of the indifferents, who go through life with no large thoughts or intense feelings of any kind, the best that can be said of them being that they serve to dilute the too fierce activities of the other two. Into the callous ears of these indifferents, nevertheless, the opposing voices of conservative and radical are continually shouting; and for years, for centuries, the conservative wins the day, not because he really touches the consciences of the indifferent so much (though in a measure he does that) as because his way causes his hearer the least mental trouble. It is easier to this lazy, inert mentality to nod its head and approve the continuance of things as they are, than to listen to proposals for change, to consider, to question, to make an innovating decision. These require activity, application,—and nothing is so foreign to the hibernating social conscience of your ordinary individual. I say "social" conscience, because I by no means wish to say that these are conscienceless people; they have, for active use, sufficient conscience to go through their daily parts in life, and they think that is all that is required. Of the lives of others, of the effects of their attitude in cursing the existences of thousands whom they do not know, they have no conception; they sleep; and they hear the voices of those who cry aloud about these things, dimly, as in dreams; and they do not wish to awaken. Nevertheless, at the end of the centuries they always awaken. It is the radical who always wins at last. At the end of the centuries institutions are reviewed by this aroused social conscience, are revised, sometimes are utterly rooted out.

Thus it is with the institutions of Crime and Punishment. The conservative holds that these things have been decided from all time; that crime is a thing-in-itself, with no other cause than the viciousness of man; that punishment was decreed from Mt. Sinai, or whatever holy mountain happens to be believed in in his country; that society is best served by strictness and severity of judgment and punishment. And he wishes only to make his indifferent brothers keepers of other men's consciences along these lines. He would have all men be hunters of men, that crime may be tracked down and struck down.

The radical says: All false, all false and wrong. Crime has not been decided from all time: crime, like everything else, has had its evolution according to place, time, and circumstance. "The demons of our sires become the saints that we adore,"—and the saints, the saints and the heroes of our fathers, are criminals according to our codes. Abraham, David, Solomon,—could any respectable member of society admit that he had done the things they did? Crime is not a thing-in-itself, not a plant without roots, not a something proceeding from nothing; and the only true way to deal with it is to seek its causes as earnestly, as painstakingly, as the astronomer seeks the causes of the perturbations in the orbit of the planet he is observing, sure that there must be one, or many, some· where.   And Punishment, too, must be studied.   The holy mountain theory is a failure.   Punishment is a failure.   And it is a failure not because men do not hunt down and strike enough, but because they hunt down and strike at all; because in the chase of those who do ill, they do ill themselves; they brutalize their own characters, and so much the more so because they are convinced that this time the brutal act is done in accord with conscience.   The murderous deed of the criminal was *against* conscience, the torture or the murder of the criminal by the official is *with* conscience.   Thus the conscience is diseased and perverted, and a new class of imbruted men created.   We have punished and punished for untold thousands of years, and we have not gotten rid of crime, we have not diminished it.   Let us consider then.

The indifferentist shrugs his shoulders and remarks to the conservative: "What have I to do with it?   I will hunt nobody and I will save nobody.   Let every one take care of himself.   I pay my taxes; let the judges and the lawyers take care of the criminals.   And as for you, Mr. Radical, you weary me.   Your talk is too heroic.   You want to play Atlas and carry the heavens on your shoulders.   Well, do it if you like.   But don't imagine I am going to act the stupid Hercules and transfer your burden to my shoulders.   Rave away until you are tired, but let me alone."

"I will not let you alone.   I am no Atlas.   I am no more than a fly; but I will annoy you, I will buzz in your ears; I will not let you sleep.   You must think about this."

That is about the height and power of my voice, or of any individual voice, in the present state of the question. I do not deceive myself. I do not imagine that the question of crime and punishment will be settled till long, long after the memory of me shall be as completely swallowed up by time as last year's snow is swallowed by the sea. Two thousand years ago a man whose soul revolted at punishment, cried out: "Judge not, that ye be not judged," and yet men and women who have taken his name upon their lips as holy, have for all those two thousand years gone on judging as if their belief in what he said was only lip-belief; and they do it to-day. And judges sit upon benches and send men to their death,—even judges who do not themselves believe in capital punishment; and prosecutors exhaust their eloquence and their tricks to get men convicted; and women and men bear witness against sinners; and then they all meet in church and pray, "Forgive us our trespasses *as* we forgive those who trespass against us!"

Do they mean anything at all by it?

And I know that just as the voice of Jesus was not heard, and is not heard, save here and there; just as the voice of Tolstoy is not heard, save here and there; and others great and small are lost in the great echoless desert of indifferentism, having produced little perceptible effect, so my voice also will be lost, and barely a slight ripple of thought be propagated over that dry and fruitless expanse; even that the next wind of trial will straighten and leave as unimprinted sand.

Nevertheless, by the continued and unintermitting action of forces infinitesimal compared with the human voice, the greatest effects are at length accomplished. A wave-length of light is but the fifty-thousandth part of an inch, yet by the continuous action of waves like these have been produced all the creations of light, the entire world of sight, out of masses irresponsive, dark, colorless. And doubt not that in time this cold and irresponsive mass of indifference will feel and stir and realize the force of the great sympathies which will change the attitude of the human mind as a whole towards Crime and Punishment, and erase both from the world.

Not by lawyers and not by judges shall the final cause of the criminal be tried; but lawyer and judge and criminal together shall be told by the Social Conscience, "Depart in peace."

A great ethical teacher once wrote words like unto these: "I have within me the capacity for every crime."

Few, reading them, believe that he meant what he said. Most take it as the sententious utterance of one who, in an abandonment of generosity, wished to say something large and leveling. But I think he meant exactly what he said. I think that with all his purity Emerson had within him the turbid stream of passion and desire; for all his hard-cut granite features he knew the instincts of the weakling and the slave; and for all the sweetness, the tenderness, and the nobility of his nature, he had the tiger and the jackal in his soul. I think that within every bit of human flesh and spirit that has ever crossed the enigma bridge of life, from the prehistoric racial morning until now, all crime and all virtue were germinal. Out of one great soul-stuff are we sprung, you and I and all of us; and if in you the virtue has grown and not the vice, do not therefore conclude that you are essentially different from him whom you have helped to put in stripes and behind bars. Your balance may be more even, you may be mixed in smaller proportions altogether, or the outside temptation has not come upon you.

I am no disciple of that school whose doctrine is summed up in the teaching that Man's Will is nothing, his Material Surroundings all. I do not accept that popular socialism which would make saints out of sinners only by filling their stomachs. I am no apologist for characterlessness, and no petitioner for universal moral weakness. I believe in the individual. I believe that the purpose of life (in so far as we can give it a purpose, and it has none save what we give it) is the assertion and the development of strong, self-centered personality. It is therefore that no religion which offers vicarious atonement for the misdoer, and no philosophy which rests on the cornerstone of irresponsibility, makes any appeal to me. I believe that immeasurable mischief has been wrought by the ceaseless repetition for the last two thousand years of the formula: "Not through any merit of mine shall I enter heaven, but through the sacrifice of Christ."—Not through the sacrifice of Christ, nor any other sacrifice, shall any one attain strength, save in so far as he takes the spirit and the purpose of the sacrifice into his own life and lives it. Nor do I see anything as the result of the teaching that all men are the helpless victims of external circumstance and under the same conditions will act precisely alike, than a lot of spineless, nerveless, bloodless crawlers in the tracks of stronger men,—too desirous of ease to be honest, too weak to be successful rascals.

Let this be put as strongly as it can now, that nothing I shall say hereafter may be interpreted as a gospel of shifting and shirking.

But the difference between us, the Anarchists, who preach self-government and none else, and Moralists who in times past and present have asked for individual responsibility, is this, that while they have always framed creeds and codes for the purpose of *holding others to account,* we draw the line upon ourselves. Set the standard as high as you will; live to it as near as you can; and if you fail, try yourself, judge yourself, condemn yourself, if you choose. Teach and persuade your neighbor if you can; consider and compare his conduct if you please; speak your mind if you desire; but if he fails to reach your standard or his own, try him not, judge him not, condemn him not. He lies beyond your sphere; you cannot know the temptation nor the inward battle nor the weight of the circumstances upon him. You do not know how long he fought before he failed. Therefore you cannot be just. Let him alone.

This is the ethical concept at which we have arrived, not by revelation from any superior power, not through the reading of any inspired book, not by special illumination of our inner consciousness; but by the study of the results of social experiment in the past as presented in the works of historians, psychologists, criminologists, sociologists and legalists.

Very likely so many "ists" sound a little oppressive, and there may be those to whom they may even have a savor of pedantry. It sounds much simpler and less ostentatious to say "Thus saith the Lord," or "The Good Book says." But in the meat and marrow these last are the real presumptions, these easy-going claims of familiarity with the will and intent of Omnipotence. It may sound more pedantic to you to say, "I have studied the accumulated wisdom of man, and drawn certain deductions therefrom," than to say "I had a talk with God this morning and he said thus and so"; but to me the first statement is infinitely more modest. Moreover there is some chance of its being true, while the other is highly imaginative fiction.

This is not to impugn the honesty of those who inherit
this survival of an earlier mental state of the race, and
who accept it as they accept their appetites or anything
else they find themselves born with.   Nor is it to belittle
those past efforts of active and ardent souls who claimed
direct divine inspiration as the source of their doctrines.
All religions have been, in their great general outlines,
the intuitive graspings of the race at truths which it had
not yet sufficient knowledge to demonstrate,—rude and
imperfect statements of ideas which were yet but germinal, but which, even then, mankind had urgent need to
conceive, and upon which it afterwards spent the efforts
of generations of lives to correct and perfect.   Thus the
very ethical concept of which I have been speaking as
peculiarly Anarchistic, was preached as a religious doctrine by the fifteenth century Tolstoy, Peter Chilciky;
and in the sixteenth century, the fanatical sect of the
Anabaptists shook Germany from center to circumfer-
ence by a doctrine which included the declaration that
"pleadings in courts of law, oaths, capital punishment,
and all absolute power were incompatible with the
Christian faith."   It was an imperfect illumination of
the intellect, such only as was possible in those less enlightened days, but an illumination that defined certain
noble conceptions of justice.   They appealed to all they
had, the Bible, the inner light, the best that they knew,
to justify their faith.   We to whom a wider day is given,
who can appeal not to one book but to thousands, who
have the light of science which is free to all that can
command the leisure and the will to know, shining white
and open on these great questions, dim and obscure in
the days of Peter Chilciky, we should be the last to cast
a sreer at them for their heroic struggle with tyranny and
cruelty; though to-day the man who would claim their

claims on their grounds would justly be rated atavist or charlatan.

Nothing or next to nothing did the Anabaptists know of history. For genuine history, history which records the growth of a whole people, which traces the evolution of its mind as seen in its works of peace,—its literature, its art, its constructions—is the creation of our own age. Only within the last seventy-five years has the purpose of history come to have so much depth as this. Before that it was a mere register of dramatic situations, with no particular connection, a chronicle of the deeds of prominent persons, a list of intrigues, scandals, murders big and little; and the great people, the actual builders and preservers of the race, the immense patient, silent mass who painfully filled up all the waste places these destroyers made, almost ignored. And no man sought to discover the relations of even the recorded acts to any general causes; no man conceived the notion of discovering what is political and moral growth or political and moral suicide. That they did not do so is because writers of history, who are themselves incarnations of their own time spirit, could not get beyond the unscientific attitude of mind, born of ignorance and fostered by the Christian religion, that man is something entirely different from the rest of organized life; that he is a free moral agent, good if he pleases and bad if he pleases, that is, according as he accepts or rejects the will of God; that every act is isolated, having no antecedent, morally, but the will of its doer. Nor until modern science had fought its way past prisons, exilements, stakes, scaffolds, and tortures, to the demonstration that man is no free-will freak thrust by an omnipotent joker upon a world of cause and sequence to play havoc therein, but just a poor differentiated bit of protoplasm as much subject to the general processes of matter and mind as his ancient progenitor in the depths of the Silurian sea, not until then was it possible for any real conception of the scope of history to begin. Not until then was it said: "The actions of men are the effects of large and general causes. Humanity as a whole has a regularity of movement as fixed as the movement of the tides; and given certain physical and social environments, certain developments may be predicted with the certainty of a mathematical calculation." Thus crime, which for so many ages men have gone on punishing more or less light-heartedly, so far from having its final cause in individual depravity, bears a steady and invariable relation to the production and distribution of staple food supplies, a thing over which society itself at times can have no control (as on the occasion of great natural disturbances), and in general does not yet know how to manage wisely: how much less, then, the individual! This regularity of the recurrence of crime was pointed out long before by the greatest statisticians of Europe, who, indeed, did not go so far as to question why it was so, nor to compare these regularities with other regularities, but upon whom the constant repetition of certain figures in the statistics of murder, suicide, assault, etc., made a profound impression. It was left to the new historians, the great pioneer among whom was H. T. Buckle in England, to make the comparisons in the statistics, and show that individual crimes as well as virtues are always calculable from general material conditions.

This is the basis from which we argue, and it is a basis established by the comparative history of civilizations. In no other way could it have been really established. It might have been guessed at, and indeed was. But only when the figures are before us, figures obtained "by millions of observations extending over different grades of civilization, with different laws, different opinions, different habits, different morals" (I am quoting Buckle), only then are we able to say surely that the human mind proceeds with a regularity of operation overweighing all the creeds and codes ever invented, and that if we would begin to understand the problem of the treatment of crime, we must go to something far larger than the moral reformation of the criminal. No prayers, no legal enactments, will ever rid society of crime. If they would, there have been prayers enough and preachments enough and laws enough and prisons enough to have done it long ago. But pray that the attraction of gravitation shall cease. Will it cease? Enact that water shall freeze at 100° heat. Will it freeze? And no more will men be sane and honest and just when they are compelled to live in an insane, dishonest, and unjust society, when the natural operation of the very elements of their being is warred upon by statutes and institutions which must produce outbursts destructive both to themselves and to others.

Away back in 1835 Quetelet, the French statistician, wrote: "Experience demonstrates, in fact, by every possible evidence, this opinion, which may seem paradoxical at first, that it is society which prepares the crime, and that the guilty one is but the instrument which executes it." Every crime, therefore, is a charge against society which can only be rightly replied to when society consents to look into its own errors and rectify the wrong it has done. This is one of the results which must, in the end, flow from the labors of the real historians; one of the reasons why history was worth writing at all.

Now the next point in the problem is the criminal himself. Admitting what cannot be impeached, that there is cause and sequence in the action of man; admitting the pressure of general causes upon all alike, what is the reason that one man is a criminal and another not?

From the days of the Roman jurisconsults until now the legalists themselves have made a distinction between crimes against the law of nature and crimes merely against the law of society. From the modern scientific standpoint no such distinction can be maintained. Nature knows nothing about crime, and nothing ever was a crime until the social Conscience made it so. Neither is it easy when one reads their law books, even accepting their view-point, to understand why certain crimes were catalogued as against the law of nature, and certain others as of the more artificial character. But I presume what were in general classed as crimes against nature were Acts of Violence committed against persons. Aside from these we have a vast, an almost interminable number of offenses big and little, which are in the main attacks upon the institution of property, concerning which some very different things have to be said than concerning the first. As to these first there is no doubt that these are real crimes, by which I mean simply anti-social acts. Any action which violates the life or liberty of any individual is an anti-social act, whether done by one person, by two, or by a whole nation. And the greatest crime that ever was perpetrated, a crime beside which all individual atrocities diminish to nothing, is War; and the greatest, the least excusable of murderers are those who order it and those who execute it. Nevertheless, this chiefest of murderers, the Government, its own hands red with the blood of hundreds of thousands, assumes to correct the individual offender, enacting miles of laws to define the varying degrees of his offense and punishment, and putting beautiful building stone to very hideous purposes for the sake of caging and tormenting him therein.

We do get a fig from a thistle—sometimes! Out of this noisome thing, the prison, has sprung the study of criminology. It is very new, and there is considerable painstaking nonsense about it. But the main results are interesting and should be known by all who wish to form an intelligent conception of what a criminal is and how he should be treated. These men who are cool and quiet and who move among criminals and study them as Darwin did his plants and animals, tell us that these prisoners are reducible to three types: The Born Criminal, the Criminaloid, and the Accidental Criminal. I am inclined to doubt a great deal that is said about the born criminal. Prof. Lombroso gives us very exhaustive reports of the measurements of their skulls and their ears and their noses and their thumbs and their toes, etc. But I suspect that if a good many respectable, decent, never-did-a-wrong-thing-in-their-lives people were to go up for measurement, malformed ears and disproportionately long thumbs would be equally found among them if they took the precaution to represent themselves as criminals first. Still, however few in number (and they are really very few), there are some born criminals,—people who through some malformation or deficiency or excess of certain portions of the brain are constantly impelled to violent deeds. Well, there are some born idiots and some born cripples. Do you punish them for their idiocy or for their unfortunate physical condition? On the contrary, you pity them, you realize that life is a long infliction to them, and your best and tenderest sympathies go out to them. Why not to the other, equally a helpless victim of an evil inheritance? Granting for the moment that you have the right to punish the mentally responsible, surely you will not claim the right to punish the mentally irresponsible! Even the law does not hold the insane man guilty. And the born criminal is irresponsible; he is a sick man, sick with the most pitiable chronic disease; his treatment is for the medical world to decide, and the best of them,—not for the prosecutor, the judge, and the warden.

It is true that many criminologists, including Prof. Lombroso himself, are of opinion that the best thing to do with the born criminal is to kill him at once, since he can be only a curse to himself and others. Very heroic treatment. We may inquire, Is he to be exterminated at birth because of certain physical indications of his criminality? Such neo-Spartanism would scarcely commend itself to any modern society Moreover the diagnosis might be wrong, even though we had a perpetual and incorruptible commission of the learned to sit in inquiry upon every pink-skinned little suspect three days old! What then? Is he to be let go, as he is now, until he does some violent deed and then be judged more hardly because of his natural defect? Either proposition seems not only heartless and wicked but,—what the respectable world is often more afraid of being than either,—ludicrous. If one is really a born criminal he will manifest criminal tendencies in early life, and being so recognized should be cared for according to the most humane methods of treating the mentally afflicted.

The second, or criminaloid, class is the most numerous of the three. These are criminals, first, because being endowed with strong desires and unequal reasoning powers they cannot maintain the uneven battle against a society wherein the majority of individuals must all the time deny their natural appetites, if they are to remain unstained with crime. They are, in short, the ordinary man (who, it must be admitted, has a great deal of paste in him) plus an excess of wants of one sort and another, but generally physical. Society outside of prisons is full of these criminaloids, who sometimes have in place of the power of genuine moral resistance a sneaking cunning by which they manage to steer a shady course between the crime and the punishment.

It is true these people are not pleasant subjects to contemplate; but then, through that very stage of development the whole human race has had to pass in its progress from the beast to the man,—the stage, I mean, of overplus of appetite opposed by weak moral resistance; and if now some, it is not certain that their number is very great, have reversed the proportion, it is only because they are the fortunate inheritors of the results of thousands of years of struggle and failure, struggle and failure, but *struggle* again. It is precisely these criminaloids who are most sinned against by society, for they are the people who need to have the right of doing things made easy, and who, when they act criminally, need the most encouragement to help the feeble and humiliated moral sense to rise again, to try again.

The third class, the Accidental or Occasional Criminals, are perfectly normal, well balanced people, who, through tremendous stress of outward circumstance, and possibly some untoward mental disturbance arising from those very notions of the conduct of life which form part of their moral being, suddenly commit an act of violence which is at utter variance with their whole former existence; such as, for instance, the murder of a seducer by the father of the injured girl, or of a wife's paramour by her husband. If I believed in severity at all I should say that these were the criminals upon whom society should look with most severity, because they are the ones who have most mental responsibility. But that also is nonsense; for such an individual has within him a severer judge, a more pitiless jailer than any court or prison,—his conscience and his memory. Leave him to these; or no, in mercy take him away from these whenever you can; he will suffer enough, and there is no fear of his action being repeated.

Now all these people are with us, and it is desirable that something be done to help the case. What does Society do? Or rather what does Government do with them? Remember we are speaking now only of crimes of violence. It hangs, it electrocutes, it exiles, it imprisons. Why? For punishment. And why punishment? "Not," says Blackstone, "by way of atonement or expiation for the crime committed, for that must be left to the just determination of the Supreme Being, but as a precaution against future offenses of the same kind." This is supposed to be effected in three ways: either by reforming him, or getting rid of him altogether, or by deterring others by making an example of him.

Let us see how these precautions work. Exile, which is still practised by some governments, and imprisonment are, according to the theory of law, for the purpose of reforming the criminal that he may no longer be a menace to society. Logic would say that anyone who wished to obliterate cruelty from the character of another must himself show no cruelty; one who would teach regard for the rights of others must himself be regardful. Yet the story of exile and prison is the story of the lash, the iron, the chain and every torture that the fiendish ingenuity of *the non-criminal class can devise by way of teaching criminals to be good!* To teach men to be good, they are kept in airless cells, made to sleep on narrow planks, to look at the sky through iron grates, to eat food that revolts their palates, and destroys their stomachs,—

battered and broken down in body and soul; and this is what they call reforming men!

Not very many years ago the Philadelphia dailies told us (and while we cannot believe all of what they say, and are bound to believe that such cases are exceptional, yet the bare facts were true) that Judge Gordon ordered an investigation into the workings of the Eastern Penitentiary officials; and it was found that an insane man had been put into a cell with two sane ones, and when he cried in his insane way and the two asked that he be put elsewhere, the warden gave them a strap to whip him with; and they tied him in some way to the heater, with the strap, so that his legs were burned when he moved; all scarred with the burns he was brought into the court, and the other men frankly told what they had done and why they had done it. This is the way they reform men.

Do you think people come out of a place like that better? with more respect for society? with more regard for the rights of their fellow men? I don't. I think they come out of there with their hearts full of bitterness, much harder than when they went in. That this is often the case is admitted by those who themselves believe in punisment, and practice it. For the fact is that out of the Criminaloid class there develops the Habitual Criminal, the man who is perpetually getting in prison; no sooner is he out than he does something else and gets in again. The brand that at first scorched him has succeeded in searing. He no longer feels the ignominy. He is a "jail-bird," and he gets to have a cynical pride in his own degradation. Every man's hand is against him, and his hand is against every man's. Such are the reforming effects of punishment. Yet there was a time when he, too, might have been touched, had the right word been spoken. It is for society to find and speak that word.

This for prison and exile. Hanging? electrocution? These of course are not for the purpose of reforming the criminal. These are to deter others from doing as he did; and the supposition is that the severer the punishment the greater the deterrent effect. In commenting upon this principle Blackstone says: "We may observe that punishments of unreasonable severity . . . . have less effect in preventing crimes and amending the manners of a people than such as are more merciful in general . . . ." He further quotes Montesquieu: "For the excessive severity of laws hinders their execution; when the punishment surpasses all measure, the public will frequently, out of humanity, prefer impunity to it." Again Blackstone: "It is a melancholy truth that among the variety of actions which men are daily liable to commit, no less than one hundred and sixty have been declared by act of Parliament to be felonies . . . worthy of instant death. So dreadful a list instead of diminishing *increases* the number of offenders."

Robert Ingersoll, speaking on "Crimes Against Criminals" before the New York Bar Association, a lawyer addressing lawyers, treating of this same period of which Blackstone writes, says: "There is something in injustice, in cruelty, which tends to defeat itself. There never were so many traitors in England as when the traitor was drawn and quartered, when he was tortured in every possible way,—when his limbs, torn and bleeding, were given to the fury of mobs, or exhibited pierced by pikes or hung in chains. The frightful punishments produced intense hatred of the government, and traitors increased until they became powerful enough to decide what treason was and who the traitors were and to inflict the same torments on others."

The fact that Blackstone was right and Ingersoll was right in saying that severity of punishment increases crime, is silently admitted in the abrogation of those severities by acts of Parliament and acts of Congress. It is also shown by the fact that there are no more murders, proportionately, in States where the death penalty does not exist than in those where it does. Severity is therefore admitted by the State itself to have no deterrent influence on the intending criminal. And to take the matter out of the province of the State, we have only to instance the horrible atrocities perpetrated by white mobs upon negroes charged with outrage. Nothing more fiendishly cruel can be imagined; yet these outrages multiply. It would seem, then, that the notion of making a horrible example of the misdoer is a complete failure. As a specific example of this, Ingersoll (in this same lecture) instanced that "a few years before a man was hanged in Alexandria, Va. One who witnessed the execution on that very day murdered a peddler in the Smithsonian grounds at Washington. He was tried and executed; and one who witnessed his hanging went home and on the same day murdered his wife." Evidently the brute is rather aroused than terrified by scenes of execution.

What then? If extreme punishments do not deter, and if what are considered mild punishments do not reform, is any measure of punishment conceivable or attainable which will better our case?

Before answering this question let us consider the class of crimes which so far has not been dwelt upon, but which nevertheless comprises probably nine-tenths of all offenses committed. These are all the various forms of stealing,—robbery, burglary, theft, embezzlement, forgery, counterfeiting, and the thousand and one ramifications and offshoots of the act of taking what the law defines as another's. It is impossible to consider crimes of violence apart from these, because the vast percentage of murders and assaults committed by the criminaloid class are simply incidental to the commission of the so-called lesser crime. A man often murders in order to escape with his booty, though murder was no part of his original intention. Why, now, have we such a continually increasing percentage of stealing?

Will you persistently hide your heads in the sand and say it is because men grow worse as they grow wiser? that individual wickedness is the result of all our marvelous labors to compass sea and land, and make the earth yield up her wealth to us? Dare you say that?

It is not so. THE REASON MEN STEAL IS BECAUSE THEIR RIGHTS ARE STOLEN FROM THEM BEFORE THEY ARE BORN.

A human being comes into the world; he wants to eat, he wants to breathe, he wants to sleep; he wants to use his muscles, his brain; he wants to love, to dream, to create. These wants constitute him, the whole man; he can no more help expressing these activities than water can help running down hill. If the freedom to do any of these things is denied him, then by so much he is a crippled creature, and his energy will force itself into some abnormal channel or be killed altogether. Now I do not mean that he has a "natural right" to do these things inscribed on any lawbook of Nature. Nature knows nothing of rights, she knows power only, and a louse has as much natural right as a man to the extent of its power. What I do mean to say is that man, in common with many other animals, has found that by associative life he conquers the rest of nature, and that this society is slowly being perfected; and that this perfectionment consists in realizing that the solidarity and safety of the whole arises from the freedom of the parts; that such freedom constitutes Man's Social Right; and that any institution which interferes with this right will be destructive of the association, will breed criminals, will work its own ruin. This is the word of the sociologist, of the greatest of them, Herbert Spencer.

Now do we see that all men eat,—eat well? You know we do not. Some have so much that they are sickened with the extravagance of dishes, and know not where next to turn for a new palatal sensation. They cannot even waste their wealth. Some, and they are mostly the hardest workers, eat poorly and fast, for their work allows them no time to enjoy even what they have. Some,—I have seen them myself in the streets of New York this winter, and the look of their wolfish eyes was not pleasant to see—stand in long lines waiting for midnight and the plate of soup dealt out by some great newspaper office, stretching out, whole blocks of them, as other men wait on the first night of some famous star at the theater! Some die because they cannot eat at all. Pray tell me what these last have to lose by becoming thieves. And why shall they not become thieves? And is the action of the man who takes the necessities which have been denied to him really criminal? Is he morally worse than the man who crawls in a cellar and dies of starvation? I think not. He is only a little more assertive. Cardinal Manning said: "A starving man has a natural right to his neighbor's bread." The Anarchist says: "A hungry man has a social right to bread." And there have been whole societies and races among whom that right was never questioned. And whatever were the mistakes of those societies, whereby they perished, this was not a mistake, and we shall do well to take so much wisdom from the dead and gone, the simple ethics of the stomach which with all our achievement we cannot despise, or despising, shall perish as our reward.

"But," you will say, and say truly, "to begin by taking loaves means to end by taking everything and murdering, too, very often." And in that you draw the indictment against your own system. If there is no alternative between starving and stealing (and for thousands there is none), then there is no alternative between society's murdering its members, or the members disintegrating society. Let Society consider its own mistakes, then: let it answer itself for all these people it has robbed and killed: let it cease its own crimes first!

To return to the faculties of Man. All would breathe; and some do breathe. They breathe the air of the mountains, of the seas, of the lakes,—even the atmosphere in the gambling dens of Monte Carlo, for a change! Some, packed thickly together in closed rooms where men must sweat and faint to save tobacco, breathe the noisome reek that rises from the spittle of their consumptive neighbors. Some, mostly babies, lie on the cellar doors along Bainbridge street, on summer nights, and bathe their lungs in that putrid air where a thousand lungs have breathed before, and grow up pale and decayed looking as the rotting vegetables whose exhalations they draw in. Some, far down underground, meet the choke-damp, and—do not breathe at all! Do you expect healthy morals out of all these poisoned bodies?

Some sleep. They have so much time that they take all manner of expensive drugs to try what sleeping it off a different way is like! Some sleep upon none too easy beds a few short hours, too few not to waken more tired than ever, and resume the endless grind of waking life. Some sleep bent over the books they are too tired to study, though the mind clamors for food after the long day's physical toil. Some sleep with hand upon the throttle of the engine, after twenty-six hours of duty, and—crash!—they have sleep enough!

Some use their muscles: they use them to punch bags, and other gentlemen's stomachs when their heads are full of wine. Some use them to club other men and women, at $2.50 a day. Some exhaust them welding them into iron, or weaving them into wool, for ten or eleven hours a day. And some become atrophied sitting at desks till they are mere specters of men and women.

Some love; and there is no end to the sensualities of their love, because all normal expressions have lost their savor through excess. Some love, and see their love tried and worn and threadbare, a skeleton of love, because the practicality of life is always there to repress the purely emotional. Some are stricken in health, so robbed of power to feel, that they never love at all.

And some dream, think, create; and the world is filled with the glory of their dreams. But who knows the glory of the dream that never was born, lost and dead and buried away somewhere there under the roofs where the exquisite brain was ruined by the heavy labor of life? And what of the dream that turned to madness and destroyed the thing it loved the best?

These are the things that make criminals, the perverted forces of man, turned aside by the institution of property, which is the giant social mistake to-day. It is your law which keeps men from using the sources and the means of wealth production unless they pay tribute to other men; it is this, and nothing else, which is responsible for all the second class of crimes and all those crimes of violence incidentally committed while carrying out a robbery. Let me quote here a most sensible and appropriate editorial which recently appeared in the Philadelphia *North American,* in comment upon the proposition of some foolish preacher to limit the right of reproduction to rich families:

"The earth was constructed, made habitable, and populated without the advice of a commission of superior persons, and until they appeared and began meddling with affairs, making laws and setting themselves up as rulers, poverty and its evil consequences were unknown to humanity. When social science finds a way to remove obstructions to the operation of natural law and to the equitable distribution of the products of labor, poverty will cease to be the condition of the masses of people, and misery, CRIME and problems of population will disappear."

And they will never disappear until it does. All hunting down of men, all punishments, are but so many ineffective efforts to sweep back the tide with a broom. The tide will fling you, broom and all, against the idle walls that you have built to fence it in. Tear down those walls or the sea will tear them down for you.

Have you ever watched it coming in,—the sea? When the wind comes roaring out of the mist and a great bellowing thunders up from the water? Have you watched the white lions chasing each other towards the walls, and leaping up with foaming anger as they strike, and turn and chase each other along the black bars of their cage in rage to devour each other? And tear back? And leap in again? Have you ever wondered in the midst of it all *which particular drops of water* would strike the wall? If one could know all the factors one might calculate even that. But who can know them all? Of one thing only we are sure; *some must strike it.*

They are the criminals, those drops of water pitching against that silly wall and broken. Just why it was these particular ones we cannot know; but some had to go. Do not curse them; you have cursed them enough. Let the people free.

There is a class of crimes of violence which arises from another set of causes than economic slavery—acts which are the result of an antiquated moral notion of the true relations of men and women. These are the Nemesis of the institution of property in love. If every one would learn that the limit of his right to demand a certain course of conduct in sex relations is himself; that the relation of his beloved ones to others is not a matter for him to regulate, any more than the relations of those whom he does not love; if the freedom of each is unquestioned, and whatever moral rigors are exacted are exacted of oneself only; if this principle is accepted and followed, crimes of jealousy will cease. But religions and governments uphold this institution and constantly tend to create the spirit of ownership, with all its horrible consequences.

Ah, you will say, perhaps it is true; perhaps when this better social condition is evolved, and this freer social spirit, we shall be rid of crime,—at least nine-tenths of it. But meanwhile must we not punish to protect ourselves?

The protection does not protect. The violent man does not communicate his intention; when he executes it, or attempts its execution, more often than otherwise it is some unofficial person who catches or stops him. If he is a born criminal, or in other words an insane man, he should, I reiterate, be treated as a sick person—not punished, not made to suffer. If he is one of the accidental criminals, his act will not be repeated; his punishment will always be with him. If he is of the middle class, your punishment will not reform him, it will only harden him; and it will not deter others.

As for thieves, the great thief is within the law, or he buys it; and as for the small one, see what you do! To protect yourself against him, you create a class of persons who are sworn to the service of the club and the revolver; a set of spies; a set whose business it is to deal constantly with these unhappy beings, who in rare instances are softened thereby, but in the majority of cases become hardened to their work as butchers to the use of the knife; a set whose business it is to serve cell and lock and key; and lastly, the lowest infamy of all, the hangman. Does any one want to shake his hand, the hand that kills for pay?

Now against all these persons individually there is nothing to be said: they may probably be very humane, well-intentioned persons when they start in; but the end of all this is imbrutement. One of our dailies recently observed that "the men in charge of prisons have but too often been men who ought themselves to have been prisoners." The Anarchist does not agree with that. He would have no prisons at all. But I am quite sure that if that editor himself were put in the prison-keeper's place, he too would turn hard. And the opportunities of the official criminal are much greater than those of the unofficial one. Lawyer and governmentalist as he was, Ingersoll said: "It is safe to say that governments have committed far more crimes than they have prevented." Then why create a second class of parasites worse than the first? Why not put up with the original one?

Moreover, you have another thing to consider than the simple problem of a wrong inflicted upon a guilty man. How many times has it happened that the innocent man

has been convicted! I remember an instance of a man
so convicted of murder in Michigan. He had served
twenty-seven years in Jackson penitentiary (for Michigan is not a hang-State) when the real murderer, dying,
confessed. And the State *pardoned* that innocent man!
Because it was the quickest legal way to let him out!
I hope he has been able to pardon the State.

Not very long ago a man was hanged here in this city.
He had killed his superintendent. Some doctors said
he was insane; the government experts said he was not.
They said he was faking insanity when he proclaimed
himself Jesus Christ. And he was hanged. Afterwards
the doctors found two cysts in his brain. The State of
Pennsylvania had killed a sick man! And as long as
punishments exist, these mistakes will occur. If you
accept the principle at all, you must accept with it the
blood-guilt of innocent men.

Not only this, but you must accept also the responsibility for all the misery which results to others whose
lives are bound up with that of the convict, for even he
is loved by some one, much loved perhaps. It is a foolish thing to turn adrift a house full of children, to
become criminals in turn, perhaps, in order to frighten
some indefinite future offender by making an example
of their father or mother. Yet how many times has it
not happened!

And this is speaking only from the practical, selfish
side of the matter. There is another, one from which
I would rather appeal to you, and from which I think
you would after all prefer to be appealed to. Ask yourselves, each of you, whether you are quite sure that you
have feeling enough, understanding enough, and *have
you suffered* enough, to be able to weigh and measure
out another man's life or liberty, no matter what he has
done? And if you have not yourself, are you able to

delegate to any judge the power which you have not? The great Russian novelist, Dostoyevsky, in his psychological study of this same subject, traces the sufferings of a man who had committed a shocking murder; his whole body and brain are a continual prey to torture. He gives himself up, seeking relief in confession. He goes to prison, for in barbarous Russia they have not the barbarity of capital punishment for murderers, unless political ones. But he finds no relief. He remains for a year, bitter, resentful, a prey to all miserable feelings. But at last he is touched by love, the silent, unobtrusive, all-conquering love of one who knew it all and forgave it all. And the regeneration of his soul began.

"The criminal slew," says Tolstoy: "are you better, then, when you slay? He took another's liberty; and is it the right way, therefore, for you to take his? Violence is no answer to violence."

> "Have good will
> To all that lives, letting unkindness die,
> And greed and wrath; so that your lives be made
> As soft airs passing by."

So said Lord Buddha, the Light of Asia.

And another said: "Ye have heard that it hath been said 'an eye for an eye, and a tooth for a tooth'; but I say unto you, resist not him that is evil."

Yet the vengeance that the great psychologist saw was futile, the violence that the greatest living religious teacher and the greatest dead ones advised no man to wreak, that violence is done daily and hourly by every little-hearted prosecutor who prosecutes at so much a day, by every petty judge who buys his way into office with common politicians' tricks, and deals in men's lives and liberties as a trader deals in pins, by every neat-souled and cheap-souled member of the "unco guid" whose respectable bargain-counter maxims of morality have as much effect to stem the great floods and storms that shake the human will as the waving of a lady's kid glove against the tempest. Those who have not suffered cannot understand how to punish; those who have understanding *will* not.

I said at the beginning and I say again, I believe that in every one of us all things are germinal: in judge and prosecutor and prison-keeper too, and even in those small moral souls who cut out one undeviating pattern for all men to fit, even in them there are the germs of passion and crime and sympathy and forgiveness. And some day things will stir in them and accuse them and awaken them. And that awakening will come when suddenly one day there breaks upon them with realizing force the sense of the unison of life, the irrevocable relationship of the saint to the sinner, the judge to the criminal; that all personalities are intertwined and rushing upon doom together. Once in my life it was given to me to see the outward manifestation of this unison. It was in 1897. We stood upon the base of the Nelson monument in Trafalgar Square. Below were ten thousand people packed together with upturned faces. They had gathered to hear and see men and women whose hands and limbs were scarred all over with the red-hot irons of the tortures in the fortress of Montjuich. For the crime of an unknown person these twenty-eight men and women, together with four hundred others, had been cast into that terrible den and tortured with the infamies of the inquisition to make them reveal that of which they knew nothing. After a year of such suffering as makes the decent human heart sick only to contemplate, with nothing proven against them, some even without trial, they were suddenly released with orders to leave the country within twenty-four hours. They were then in Trafalgar Square, and to the credit of old England be it said, harlot and mother of harlots though she is, for there was not another country among the great nations of the earth to which those twenty-eight innocent people could go. For they were paupers impoverished by that cruel State of Spain in the terrible battle for their freedom; they would not have been admitted to free America. When Francesco Gana, speaking in a language which most of them did not understand, lifted his poor, scarred hands, the faces of those ten thousand people moved together like the leaves of a forest in the wind. They waved to and fro, they rose and fell; the visible moved in the breath of the invisible. It was the revelation of the action of the Unconscious, the fatalistic unity of man.

Sometimes, even now as I look upon you, it is as if the bodies that I see were as transparent bubbles wherethrough the red blood boils and flows, a turbulent stream churning and tossing and leaping, and behind us and our generation, far, far back, endlessly backwards, where all the bubbles are broken and not a ripple remains, the silent pouring of the Great Red River, the unfathomable River,—backwards through the unbroken forest and the untilled plain, backwards through the forgotten world of savagery and animal life, back somewhere to its dark sources in deep Sea and old Night, the rushing River of Blood—no fancy—real, tangible blood, the blood that hurries in your veins while I speak, bearing with it the curses and the blessings of the Past. Through what infinite shadows has that river rolled! Through what desolate wastes has it not spread its ooze! Through what desperate passages has it been forced! What strength, what invincible strength is in that hot stream! You are just the bubble on its crest; where will the current fling you ere you die? At what moment will the fierce impurities borne from its somber and tenebrous past be hurled up in you? Shall you then cry out for punish-

ment if they are hurled up in another? if, flung against
the merciless rocks of the channel, while you swim easily
in the midstream, they fall back and hurt other bubbles?

Can you not feel that

"Men are the heart-beats of Man, the plumes that feather his
     wings,
Storm-worn since being began with the wind and the thunder
     of things.
Things are cruel and blind; their strength detains and deforms.
And the wearying wings of the mind still beat up the stream
     of their storms.
Still, as one swimming up-stream, they strike out blind in the
     blast,
In thunder of vision and dream, and lightning of future and
     past.
We are baffled and caught in the current and bruised upon
     edges of shoals:
As weeds or as reeds in the torrent of things are the wind-
     shaken souls.
Spirit by spirit goes under, a foam-bell's bubble of breath,
That blows and opens asunder and blurs not the mirror of
     Death."

Is it not enough that "things are cruel and blind"?
Must we also be cruel and blind? When the whole thing
amounts to so little at the most, shall we embitter it
more, and crush and stifle what must so soon be crushed
and stifled anyhow? Can we not, knowing what rem-
nants of things dead and drowned are floating through
us, haunting our brains with specters of old deeds and
scenes of violence, can we not learn to pardon our brother
to whom the specters are more real, upon whom greater
stress was laid? Can we not, recalling all the evil things
that we have done, or left undone only because some
scarcely perceptible weight struck down the balance, or
because some kindly word came to us in the midst of our
bitterness and showed that not all was hateful in the

world; can we not understand him for whom the balance
was not struck down, the kind word unspoken? Believe me, forgiveness is better than wrath,—better for
the wrong-doer, who will be touched and regenerated by
it, and better for you.   And you are wrong if you think
it is hard: it is easy, far easier than to hate.   It may
sound like a paradox, but the greater the injury the
easier the pardon.

Let us have done with this savage idea of punishment,
which is without wisdom.   Let us work for the freedom
of man from the oppressions which make criminals, and
for the enlightened treatment of all the sick.   And though
we may never see the fruit of it, we may rest assured
that the great tide of thought is setting our way, and
that

> "While the tired wave, vainly breaking,
>   Seems here no painful inch to gain,
> Far back, through creeks and inlets making,
>   Comes silent, flooding in, the main."

In Defence of
Emma Goldman and the Right
of Expropriation

THE light is pleasant, is it not, my friends? It is good to look into each other's faces, to see the hands that clasp our own, to read the eyes that search our thoughts, to know what manner of lips give utterance to our pleasant greetings. It is good to be able to wink defiance at the Night, the cold, unseeing Night. How weird, how gruesome, how chilly it would be if I stood here in blackness, a shadow addressing shadows, in a house of blindness! Yet each would know that he was not alone; yet might we stretch hands and touch each other, and feel the warmth of human presence near. Yet might a sympathetic voice ring thro' the darkness, quickening the dragging moments.—The lonely prisoners in the cells of Blackwell's Island have neither light nor sound! The short day hurries across the sky, the short day still more shortened in the gloomy walls. The long chill night creeps up so early, weaving its sombre curtain before the imprisoned eyes. And thro' the curtain comes no sympathizing voice, beyond the curtain lies the prison silence, beyond that the cheerless, uncommunicating land, and still beyond the icy, fretting river, black and menacing, ready to drown. A wall of night, a wall of stone, a wall of water! Thus has the great State of New York answered EMMA GOLDMAN; thus have the classes replied to the masses; thus do the rich respond to the poor; thus does the Institution of Property give its ultimatum to Hunger!

"Give us work," said EMMA GOLDMAN; "if you will not give us work, then give us bread; if you do not give us either work or bread, then we shall take bread." It wasn't a very wise remark to make to the State of New York, that is—Wealth and its watch-dogs, the Police. But I fear me much that the apostles of liberty, the fore-runners of revolt, have never been very wise. There is a record of a seditious person, who once upon a time went about with a few despised followers in Palestine, taking corn out of other people's corn-fields, (on the Sabbath day, too). That same person, when he wished to ride into Jerusalem told his disciples to go forward to where they would find a young colt tied, to unloose it and bring it to him, and if any one interfered or said anything to them, were to say: "My master hath need of it." That same person said: "Give to him that asketh of thee, and from him that taketh away thy goods ask them not back again." That same person once stood before the hungry multitudes of Galilee and taught them, saying: "The Scribes and the Pharisees sit in Moses' seat; therefore whatever they bid you observe, that observe and do. But do not ye after their works, for they say, and do not. For they bind heavy burdens, and grievous to be borne, and lay them on men's shoulders; but they themselves will not move them with one of their fingers. But all their works they do to be seen of men; they make broad their phylacteries, and enlarge the borders of their garments: and love the uppermost rooms at feasts, and the chief seats in the synagogues, and greeting in the markets, and to be called of men, 'Rabbi, Rabbi.'" And turning to the Scribes and the Pharisees, he continued: "Woe unto you, Scribes and Pharisees, hypocrites! for ye devour widows' houses, and for a pretense make long prayers: therefore shall ye receive the greater damnation. Woe unto you Scribes and Pharisees, hypocrites! for ye pay tithe of mint, and anise, and cummin, and have omitted the weightier matters of the law, judgement, and mercy, and faith: these ought ye to have done and not left the other undone. Ye blind guides, that strain at a gnat and swallow a camel! Woe unto you, Scribes and Pharisees, hypocrites! for ye make clean the outside of the cup and platter, but within they are full of extortion and excess. Woe unto you, Scribes and Pharisees, hypocrites! For ye are like unto whited sepulchres, which indeed appear beautiful outward, but within are full of dead men's bones and all uncleanness. Even so ye outwardly appear righteous unto men, but within ye are full of hypocrisy and iniquity. Woe unto you, Scribes and Pharisees, hypocrites! Because ye build the tombs of the prophets and garnish the sepulchres of the righteous; and say 'If we had been in the days of our fathers we would not have been partakers with them in the blood of the prophets'. Wherefore ye be witnesses unto yourselves that ye are the children of them which killed the prophets. Fill ye up then the measure of your fathers! Ye serpents! Ye generation of vipers! How can ye escape the damnation of hell!"

Yes; these are the words of the outlaw who is alleged to form the foundation stone of modern civilization, to the authorities of his day. Hypocrites, extortionists, doers of iniquity, robbers of the poor, blood-partakers, serpents, vipers, fit for hell!

It wasn't a very wise speech, from beginning to end. Pe haps he knew it when he stood before Pilate to receive his sentence, when he bore his heavy crucifix up Calvary, when nailed upon it, stretched in agony, he cried: "My God, my God, why hast thou forsaken me!"

No, it wasn't wise—but it was very grand.

This grand, foolish person, this beggar-tramp, this thief who justified the action of hunger, this man who set the Right of Property beneath his foot, this Individual who defied the State, do you know why he was so feared and hated, and punished? Because, as it is said in the record, "the common people heard him gladly"; and the accusation before Pontius Pilate was, "we found this fellow perverting the whole nation. He stirreth up the people, teaching throughout all Jewry."

Ah, the dreaded "common people"!

When Cardinal Manning wrote: "Necessity knows no law, and a starving man has a natural right to a share of his neighbor's bread," who thought of arresting Cardinal Manning? His was a carefully written article in the *Fortnightly Review*. Who read it? Not the people who needed bread. Without food in their stomachs, they had not fifty cents to spend for a magazine. It was not the voice of the people themselves asserting their rights. No one for one instant imagined that Cardinal Manning would put himself at the head of ten thousand hungry men to loot the bakeries of London. It was a piece of ethical hair-splitting to be discussed in after-dinner speeches by the wine-muddled gentlemen who think themselves most competent to consider such subjects when their dress-coats are spoiled by the vomit of gluttony and drunkenness. But when EMMA GOLDMAN stood in Union Square and said, "If they do not give you work or bread, take bread," the common people heard her gladly; and as of old the wandering carpenter of Nazareth addressed his own class, teaching throughout all Jewry, stirring up the people against the authorities, so the dressmaker of New York addressing the unemployed working-people of New York was the menace of the depths of society, crying in its own tongue. The authorities heard and were afraid: therefore the triple wall.

It is the old, old story. When Thomas Paine, one hundred years ago, published the first part of "The Rights of Man," the part in which he discusses principles only, the edition was a high-priced one, reaching comparatively few readers. It created only a literary furore. When the second part appeared, the part in which he treats of the application of principles, in which he declares that "men should not petition for rights but take them," it came out in a cheap form, so that one hundred thousand copies were sold in a few weeks. That brought down the prosecution of the government. It had reached the people that might act, and prosecution followed prosecution till Botany Bay was full of the best men of England. Thus were the limitations of speech and press declared, and thus will they ever be declared so long as there are antagonistic interests in human society.

Understand me clearly. I believe that the term "constitutional right of free speech" is a meaningless phrase, for this reason: the Constitution of the United States, and the Declaration of Independence, and particularly the latter, were, in their day, progressive expressions of progressive ideals. But they are, throughout, characterized by the metaphysical philosophy which dominated the thought of the last century. They speak of "inherent rights," "inalienable rights," "natural rights," etc. They declare that men are equal because of a supposed metaphysical something-or-other, called equality, existing in some mysterious way apart from material conditions, just as the philosophers of the eighteenth century accounted for water being wet by alleging a metaphysical wetness, existing somehow apart from matter. I do not say this to disparage those grand men who dared to put themselves against the authorities of the monarchy, and to conceive a better ideal of society, one which they certainly thought would secure equal rights to men; because I realize fully that no one can live very far in advance of the time-spirit, and I am positive in my own mind that, unless some cataclysm destroys the human race before the end of the twentieth century, the experience of the next hundred years will explode many of our own theories. But the experience of this age has proven that metaphysical quantities do not exist apart from materials, and hence humanity can not be made equal by declarations on paper. Unless the material conditions for equality exist, it is worse than mockery to pronounce men equal. And unless there is equality (and by equality I mean equal chances for every one to make the most of himself), unless, I say, these equal chances exist, freedom, either of thought, speech, or action, is equally a mockery.

I once read that one million angels could dance at the same time on the point of a needle; possibly one million angels might be able to get a decent night's lodging by virtue of their constitutional rights; one single tramp couldn't. And whenever the tongues of the non-possessing class threaten the possessors, whenever the disinherited menace the privileged, that moment you will find that the Constitution isn't made for you. Therefore I think Anarchists make a mistake when they contend for their constitutional rights. As a prominent lawyer, Mr. Thomas Earle White, of Philadelphia, himself an An-

archist, said to me not long since: "What are you going
to do about it? Go into the courts, and fight for your
legal rights? Anarchists haven't got any." "Well," says
the governmentalist, "you can't consistently claim any.
You don't believe in constitutions and laws." Exactly
so; and if any one will right my constitutional wrongs,
I will willingly make him a present of my constitutional
rights. At the same time I am perfectly sure no one
will ever make this exchange; nor will any help ever
come to the wronged class from the outside. Salvation
on the vicarious plan isn't worth despising. Redress of
wrongs will not come by petitioning "the powers that
be." "He has rights who dare maintain them." "The
Lord helps them who help themselves." (And when
one is able to help himself, I don't think he is apt to
trouble the Lord much for his assistance.) As long as
the working people fold hands and pray the gods in
Washington to give them work, so long they will not
get it. So long as they tramp the streets, whose stones
they lay, whose filth they clean, whose sewers they dig,
yet upon which they must not stand too long lest the
policeman bid them "move on"; so long as they go
from factory to factory, begging for the opportunity to
be a slave, receiving the insults of bosses and foremen,
getting the old "No," the old shake of the head, in these
factories which they build, whose machines they wrought;
so long as they consent to herd like cattle, in the cities,
driven year after year, more and more, off the mortgaged
land, the land they cleared, fertilized, cultivated, rendered of value; so long as they stand shivering, gazing
through plate glass windows at overcoats, which they
made but cannot buy, starving in the midst of food they
produced but cannot have; so long as they continue to do
these things vaguely relying upon some power outside

themselves, be it god, or priest, or politician, or employer, or charitable society, to remedy matters, so long deliverance will be delayed. When they conceive the possibility of a complete international federation of labor, whose constituent groups shall take possession of land, mines, factories, all the instruments of production, issue their own certificates of exchange, and, in short, conduct their own industry without regulative interference from law-makers or employers, then we may hope for the only help which counts for aught—self-help; the only condition which can guarantee free speech (and no paper guarantee needed).

But meanwhile, while we are waiting, for there is yet much grist of the middle class to be ground between the upper and nether millstones of economic evolution; while we await the formation of the international labor trust; while we watch for the day when there are enough of people with nothing in their stomachs and desperation in their heads, to go about the work of expropriation; what shall those do who are starving now?

That is the question which EMMA GOLDMAN had to face; and she answered it by saying: "Ask, and if you do not receive, take—take bread."

I do not give you that advice. Not because I do not think the bread belongs to you; not because I do not think you would be morally right in taking it; not that I am not more shocked and horrified and embittered by the report of one human being starving in the heart of plenty, than by all the Pittsburgs, and Chicagos, and Homesteads, and Tennessees, and Cœur d'Alenes, and Buffalos, and Barcelonas, and Parises; not that I do not think one little bit of sensitive human flesh is worth all the property rights in New York city; not that I do not think the world will ever be saved by the sheep's virtue of going patiently to the shambles; not that I do not believe the expropriation of the possessing classes is inevitable, and that that expropriation will begin by just such acts as EMMA GOLDMAN advised, viz.: the taking possession of wealth already produced; not that I think you owe any consideration to the conspirators of Wall Street, or those who profit by their operations, as such, nor ever will till they are reduced to the level of human beings having equal chances with you to earn their share of social wealth, and no more.

I have said that I do not give you the advice given by EMMA GOLDMAN, not that I would have you forget the consideration the expropriators have shown to you; that they have advised lead for strikers, strychnine for tramps, bread and water as good enough for working people; not that I cannot hear yet in my ears the words of one who said to me of the Studebaker Wagon Works' strikers, "If I had my way I'd mow them down with Gatling guns", not that I would have you forget the electric wire of Fort Frick, nor the Pinkertons, nor the militia, nor the prosecutions for murder and treason; not that I would have you forget the 4th of May, when your constitutional right of free speech was vindicated, nor the 11th of November when it was assassinated; not that I would have you forget the single dinner at Delmonico's which Ward McAllister tells us cost ten thousand dollars! Would I have you forget that the wine in the glasses was your children's blood? It must be a rare drink—children's blood! I have read of the wonderful sparkle on costly champagne—I have never seen it. If I did I think it would look to me like mothers' tears over the little, white, wasted forms of dead babies— dead because there was no milk in their breasts! Yes, I want you to remember that these rich are blood-drinkers, tearers of human flesh, gnawers of human bones! Yes, if I had the power I would burn your wrongs upon your hearts in characters that should glow like coals in the night!

I have not a tongue of fire as EMMA GOLDMAN has; I cannot "stir the people"; I must speak in my own cold, calculated way. (Perhaps that is the reason I am allowed to speak at all.) But if I had the power, my will is good enough. You know how Shakespeare's Marc Antony addressed the populace at Rome:

> "I am no orator, as Brutus is,
> But as you know me well, a plain blunt man
> That love my friend. And that they know full well
> That gave me public leave to speak of him.
> For I have neither wit, nor words, nor worth,
> Action, nor utterance, nor the power of speech
> To stir men's blood. I only speak right on.
> I tell you that which you yourselves do know,
> Show you sweet Cæsar's wounds, poor, poor dumb mouths,
> And bid them speak for me. But were I Brutus
> And Brutus Antony, there were an Antony
> Would ruffle up your spirits, and put a tongue
> In every wound of Cæsar's, that should move
> The stones of Rome to rise and mutiny."

If, therefore, I do not give you the advice which EMMA GOLDMAN gave, let not the authorities suppose it is because I have any more respect for their constitution and their law than she has, or that I regard them as having any rights in the matter.

No! My reasons for not giving that advice are two. First, if I were giving advice at all, I would say: "My friends, that bread belongs to you. It is you who toiled and sweat in the sun to sow and reap the wheat; it is you who stood by the thresher, and breathed the chaff-filled atmosphere in the mills, while it was ground to flour; it is you who went into the eternal night of the mine and risked drowning, fire damp, explosion, and cave-in, to get the fuel for the fire that baked it; it is you who stood in the hell-like heat, and struck the blows that forged the iron for the ovens wherein it is baked; it is you who stand all night in the terrible cellar shops, and tend the machines that knead the flour into dough; it is you, you, you, farmer, miner, mechanic, who make the bread; but you haven't the power to take it. At every transformation wrought by toil, some one who didn't toil has taken part from you; and now he has it all, and you haven't the power to take it back! You are told you have the power because you have the numbers. Never make so silly a blunder as to suppose that power resides in numbers. One good, level-headed policeman with a club, is worth ten excited, unarmed men; one detachment of well-drilled militia has a power equal to that of the greatest mob that could be raised in New York City. Do you know I admire compact, concentrated power. Let me give you an illustration. Out in a little town in Illinois there is a certain capitalist, and if ever a human creature sweat and ground the grist of gold from the muscle of man, it is he. Well, once upon a time, his workmen, (not his slaves, his workmen,) were on strike; and fifteen hundred muscular Polacks armed with stones, brick-bats, red-hot pokers, and other such crude weapons as a mob generally collects, went up to his house for the purpose of smashing the windows, and so forth; possibly to do as those people in Italy did the other day with the sheriff who attempted to collect the milk tax. He alone, one man, met them on the steps of his porch, and for two mortal hours, by threats, promises, cajoleries held those fifteen hundred Poles at bay. And finally they went away, without smashing a pane of glass or harming a hair of his head. Now that was power; and you can't help but admire it, no matter if it was your enemy who displayed it; and you must admit that so long as numbers can be overcome by such relative quantity, power does not reside in numbers. Therefore, if I were giving advice, I would not say, "take bread," but take counsel with yourselves how to get the power to take bread.

There is no doubt but that power is latently in you; there is no doubt it can be developed; there is no doubt the authorities know this, and fear it, and are ready to exert as much force as is necessary to repress any signs of its development. And this is the explanation of EMMA GOLDMAN's imprisonment. The authorities do not fear you as you are; they only fear what you may become. The dangerous thing was "the voice crying in the wilderness", foretelling the power which was to come after it. You should have seen how they feared it in Philadelphia. They got out a whole platoon of police and detectives, and executed a military manœuvre to catch the woman who had been running around under their noses for three days. And when she walked up to them, then they surrounded and captured her, and guarded the city hall where they kept her over night, and put a detective in the next cell to make notes. Why so much fear? Did they shrink from the stab of the dressmaker's needle? Or did they dread some stronger weapon?

Ah! the accusation before the New York Pontius Pilate was: "She stirreth up the people." And Pilate sentenced her to the full limit of the law, because, he said, "You are more than ordinarily intelligent." Why is intelligence dealt thus harshly with? Because it is the beginning of power. Strive, then, for power.

My second reason for not repeating EMMA GOLDMAN's

words is, that I, as an Anarchist, have no right to advise another to do anything involving a risk to himself; nor would I give a fillip for an action done by the advice of some one else, unless it is accompanied by a well-argued, well settled conviction on the part of the person acting, that it really is the best thing to do. Anarchism, to me, means not only the denial of authority, not only a new economy, but a revision of the principles of morality. It means the development of the individual, as well as the assertion of the individual. It means self-responsibility, and not leader-worship. I say it is your business to decide whether you will starve and freeze in sight of food and clothing, outside of jail, or commit some overt act against the institution of property and take your place beside Timmermann and Goldman. And in saying this I mean to cast no reflection whatever upon Miss Goldman for doing otherwise. She and I hold many different views on both Economy and Morals; and that she is honest in her's she has proved better than I have proved mine. Miss Goldman is a Communist; I am an Individualist. She wishes to destroy the right of property; I wish to assert it. I make my war upon privilege and authority, whereby the right of property, the true right in that which is proper to the individual, is annihilated. She believes that co-operation would entirely supplant competition; I hold that competition in one form or another will always exist, and that it is highly desirable it should. But whether she or I be right, or both of us be wrong, of one thing I am sure: *the spirit which animates Emma Goldman is the only one which will emancipate the slave from his slavery, the tyrant from his tyranny—the spirit which is willing to dare and suffer.*

That which dwells in the frail body in the prison-room

to-night is not the New York dressmaker alone. Transport yourselves there in thought a moment; look steadily into those fair, blue eyes, upon the sun-brown hair, the sea-shell face, the restless hands, the woman's figure; look steadily till in place of the person, the individual of time and place, you see that which transcends time and place, and flits from house to house of life, mocking at death. Swinburne in his magnificent "Before a Crucifix," says:

> "With iron for thy linen bands,
>   And unclean cloths for winding-sheet,
>   They bind the people's nail-pierced hands,
>   They hide the people's nail-pierced feet:
>   And what man, or what angel known
>   Shall roll back the sepulchral stone?"

Perhaps in the presence of this untrammeled spirit we shall feel that something has rolled back the sepulchral stone; and up from the cold wind of the grave is borne the breath that animated ANAXAGORAS, SOCRATES, CHRIST, HYPATIA, JOHN HUSS, BRUNO, ROBERT EMMET, JOHN BROWN, SOPHIA PEROVSKAYA, PARSONS, FISCHER, ENGEL, SPIES, LINGG, BERKMAN, PALLAS; and all those, known and unknown, who have died by tree, and axe, and fagot, or dragged out forgotten lives in dungeons, derided, hated, tortured by men. Perhaps we shall know ourselves face to face with that which leaps from the throat of the strangled when the rope chokes, which smokes up from the blood of the murdered when the axe falls; that which has been forever hunted, fettered. imprisoned, exiled, executed, and never conquered. Lo, from its many incarnations it comes forth again, the immortal Race-Christ of the Ages! The gloomy walls are glorified thereby, the prisoner is transfigured, and we say, reverently we say:

> "O sacred Head, O desecrate,
> O labor-wounded feet and hands,
> O blood poured forth in pledge to fate
> Of nameless lives in divers lands!
> O slain, and spent, and sacrificed
> People! The grey-grown, speechless Christ."

Direct Action

FROM the standpoint of one who thinks himself capable of discerning an undeviating route for human progress to pursue, if it is to be progress at all, who, having such a route on his mind's map, has endeavored to point it out to others; to make them see it as he sees it; who in so doing has chosen what appeared to him clear and simple expressions to convey his thoughts to others,—to such a one it appears matter for regret and confusion of spirit that the phrase "Direct Action" has suddenly acquired in the general mind a circumscribed meaning, not at all implied in the words themselves, and certainly never attached to it by himself or his co-thinkers.

However, this is one of the common jests which Progress plays on those who think themselves able to set metes and bounds for it. Over and over again, names, phrases, mottoes, watchwords, have been turned inside out, and upside down, and hindside before, and sideways, by occurrences out of the control of those who used the expressions in their proper sense; and still, those who sturdily held their ground, and insisted on being heard, have in the end found that the period of misunderstanding and prejudice has been but the prelude to wider inquiry and understanding.

I rather think this will be the case with the present misconception of the term Direct Action, which through the misapprehension, or else the deliberate misrepresentation, of certain journalists in Los Angeles, at the time the McNamaras pleaded guilty, suddenly acquired in the popular mind the interpretation, "Forcible Attacks on Life and Property." This was either very ignorant or very dishonest of the journalists; but it has had the effect of making a good many people curious to know all about Direct Action.

As a matter of fact, those who are so lustily and so inordinately condemning it, will find on examination that they themselves have on many occasions practised direct action, and will do so again.

Every person who ever thought he had a right to assert, and went boldly and asserted it, himself, or jointly with others that shared his convictions, was a direct actionist. Some thirty years ago I recall that the Salvation Army was vigorously practising direct action in the maintenance of the freedom of its members to speak, assemble, and pray. Over and over they were arrested, fined, and imprisoned; but they kept right on singing, praying, and marching, till they finally compelled their persecutors to let them alone. The Industrial Workers are now conducting the same fight, and have, in a number of cases, compelled the officials to let them alone by the same direct tactics.

Every person who ever had a plan to do anything, and went and did it, or who laid his plan before others, and won their co-operation to do it with him, without going to external authorities to please do the thing for them, was a direct actionist. All co-operative experiments are essentially direct action.

Every person who ever in his life had a difference with any one to settle, and went straight to the other persons involved to settle it, either by a peaceable plan or otherwise, was a direct actionist. Examples of such action are strikes and boycotts; many persons will recall the action of the housewives of New York who boycotted the butchers, and lowered the price of meat; at the present moment a butter boycott seems looming up, as a direct reply to the price-makers for butter.

These actions are generally not due to any one's reasoning overmuch on the respective merits of directness or indirectness, but are the spontaneous retorts of those who feel oppressed by a situation. In other words, all people are, most of the time, believers in the principle of direct action, and practisers of it. However, most people are also indirect or political actionists. And they are both these things at the same time, without making much of an analysis of either. There are only a limited number of persons who eschew political action under any and all circumstances; but there is nobody, nobody at all, who has ever been so "impossible" as to eschew direct action altogether.

The majority of thinking people are really opportunists, leaning, some, perhaps, more to directness, some more to indirectness, as a general thing, but ready to use either means when opportunity calls for it. That is to say, there are those who hold that balloting governors into power is essentially a wrong and foolish thing; but who, nevertheless, under stress of special circumstance, might consider it the wisest thing to do, to vote some individual into office at that particular time. Or there are those who believe that, in general, the wisest way for people to get what they want is by the indirect method of voting into power some one who will make what they want legal; yet who, all the same, will occasionally, under exceptional conditions, advise a strike; and a strike, as I have said, is direct action.

Or they may do as the Socialist Party agitators, who are mostly declaiming now against direct action, did last summer, when the police were holding up their meetings. They went in force to the meeting-places, prepared to speak whether-or-no; and they made the police back down. And while that was not logical on their part, thus to oppose the legal executors of the majority's will, it was a fine, successful piece of direct action.

Those who, by the essence of their belief, are committed to Direct Action only are—just who? Why, the non-resistants; precisely those who do not believe in violence at all! Now do not make the mistake of inferring that I say direct action means non-resistance; not by any means. Direct action may be the extreme of violence, or it may be as peaceful as the waters of the Brook of Siloa that go softly. What I say is, that the real non-resistants can believe in direct action only, never in political action. For the basis of all political action is coercion; even when the State does good things, it finally rests on a club, a gun, or a prison, for its power to carry them through.

Now every school child in the United States has had the direct action of certain non-resistants brought to his notice by his school history. The case which every one instantly recalls is that of the early Quakers who came to Massachusetts. The Puritans had accused the Quakers of "troubling the world by preaching peace to it." They refused to pay church taxes; they refused to bear arms; they refused to swear allegiance to any government. (In so doing, they were direct actionists; what we may call negative direct actionists.) So the Puritans, being political actionists, passed laws to keep them out, to deport, to fine, to imprison, to mutilate, and finally, to hang them. And the Quakers just kept on coming (which was positive direct action); and history records that after the hanging of four Quakers, and the flogging of Margaret Brewster at the cart's tail through the streets of Boston, "the Puritans gave up trying to silence the new missionaries"; that "Quaker persistence and Quaker non-resistance had won the day."

Another example of direct action in early colonial history, but this time by no means of the peaceable sort, was the affair known as Bacon's Rebellion. All our historians certainly defend the action of the rebels in that matter, as reason is, for they were right. And yet it was a case of violent direct action against lawfully constituted authority. For the benefit of those who have forgotten the details, let me briefly remind them that the Virginia planters were in fear of a general attack by the Indians; with reason. Being political actionists, they asked, or Bacon as their leader asked, that the governor grant him a commission to raise volunteers in their own defense. The governor feared that such a company of armed men would be a threat to him; also with reason. He refused the commission. Whereupon the planters resorted to direct action. They raised the volunteers without the commission, and successfully fought off the Indians. Bacon was pronounced a traitor by the governor; but the people being with him, the governor was afraid to proceed against him. In the end, however, it came so far that the rebels burned Jamestown; and but for the untimely death of Bacon, much more might have been done. Of course the reaction was very dreadful, as it usually is where a rebellion collapses, or is crushed. Yet even during the brief period of success, it had corrected a good many abuses. I am quite sure that the political-action-at-all-costs advocates of those times, after the reaction came back into power, must have said: "See to what evils direct action brings us! Behold, the progress of the colony has been set back twenty-five years"; forgetting that if the colonists had not resorted to direct action, their scalps would have been taken by the Indians a year sooner, instead of a number of them being hanged by the governor a year later.

In the period of agitation and excitement preceding the revolution, there were all sorts and kinds of direct action from the most peaceable to the most violent; and I believe that almost everybody who studies United States history finds the account of these performances the most interesting part of the story, the part which dents into his memory most easily.

Among the peaceable moves made, were the non-importation agreements, the leagues for wearing home-spun clothing and the "committees of correspondence." As the inevitable growth of hostility progressed, violent direct action developed; e. g., in the matter of destroying the revenue stamps, or the action concerning the tea-ships, either by not permitting the tea to be landed, or by putting it in damp storage, or by throwing it into the harbor, as in Boston, or by compelling a tea-ship owner to set fire to his own ship, as at Annapolis. These are all actions which our commonest text-books record, certainly not in a condemnatory way, not even in an apologetic one, though they are all cases of direct action against legally constituted authority and property rights. If I draw attention to them, and others of like nature, it is to prove to unreflecting repeaters of words that *direct action has always been used, and has the historical sanction of the very people now reprobating it.*

George Washington is said to have been the leader of the Virginia planters' non-importation league: he would now be "enjoined," probably, by a court, from forming any such league; and if he persisted, he would be fined for contempt.

When the great quarrel between the North and the South was waxing hot and hotter, it was again direct action which preceded and precipitated political action. And I may remark here that political action is never taken, nor even contemplated, until slumbering minds have first been aroused by direct acts of protest against existing conditions.

The history of the anti-slavery movement and the Civil War is one of the greatest of paradoxes, although history is a chain of paradoxes. Politically speaking, it was the slave-holding States that stood for greater political freedom, for the autonomy of the single State against the interference of the United States; politically speaking, it was the non-slave-holding States that stood for a strong centralized government, which, Secessionists said, and said truly, was bound progressively to develop into more and more tyrannical forms. Which happened. From the close of the Civil War on, there has been continuous encroachment of the federal power upon what was formerly the concern of the States individually. The wage-slaves, in their struggles of to-day, are continually thrown into conflict with that centralized power, against which the slave-holder protested (with liberty on his lips but tyranny in his heart). Ethically speaking, it was the non-slave-holding States that, in a general way, stood for greater human liberty, while the Secessionists stood for race-slavery. In a general way only; that is, the majority of northerners, not being accustomed to the actual presence of negro slavery about them, thought it was probably a mistake; yet they were in no great ferment of anxiety to have it abolished. The

Abolitionists only, and they were relatively few, were the genuine ethicals, to whom slavery itself—not secession or union—was the main question. In fact, so paramount was it with them, that a considerable number of them were themselves for the dissolution of the union, advocating that the North take the initiative in the matter of dissolving, in order that the northern people might shake off the blame of holding negroes in chains.

Of course, there were all sorts of people with all sorts of temperaments among those who advocated the abolition of slavery. There were Quakers like Whittier (indeed it was the peace-at-all-costs Quakers who had advocated abolition even in early colonial days); there were moderate political actionists, who were for buying off the slaves, as the cheapest way; and there were extremely violent people, who believed and did all sorts of violent things.

As to what the politicians did, it is one long record of "how-not-to-do-it," a record of thirty years of compromising, and dickering, and trying to keep what was as it was, and to hand sops to both sides when new conditions demanded that something be done, or be pretended to be done. But "the stars in their courses fought against Sisera"; the system was breaking down from within, and the direct actionists from without, as well, were widening the cracks remorselessly.

Among the various expressions of direct rebellion was the organization of the "underground railroad." Most of the people who belonged to it believed in both sorts of action; but however much they theoretically subscribed to the right of the majority to enact and enforce laws, they didn't believe in it on that point. My grandfather was a member of the "underground"; many a fugitive slave he helped on his way to Canada. He was a very patient, law-abiding man, in most respects, though I have often thought he probably respected it because he didn't have much to do with it; always leading a pioneer life, law was generally far from him, and direct action imperative. Be that as it may, and law-respecting as he was, he had no respect whatever for slave laws, no matter if made by ten times of a majority; and he conscientiously broke every one that came in his way to be broken.

There were times when in the operation of the "underground", violence was required, and was used. I recollect one old friend relating to me how she and her mother kept watch all night at the door, while a slave for whom a posse was searching hid in the cellar; and though they were of Quaker descent and sympathies, there was a shot-gun on the table. Fortunately it did not have to be used that night.

When the fugitive slave law was passed, with the help of the political actionists of the North who wanted to offer a new sop to the slave-holders, the direct actionists took to rescuing recaptured fugitives. There was the "rescue of Shadrach," and the "rescue of Jerry," the latter rescuers being led by the famous Gerrit Smith; and a good many more successful and unsuccessful attempts. Still the politicals kept on pottering and trying to smooth things over, and the Abolitionists were denounced and decried by the ultra-law-abiding pacificators, pretty much as Wm. D. Haywood and Frank Bohn are being denounced by their own party now.

The other day I read a communication in the Chicago *Daily Socialist* from the secretary of the Louisville local, Socialist Party, to the national secretary, requesting that some safe and sane speaker be substituted for Bohn, who had been announced to speak there. In explaining why,

Mr. Dobbs, secretary, makes this quotation from Bohn's lecture: "Had the McNamaras been successful in defending the interests of the working class, they would have been right, just as John Brown would have been right, had he been successful in freeing the slaves. Ignorance was the only crime of John Brown, and ignorance was the only crime of the McNamaras."

Upon this Mr. Dobbs comments as follows: "We dispute emphatically the statements here made. The attempt to draw a parallel between the open—if mistaken —revolt of John Brown on the one hand, and the secret and murderous methods of the McNamaras on the other, is not only indicative of shallow reasoning, but highly mischievous in the logical conclusions which may be drawn from such statements."

Evidently Mr. Dobbs is very ignorant of the life and work of John Brown. John Brown was a man of violence; he would have scorned anybody's attempt to make him out anything else. And when once a person is a believer in violence, it is with him only a question of the most effective way of applying it, which can be determined only by a knowledge of conditions and means at his disposal. John Brown did not shrink at all from conspiratical methods. Those who have read the autobiography of Frederick Douglas and the Reminiscences of Lucy Colman, will recall that one of the plans laid by John Brown was to organize a chain of armed camps in the mountains of West Virginia, North Carolina, and Tennessee, send secret emissaries among the slaves inciting them to flee to these camps, and there concert such measures as times and conditions made possible for further arousing revolt among the negroes. That this plan failed was due to the weakness of the desire for liberty among the slaves themselves, more than anything else.

Later on, when the politicians in their infinite devious-
ness contrived a fresh proposition of how-not-to-do-it,
known as the Kansas-Nebraska Act, which left the question of slavery to be determined by the settlers, the direct
actionists on both sides sent bogus settlers into the territory, who proceeded to fight it out. The pro-slavery
men, who got in first, made a constitution recognizing
slavery, and a law punishing with death any one who
aided a slave to escape; but the Free Soilers, who were
a little longer in arriving, since they came from more
distant States, made a second constitution, and refused
to recognize the other party's laws at all. And John
Brown was there, mixing in all the violence, conspiratical
or open; he was "a horse-thief and a murderer," in the
eyes of decent, peaceable, political actionists. And there
is no doubt that he stole horses, sending no notice in
advance of his intention to steal them, and that he killed
pro-slavery men. He struck and got away a good many
times before his final attempt on Harper's Ferry. If
he did not use dynamite, it was because dynamite had
not yet appeared as a practical weapon. He made a great
many more intentional attacks on life than the two
brothers Secretary Dobbs condemns for their "murderous methods." And yet, history has not failed to understand John Brown. Mankind knows that though he was
a violent man, with human blood upon his hands, who
was guilty of high treason and hanged for it, yet his
soul was a great, strong, unselfish soul, unable to bear
the frightful crime which kept 4,000,000 people like dumb
beasts, and thought that making war against it was a
sacred, a God-called duty, (for John Brown was a very
religious man—a Presbyterian).

It is by and because of the direct acts of the fore-
runners of social change, whether they be of peaceful

or warlike nature, that the Human Conscience, the conscience of the mass, becomes aroused to the need for
change. It would be very stupid to say that no good results are ever brought about by political action; sometimes good things do come about that way. But never
until individual rebellion, followed by mass rebellion,
has forced it. Direct action is always the clamorer, the
initiator, through which the great sum of indiffer-
entists become aware that oppression is getting intolerable.

We have now an oppression in the land,—and not only
in this land, but throughout all those parts of the world
which enjoy the very mixed blessings of Civilization.
And just as in the question of chattel slavery, so this
form of slavery has been begetting both direct action and
political action. A certain per cent. of our population
(probably a much smaller per cent. than politicians are
in the habit of assigning at mass meetings) is producing the material wealth upon which all the rest of us live;
just as it was the 4,000,000 chattel blacks who supported
all the crowd of parasites above them. These are the
land workers and the *industrial workers.*

Through the unprophesied and unprophesiable operation of institutions which no individual of us created, but
found in existence when he came here, these workers,
the most absolutely necessary part of the whole social
structure, without whose services none can either eat,
or clothe, or shelter himself, are just the ones who get
the least to eat, to wear, and to be housed withal—to
say nothing of their share of the other social benefits
which the rest of us are supposed to furnish, such as
education and artistic gratifications.

These workers have, in one form or another, mutually
joined their forces to see what betterment of their con-

dition they could get; primarily by direct action, secondarily through political action. We have had the Grange, the Farmers' Alliance, Co-operative Associations, Colonization Experiments, Knights of Labor, Trade Unions, and Industrial Workers of the World. All of them have been organized for the purpose of wringing from the masters in the economic field a little better price, a little better conditions, a little shorter hours; or on the other hand, to resist a reduction in price, worse conditions, or longer hours. None of them has attempted a final solution of the social war. None of them, except the Industrial Workers, has recognized that there is a social war, inevitable so long as present legal-social conditions endure. They accepted property institutions as they found them. They were made up of average men, with average desires, and they undertook to do what appeared to them possible and very reasonable things. They were not committed to any particular political policy when they were organized, but were associated for direct action of their own initiation, either positive or defensive.

Undoubtedly there were, and are, among all these organizations, members who looked beyond immediate demands; who did see that the continuous development of forces now in operation was bound to bring about conditions to which it is impossible that life continue to submit, and against which, therefore, it will protest, and violently protest; that it will have no choice but to do so; that it must do so, or tamely die; and since it is not the nature of life to surrender without struggle, it will not tamely die. Twenty-two years ago I met Farmers' Alliance people who said so, Knights of Labor who said so, Trade Unionists who said so. They wanted larger aims than those to which their organizations were looking; but they had to accept their fellow members as they were, and try to stir them to work for such things as it was possible to make them see. And what they could see was better prices, better wages, less dangerous or tyrannical conditions, shorter hours. At the stage of development when these movements were initiated, the land workers could not see that their struggle had anything to do with the struggle of those engaged in the manufacturing or transporting service; nor could these latter see that theirs had anything to do with the movement of the farmers. For that matter very few of them see it yet. They have yet to learn that there is one common struggle against those who have appropriated the earth, the money, and the machines.

Unfortunately the great organization of the farmers frittered itself away in a stupid chase after political power. It was quite successful in getting the power in certain States; but the courts pronounced its laws unconstitutional, and there was the burial hole of all its political conquests. Its original program was to build its own elevators, and store the products therein, holding these from the market till they could escape the speculator. Also, to organize labor exchanges, issuing credit notes upon products deposited for exchange. Had it adhered to this program of direct mutual aid, it would, to some extent, for a time at least, have afforded an illustration of how mankind may free itself from the parasitism of the bankers and the middlemen. Of course, it would have been overthrown in the end, unless it had so revolutionized men's minds by the example as to force the overthrow of the legal monopoly of land and money; but at least it would have served a great educational purpose. As it was, it "went after the red herring," and disintegrated merely from its futility.

The Knights of Labor subsided into comparative in-significance, not because of failure to use direct action, nor because of its tampering with politics, which was small, but chiefly because it was a heterogeneous mass of workers who could not associate their efforts effect-ively.

The Trade Unions grew strong about as the K. of L. subsided, and have continued slowly but persistently to increase in power. It is true the increase has fluctuated; that there have been set-backs; that great single organiza-tions have been formed and again dispersed. But on the whole, trade unions have been a growing power. They have been so because, poor as they are, inefficient as they are, they have been a means whereby a certain section of the workers have been able to bring their united force to bear directly upon their masters, and so get for themselves some portion of what they wanted,—of what their conditions dictated to them they must try to get. The strike is their natural weapon, that which they them-selves forged. It is the direct blow of the strike which nine times out of ten the boss is afraid of. (Of course there are occasions when he is glad of one, but that's unusual.) And the reason he dreads a strike is not so much because he thinks he cannot win out against it, but simply and solely because he does not want an in-terruption of his business. The ordinary boss isn't in much dread of a "class-conscious vote"; there are plenty of shops where you can talk Socialism or any other po-litical program all day long; but if you begin to talk Unionism, you may forthwith expect to be discharged, or at best warned to shut up. Why? Not because the boss is so wise as to know that political action is a swamp in which the workingman gets mired, or because he understands that political Socialism is fast becoming a middle-class movement; not at all. He thinks Socialism is a very bad thing; but it's a good way off! But he knows that if his shop is unionized, he will have trouble right away. His hands will be rebellious, he will be put to expense to improve his factory conditions, he will have to keep workingmen that he doesn't like, and in case of strike he may expect injury to his machinery or his buildings.

It is often said, and parrot-like repeated, that the bosses are "class-conscious," that they stick together for their class interest, and are willing to undergo any sort of personal loss rather than be false to those interests. It isn't so at all. The majority of business people are just like the majority of workingmen; they care a whole lot more about their individual loss or gain than about the gain or loss of their class. And it is his individual loss the boss sees, when threatened by a union.

Now everybody knows that a strike of any size means violence. No matter what any one's ethical preference for peace may be, he knows it will not be peaceful. If it's a telegraph strike, it means cutting wires and poles, and getting fake scabs in to spoil the instruments. If it is a steel rolling mill strike, it means beating up the scabs, breaking the windows, setting the guages wrong, and ruining the expensive rollers together with tons and tons of material. If it's a miners' strike, it means destroying tracks and bridges, and blowing up mills. If it is a garment workers' strike, it means having an unaccountable fire, getting a volley of stones through an apparently inaccessible window, or possibly a brickbat on the manufacturer's own head. If it's a street-car strike, it means tracks torn up or barricaded with the contents of ash-carts and slop-carts, with overturned wagons or stolen fences, it means smashed or incinerated cars and turned switches. ' If it is a system federation strike, it means "dead" engines, wild engines, derailed freights, and stalled trains. If it is a building trades strike, it means dynamited structures. And always, everywhere, all the time, fights between strike-breakers and scabs against strikers and strike-sympathizers, between People and Police.

On the side of the bosses, it means search-lights, electric wires, stockades, bull-pens, detectives and provocative agents, violent kidnapping and deportation, and every device they can conceive for direct protection, besides the ultimate invocation of police, militia, State constabulary, and federal troops.

Everybody knows this; everybody smiles when union officials protest their organizations to be peaceable and law-abiding, because everybody knows they are lying. They know that violence is used, both secretly and openly; and they know it is used because the strikers cannot do any other way, without giving up the fight at once. Nor do they mistake those who thus resort to violence under stress for destructive miscreants who do what they do out of innate cussedness. The people in general understand that they do these things, through the harsh logic of a situation which they did not create, but which forces them to these attacks in order to make good in their struggle to live, or else go down the bottomless descent into poverty, that lets Death find them in the poorhouse hospital, the city street, or the river-slime. This is the awful alternative that the workers are facing; and this is what makes the most kindly disposed human beings,—men who would go out of their way to help a wounded dog, or bring home a stray kitten and nurse it, or step aside to avoid walking on a worm— resort to violence against their fellow-men. They know, for the facts have taught them, that this is the only way to win, if they can win at all. And it has always appeared to me one of the most utterly ludicrous, absolutely irrelevant things that a person can do or say, when approached for relief or assistance by a striker who is dealing with an immediate situation, to respond with, "Vote yourself into power!" when the next election is six months, a year, or two years away.

Unfortunately, the people who know best how violence is used in union warfare, cannot come forward and say: "On such a day, at such a place, such and such a specific action was done, and as the result such and such a concession was made, or such and such a boss capitulated." To do so would imperil their liberty, and their power to go on fighting. Therefore those that know best must keep silent, and sneer in their sleeves, while those that know little prate. Events, not tongues, must make their position clear.

And there has been a very great deal of prating these last few weeks. Speakers and writers, honestly convinced, I believe, that political action, and political action only, can win the workers' battle, have been denouncing what they are pleased to call "direct action" (what they really mean is conspiratical violence) as the author of mischief incalculable. One Oscar Ameringer, as an example, recently said at a meetng in Chicago that the Haymarket bomb of '86 had set back the eight-hour movement twenty-five years, arguing that the movement would have succeeded then but for the bomb. It's a great mistake. No one can exactly measure in years or months the effect of a forward push or a reaction. No one can demonstrate that the eight-hour movement could have been won twenty-five years ago. We know that the eight-hour day was put on the statute books of Illinois in 1871, by political action, and has remained a dead letter. That the direct action of the workers could have won it, then, can not be proved; but it can be shown that many more potent factors than the Haymarket bomb worked against it. On the other hand, if the reactive influence of the bomb was really so powerful, we should naturally expect labor and union conditions to be worse in Chicago than in the cities where no such thing happened. On the contrary, bad as they are, the general conditions of labor are better in Chicago than in most other large cities, and the power of the unions is more developed there than in any other American city except San Francisco. So if we are to conclude anything for the influence of the Haymarket bomb, keep these facts in mind. Personally I do not think its influence on the labor movement, as such, was so very great.

It will be the same with the present furore about violence. Nothing fundamental has been altered. Two men have been imprisoned for what they did (twenty-four years ago they were hanged for what they did not do) ; some few more may yet be imprisoned. But the forces of life will continue to revolt against their economic chains. There will be no cessation in that revolt, no matter what ticket men vote or fail to vote, until the chains are broken.

How will the chains be broken?

Political actionists tell us it will be only by means of working-class party action at the polls; by voting themselves into possession of the sources of life and the tools; by voting that those who now command forests, mines, ranches, waterways, mills and factories, and likewise command the military power to defend them, shall hand over their dominion to the people.

And meanwhile?

Meanwhile be peaceable, industrious, law-abiding, patient, and frugal (as Madero told the Mexican peons to be, after he had sold them to Wall Street)! Even if some of you are disfranchised, don't rise up even against that, for it might "set back the party."

Well, I have already stated that some good is occasionally accomplished by political action,—not necessarily working-class party action either. But I am abundantly convinced that the occasional good accomplished is more than counterbalanced by the evil; just as I am convinced that though there are occasional evils resulting from direct action, they are more than counterbalanced by the good.

Nearly all the laws which were originally framed with the intention of benefiting the workers, have either turned into weapons in their enemies' hands, or become dead letters, unless the workers through their organizations have directly enforced the observance. So that in the end, it is direct action that has to be relied on anyway. As an example of getting the tarred end of a law, glance at the anti-trust law, which was supposed to benefit the people in general, and the working class in particular. About two weeks since, some 250 union leaders were cited to answer to the charge of being trust formers, as the answer of the Illinois Central to its strikers.

But the evil of pinning faith to indirect action is far greater than any such minor results. The main evil is that it destroys initiative, quenches the individual rebellious spirit, teaches people to rely on some one else to do for them what they should do for themselves, what they alone can do for themselves; finally renders organic the anomalous idea that by massing supineness together until a majority is acquired, then, through the peculiar magic of that majority, this supineness is to be transformed into energy. That is, people who have lost the habit of striking for themselves as individuals, who have submitted to every injustice while waiting for the majority to grow, are going to become metamorphosed into human high-explosives by a mere process of packing!

I quite agree that the sources of life, and all the natural wealth of the earth, and the tools necessary to co-operative production, must become free of access to all. It is a positive certainty to me that unionism must widen and deepen its purposes, or it will go under; and I feel sure that the logic of the situation will force them to see it gradually. They must learn that the workers' problem can never be solved by beating up scabs, so long as their own policy of limiting their membership by high initiation fees and other restrictions helps to make scabs. They must learn that the course of growth is not so much along the line of higher wages, but shorter hours, which will enable them to increase membership, to take in everybody who is willing to come into the union. They must learn that if they want to win battles, all allied workers must act together, act quickly (serving no notice on bosses), and retain their freedom so to do at all times. And finally they must learn that even then (when they have a complete organization), they can win nothing permanent unless they strike for everything,—not for a wage, not for a minor improvement, but for the whole natural wealth of the earth. And proceed to the direct expropriation of it all!

They must learn that their power does not lie in their voting strength, that their power lies in their ability to stop production. It is a great mistake to suppose that the wage-earners constitute a majority of the voters. Wage-earners are here to-day and there to-morrow, and that hinders a large number from voting; a great percentage of them in this country are foreigners without a voting right. The most patent proof that Socialist leaders know this is so, is that they are compromising their propaganda at every point to win the support of the business class, the small investor. Their campaign papers proclaimed that their interviewers had been assured by Wall Street bond purchasers that they would be just as ready to buy Los Angeles bonds from a socialist as a capitalist administration; that the present Milwaukee administration has been a boon to the small investor; their reading notices assure their readers in this city that we need not go to the great department stores to buy,—buy rather of So-and-so on Milwaukee Avenue, who will satisfy us quite as well as a "big business" institution. In short, they are making every desperate effort to win the support, and to prolong the life, of that middle-class which socialistic economy says must be ground to pieces, because they know they cannot get a majority without them.

The most that a working-class party could do, even if its politicians remained honest, would be to form a strong faction in the legislatures, which might, by combining its vote with one side or the other, win certain political or economic palliatives.

But what the working-class can do, when once they grow into a solidified organization, is to show the possessing classes, through a sudden cessation of all work, that the whole social structure rests on them; that the possessions of the others are absolutely worthless to them without the workers' activity; that such protests, such strikes, are inherent in the system of property, and will continually recur until the whole thing is abolished,— and having shown that, effectively, proceed to expropriate.

"But the military power," says the political actionist; "we must get political power, or the military will be used against us!"

Against a real General Strike, the military can do

nothing. Oh, true, if you have a Socialist Briand in power, he may declare the workers "public officials" and try to make them serve against themselves! But against the solid wall of an immobile working-mass, even a Briand would be broken.

Meanwhile, until this international awakening, the war will go on as it has been going, in spite of all the hysteria which well-meaning people, who do not understand life and its necessities, may manifest; in spite of all the shivering that timid leaders have done; in spite of all the reactionary revenges that may be taken; in spite of all the capital politicians make out of the situation. It will go on because Life cries to live, and Property denies its freedom to live; and Life will not submit.

And should not submit.

It will go on until that day when a self-freed Humanity is able to chant Swinburne's Hymn of Man:

> "Glory to Man in the highest,
>   For Man is the master of Things."

The Paris Commune

THE Paris Commune, like other spectacular events in human history, has become the clinging point for many legends, alike among its enemies and among its friends. Indeed, one must often question which was the real Commune, the legend or the fact,—what was actually lived, or the conception of it which has shaped itself in the world-mind during those forty odd years that have gone since the 18th of March, 1871.

It is thus with doctrines, it is thus with personalities, it is thus with events.

Which is the real Christianity, the simple doctrine attributed to Christ or the practical preaching and realizing of organized Christianity? Which is the real Abraham Lincoln,—the clever politician who emancipated the chattel slaves as an act of policy, or the legendary apostle of human liberty, who rises like a gigantic figure of iconoclastic right smiting old wrongs and receiving the martyr's crown therefor?

Which is the real Commune,—the thing that was, or the thing our orators have painted it? Which will be the influencing power in the days that are to come? Our Commune commemorators are wont to say, and surely they believe, that the declaration of the Commune was the spontaneous assertion of independence by the Parisian masses, consciously alive to the fact that the national government of France had treated them most outrageously in the matter of defense against the Prussian army. They believe that the farce of the situation in which the city found itself, had opened the eyes of the general populace to the fact that the national government, so far from serving the supposed prime purpose of government, viz., as a means of defense against a foreign invader, was in reality a thing so apart from them and their interests that it preferred to leave them to the mercy of the Prussians, to endangering its own supremacy by assisting in their defense, or permitting them to defend themselves.

It is a pity that this legendary figure of Awakened Paris is not a true one. The Commune, in fact, was not the work of the whole people of Paris, nor of a majority of the people of Paris. The Commune was really established by a comparatively small number of able, nay brilliant, and supremely devoted men and women from *every* walk in life, but with a relatively high percentage of military men, engineers, and political journalists, some of whom had time and again been in prison before for seditious writing or acts of rebellion. They flocked in from their exile in the neighboring countries, thinking that now they saw the opportunity for retrieving former errors, and arousing the people to renew and to extend the struggle of 1848. It is true that there were also teachers, artists, designers, architects and builders, skilled craftsmen of every sort. And perhaps no chapter in the whole story is more inspiring than the description of the gatherings of the workers, which took place night after night in every quarter of the beleaguered city, previous to the 18th of March and thereafter. To such meetings went those who burned with fervor of faith in what the people might and would accomplish, and, with the radiant vision of a new social day shining in their eyes, endeavored to make it clear to those who listened. One almost catches the redolence of outbursting faith, that rising of the sap of hope and courage and daring, like an incense of spring; almost feels himself there, partaking in the work, the danger, the glorious, mistaken assurance which was theirs.

And yet the truth must have been that these apostles of the Commune were blinded by their own enthusiasm, deafened by the enthusiasm they evoked in others, to the fact that the great unvoiced majority who did not attend public meetings, who sat within their houses or kept silent in the shops, were not converted or affected by their teachings.

We are told by those who should know, the survivors among the Communards themselves, that the actual number of persons who were aggressive, moving spirits in the great uprising was not greatly above 2,000. The mass of the people were, as they would probably be in this city to-day under like circumstances, indifferent as to what went on over their heads, so that the peace and quiet of their individual lives was restored, so that the siege of the Prussians was raised, and themselves permitted to go about their business. If the Commune could assure that, good luck to it! They were tired of the siege; and they longed for their old familiar miseries to which they were in some respect accustomed; they hardly dreamed of anything better.

But, as is usually the case when strategic moments arise, these same plain, stolid, indifferent people, who neither know nor care about fine theories of political right, municipal sovereignty, and so forth, see more directly into the logic of a situation than those who have confused their minds with much theorizing. Likewise the people of Paris in general, when the Commune had become an established fact, saw that the only consequent proceeding would be to make war economically as well as politically, to cut off any source of supply to the national army which lay within the city. Instead of doing that, the government of the Commune, anxious to prove itself more law-abiding than the old regime, stupidly defended the property right of its enemies, and continued to let the Bank of France furnish supplies to those who were financing the army of Versailles, the very army which was to cut their throats.

Naturally, the plain people grew disgusted with so senseless a program, and in the main took no part in the final struggle with the Versailles troops, nor even opposed the idea of their entrance into the city. Probably a goodly number even drew a sigh of relief at the prospect of a return to the smaller evil of the two. Little enough did they dream that the way back lay through their own blood, and that they, who had never lifted hand or voice for the Commune, would become its martyrs. Little did they conceive the wild revenge of Law and Order upon Rebellion, the saturnalia of restored Power.

Did they sleep, I wonder, on the night before the 20th of May, when that dark thunder of vengeance was gathering to break? Many slept well the next night, and still sleep; for "then began a murder grim and great,"—a murder whose painted image, even after these forty years have risen and sunk upon it, sends the blood shuddering backward, and sets the teeth in uttermost horror and hate. MacMahon placarded the streets with peace and sent his troops to make it; in the name of that Peace, Gallifet, an incarnation of hell, set his men the example and rode up and down the streets of Paris, dashing out children's brains. Did a hand appear at a shutter, the window was riddled with bullets. Did a cry of protest escape from any throat, the house was invaded, its inhabitants driven out, lined against the walls, and shot where they stood. The doctors and the nurses at the bedsides of the wounded, the very sick in the hospitals, themselves were slaughtered where they lay. Such was MacMahon's peace.

After the street massacres, the organized massacres at the bastions, the stakes of Satory, the huddled masses of prisoners, the grim visitor with the lantern, the ghastly call to rise and follow, the trenches dug by the condemned in the slippery, blood-soaked ground for their own corpses to fall in. Thirty thousand people butchered! Butchered by the sateless vengeance of authority and the insane blood-lust of the professional soldier! Butchered without a pretence of reason, a shadow of inquiry, merely as the gust of insensate rage blew!

After the orgy of fury, the orgy of the inquisition. The gathering of the prisoners in cellar holes, where they must squat or lie upon damp earth, and see the light daily only for some short half hour when an unexpellable sun ray shot through some unstopped crevice. The shifting of them day and night across the country, sometimes in stock yard wagons, stifled, starved, and jammed together, as even our butchering civilization is ashamed to jam pigs for the slaughter; sometimes by dreadful marches, mostly by night, often with the rain beating on them, the butts of the soldiers' muskets striking them, as they lagged through weakness or through lameness.

Then the detention prisons, with their long-drawn agonies of hunger, cold, vermin, and disease, and the ever-looming darkness of waiting death. Follow the tortures of friends and relatives of Communards or suspected Communards, to make them betray the whereabouts of their friends.

Could they who had seen these things "forgive and forget"? They who had seen ten year old children lashed to make them tell where their fathers were? Women driven mad before the terrible choice of giving up their sons who had fought, or their daughters who had not, to the brutality of the soldiery.

After the tortures of the hunt, the tortures of the trials, solemn farces, cat-like cruelties. Then the long hopeless line of exiles marching from the prison to the port, crowded on the transport ships, watched like caged animals, forbidden to speak, the cannon always threatening above them, and so drifted away, away to exile lands, to barren islands and fever shores—there to waste away in loneliness, in uselessness, in futile dreams of freedom that ended in chains upon the ankles or death on the coral reefs—all this was the Mercy and the Wisdom shown by the national government to the rebel city whose works are the glory of France, and whose beauty is the Beauty of the World. Whatever other lesson we have to learn, this one is certain: the glutless revenge of restored Authority. If ever one rebels, let him rebel to the end; there is no hope so futile as hope in either the justice or the mercy of a power against which a rebellion has been raised. No faith so simple or so foolish as faith in the discrimination, the judgement, or the wisdom of a re-conquering government.

Whether at that time the essential principle of the independent Commune could have been realized or not, through a general response of the other cities of France by like action (in case Paris had continued to maintain the struggle some months longer), I am not historian enough, nor historic prophet enough, to say. I incline to think not. But certainly the struggle would have been far other, far more fruitful in its results, both then and later, (even if finally overthrown), had it really been a movement of all those people who were so indiscriminately murdered for it, so vilely tortured, so mercilessly exiled. For had it really been the deliberate expression of a million people's will to be free, they would have seized whatever supplies were being furnished the enemy from within their own gates; they would have repudiated property rights created by the very power they were seeking to overthrow. They would have seen what was necessary, and done it.

Had the real Communards themselves seen the logic of their own effort, and understood that to overset the political system of dependence which enslaves the Communes they must overset the economic institutions which beget the centralized State; had they proclaimed a general communalization of the city's resources they might have won the people to full faith in the struggle and aroused a ten-fold effort to win out. If that again had been followed by a like contagion in the other cities of France, (which was a possibility) the flame might have caught throughout Latin Europe, and those countries might now be giving a practical example of the extension of a modified Socialism and local autonomy. This is what is likely to happen at the next similar outbreak, if politicians are so impolitic as to provoke the like. There are those among the best social students who feel sure that such will be the course of progress.

I frankly say that I cannot see the path of future progress,—my vision is not large enough, nor my viewpoint high enough. Where others perhaps behold the morning sunlight, I can discern only mists—blowing dust and moving glooms which obscure the future. I do not know where the path leads nor how it goes. Only when looking backward, I can catch glimpses of that long, terrible, toilsome way by which humanity has gone forward; even that I do not see clearly,—just stretches of it here and there. But I see enough of it to know that never has it been a straight, undeviating line. Always the path winds and returns, and even in the moment of gaining something, there is something lost.

Against the onslaught of Nature, Man collects his social strength, and loses thereby the freedom of his more isolated condition. Against the inconveniences of primitive society, he hurls his inventive genius,—compasses land, sea, and air,—and by the very act of conquering his limitations binds fresh fetters on himself, creating a wealth which he enslaves himself to produce!

And this is the Path of Progress, which there was no foreseeing!

What waits them? And what hope is there? And what help is there?

What waits? The Unknown waits, as it has always waited,—dark, vague, immense, impenetrable—the Mystery which allures the young and strong saying, "Come and cope with me"; the Mystery from which the old and wise shrink back, saying, "Better to endure the evils that we have than fly to others that we know not of"; the old and wise, but alas! the cold-blooded! The Mystery of the still unbound strengths of earth, sun, and depths, the loosing of any one of which may so alter the face of all that has been done that what now we think a guarantee of liberty may become the very chain of slavery, as has been the case before with freedoms laboriously won by act, and then set down in words for unborn men to abide by. And yet—It waits.

Are you strong and courageous? The Unknown invites you to the struggle, dares you to its conquering. Nay, it is perhaps your future beloved, waiting to reward your daring passion with the fervors of fresh creation. Are you feeble and timid of spirit? Bow your head to the ground. Still you must meet the future; still you must go in the track of the others. You may hinder them, you may make them lag; you cannot stop them, nor yourself.

Struggle waits—abortive struggle, crushed struggle, mistaken struggle, long and often. And worse than all this, *Waiting waits,*—the long dead-level of inaction, when no one does anything, when even the daring can only move in self-returning circles; when no one knows what to do, except to endure the ever-tightening pressure of intolerable conditions, how to better which he knows not; when living appears a monotonous journey through a featureless wilderness, wherein the same pitiless word "Useless" stares at one from every aimless path one seeks to follow in the despairing search for a way out. And happier is he who perishes in the mistaken struggle than he who, with a hot and chafing soul, but with clear discernment, sees that he is doomed to go on indefinitely in submission to the wrongs that are.

What hope is there? That the increasing pressure of conditions may quicken intelligences; that even out of mistaken struggle, frustrate struggle, unforeseen *good* consequences may flow, just as out of undeniable improvements in material life, unforeseeable ill results are consequent.

The Commune hoped to free Paris, and by so setting an example free many other cities. It went down in utter defeat, and no city was freed thereby. But out of this defeat the knowledge and skill of craftsmanship of its people went abroad over other lands, both into civilized centers and to wild waste places; and wherever its art went, its idea went also, so that the "Commune," the idealized Commune, has become a watchword through the workshops of the world, wherever there are even a few workers seeking to awaken their fellows.

There are those who have definite hopes; those who think they know precisely how overwork and underwork and poverty, and all their consequences of spiritual enslavement, are to be abolished. Such are they who think they can see the way of progress broad and clear through the slit in a ballot box. I fear their works will have some uncalculated consequences also, if ever they execute them; I fear their narrowly enclosed view deceives them much. Climbing a hill is a different affair from voting oneself at the top.

No matter: Man always hopes; Life always hopes. When a definite object cannot be outlined, the indomitable spirit of hope still impels the living mass to move toward something—something that shall somehow be better.

What help is there? No help from outside power; no help from overhead; no help from the Sky, pray to it ever so much; no help from the strong hand of wise men, nor of good men, however wise or good. Such help always ends in despotism. Nor yet is there help in the abnegation of generous fanatics whose efforts end in deplorable fiasco, as did the Commune. Help lies only in the general will of those who do the work to say how, when, and where they shall do it.

The force of the lesson of the Commune is that people cannot be made free who have not conceived freedom; yet through such examples they may learn to conceive it. It cannot be bestowed as a gift; it must be taken by those who want it. Let us hope that those who would have given it, bought that much by their sacrifice, that they touched the unseeing eyes of the somnambulist proletariat with a light which has made them dream, at least, of waking.

The Mexican Revolution

THAT a nation of people considering themselves enlightened, informed, alert to the interests of the hour, should be so generally and so profoundly ignorant of a revolution taking place in their backyard, so to speak, as the people of the United States are ignorant of the present revolution in Mexico, can be due only to profoundly and generally acting causes. That people of revolutionary principles and sympathies should be so, is inexcusable.

It is as one of such principles and sympathies that I address you,—as one interested in every move the people make to throw off their chains, no matter where, no matter how,—though naturally my interest is greatest where the move is such as appears to me to be most in consonance with the general course of progress, where the tyranny attacked is what appears to me the most fundamental, where the method followed is to my thinking most direct and unmistakable. And I add that those of you who have such principles and sympathies are in the logic of your own being bound, first, to inform yourselves concerning so great a matter as the revolt of millions of people—what they are struggling for, what they are struggling against, and how the struggle stands—from day to day, if possible; if not, from week to week, or month to month, as best you can; and second, to spread this knowledge among others, and endeavor to do what little you can to awaken the consciousness and sympathy of others.

One of the great reasons why the mass of the American people know nothing of the Revolution in Mexico, is, that they have altogether a wrong conception of what "revolution" means. Thus ninety-nine out of a hundred persons to whom you broach the subject will say, "Why, I thought that ended long ago. That ended last May"; and this week the press, even the *Daily Socialist*, reports, "A *new* revolution in Mexico." It isn't a new revolution at all; it is the same revolution, which did not begin with the armed rebellion of last May, which has been going on steadily ever since then, and before then, and is bound to go on for a long time to come, if the other nations keep their hands off and the Mexican people are allowed to work out their own destiny.

What is *a* revolution? and what is *this* revolution?

A revolution means some great and subversive change in the social institutions of a people, whether sexual, religious, political, or economic.

The movement of the Reformation was a great religious revolution; a profound alteration in human thought—a refashioning of the human mind. The general movement towards political change in Europe and America about the close of the eighteenth century, was a revolution. The American and the French revolutions were only prominent individual incidents in it, culminations of the teachings of the Rights of Man. The present unrest of the world in its economic relations, as manifested from day to day in the opposing combinations of men and money, in strikes and bread-riots, in literature and movements of all kinds demanding a readjustment of the whole or of parts of our wealth-owning and wealth-distributing system,—this unrest is the revolution of our time, the economic *revolution*, which is seeking social change, and will go on until it is accomplished. We are in it; at any moment of our lives it may invade our own homes with its stern demand for self-sacrifice and suffering. Its more violent manifestations are in Liverpool and London to-day, in Barcelona and Vienna to-morrow, in New York and Chicago the day after. Humanity is a seething, heaving mass of unease, tumbling like surge over a slipping, sliding, shifting bottom; and there will never be any ease until a rock bottom of economic justice is reached.

The Mexican revolution is one of the prominent manifestations of this world-wide economic revolt. It possibly holds as important a place in the present disruption and reconstruction of economic institutions, as the great revolution of France held in the eighteenth century movement. It did not begin with the odious government of Diaz nor end with his downfall, any more than the revolution in France began with the coronation of Louis XVI, or ended with his beheading. It began in the bitter and outraged hearts of the peasants, who for generations have suffered under a ready-made system of exploitation, imported and foisted upon them, by which they have been dispossessed of their homes, compelled to become slave-tenants of those who robbed them; and under Diaz, in case of rebellion to be deported to a distant province, a killing climate, and hellish labor. It will end only when that bitterness is assuaged by very great alteration in the land-holding system, or until the people have been absolutely crushed into subjection by a strong military power, whether that power be a native or a foreign one.

Now the political overthrow of last May, which was followed by the substitution of one political manager for another, did not at all touch the economic situation. It promised, of course; politicians always promise. It promised to consider measures for altering conditions; in the meantime, proprietors are assured that the new government intends to respect the rights of landlords and capitalists, and exhorts the workers to be patient and— *frugal!*

Frugal! Yes, that was the exhortation in Madero's paper to men who, when they are able to get work, make twenty-five cents a day. A man owning 5,000,000 acres of land exhorts the disinherited workers of Mexico to be frugal!

The idea that such a condition can be dealt with by the immemorial remedy offered by tyrants to slaves, is like the idea of sweeping out the sea with a broom. And unless that frugality, or in other words, starvation, is forced upon the people by more bayonets and more strategy than appear to be at the government's command, the Mexican revolution will go on to the solution of Mexico's land question with a rapidity and directness of purpose not witnessed in any previous upheaval.

For it must be understood that the main revolt is a revolt against the system of land tenure. The industrial revolution of the cities, while it is far from being silent, is not to compare with the agrarian revolt.

Let us understand why. Mexico consists of twenty-seven states, two territories and a federal district about the capital city. Its population totals about 15,000,000. Of these, 4,000,000 are of unmixed Indian descent, people somewhat similar in character to the Pueblos of our own southwestern states, primitively agricultural for an immemorial period, communistic in many of their social customs, and like all Indians, invincible haters of authority. These Indians are scattered throughout the rural districts of Mexico, one particularly well-known and much talked of tribe, the Yaquis, having had its father-land in the rich northern state of Sonora, a very valuable agricultural country.

The Indian population—especially the Yaquis and the Moquis—have always disputed the usurpations of the invaders' government, from the days of the early conquest until now, and will undoubtedly continue to dispute them as long as there is an Indian left, or until their right to use the soil out of which they sprang *without paying tribute in any shape* is freely recognized.

The communistic customs of these people are very interesting, and very instructive too; they have gone on practising them all these hundreds of years, in spite of the foreign civilization that was being grafted upon Mexico (grafted in all senses of the word); and it was not until forty years ago (indeed the worst of it not till twenty-five years ago), that the increasing power of the government made it possible to destroy this ancient life of the people.

By them, the woods, the waters, and the lands were held in common. Any one might cut wood from the forest to build his cabin, make use of the rivers to irrigate his field or garden patch (and this is a right whose acknowledgment none but those who know the aridity of the southwest can fully appreciate the imperative necessity for). Tillable lands were allotted by mutual agreement before sowing, and reverted to the tribe after harvesting, for reallotment. Pasturage, the right to collect fuel, were for all. The habits of mutual aid which always arise among sparsely settled communities were instinctive with them. Neighbor assisted neighbor to build his cabin, to plough his ground, to gather and store this crop.

No legal machinery existed—no taxgatherer, no justice, no jailer. All that they had to do with the hated foreign civilization was to pay the periodical rent-collector, and to get out of the way of the recruiting officer when he came around. Those two personages they regarded with spite and dread; but as the major portion of their lives was not in immediate contact with them, they could still keep on in their old way of life in the main.

With the development of the Diaz regime, which came into power in 1876 (and when I say the Diaz regime I do not especially mean the man Diaz, for I think he has been both overcursed and overpraised, but the whole force which has steadily developed centralized power from then on, and the whole policy of "civilizing Mexico," which was the Diaz boast), with its development, I say, this Indian life has been broken up, violated with as ruthless a hand as ever tore up a people by the roots and cast them out as weeds to wither in the sun.

Historians relate with horror the iron deeds of William the Conqueror, who in the eleventh century created the New Forest by laying waste the farms of England, destroying the homes of the people to make room for the deer. But his edicts were mercy compared with the action of the Mexican government toward the Indians. In order to introduce "progressive civilization" the Diaz regime granted away immense concessions of land, to native and foreign capitalists—chiefly foreign indeed, though there were enough of native sharks as well. Mostly these concessions were granted to capitalistic combinations, which were to build railroads (and in some cases did so in a most uncalled for and uneconomic way), "develop" mineral resources, or establish "modern industries."

The government took no note of the ancient tribal rights or customs, and those who received the concessions proceeded to enforce their property rights. They intro-duced the unheard of crime of "trespass." They forbade the cutting of a tree, the breaking of a branch, the gather-ing of the fallen wood in the forests. They claimed the watercourses, forbidding their free use to the people; and it was as if one had forbidden to us the rains of heaven. The unoccupied land was theirs; no hand might drive a plow into the soil without first obtaining permission from a distant master—a permission granted on the condition that the product be the landlord's, a small, pitifully small, wage, the worker's.

Nor was this enough: in 1894 was passed "The Law of Unappropriated Lands." By that law, not only were the great stretches of *vacant,* in the old time *common,* land appropriated, but the occupied lands themselves to *which the occupants could not show a legal title* were to be "denounced"; that is, the educated and the power-ful, who were able to keep up with the doings of the gov-ernment, went to the courts and said that there was no legal title to such and such land, and put in a claim for it. And the usual hocus-pocus of legality being complied with (the actual occupant of the land being all the time blissfully unconscious of the law, in the innocence of his barbarism supposing that the working of the ground by his generations of forbears was title all-sufficient) one fine day the sheriff comes upon this hapless dweller on the heath and drives him from his ancient habitat to wander an outcast.

Such are the blessings of education.

Mankind invents a written sign to aid its intercommu-nication; and forthwith all manner of miracles are wrought with the sign. Even such a miracle as that a part of the solid earth passes under the mastery of an impotent sheet of paper; and a distant bit of animated flesh which never even saw the ground, acquires the power to expel hundreds, thousands, of like bits of flesh, though they grew upon that ground as the trees grow, labored it with their hands, and fertilized it with their bones for a thousand years.

"This law of unappropriated lands," says William Archer, "has covered the country with Naboth's Vineyards." I think it would require a Biblical prophet to describe the "abomination of desolation" it has made.

It was to become lords of this desolation that the men who play the game—landlords who are at the same time governors and magistrates, enterprising capitalists seeking investments—connived at the iniquities of the Diaz regime; I will go further and say devised them.

The Madero family alone owns some 8,000 square miles of territory; more than the entire state of New Jersey. The Terrazas family, in the state of Chihuahua, owns 25,000 square miles; rather more than the entire state of West Virginia, nearly one-half the size of Illinois. What was the plantation owning of our southern states in chattel slavery days, compared with this? And the peon's share for his toil upon these great estates is hardly more than was the chattel slave's—wretched housing, wretched food, and wretched clothing.

It is to slaves like these that Madero appeals to be "frugal."

It is of men who have thus been disinherited that our complacent fellow-citizens of Anglo-Saxon origin, say: "Mexicans! What do you know about Mexicans? Their whole idea of life is to lean up against a fence and smoke cigarettes". And pray, what idea of life should a people have whose means of life in their own way have been taken from them? Should they be so mighty anxious to convert their strength into wealth for some other man to loll in?

It reminds me very much of the answer given by a negro employee on the works at Fortress Monroe to a companion of mine who questioned him good-humoredly on his easy idleness when the foreman's back was turned. "Ah ain't goin' to do no white man's work, fo' Ah don' get no white man's pay."

But for the Yaquis, there was worse than this. Not only were their lands seized, but they were ordered, a few years since, to be deported to Yucatan. Now Sonora, as I said, is a northern state, and Yucatan one of the southernmost. Yucatan hemp is famous, and so is Yucatan fever, and Yucatan slavery on the hemp plantations. It was to that fever and that slavery that the Yaquis were deported, in droves of hundreds at a time, men, women and children—droves like cattle droves, driven and beaten like cattle. They died there, like flies, as it was meant they should. Sonora was desolated of her rebellious people, and the land became "pacific" in the hands of the new landowners. Too pacific in spots. They had not left people enough to reap the harvests.

Then the government suspended the deportation act, but with the provision that for every crime committed by a Yaqui, five hundred of his people be deported. This statement is made in Madero's own book.

Now what in all conscience would any one with decent human feeling expect a Yaqui to do? Fight! As long as there was powder and bullet to be begged, borrowed, or stolen; as long as there is a garden to plunder, or a hole in the hills to hide in!

When the revolution burst out, the Yaquis and other Indian peoples, said to the revolutionists: "Promise us our lands back, and we will fight with you." And they are keeping their word, magnificently. All during the summer they have kept up the warfare. Early in September, the Chihuahua papers reported a band of 1,000 Yaquis in Sonora about to attack El Anil; a week later 500 Yaquis had seized the former quarters of the federal troops at Pitahaya. This week it is reported that federal troops are dispatched to Ponoitlan, a town in Jalisco, to quell the Indians who have risen in revolt again because their delusion that the Maderist government was to restore their land has been dispelled. Like reports from Sinaloa. In the terrible state of Yucatan, the Mayas are in active rebellion; the reports say that "the authorities and leading citizens of various towns have been seized by the malcontents and put in prison." What is more interesting is, that the peons have seized not only "the leading citizens," but still more to the purpose have seized the plantations, parceled them, and are already gathering the crops for themselves.

Of course, it is not the pure Indians alone who form the peon class of Mexico. Rather more than double the number of Indians are mixed breeds; that is, about 8,000,-000, leaving less than 3,000,000 of pure white stock. The mestiza, or mixed breed population, have followed the communistic instincts and customs of their Indian forbears; while from the Latin side of their make-up, they have certain tendencies which work well together with their Indian hatred of authority.

The mestiza, as well as the Indians, are mostly ignorant in book-knowledge, only about sixteen per cent. of the whole population of Mexico being able to read and write. It was not within the program of the "civilizing" regime to spend money in putting the weapon of learning in the people's hands. But to conclude that people are necessarily unintelligent because they are illiterate, is in itself a rather unintelligent proceeding.

Moreover, a people habituated to the communal customs of an ancient agricultural life do not need books or papers to tell them that the soil is the source of wealth, and they must "get back to the land," even if their intelligence is limited.

Accordingly, they have got back to the land. In the state of Morlos, which is a small, south-central state, but a very important one—being next to the Federal District, and by consequence to the city of Mexico—there has been a remarkable land revolution. General Zapata, whose name has figured elusively in newspaper reports now as having made peace with Madero, then as breaking faith, next wounded and killed, and again resurrected and in hiding, then anew on the warpath and proclaimed by the provisional government the arch-rebel who must surrender unconditionally and be tried by court-martial; who has seized the strategic points on both the railroads running through Morelos, and who just a few days ago broke into the federal district, sacked a town, fought successfully at two or three points, with the federals, blew out two railroad bridges and so frightened the deputies in Mexico City that they are clamoring for all kinds of action; this Zapata, the fires of whose military camps are springing up now in Guerrero, Oaxaca and Puebla as well, is an Indian with a long score to pay, and all an Indian's satisfaction in paying it. He appears to be a fighter of the style of our revolutionary Marion and Sumter; the country in which he is operating is mountainous, and guerilla bands are exceedingly difficult of capture; even when they are defeated, they have usually succeeded in inflicting more damage than they have received, and they always get away.

Zapata has divided up the great estates of Morelos from end to end, telling the peasants to take possession. They have done so. They are in possession, and have already harvested their crops. Morelos has a population of some 212,000.

In Puebla reports in September told us that eighty leading citizens had waited on the governor to protest against the taking possession of the land by the peasantry. The troops were deserting, taking horses and arms with them. It is they no doubt who are now fighting with Zapata. In Chihuahua, one of the largest states, prisons have been thrown open and the prisoners recruited as rebels; a great hacienda was attacked and the horses run off, whereupon the peons rose and joined the attacking party. In Sinaloa, a rich northern state—famous in the southwestern United States some years ago as the field of a great co-operative experiment in which Mr. C. B. Hoffman, one of the former editors of *The Chicago Daily Socialist*, was a leading spirit—this week's paper reports that the former revolutionary general, Juan Banderas, is heading an insurrection second in importance only to that led by Zapata.

In the southern border state of Chiapas, the taxes in many places could not be collected. Last week news items said that the present government had sent General Paz there, with federal troops, to remedy that state of affairs. In Tabasco, the peons refused to harvest the crops for their masters; let us hope they have imitated their brothers in Morelos and gathered them for themselves.

The Maderists have announced that a stiff repressive campaign will be inaugurated at once; if we are to believe the papers, we are to believe Madero guilty of the imbecility of saying, "Five days after my inauguration the rebellion will be crushed." Just why the crushing has to wait till five days after the inauguration does not appear. I conceive there must have been some snickering among the reactionary deputies if such an announcement was really made; and some astonished query among his followers.

What are we to conclude from all these reports? That the Mexican people are satisfied? That it's all good and settled? What should we think if we read that the people, not of Lower but of Upper, California had turned out the ranch owners, had started to gather in the field products for themselves and that the Secretary of War had sent United States troops to attack some thousands of armed men (Zapata has had 3,000 under arms the whole summer and that force is now greatly increased) who were defending that expropriation? if we read that in the state of Illinois the farmers had driven off the tax collector? that the coast states were talking of secession and forming an independent combination? that in Pennsylvania a division of the federal army was to be dispatched to overpower a rebel force of fifteen hundred armed men doing guerilla work from the mountains? that the prison doors of Maryland, within hailing distance of Washington City, were being thrown open by armed revoltees? Should we call it a condition of peace? Regard it a proof that the people were appeased? We would not: we would say that revolution was in full swing. And the reason you have thought it was all over in Mexico, from last May till now, is that the Chicago press, like the eastern, northern, and central press in general, has said nothing about this steady march of revolt. Even *The Socialist* has been silent. Now that the flame has shot up more spectacularly for the moment, they call it "a new revolution."

That the papers pursue this course is partly due to the generally acting causes that produce our northern indifference, which I shall presently try to explain, and partly to the settled policy of capitalized interest in controlling its mouthpieces in such a manner as to give their present henchmen, the Maderists, a chance to pull their chestnuts out of the fire. They invested some $10,000,000 in this bunch, in the hope that they may be able to accomplish the double feat of keeping capitalist possessions intact and at the same time pacifying the people with specious promises. They want to lend them all the countenance they can, till the experiment is well tried; so they deliberately suppress revolutionary news.

Among the later items of interest reported by the *Los Angeles Times* are those which announce an influx of ex-officials and many-millioned landlords of Mexico, who are hereafter to be residents of Los Angeles. What is the meaning of it? Simply that life in Mexico is not such a safe and comfortable proposition as it was, and that for the present they prefer to get such income as their agents can collect wthout themselves running the risk of actual residence.

Of course it is understood that some of this notable efflux (the supporters of Reyes, for example, who have their own little rebellions in Tabasco and San Luis Potosi this week) are political reactionists, scheming to get back the political loaves and fishes into their own hands. But most are simply those who know that their property right is safe enough to be respected by the Maderist government, but that the said government is not strong enough to put down the innumerable manifestations of popular hatred which are likely to terminate fatally to themselves if they remain there.

Nor is all of this fighting revolutionary; not by any

means. Some is reactionary, some probably the satisfaction of personal grudge, much, no doubt, the expression of general turbulency of a very unconscious nature. But granting all that may be thrown in the balance, the main thing, the mighty thing, the regenerative revolution is the *Reappropriation of the land by the peasants.* Thousands upon thousands of them are doing it.

Ignorant peasants: peasants who know nothing about the jargon of land reformers or of Socialists. Yes: that's just the glory of it! Just the fact that it is done by ignorant people; that is, people ignorant of book theories; but *not* ignorant, not so ignorant by half, of life on the land, as the theory-spinners of the cities. Their minds are simple and direct; they act accordingly. For them, there is *one way* to "get back to the land"; i. e., to ignore the machinery of paper land-holding (in many instances they have burned the records of the title-deeds) and proceed to plough the ground, to sow and plant and gather, and *keep the product themselves.*

Economists, of course, will say that these ignorant people, with their primitive institutions and methods, will not develop the agricultural resources of Mexico, and that they must give way before those who will so develop its resources; that such is the law of human development.

In the first place, the abominable political combination, which gave away, as recklessly as a handful of soap-bubbles, the agricultural resources of Mexico—gave them away to the millionaire speculators who were to *develop the country*—were the educated men of Mexico. And this is what they saw fit to do with their higher intelligence and education. So the ignorant may well distrust the good intentions of educated men who talk about improvements in land development.

In the second place, capitalistic land-ownership, so far from developing the land in such a manner as to support a denser population, has depopulated whole districts, immense districts.

In the third place, what the economists do not say is, that the only justification for intense cultivation of the land is, that the product of such cultivation may build up the bodies of men (by consequence their souls) to richer and fuller manhood. It is not merely to pile up figures of so many million bushels of wheat and corn produced in a season; but that this wheat and corn shall first go into the stomachs of those who planted it—and in abundance; to build up the brawn and sinew of the arms that work the ground, not meanly maintaining them in a half-starved condition. And second, to build up the strength of the rest of the nation who are willing to give needed labor in exchange. But never to increase the fortunes of idlers who dissipate it. This is the purpose, and the only purpose, of tilling soil; and the working of it for any other purpose is *waste,* waste both of land and of men.

In the fourth place, no change ever was, or ever can be, worked out in any society, except by the mass of the people. Theories may be propounded by educated people, and set down in books, and discussed in libraries, sitting-rooms and lecture-halls; but they will remain barren, unless the people in mass work them out. If the change proposed is such that it is not adaptable to the minds of the people for whose ills it is supposed to be a remedy, then it will remain what it was, a barren theory.

Now the conditions in Mexico have been and are so desperate that some change is imperative. The action of the peasants proves it. Even if a strong military dictator shall arise, he will have to allow some provision going towards peasant proprietorship. These unlettered, but determined, people must be dealt with *now;* there is no such thing as "waiting till they are educated up to it." Therefore the wisdom of the economists is wisdom out of place—rather, *relative unwisdom.* The people never *can* be educated, if their conditions are to remain what they were under the Diaz regime. Bodies and minds are both too impoverished to be able to profit by a spread of theoretical education, even if it did not require unavailable money and indefinite time to prepare such a spread. Whatever economic change is wrought, then, must be such as the people in their present state of comprehension can understand and make use of. And we see by the reports what they understand. They understand they have a right upon the soil, a right to use it for themselves, a right to drive off the invader who has robbed them, to destroy landmarks and title-deeds, to ignore the tax-gatherer and his demands.

And however primitive their agricultural methods may be, one thing is sure; that they are more economical than any system which heaps up fortunes by destroying men.

Moreover, who is to say how they may develop their methods once they have a free opportunity to do so? It is a common belief of the Anglo-Saxon that the Indian is essentially lazy. The reasons for his thinking so are two: under the various tyrannies and robberies which white men in general, and Anglo-Saxons in particular (they have even gone beyond the Spaniard) have inflicted upon Indians, there is no possible reason why an Indian should want to work, save the idiotic one that work in itself is a virtuous and exalted thing, even if by it the worker increases the power of his tyrant. As William Archer says: "If there are men, *and this is not denied,* who work for no wage, and with no prospect or hope of any reward, it would be curious to know by what motive other than the lash or the fear of the lash, they are induced to go forth to their labor in the morning." The second reason is, that an Indian really has a different idea of what he is alive for than an Anglo-Saxon has. And so have the Latin peoples. This different idea is what I meant when I said that the mestiza have certain tendencies inherited from the Latin side of their make-up which work well together with their Indian hatred of authority. The Indian likes to *live;* to be his own master; to work when he pleases and stop when he pleases. He does not crave many things, but he craves the enjoyment of the things that he has. He feels himself more a part of nature than a white man does. All his legends are of wanderings with nature, of forests, fields, streams, plants, animals. He wants to live with the same liberty as the other children of earth. His philosophy of work is, Work so as to live care-free. This is not laziness; this is sense—to the person who has that sort of make-up.

Your Latin, on the other hand, also wants to live; and having artistic impulses in him, his idea of living is very much in gratifying them. He likes music and song and dance, picture-making, carving, and decorating. He doesn't like to be forced to create his fancies in a hurry; he likes to fashion them, and admire them, and improve and refashion them, and admire again; and all for the fun of it. If he is ordered to create a certain design or a number of objects at a fixed price in a given time, he loses his inspiration; the play becomes work, and hateful work. So he, too, does not want to work, except what is requisite to maintain himself in a position to do those things that he likes better.

Your Anglo-Saxon's idea of life, however, is to create the useful and the profitable—whether he has any use or profit out of it or not—and to keep busy, busy; to bestir himself "like the Devil in a holy water font." Like all other people, he makes a special virtue of his own natural tendencies, and wants all the world to "get busy"; it doesn't so much matter to what end this business is to be conducted, provided the individual—*scrabbles*. Whenever a true Anglo-Saxon seeks to enjoy himself, he makes work out of that too, after the manner of a certain venerable English shopkeeper who in company with his son visited the Louvre. Being tired out with walking from room to room, consulting his catalogue, and reading artists' names, he dropped down to rest; but after a few moments rose resolutely and faced the next room, saying, "Well, Alfred, we'd better be getting through our work."

There is much question as to the origin of the various instincts. Most people have the impression that the chief source of variation lies in the difference in the amount of sunlight received in the native countries inhabited of the various races. Whatever the origin is, these are the broadly marked tendencies of the people. And "Business" seems bent not only upon fulfilling its own foreordained destiny, but upon making all the others fulfill it too. Which is both unjust and stupid. There is room enough in the world for the races to try out their several tendencies and make their independent contributions to the achievements of humanity, without imposing them on those who revolt at them.

Granting that the population of Mexico, if freed from this foreign "busy" idea which the government imported from the north and imposed on them with such severity in the last forty years, would not immediately adopt improved methods of cultivation, even when they should have free opportunity to do so, still we have no reason

to conclude that they would not adopt so much of it as
would fit *their* idea of what a man is alive for; and if
that actually proved good, it would introduce still further
development. So that there would be a natural, and
therefore solid, economic growth which would stick;
while a forced development of it through the devastation
of the people is no true growth. The only way to make
it go, is to kill out the Indians altogether, and transport
the "busy" crowd there, and then keep on transporting
for several generations, to fill up the ravages the climate
will make on such an imported population.

The Indian population of our states was in fact dealt
with in this murderous manner. I do not know how
grateful the reflection may be to those who materially
profited by its extermination; but no one who looks forward to the final unification and liberation of man, to the
incorporation of the several goodnesses of the various
races in the one universal race, can ever read those pages
of our history without burning shame and fathomless
regret.

I have spoken of the meaning of revolution in general;
of the meaning of the Mexican revolution—chiefly an
agrarian one; of its present condition. I think it should
be apparent to you that in spite of the electoral victory of
the now ruling power, it has not put an end even to the
armed rebellion, and cannot, until it proposes some plan
of land restoration; and that it not only has no inward
disposition to do, but probably would not dare to do, in
view of the fact that immense capital financed it into
power.

As to what amount of popular sentiment was actually
voiced in the election, it is impossible to say. The dailies
informed us that in the Federal District where there are
1,000,000 voters, the actual vote was less than 450,000.

They offered no explanation. It is impossible to explain it on the ground that we explain a light vote in our own communities, that the people are indifferent to public questions; for the people of Mexico are not now *indifferent,* whatever else they may be. Two explanations are possible: the first, and most probable, that of *governmental* intimidation; the second, that the people are convinced of the uselessness of voting as a means of settling their troubles. In the less thickly populated agricultural states, *this is* very largely the case; they are relying upon direct revolutionary action. But although there was guerilla warfare in the Federal District, even before the election, I find it unlikely that more than half the voting population there abstained from voting out of conviction, though I should be glad to be able to believe they did.

However, Madero and his aids are in, as was expected; the question is, how will they stay in? As Diaz did, and in no other way—if they succeed in developing Diaz's sometime ability; which so far they are wide from having done, though they are resorting to the most vindictive and spiteful tactics in their persecution of the genuine revolutionists, wherever such come near their clutch.

To this whole turbulent situation three outcomes are possible:

1. A military dictator must arise, with sense enough to make some substantial concessions, and ability enough to pursue the crushing policy ably; or

2. The United States must intervene in the interests of American capitalists and landholders, in case the peasant revolt is not put down by the Maderist power. And that will be the worst thing that can possibly happen, and against which every worker in the United States should protest with all his might; or

3. The Mexican peasantry will be successful, and free

dom in land become an actual fact. And that means the death-knell of great landholding in this country also, for what people is going to see its neighbor enjoy so great a triumph, and sit on tamely itself under landlordism?

Whatever the outcome be, one thing is certain: it is a *great* movement, which all the people of the world should be eagerly watching. Yet as I said at the beginning, the majority of our population know no more about it than of a revolt on the planet Jupiter. First because they are so, so, *busy;* they scarcely have time to look over the baseball score and the wrestling match; how *could* they read up on a revolution! Second, they are supremely egotistic and concerned in their own big country with its big deeds—such as divorce scandals, vice-grafting, and auto races. Third, they do not read Spanish, and they have an ancient hostility to all that smells Spanish. Fourth, from our cradles we were told that whatever happened in Mexico was a joke. Revolutions, or rather rebellions, came and went, about like April showers, and they never meant anything serious. And in this indeed there was only too much truth—it was usually an excuse for one place-hunter to get another one's scalp. And lastly, as I have said, the majority of our people do not know that a revolution means a fundamental change in social life, and not a spectacular display of armies.

It is not much a few can do to remove this mountain of indifference; but to me it seems that every reformer, of whatever school, should wish to watch this movement with the most intense interest, as a practical manifestation of a wakening of the landworkers themselves to the recognition of what all schools of revolutionary economics admit to be the primal necessity—the social repossession of the land.

And whether they be victorious or defeated, I, for one, bow my head to those heroic strugglers, no matter how ignorant they are, who have raised the cry Land and Liberty, and planted the blood-red banner on the burning soil of Mexico.

Thomas Paine

TO speak of Thomas Paine is to mention in one breath daring tempered by judgment, courage both mental and physical, foresight and prudence coupled with unstinted generosity, patience and endurance for the long race, constancy to the unwon ideal, that superior power over men, conferred by no extrinsic dictum, typified best perhaps by the loadstone, which always bursts forth in times of revolution from the unexpected place, the unbought and the unsought glory of the man who is a hero because a hero is required and does not measure his services nor reckon on their reward; not that he underrates himself; (it is as impossible as it is undesirable that a powerful personality should not know itself as such) but simply that in the moment of decisions the value of self is abandoned. So far as any or all of these qualities are concerned Thomas Paine is a name for them all, in their highest expression. And one feels in approaching him that there is something like treason in paying him any but a perfect tribute. Yet such is the position into which I am forced,—to say less than I should, less than I would had not words and the art of using them almost failed me.

I do not like lecturers who come before the public with apologies, nor do I propose to make any; I simply say this to let you know that I shall feel, perhaps more keenly than any of you, my failure to do Paine justice. For the half century that his history has been being unmined from the cellar of calumny and filth that the orthodox had cast upon it, unmined chiefly by small groups of freethinkers scattered here and there and spreading his words among men, like the little foxes with the firebrands going in among the corn, the principal endeavor has been to establish Paine's reputation as a great reformer in religion. And such he undoubtedly was. Whoever reads his "Age of Reason" in anything but a spirit of predisposition against it, must feel this, however much he may disagree with Paine's criticism, or consider that he has come short in his constructive philosophy. And it is meet, too, that the book that cost him most, both before and after death, should be the one selected for defense. Nevertheless the effect has been rather to lose sight of what appear to me greater thoughts and acts. For just as the orthodox have forgotten, so have many freethinkers forgotten, his immense labors in the field of active struggle against the domination of man by man. It is true that his mind did not transcend the mental vesture of the time, and it was all the better in one of his marvelous capacities for *swinging* masses of men that it did not. The lonely heralds of the opening dawn go upon their paths solitary; no matter how much they desire to draw others with them, they cannot. And had Paine been one of these that break through the forms of thought such as was Copernicus, or Kant, or Darwin, he would have been at constant war with himself. Half his nature would have chosen the lonely path; the other half, the zealot, the propagandist, would have cried out, they *must* go with me; I must do something to make them *go with* me. Now the secret of Paine's success was that he was so thoroughly at one with himself, he believed so utterly what he preached, he had faith, he hoped, and so strongly that others were drawn to believe and to hope. For spite of all intellectual pride this is the man whom we love and admire; this is the man who overcomes us, who gets his way; this man consistent in himself, who has a remedy for the world's wrongs and hopes *everything* from it!

From the point of vantage of 100 years' experience it is seen that Paine's political creed, like his religious one, will no longer fit. But that does not matter. Neither will ours fit in a hundred years, and none of us, no, not one, is great enough to foresee where the misfit will arise. It is not our business to bear the evils of the thrice unborn upon our necks; nor was it Paine's to bear ours.

Yet while not claiming for him the prophetic gift, it is still true that he did see the moral patchwork in our constitution, the trouble of 1812 brewing, and the greater trouble of '61-'65.

When he first came to this country he wrote a number of contributions to the *Pennsylvania Magazine,* in one of which he pleaded justice for the negro, basing his plea then as always upon the natural equality of man irrespective of color. Afterwards when the constitution was framed, he objected that nothing had been done for the negro, and in his letters to the American people, written after his imprisonment in France, in which the constitution was caustically reviewed, he cries out again for this yoked man not yet to be freed for more than half a hundred years,—foreseeing that nothing good can in the end come from slavery, that every evil must bring a compensating evil. The soldiers' graves in the National cemeteries, the thousands of limping, haggard tatters and rags of white men attest how well Paine foresaw Time's revenges.

In the letter to Washington, partially unjust as it is in view of the fact that Gouverneur Morris and not Washington was responsible for the failure to save Paine from prison in France, as we now know, thanks to Moncure

Conway, but which Paine did *not* know,—in this letter, I say, will be found the most terrible arraignment of the constitution ever penned. We who are Anarchists are called traitors for much calmer talk. Yet here was the man "whose pen had done more for the revolution than Washington's sword," as his bitterest enemy declared; who believed heart and soul in the republic, who had given his money and his substance and taken the chances of his life in battle for it; the man whose devotion to America could not be gainsaid; this man declared that the American constitution was the mirror of the most vicious features of the British constitution, a fecund soil for monopolies with all their ills. It is we who experience those ills, we who know what a gigantic tool of oppression the constitution and the cumbersome machinery of the lawmaking power have become. Yet probably even we do not feel so keenly as he the fatal blunder; for while we know how it grinds us in our flesh and souls, rears its prisons and scaffolds for us, we have had the yoke about our necks always,—while he *had once seen* the country free. He had been through all the battle, had fought his fight and won his victory, only to see it lost through cowardice of thought. That was indeed bitter; and it is that bitter outcry against this sacrifice which marks Paine out among most of his time for influence on future history. The fact that he was the initiator of the direct movement for political independence in America, in the famous meeting where Adams, Franklin and Washington all shrank from uttering the thought heavy upon their souls, is a matter of past history. The fact that he was the one man in America to write the right thing at the right time, his voice the wind to sweep the scattering flames of insubordination and revolt into the conflagration of revolution; the fact that he proposed and headed with the whole contents of his purse the subscription to save the army when even Washington was in despair at the prospect of mutiny and desertion among the soldiers; the fact that he raised all the feeling possible against the fiction of divine rights and so got himself hunted out of England; the fact that he took the most active part possible in aiding the work of the French revolutionists, which he believed would be the beginning of the breakdown of monarchy throughout Europe and the building up either of one universal continental republic or a confederation of sister republics; the fact that he was the one man in the convention who dared to stand for the life of Louis the XVI, and thereby got himself suspected, thrown into prison, and condemned to death —all these facts are of import in reading the character of the man, and in comprehending the record of those days when they were making history fast. Yet none of these has so much influence upon the demands of to-day as the voice of discontent crying for eternal vigilance, which sounds through these almost unknown letters. These are the things which it will pay to reprint in the day when American liberty feels in its tomb the first stirrings of the resurrection. Did we like Paine believe in God, we might say "Pray God it may not be far away."

Such are the characters whose historic influence is greatest; they who hew, and hew hard to the line laid down for them by the events of their time; yet are not blinded by the stir and roll of things; who see clearly where the deflection from the line is likely to occur, and where it will lead; who raise the warning treble that goes shrilling to the future, startling, waking with its eerie cry custom-dulled ears, and sodden souls, who start to ask, was it not a ghost of the Revolution? In that day which may not be so distant as we fear, Paine will be more alive than ever; he will be watching at a million firesides with the old keen, strong eyes.

While I have deprecated the fact that the religious reformer has been exalted to the neglect of the political one, I cannot omit that part of his life-work so well-known to all, yet never old. The "Age of Reason" has long been both exaggerated and despised as an iconoclastic work. But we are indebted to Conway, the greatest of Paine students, who out of the many biographies he has written has chosen that of Paine to be the masterpiece of his life (and it is a work which any author might be proud to regard his master-piece), to him I say we are indebted for a different view of the "Age of Reason."

I know not whether Mr. Conway's own Unitarian bias may not have influenced him; it is possible. It is possible that his eager search for positivism may have unconsciously determined his attitude towards the great hero, and modified his interpretation of Paine's words. I believe it has; because I believe *that* is inevitable. I believe we read our own ideals into other people, and must do so if we think at all. But making all allowance for the biographer's prejudgment, Conway has still a magnificent argument for putting Paine in the defendant's position. We are no longer to view the book as an attack upon religion but as its defense,—the defense of what is beneficial, permanent, necessary, in the religious element of human nature against the scribes and pharisees on the one hand and the philistines on the other. It was the plea for the redemption of the edifice from the dirt and cobwebs, the protest against smashing the stones to kill the spiders. The great prerequisite to the understanding of the "Age of Reason" is an acquaintance with the literature of that time—especially French literature. The pamphlets, periodicals, and books are the crystals wherein *the Zeitgeist* of the 18th century is preserved. Without this acquaintance we cannot realize how the people continually thought, and what was new and what was old, what was acceptable and what unacceptable to them. And we shall find by it that the fashion of sneering popularized by Voltaire, and so admirably embodied by the *finesse* of the French language (always a language of double meanings and hemi-demi-semi-shaded insinuations), the still more reprehensible habit of deducing immense generals from very scanty particulars, or in fact contriving the generals first and then fitting in or suavely waiving the particulars altogether, had so permeated not only French philosophy, but the heads of the common people as well, that religion had become almost a byword, a baseless superstition unaccounted for by, and unnecessary according to, the all-accepted theory of Natural Law. To defend it, to maintain that there was something else in it, was equivalent to pleading for the life of the King before the convention! That was to maintain that there were claims of the human—after the King had been stripped; this was to say that underneath the gewgaws and tinsel of religions the undying heart of man, the man of all the past, had been expressing its noblest aspirations. And Paine stripped off the tinsel and said, "Put your hand here,—it beats"; and because he tore the tinsel, the orthodox would have stoned him; and because he said "it beats," the philosophers would have whetted the knife. And between the two he stood firm, proclaiming what he believed, not counting the cost. We may not believe as he; most of us do not. But that is the man we love: who has something in him superior to the judgments of men; who holds steadfast—steadfast even in persecution, even to death.

Perhaps there is no more pathetic thing than the last years, the death, and the burial of Paine. The world would have been poorer had he died sooner; but to him, to the man, the gun-shot or the guillotine had been kinder than the unhappy life rejected by the nation he had given all to free, shunned by political cowards and persecuted by religious bigots,—even on his death-bed. But though so lonely, so pathetically lonely, there is something that sends a fine, cold thrill along the nerves in that strange procession and burial—that poor procession, that procession of the Hicksite Quaker, the two negroes, the widowed Frenchwoman and her son. I wonder what sort of day it was; whether the sun shone or the clouds lowered over the solitary grave on the little farm, when Margaret Bonneville said to her child, "Stand you there at his feet, for France; and I will here, for America." I do not know where the negroes and the Hicksite stood when that august corpse was lowered to the depths, but there, close, somewhere, stood the unfreed race, for whom he had vainly plead, and there, close, somewhere, the soul's revolt at spiritual masters. And from that tomb there went away the scattering fires, of the risen ghost, the '61 living Paine, the Grand Reality.

Dyer D. Lum

February 15, 1839—April 6, 1893)

O NE of the silent martyrs whose graves are trodden to the level by their fellows' feet, almost before it is seen that they have fallen, completed his martyrdom one year ago to-night.

There are thousands of such, why then commemorate this one?

Let our answer be that in this one we commemorate all the others, and if we have chosen his day and name, it is because his genius, his work, his character was one of those rare gems produced in the great mine of suffering and flashing backward with all its changing lights the hopes, the fears, the gaieties, the griefs, the dreams, the doubts, the loves, the hates, the sum of that which is buried, low down there, in the human mine.

No more modest a man than Dyer D. Lum ever lived; partly, nay mostly, indeed, it was inborn, instinctive; but it was also fostered by his conception of life, which led him to consider self as the veriest of soap-bubbles, a thing to be dispelled by the merest whiff of wind, so to speak; and therefore, personal recognition or personal gain as the most silly, as well as unworthy, of motives. For this reason his works have often gone where his name did not, and thousands of persons have been influenced by his logic and his sentiments who never heard of his personality. Indeed there were some of us who wondered when he died, what certain labor leaders would henceforth do for a cheap scribe to furnish them brains.

I have often heard him quote as his motto, both for organization and for literary effort, the expressive sentence: *"Get in your work."* "Let fools take the credit if they want it," was the implication of his tone, and I shall never forget the delightful smile with which he repeated Charles Mackay's lines, most singularly transposing the author's meaning: "Grub little moles——." He took an especial pleasure in grubbing, and smiling when a streak of sunlight fell on some one else.

I have said that this distinguishing characteristic, so fruitful in results in his later life, was partly instinctive and partly a philosophic conviction. The instinctive side may be best understood by a brief sketch of his ancestry. It is generally complained that the troublesome people who are never satisfied to let society alone, must necessarily be foreigners; at least they can never belong to the same nation as we, the good, the respectable. The easy method of laying everything pestilent to the charge of the foreigner, will not serve a conservative American against Dyer D. Lum. The first of the Lums to set foot in this country was Samuel L., a Scotchman, in the year 1732. They rooted in New England soil, and at the time of the Revolution, Dyer's great grandfather was a minute-man in the very town, Northampton, where his own corpse was laid a year ago. On the maternal side the Tappan family were also revolutionists, and back of revolutionists Reformationists in the days of Queen Elizabeth, and still back of that, Crusaders. All this would be important enough and indeed even distinguishing, were I relating it by way of "gilding refined gold"; but they acquire meaning the moment we regard them as data for a character. They are fraught with mysterious symbolism, and he himself becomes a symbol of the deep-rooted faith of humanity, when we see that subterranean stream of blood running from Jerusalem through Europe and across the sea to America. It shows how profound is the well-spring of devotion to cause in the human heart; through how many centuries the spirit of rebellion lives. But what, say you, had it to do with his instinctive modesty? This: *the devotee of a cause is never the devotee of self.*

Now as to his philosophic convictions, it would be easy to deliver a whole lecture upon them; and unfortunately his profoundest work on that subject has not yet been printed. Of course, I can present them but briefly. I must preface that, as you will no doubt observe later on, his beliefs were in his own case a plain testimony to their own correctness. It sounds ridiculous to say that a thing can prove itself; but you will understand me when I explain that he regarded the conscious life of man, which includes, of course, his processes of reasoning and therefore his philosophy, as the merest fragment of him; that this process itself, which we are wont so fondly to consider as setting us higher than the brute, is but an upgrowth of our instincts. Man, the race Man, psychologically as well as bodily, might be likened to a tree, which every year adds small new growths whose bright green verdure opens to the sunlight, while below and supporting them quivers the great dark green mass of the tree, which year after year repeats itself, whispering in its shadows the old whispers of the centuries. The new verdure would represent the conscious life and growth of individuals, budding upward in response to the conditions surrounding them and adding what tiny mite they may to the experience of the race; but beneath and through, and all about them rustle the traditions of the dead—dead as individuals, but living, more potently living than ever, in the great trunk and branches of unconscious, or instinctive life. And as the shape of the newly budding leaf, the shade of its green, the length of its stem, its size, are determined more by the nature of the tree than by surrounding circumstances, so the philosophy of the individual is determined by the instinctive life of the race.

The winter of death comes; the individual withers like the leaf; but the small item of growth that he has added is there, brown and barren though the twig appear. From him new buds will shoot, though its own leaves hereafter rustle in the deep green shadows of unconsciousness. As time passes away useless boughs wither and die, and are stricken utterly from the life of the race; such are the worthless lives, the abnormal growths, which no longer add anything either to the beauty or the service of the whole.

Or, to adopt one of Comrade Lum's own figures, the useless or brutish elements in man slowly sink down like sediment deposited by the moving current. Now, in a case where we are able to trace a strain of blood as far back as this of his, and further are able to look at the conscious work of the man, and see that the one was the offspring of the other, modified of course by circumstances, we are able to make the seemingly absurd statement that the belief proves its own correctness.

Let me particularize concerning this belief. First he was in all his writings the advocate of resistance, the champion of rebellion. But long before he had reduced the matter to a syllogism, he was a resistant in fact. What else could you expect from the Crusader, the Reformationist, the Revolutionist? It might be said by the people who believe in the supreme influence of circumstances, that it was his social environment which made him such—that given the ideal social order and he would have been as mild a pacificator as Jesus: which is equivalent to saying that given the outward circumstances and an ear of wheat will grow from a seed corn.

Lum was the resistant, the man of action; the man who while scarcely more than a boy, enlisted as a volunteer in the 125th New York infantry to fight a cause he then deemed just; who being taken prisoner, twice effected his escape; who sick of the inaction of superiors, while a third-time prisoner waiting to be exchanged, took his exchange in his own hands, at the risk of death for desertion, and within a month re-enlisted in the cavalry, where by sheer force of daring he rose from private to captain; the man who smashed the idol of the Greenback movement, sooner than let him betray its voters, reckless himself of the rebound of hate from the politicians; the man who cast all business prospects and journalistic hopes aside as so much chaff, when he picked up the fallen banner of the fight in Chicago, by editing the paper of Albert Parsons, then in prison and doomed to die; the man who could say to his well-beloved friend, when that friend asked him whether he should petition Governor Oglesby for his life, knowing that that petition would be granted, the man who, under these circumstances could say: "Die, Parsons"; the man who poor, defeated, dirty, ragged, hungry, could proudly refuse the proffered hand of the then king of the labor movement, that king who had kept his kingdom by repudiating the martyrs of Chicago from the limitless height of one soul over another, answer "there's blood on it, Powderly"; the man who faced a public audience to defend the shooting of Frick by Alexander Berkman, a few days after the occurrence, because he felt that when another has done a thing which you approve as leading in the direction of your own aspirations, it is your duty to share the effects of the counterblast his action may have provoked; the man who seized the unknown Monster, Death, with a smile on his lips—all of this man was germinating in the child of the pious home who even when a mere boy had dared Jehovah.

Having "weighed Him, tried Him, found Him naught," he threw the Jewish God and cosmogony overboard with as much equanimity as he would have eaten his dinner, and set about finding a more reasonable explanation of phenomena. In this, as in all other matters, the man of action has a certain advantage over a pure theorist, which is this: he plunges immediately into the conflict, he throws the gauntlet, rashly sometimes, but boldly; he settles the question at once; if there is any suffering attached to the attempt, he suffers once and has done with it; while the theorist, the fellow who walks tiptoe round the edge of the battle-field, dies a hundred times and still suffers on.

My own conversion from orthodoxy to freethought was of this latter sort. I never dared God; I always tried to propitiate him with prayers and tears even while I was doubting his existence; I suffered hell a thousand times while I was wondering where it was located. But my teacher winked at the heavens, braved hell, and then tossed the whole affair aside with a joke.

Nevertheless, he did not, as nearly all of our modern image-breakers have done, deny all religions in their entirety, because he had run a lance through a stuffed Mumbo-Jumbo. Indeed, the spirit of devotion to something greater than Self, which will be found as the kernel of every religion, was so thoroughly in him, or indeed *was* he himself that whether he fancied himself *willing* it or not, his inclinations directed all his conscious efforts to read the riddle of life into the channel of Buddhism. I do not know whether he ever accepted its peculiarly fanciful side or not; but if he did, it was early corrected by a no less characteristic trait, also an inheritance of the Tappan family, that of critical analysis. An omnivorous reader, he was always abreast of the times in matters of scientific discovery; and his inexorable logic would never have permitted him to retain a creed which necessitated any doctoring of facts; he rather doctored the creed to fit the facts and thus evolved a species of modern Buddhism which he called "Evolutional Ethics," whose principles may be briefly stated as follows:

Man is the continuation of the process of evolution up to date. He is thus united to all other products of evolution, and is governed by the same laws. The two factors which determine form in the organic world are *adaptation* and *inheritance;* and since evolution is no less a matter of psychology than physiology, the soul of man as well as the soul of animals and plants, must be moulded by these factors. That inheritance tends to crystallize existing forms, while *adaptation,* or the influence of environment, ever tends to modification of forms, whether physical or intellectual. That mind as much as body is unconscious, so far as there is perfect adaptation to surroundings; and that only when inharmony of the organism with the environment as the result of change in the latter, arises, can there be *consciousness.* That this consciousness is a state of pain, more or less sharply defined; and will continue to increase in intensity until the necessary adaptation is accomplished, when *as a result* a feeling of satisfaction or pleasure will ensue, gradually sinking into the blissful unconsciousness of perfect harmony. That progress thus demands this stepping constantly up the rough stairway of pain; and that not even one step is passed until moistened by the blood of many generations. That the path up the mountain side is not laid out *by* us, but *for* us, and that we *must* travel there whether it pleases us or not. That the chances are it will *not* please us; that our whole lives, in so far as they are conscious, will probably be one record of never achieved struggle; and that rest will come only when we descend to the unconsciousness of Death.

Thus he was a pessimist of the darkest hue; and yet he never wasted a moment's regret on the facts. He watched this passing spectre man, gliding among the whirling dance of atoms, contemplated his final extinction with composure, sneered at metaphysicians while he himself was buried in metaphysics, and cracked jokes either at his own expense or somebody else's.

The result of all this speculation was the conclusion that man, being a social animal, must adapt himself to social ends (not determined by him but for him—unconsciously); that therefore the one who sets himself and his egotistic desires against the social ideal is the supreme traitor. He had a peculiar power of expressing volumes in an epithet; and the epithet he gave to the Egoist was "Dung-Beetle." For the sake of those who may not be familiar with the insect referred to, I may explain that a dung-beetle is a sort of bug that exhibits its instincts by rolling a ball of dung, and who sometimes appears to meditate when he rolls over the ball that the universe has turned bottom up—because he has.

Now, it is well known that the greater part of the reform camp—particularly the Anarchistic camp—is made up of Dung-Beetles, I mean of Egoists; people who declare that the desire for pleasure is the motive of action, who think a great deal of their egos and don't care a rap for society. The result was they sharpened their pencils and wrote scathing editorials denouncing him. To which he answered never a word. First, because he didn't consider himself worth fighting about; and second, if he had, he was altogether too good a general to do it. His opponents were a disputatious sort, who liked nothing better than argument; he knew what his enemy wanted and *didn't do it*.

But when a question worth discussing arose, then woe to those who had courted the rapier of his wit, or challenged to duel with the diamond-tipped dagger of his sarcasm. He could answer columns with a paragraph.

I do not know whether this philosophy of his had crystallized in his own mind before he became an Anarchist or not. I believe, however, it had not; I think it grew along with his other conceptions, being broadened and corrected, and in turn broadening and correcting his thought in other channels. But at any rate, fully developed or not, it certainly influenced his conclusions on economic subjects greatly. True to his instincts he was always at the front of battle, and when the war closed his first move was to attach himself to the Greenback party, the first widespread expression of organized protest against monopoly of the means of production in America. He still had faith in the saving grace of politics, and was active enough in the agitation to be nominated for Lieut. Governor of Massachusetts with Wendell Phillips for Governor. The fight, which besides being a demand for fiat money, embodied a short-hour movement, took on a national character; and Dyer D. Lum with five others, including Albert R. Parsons, was appointed on a committee to push the matter before Congress. This was in 1880. Six years later, time and the tide had driven both of them into the great current of Socialism, and final repudiation of politics as a means of attaining Socialistic ideals. And here came in the philosophy of the unconscious. The socialization of industry was the next step up the mountain side, not because men wished or planned it; but the pressure of surroundings made it the only possible move; but on the other hand the reactionary, system-building Socialism advocated by the great master Marx, and all his train of little repeaters, was seen to be at variance with a no less marked feature of the evolving social ideal, viz., elasticity, mobility, constantly increasing differentiation; which is only possible when units of society are left free to adapt themselves to the slightest changes, unforced by the opinions of other people who know nothing of the matters in question, but who, being in the majority (for where is ignorance not in the majority?) could suppress the free movements of the minority by enacting their ignorance into laws.

Thus it will be seen that he looked forward to free Socialism as the industrial ideal; the requirements of that ideal are laid down in his "Economics of Anarchy."

A few of his caustic sentences may here be quoted:

"The Statist assumes that rights increase in some metaphysical manner, and become incarnate in half the whole plus one."

"Politics discovers wisdom by taking a general poll of ignorance."

"Every appeal to legislation to do aught but *undo* is as futile as sending a flag of truce to the enemy for munitions of war."

"When Caesar conquered Greece, he subjugated Olympus, and the Gods now measure tape behind counters with Christian decorum."

Lum had faith in humankind. He always trusted

the people; the people that maligned him, the people that injured him, the people that killed him. When I asked him once why he did not get angry at an individual who industriously circulated lies about him, he answered with a twinkling laugh, "For the same reason that I don't kick the house-cat." And yet he had an abiding faith in that man, and other similar men, to work out the judgments of the human race, undisturbed by the fact that they let their only honest leaders die in garrets.

And underneath the speculative philosopher who confused you with long words; underneath the cold logician who mercilessly scouted at sentiment; underneath the pessimistic poet that sent the mournful cry of the whip-poor-will echoing through the widowed chambers of the heart, that hung and sung over the festival walls of Life the wreaths and dirges of Death; underneath the gay joker who delighted to play tricks on politicians, police and detectives; was the man who took the children on his knees and told them stories while the night was falling, the man who gave up a share of his own meagre meals to save five blind kittens from drowning; the man who lent his arm to a drunken washerwoman whom he did not know, and carried her basket for her, that she might not be arrested and locked up; the man who gathered four-leafed clovers and sent them to his friends, wishing them "all the luck which superstition attached to them"; the man whose heart was beating with the great common heart, who was one with the simplest and the poorest.

Lum held that evolutional ethics, or Anarchist ethics, in fact, must take account of both the altruistic and egoistic impulses; that while determining causes will ever lie in the mysterious realm of the unconscious life, consciousness may discern the trend of development and throw in its quota of influence for or against. That in its endeavor to comprehend the trend of development, it should take fair account of ancient truths, however enveloped in superstitious husks; should aim to extract the virtue even in the much mistaken altruistic doctrines of vicarious atonement and personal abasement; and while emphasizing the negation of human rulership as destructive of the possibilities of true growth, at the same time to acknowledge the vain conceit of self as anything more than a temporary grouping of instinct developed in beast, in plant, in man; to acknowledge the individual creature as a sort of mirrored reflection of the cosmos, constantly shifting, now scintillant, now vague and evanescent, now gone forever as Death breaks the mirror.

The notion of immortality which grows from such a conception of self is purged of the old vain conceit. It has been most beautifully voiced in George Eliot's "Choir Invisible," Mr. Lum's favorite poem; and in the lines is expressed the last great limitless shadow which engulfs even this immortality, the blind, tremendous darkness which lies at the end of all, the sense of the invincibility of which must have lain upon our teacher's soul when after the last searching, inexplicable, farewell look into a friend's eyes he went out into the April night and took his last walk in the roar of the great city—he who should soon be so silent!

Most of his comrades were surprised. They said: "I never thought Dyer D. Lum would go alone." But I who know how often and how wearily he said "What's the use," am sure that that mocking question lay at his heart, and paralyzed the *will* to *do*.

Like Olive Schreiner's stars in the African Farm, the soul about to depart sees the earth so coldly—all the ages are as one night—and like them he watches little helpless creatures of the earth come out and crawl awhile upon its skin, then go back beneath it, and it does not matter—nothing matters.

Francisco Ferrer

I N all unsuccessful social upheavals there are two
terrors: the Red—that is, the people, the mob; the
White—that is, the reprisal.

When a year ago to-day the lightning of the White
Terror shot out of that netherest blackness of Social
Depth, the Spanish Torture House, and laid in the ditch
of Montjuich a human being who but a moment before
had been the personification of manhood, in the flower of
life, in the strength and pride of a balanced intellect, full
of the purpose of a great and growing undertaking,—
that of the Modern Schools,—humanity at large received
a blow in the face which it could not understand.

Stunned, bewildered, shocked, it recoiled and stood
gaping with astonishment. How to explain it? The
average individual—certainly the average individual in
America—could not believe it possible that any group of
persons calling themselves a government, let it be of the
worst and most despotic, could slay a man for being a
teacher, a teacher of modern sciences, a builder of
hygienic schools, a publisher of text-books. No: they
could not believe it. Their minds staggered back and
shook refusal. It was not so; it could not be so. The man
was shot,—that was sure. He was dead, and there was
no raising him out of the ditch to question him. The
Spanish government had certainly proceeded in an unjus-
tifiable manner in court-martialing him and sentencing

him without giving him a chance at defense. But surely
he had been guilty of something; surely he must have
rioted, or instigated riot, or done some desperate act of
rebellion; for never could it be that in the twentieth
century a country of Europe could kill a peaceful man
whose aim in life was to educate children in geography,
arithmetic, geology, physics, chemistry, singing, and
languages.

No: it was not possible!—And, for all that, it was possible; it was done, on the 13th of October, one year ago
to-day, in the face of Europe, standing with tied hands
to look on at the murder.

And from that day on, controversy between the awakened who understood, the reactionists who likewise understood, and their followers on both sides who have half
understood, has surged up and down and left confusion
pretty badly confounded in the mind of him who did not
understand, but sought to.

The men who did him to death, and the institutions
they represent have done all in their power to create the
impression that Ferrer was a believer in violence, a teacher
of the principles of violence, a doer of acts of violence,
and an instigator of widespread violence perpetrated by
a mass of people. In support of the first they have published reports purporting to be his own writings, have
pretended to reproduce seditious pictures from the walls
of his class-rooms, have declared that he was seen
mingling with the rebels during the Catalonian uprising of
last year, and that upon trial he was found guilty of having conceived and launched the Spanish rebellion against
the Moroccan war. And that his death was a just act of
reprisal.

On the other hand, we have had a storm of indignant
voices clamoring in his defense, alternately admitting and

denying him to be a revolutionist, alternately contending that his schools taught social rebellion and that they taught nothing but pure science; we have had workmen demonstrating and professors and litterateurs protesting on very opposite grounds; and almost none were able to give definite information for the faith that was in them.

And indeed it has been very difficult to obtain exact information, and still is so. After a year's lapse, it is yet not easy to get the facts disentangled from the fancies,— the truths from the lies, and above all from the half-lies.

And even when we have the truths as to the facts, it is still difficult to valuate them, because of American ignorance of Spanish ignorance. Please understand the phrase. America has not too much to boast of in the way of its learning; but yet it has that much of common knowledge and common education that it does not enter into our minds to conceive of a population 68% of which are unable to read and write, and a good share of the remaining 32% can only read, not write; neither does it at all enter our heads to think that of this 32% of the better informed, the most powerful contingent is composed of those whose distinct, avowed, and deliberate purpose it is to keep the ignorant ignorant.

Whatever may be the sins of Government in this country, or of the Churches—and there are plenty of such sins—at least they have not (save in the case of negro slaves) constituted themselves a conspiratical force to keep out enlightenment,—to prevent the people from learning to read and write, or to acquire whatever scientific knowledge their economic circumstances permitted them to. What the unconscious conspiracy of economic circumstance has done, and what conscious manipulations the Government school is guilty of, to render higher education a privilege of the rich and a maintainer of injustice is another matter. But it cannot be charged that the rulers of America seek to render the people illiterate. People, therefore, who have grown up in a general atmosphere of thought which regards the government as a provider of education, even as a compeller of education, do not, unless their attention is drawn to the facts, conceive of a state of society in which government is a hostile force, opposed to the enlightenment of the people,—its politicians exercising all their ingenuity to sidetrack the demand of the people for schools. How much less do they conceive the hostile force and power of a Church, having behind it an unbroken descent from feudal ages, whose direct interest it is to maintain a closed monopoly of learning, and to keep out of general circulation all scientific information which would tend to destroy the superstitions whereby it thrives.

I say that the American people in general are not informed as to these conditions, and therefore the phenomenon of a teacher killed for instituting and maintaining schools staggers their belief. And when they read the assertions of those who defend the murder, that it was because his schools were instigating the overthrow of social order in Spain, they naturally exclaim: "Ah, that explains it! The man taught sedition, rebellion, riot, in his schools! That is the reason."

Now the truth is, that what Ferrer was teaching in his schools was really instigating the overthrow of the social order of Spain; furthermore it was not only instigating it, but it was making it as certain as the still coming of the daylight out of the night of the east. But not by the teaching of riot; of the use of dagger, bomb, or knife; but by the teaching of the same sciences which are taught in our public schools, through a generally diffused knowledge of which the power of Spain's despotic Church must crumble away. Likewise it was laying the primary foundation for the overthrow of such portions of the State organization as exist by reason of the general ignorance of the people.

The Social Order of Spain ought to be overthrown; must be overthrown, will be overthrown; and Ferrer was doing a mighty work in that direction. The men who killed him knew and understood it well. And they consciously killed him for what he really did; but they have let the outside world suppose they did it, for what he did not do. Knowing there are no words so hated by all governments as "sedition and rebellion," knowing that such words will make the most radical of governments align itself with the most despotic at once, knowing there is nothing which so offends the majority of conservative and peace-loving people everywhere as the idea of violence unordered by authority, they have wilfully created the impression that Ferrer's schools were places where children and youths were taught to handle weapons, and to make ready for armed attacks on the government.

They have, as I said before, created this impression in various ways; they have pointed to the fact that the man who in 1906 made the attack on Alfonso's life, had acted as a translator of books used by Ferrer in his schools; they have scattered over Europe and America pictures purporting to be reproductions of drawings in prominent wall-spaces in his schools, recommending the violent overthrow of the government.

As to the first of these accusations, I shall consider it later in the lecture; but as to the last, it should be enough to remind any person with an ordinary amount of reflection, that the schools were public places open to any one, as our schools are; and that if any such pictures had existed, they would have been sufficient cause for shutting up the schools and incarcerating the founder within a day after their appearance on the walls. The Spanish Government has that much sense of how to preserve its own existence, that it would not allow such pictures to hang in a public place for one day. Nor would books preaching sedition have been permitted to be published or circulated.—All this is foolish dust sought to be thrown in foolish eyes.

No; the real offense was the real thing that he did. And in order to appreciate its enormity, from the Spanish ruling force's standpoint, let us now consider what that ruling force is, what are the economic and educational conditions of the Spanish people, why and how Ferrer founded the Modern Schools, and what were the subjects taught therein.

Up to the year 1857 there existed no legal provision for general elementary education in Spain. In that year, owing to the liberals having gotten into power in Madrid, after a bitter contest aroused partially by the general political events of Europe, a law making elementary education compulsory was passed. This was two years before Ferrer's birth.

Now it is one thing for a political party, temporarily in possession of power, to pass a law. It is quite another thing to make that law effective, even when wealth and general sentiment are behind it. But when joined to the fact that there is a strong opposition is added the fact that this opposition is in possession of the greatest wealth of the country, that the people to be benefited are often quite as bitterly opposed to their own enlightenment as those who profit by their ignorance, and that those who do ardently desire their own uplift are extremely poor, the difficulty of practicalizing this educational law is partially appreciated.

Ferrer's own boyhood life is an illustration of how much benefit the children of the peasantry reaped from the educational law. His parents were vine dressers; they were eminently orthodox and believed what their priest (who was probably the only man in the little village of Alella able to read) told them: that the Liberals were the emissaries of Satan and that whatever they did was utterly evil. They wanted no such evil thing as popular education about, and would not that their children should have it. Accordingly, even at 13 years of age, the boy was without education,—a circumstance which in after years made him more anxious that others should not suffer as he had.

It is self-understood that if it was difficult to found schools in the cities where there existed a degree of popular clamor for them, it was next to impossible in the rural districts where people like Ferrer's parents were the typical inhabitants. The best result obtained by this law in the 20 years from 1857 to 1877 was that, out of 16,000,000 people, 4,000,000 were then able to read and write,—75% remaining illiterate. At the end of 1907 the proportion was altered to 6,000,000 literate out of 18,500,000 population, which may be considered as a fairly correct approximate of the present condition.

One of the very great accounting causes for this situation is the extreme poverty of the mass of the populace. In many districts of Spain a laborer's wages are less than $1.00 a week, and nowhere do they equal the poorest workman's wages in America. Of course, it is understood that the cost of living is likewise low; but imagine it as low as you please, it is still evident that the income of the workers is too small to permit them to save anything, even from the most frugal living. The dire struggle to secure food, clothing and shelter is such that little energy is left wherewith to aspire to anything, to demand anything, either for themselves or their children. Unless, therefore, the government provided the buildings, the books, and appliances, and paid the teachers' salaries, it is easy to see that the people most in need of education are least able, and least likely, to provide it for themselves. Furthermore the government itself, unless it can tax the wealthier classes for it, cannot out of such an impoverished source wring sufficient means to provide adequate schools and school equipments.

Now, the wealthiest classes are just the religious orders. According to the statement of Monsignor José Valeda de Gunjado, these orders own two-thirds of the money of the country and one-third of the wealth in property. These orders are utterly opposed to all education except such as they themselves furnish—a lamentable travesty on learning.

As a writer who has investigated these conditions personally, observes, in reply to the question, "Does not the Church provide numbers of schools, day and night, at its own expense?"—'It does,—unhappily for Spain.'" It provides schools whose principal aim is to strengthen superstition, follow a mediaeval curriculum, *keep out* scientific light,—and prevent other and better schools from being established.

A Spanish educational journal (*La Escuela Espanola*), not Ferrer's journal, declared in 1907 that these schools were largely "without light or ventilation, dens of death, ignorance, and bad training." It was estimated that 50,000 children died every year in consequence of the mischievous character of the school rooms. And even to schools like these, there were half a million children in Spain who could gain no admittance.

As to the teachers, they are allowed a salary ranging

from $50.00 to $100.00 a year; but this is provided, not by the State, but through voluntary donations from the parents. So that a teacher, in addition to his legitimate functions, must perform those of collector of his own salary.

Now conceive that he is endeavoring to collect it from parents whose wages amount to two or three dollars a week; and you will not be surprised at the case reported by a Madrid paper in 1903 of a master's having canvassed a district to find how many parents would contribute if he opened a school. Out of one hundred families, three promised their support!

Is it any wonder that the law of compulsory education is a mockery? How could it be anything else?

Now let us look at the products of this popular ignorance, and we shall presently understand why the Church fosters it, why it fights education; and also why the Catalonian insurrection of 1909, which began as a strike of workers in protest against the Moroccan war, ended in mob attacks upon convents, monasteries, and churches.

I have already quoted the statement of a high Spanish prelate that the religious orders of Spain own two-thirds of the money of Spain, and one-third of the wealth in property. Whether this estimate is precisely correct or not, it is sufficiently near correctness to make us aware that at least a great portion of the wealth of the country has passed into their hands,—a state not widely differing from that existing in France prior to the great Revolution. Before the insurrection of last year, the city of Barcelona alone had 165 convents, many of which were exceedingly rich. The province of Catalonia maintained 2.300 of these institutions. Aside from these religious orders with their accumulations of wealth, the Church itself, the united body of priests not in orders, is immensely wealthy. Conceive that in the Cathedral at Toledo there is an image of the Virgin whose wardrobe alone would be sufficient to build hundreds of schools. Imagine that this doll, which is supposed to symbolize the forlorn young woman who in her pain and sorrow and need was driven to seek shelter in a stable, whose life was ever lowly, and who is called the Mother of Sorrows, —imagine that this image of her has become a vulgar coquette sporting a robe whereinto are sown 85,000 pearls, besides as many more sapphires, amethysts, and diamonds!

Oh, what a decoration for the mother of the Carpenter of Nazareth! What a vision for the dying eyes on the Cross to look forward to! What an outcome of the gospel of salvation free to the poor and lowly, taught by the poorest and the lowliest,—that the humble keeper of the humble household of the despised little village of Judea should be imaged forth as a Queen of Gauds, bedizened with a crown worth $25,000 and bracelets valued at $10,000 more. The Virgin Mary, the Daughter of the Stable, transformed into a diamond merchant's showcase!

And this in the midst of men and women working for just enough to keep the skin upon the bone; in the midst of children who are denied the primary necessities of childhood.

Now I ask you, when the fury of these people burst, as under the provocation they received it was inevitable that it should burst, was it any wonder that it manifested itself in mob violence against the institutions which mock their suffering by this useless, senseless, criminal waste of wealth in the face of utter need?

Will some one now whisper in our ears that there are

women in America who decorate themselves with more jewels than the Virgin of Toledo, and throw away the price of a school on a useless decoration in a single night; while within a radius of five miles from them there are also uneducated children, for whom our School Boards can provide no place?

Yes, it is so; let them remember the mobs of Barcelona!

And let me remember I am talking about Spain!

The question naturally intrudes, How does the Church, how do the religious orders manage to accumulate such wealth? Remember first that they are old, and of unbroken continuance for hundreds of years. That various forms of acquisition, in operation for centuries, would produce immense accumulations, even supposing nothing but legitimate purchases and gifts. But when we consider the actual means whereby money is daily absorbed from the people by these institutions we receive a shock which sets all our notions of the triumph of Modern Science topsy-turvy.

It is almost impossible to realize, and yet it is true, that the Spanish Church still deals in that infamous "graft" against which Martin Luther hurled the splendid force of his wrath four hundred years ago. The Church of Spain still sells indulgences. Every Catholic bookstore, and every priest, has them for sale. They are called "bulas." Their prices range from about 15 to 25 cents, and they constitute an elastic excuse for doing pretty much what the possessor pleases to do, providing it is not a capital crime, for a definitely named period.

Probably there is no one in America so little able to believe this condition to exist, as the ordinary well-informed Roman Catholic. I have myself listened to priests of the Roman faith giving the conditions on which pardon for venal offenses might be obtained; and they had nothing to do with money. They consisted in saying a certain number of prayers at stated periods, with specified intent. While that may be a very illogical way of putting things together that have no connection, there is nothing in it to offend one's ideas of honesty. The enlightened conscience of an entire mass of people has demanded that a spiritual offense be dealt with by spiritual means. It would revolt at the idea that such grace could be written out on paper and sold either to the highest bidder or for a fixed price.

But now conceive what happens where a people are illiterate, regarding written documents with that superstitious awe which those who cannot read always have for the mysterious language of learning; regarding them besides with the combination of fear and reverence which the ignorant believer entertains for the visible sign of Supernatural Power, the Power which holds over him the threat of eternal punishment,—and you will have what goes on in Spain. Add to this that such a condition of fear and gullibility on the side of the people, is the great opportunity of the religious "grafter." Whatever number of honest, self-sacrificing, devoted people may be attracted to the service of the Church, there will certainly be found also, the cheat, the impostor, the searcher for ease and power.

These indulgences, which for 15 or 25 cents pardon the buyer for his past sins, but are good only till he sins again, constitute a species of permission to do what otherwise is forbidden; the most expensive one, the 25c-one, is practically a license to hold stolen property up to a certain amount.

Both rich and poor buy these things, the rich of course paying a good deal more than the stipulated sum, But it hardly requires the statement that an immense number of the very poor buy them also. And from this horrible traffic the Church of Spain annually draws millions.

There are other sources of income such as the sale of scapulars, agnus-deis, charms, and other pieces of trumpery, which goes on all over the Catholic world also, but naturally to no such extent as in Spain, Portugal, and Italy, where popular ignorance may be again measured by the materialism of its religion.

Now, is it reasonable to suppose that the individuals who are thriving upon these sales, want a condition of popular enlightenment? Do they not know how all this traffic would crumble like the ash of a burnt-out fire, once the blaze of science were to flame through Spain? *They* EDUCATE! Yes; they educate the people to believe in these barbaric relics of a dead time,—for *their own material interest*. Spain and Portugal are the last resort of the mediaeval church; the monasticism and the Jesuitry which have been expelled from other European countries, and compelled to withdraw from Cuba and the Philippines, have concentrated there; and there they are making their last fight. There they will go down into their eternal grave; but not till Science has invaded the dark corners of the popular intellect.

The political condition is parallel with the religious condition of the people, with the exception that the State is poor while the Church is rich.

There are some elements in the government which are opposed to the Church religiously, which nevertheless do not wish to see its power as an institution upset, because they foresee that the same people who would overthrow the Church, would later overthrow them. These, too, wish to see the people kept ignorant.

Nevertheless, there have been numerous political rebellions in Spain, having for their object the establishment of a republic.

In 1868 there occurred such a rebellion, under the leadership of Ruiz Zorilla. At that time, Ferrer was not quite 20 years old. He had acquired an education by his own efforts. He was a declared Republican, as it seems that every young, ardent, bright-minded youth, seeing what the condition of his country was, and wishing for its betterment, would be. Zorilla was for a short time Minister of Public Instruction, under the new government, and very zealous for popular education.

Naturally he became an object of admiration and imitation to Ferrer.

In the early eighties, after various fluctuations of political power, Zorilla, who had been absent from Spain, returned to it, and began the labor of converting the soldiers to republicanism. Ferrer was then a director of railways, and of much service to Zorilla in the practical work of organization. In 1885 this movement culminated in an abortive revolution, wherein both Ferrer and Zorilla took active part, and were accordingly compelled to take refuge in France upon the failure of the insurrection.

It is therefore certain that from his entrance into public agitation till the year 1885, Ferrer was an active revolutionary republican, believing in the overthrow of Spanish tyranny by violence.

There is no question that at that time he said and wrote things which, whether we shall consider them justifiable or not, were openly in favor of forcible rebellion. Such utterances charged against him at the alleged trial in 1909, which were really his, were quotations from this period. Remember he was then 26 years old. When the trial occurred, he was 50 years old. What had been his mental evolution during those 24 years?

In Paris, where, with the exception of a short intermission in 1889 when he visited Spain, he remained for about fifteen years, he naturally drifted into a method of making a living quite common to educated exiles in a foreign land; viz., giving private lessons in his native language. But while this is with most a mere temporary makeshift, which they change for something else as soon as they are able, to Ferrer it revealed what his real business in life should be; he found teaching to be his genuine vocation; so much so that he took part in several movements for popular education in Paris, giving much free service.

This participation in the labor of training the mind, which is always a slow and patient matter, began to have its effect on his conceptions of political change. Slowly the idea of a Spain regenerated through the storm blasts of revolution, mightily and suddenly, faded out of his belief, being replaced, probably almost insensibly, by the idea that a thorough educational enlightenment must precede political transformation, if that transformation were to be permanent. This conviction he voiced with strange power and beauty of expression, when he said to his old revolutionary Republican friend, Alfred Naquet: "Time respects those works alone which Time itself has helped to build."

Naquet himself, old and sinking man as he is, is at this day and hour heart and soul for forcible revolution; admitting all the evils which it engenders and all the dangers of miscarriage which accompany it, he still believes, to quote his own words, that "Revolutions are not only the marvelous accoucheurs of societies; they are also fecundating forces. They fructify men's intelligences; and if they determine the final realization of matured evolutions, they also become, through their action on

human minds, points of departure for newer evolutions."
Yet he, who thus sings the paean of the uprisen people,
with a fire of youth and an ardor of love that sound like
the singing of some strong young blacksmith marching at
the head of an insurgent column, rather than the quaver-
ing voice of an old spent man; he, who was the warm personal friend of Ferrer for many years, and who would
surely have wished that his ideal love should also have
been his friend's love, he expressly declares that Ferrer
was of those who feel themselves drawn to the field of
preparative labor, making sure the ground over which the
Revolution may march to enduring results.

This then was the ripened condition of his mind, especially after the death of Zorilla, and all his subsequent
life and labor is explicable only with this understanding of
his mental attitude.

In the confusion of deafening voices, it has been declared that not only did he not take part in last year's
manifestations, nor instigate them; but that he in fact had
become a Tolstoyan, a non-resistant.

This is not true: he undoubtedly understood that the
introduction of popular education into Spain means revolt, sooner or later. And he would certainly have been
glad to see a successful revolt overthrow the monarchy at
Madrid. He did not wish the people to be submissive; it
is one of the fundamental teachings of the schools he
founded that the assertive spirit of the child is to be encouraged; that its will is not to be broken; that the sin
of other schools is the forcing of obedience. He hoped to
help to form a young Spain which would not submit;
which would resist, resist consciously, intelligently,
steadily. He did not wish to enlighten people merely to
render them more sensitive to their pains and depriva-
tions, but that they might so use their enlightenment as to
rid themselves of the system of exploitation by Church

and State which is responsible for their miseries. By what means they would choose to free themselves, he did not make his affair.

How and when were these schools founded? It was during his long sojourn in Paris, that he had as a private pupil in Spanish, a middle-aged, wealthy, unmarried, Catholic lady. After much conflict over religion between teacher and pupil, the latter modified her orthodoxy greatly; and especially after her journeys to Spain, where she herself saw the condition of public instruction.

Eventually she became interested in Ferrer's conceptions of education, and his desire to establish schools in his own country. And when she died in 1900 (she was then somewhat over 50 years old) she devised a certain part of her property to Ferrer, to be used as he saw fit, feeling assured no doubt that he would see fit to use it not for his personal advantage, but for the purpose so dear to his heart. Which he did.

The bequest amounted to about $150,000; and the first expenditure was for the establishment of the Modern School of Barcelona, in the year 1901.

It should be said that this was not the first of the Modern School movement in Spain; for previous to that, and for several years, there had sprung up, in various parts of the country, a spontaneous movement towards self-education; a very heroic effort, in a way, considering that the teachers were generally workingmen who had spent their day in the shops, and were using the remainder of their exhausted strength to enlighten their fellow-workers and the children. These were largely night-schools. As there were no means behind these efforts, the buildings in which they were held were of course unsuitable; there was no proper plan of work; no sufficient equipment, and little co-ordination of labor. A considerable percentage of these schools were already on the decline, when Ferrer, equipped with his splendid organizing ability, his teacher's experience, and Mlle. Meunier's endowment, opened the Barcelona School, having as pupils eighteen boys and twelve girls.

So proper to the demand was this effort, that at the end of four years' earnest activity, fifty schools had been established, ten in Barcelona, and forty in the provinces.

In 1906, that is, after five years' work, a banquet was held on Good Friday, at which 1,700 pupils were present.

From 30 to 1,700,—that is something. And a banquet in Catholic Spain on Good Friday! A banquet of children who have bade good-bye to the salvation of the soul by the punishment of the stomach! We here may laugh; but in Spain it was a triumph and a menace, which both sides understood.

I have said that Ferrer brought to his work splendid organizing ability. This he speedily put to purpose by enlisting the co-operation of a number of the greatest scientists of Europe in the preparation of text-books embodying the discoveries of science, couched in language comprehensible to young minds.

So far, I am sorry to say, I have not succeeded in getting copies of these manuals; the Spanish government confiscated most of them, and has probably destroyed them. Still there are some uncaptured sets (one is already in the British Museum) and I make no doubt that within a year or so we shall have translations of most of them.

There were thirty of these manuals all told, comprising the work of the three sections, primary, intermediate, and superior, into which the pupils were divided.

From what I have been able to find out about these books, I believe the most interesting of them all would be the First Reading Book. It was prepared by Dr. Odon de Buen, and is said to be at the same time "a speller, a grammar and an illustrated manual of evolution," "the majestic story of the evolution of the cosmos from the atom to the thinking being, related in a language simple, comprehensible to the child."

20,000 copies of this book were rapidly sold.

Imagine what that meant to Catholic schools! That the babies of Spain should learn nothing about eternal punishment for their deadly sins, and *should* learn that they are one in a long line of unfolding life that started in the lowly sea-slime!

The books on geography, physics, and minerology were written in like manner and with like intent by the same author; on anthropology, Dr. Enguerrand wrote, and on evolution, Dr. Letourneau of Paris.

Among the very suggestive works was one on "The Universal Substance," a collaborate production of Albert Bloch and Paraf Javal, in which the mysteries of existence are resolved into their chemical equivalents, so that the foundations for magic and miracle are unceremoniously cleared out of the intellectual field.

This book was prepared at Ferrer's special request, as an antidote to ancestral leanings, inherited superstitions, the various outside influences counteracting the influences of the school.

The methods of instruction were modeled after earlier attempts in France, and were based on the general idea that physical and intellectual education must continually supplement each other. That no one is really educated, so long as his knowledge is merely the recollection of what he has read or seen in a book. Accordingly a lesson often consisted of a visit to a factory, a workshop, a studio, or a laboratory, where things were explained and illustrated; or in a class journey to the hills, or the sea, or the open country, where the geological or topographical conditions were studied, or botanical specimens collected and individual observation encouraged.

Very often even book classes were held out of doors, and the children insensibly put in touch with the great pervading influences of nature, a touch too often lost, or never felt at all, in our city environments.

How different was all this from the incomprehensible theology of the Catholic schools to be learned and believed but not understood, the impractical rehearsing of strings of words characteristic of mediaeval survivals! No wonder the Modern Schools grew and grew, and the hatred of the priests waxed hotter and hotter.

Their opportunity came; indeed, they did not wait long.

In the year 1906, on the 31st day of May, not so very long after that Good Friday banquet, occurred the event which they seized upon to crush the Modern School and its founder.

I am not here to speak either for or against Mateo Morral. He was a wealthy young man, of much energy and considerable learning. He had helped to enrich the library of the Modern School and being an excellent linguist, he had offered to make translations of text-books. Ferrer had accepted the offer. That is all Morral had to do with the Modern School.

But on the day of royal festivities, Morral had it in his head to throw a bomb where it would do some royal hurt. He missed his calculations, and the hurt intended did not take place; but after a short interval, finding himself about to be captured, he killed himself.

Think of him as you please: think that he was a madman who did a madman's act; think that he was a generous enthusiast who in an outburst of long chafing indignation at his country's condition wanted to strike a blow at a tyrannical monarchy, and was willing to give his own life in exchange for the tyrant's; or better than this, reserve your judgment, and say that you know not the man nor his personal condition, nor the special external conditions that prompted him; and that without such knowledge he cannot be judged. But whatever you think of Morral, pray why was Ferrer arrested and the Modern School of Barcelona closed? Why was he thrown in prison and kept there for more than a year? Why was it sought to railroad him before a Court Martial, and that attempt failing, the civil trial postponed for all that time?

WHY? WHY?

Because Ferrer taught science to the children of Spain,—and for no other thing. His enemies would have killed him then; but having been compelled to yield an open trial, by the outcry of Europe, they were also compelled to release him. But I imagine I hear, yea hear, the resolute mutter behind the closed walls of the monasteries, the day Ferrer went free. "Go, then; we shall get you again. And then——"

And then they would do what three years later they did,—*damn him to the ditch of* MONTJUICH.

Yea, they shut their lips together like the thin lips of Fate and—waited. The hatred of an order has something superb in it,—it hates so relentlessly, so constantly, so transcendently; its personnel changes, its hate never alters; it wears one priest's face or another's; itself is identical, inexorable; it pursues to the end.

Did Ferrer know this? Undoubtedly in a general way he did. And yet he was so far from conceiving its appalling remorselessness, that even when he found himself in prison again, and utterly in their power, he could not believe that he would not be freed.

What was this opportunity for which the Jesuitry of Spain waited with such terrible security? The Catalonian uprising. How did they know it would come? As any sane man, not over-optimistic, knows that uprising must come in Spain. Ferrer hoped to sap away the foundations of tyranny through peaceful enlightenment. He was right. But they are also right who say that there are other forces hurling towards those foundations; the greatest of these,—*Starvation*.

Now it was plain and simple Starvation that rose to rend its starvers when the Catalonian women rose in mobs to cry against the command that was taking away their fathers and sons to their death in Morocco. The Spanish people did not want the Moroccan war; the Government, in the interest of a number of capitalists, did; but like all governments and all capitalists, it wanted workingmen to do the dying. And they did not want to die, and leave their wives and children to die too. So they rebelled. At first it was the conscious, orderly protest of organized workingmen. But Starvation no more respects the commands of workingmen's unions, than the commands of governments, and other orderly bodies. It has nothing to lose: and it gets away, in its fury, from all management; and it riots.

Where Churches and Monasteries are offensively rich and at ease in the face of Hunger, Hunger takes its revenge. It has long fangs, it rends, and tears, and tramples—the innocent with the guilty—always. It is very horrible! But remember,—remember how much more horrible is the long, slow systematic crushing, wasting, drying of men upon their bones, which year after year, century after century, has begotten the Monster, Hunger. Remember the 50,000 innocent children annually slaughtered, the blinded and the crippled children, maimed and forsaken by social power; and behind the smoke and flame of the burning convents of July, 1909, see the staring of those sightless eyes.

Ferrer instigate that mad frenzy! Oh, no; it was a mightier than Ferrer!

"Our Lady of Pain"—Our Lady of Hunger—Our Lady with uncut nails and wolf-like teeth—Our Lady who bears the Man-flesh in her body that cannon are to tear—Our Lady the Workingwoman of Spain, ahungered. She incarnated the Red Terror.

And the enemies of Ferrer in 1906, as in 1909, knew that such things would come; and they bided their time.

It is one of those pathetic things which destiny deals, that it was only for love's sake—and most for the love of a little child—who died moreover—that the uprising found Ferrer in Spain at all. He had been in England, investigating schools and methods there from April until the middle of June. Word came that his sister-in-law and his niece were ill, so the 19th of June found him at the little girl's bedside. He intended soon after to go to Paris, but delayed to make some inquiries for a friend concerning the proceedings of the Electrical Society of Barcelona. So the storm caught him as it caught thousands of others.

He went about the business of his publishing house as usual, making the observations of an interested spectator of events. To his friend Naquet he sent a postal card on the 26th of July, in which he spoke of the heroism of the women, the lack of co-ordination in the people's movements, and the total absence of leaders, as a curious phenomenon. Hearing soon after that he was to be arrested, he secluded himself for five weeks. The "White Terror" was in full sway; 3,000 men, women, and children had been arrested, incarcerated, inhumanly treated. Then the Chief Prosecutor issued the statement that Ferrer was "the director of the revolutionary movement."

Too indignant to listen to the appeals of his friends,

he started to Barcelona to give himself up and demand trial. He was arrested on the way.

And they court-martialed him.

The proceedings were utterly infamous. No chance to confront witnesses against him; no opportunity to bring witnesses; not even the books accused of sedition allowed to offer their mute testimony in their own defense; no opportunity given to his defender to prepare; letters sent from England and France to prove what had been the doomed man's purposes and occupations during his stay there, "lost in transit"; the old articles of twenty-four years before, made to appear as if recent utterances; forgeries imposed: and with all this, nothing but hearsay evidence even from his accusers; and yet—he was sentenced to death.

Sentenced to death and shot.

And all Modern Schools closed, and his property sequestrated.

And the Virgin of Toledo may wear her gorgeous robes in peace, since the shadow of the darkness has stolen back over the circle of light he lit.

Only,—somewhere, somewhere, down in the obscurity—hovers the menacing figure of her rival, "Our Lady of Pain." She is still now,—but she is not dead. And if all things be taken from her, and the light not allowed to come to her, nor to her children,—then—some day—she will set her own lights in the darkness.

Ferrer—Ferrer is with the immortals. His work is spreading over the world; it will yet return, and rid Spain of its tyrants.

Modern Educational Reform

QUESTIONS of genuine importance to large masses of people, are not posed by a single questioner, nor even by a limited number. They are put with more or less precision, with more or less consciousness of their scope and demand by all classes involved. This is a fair test of its being a genuine question, rather than a temporary fad. Such is the test we are to apply to the present inquiry, What is wrong with our present method of Child Education? What is to be done in the way of altering or abolishing it?

The posing of the question acquired a sudden prominence, through the world-shocking execution of a great educator for alleged complicity in the revolutionary events of Spain during the Moroccan war. People were not satisfied with the Spanish government's declarations as to this official murder; they were not convinced that they were being told the truth. They inquired why the Government should be so anxious for that man's death. And they learned that as a·teacher he had founded schools wherein ideas hostile to governmental programs for learning, were put in practice. And they have gone on asking to know what these ideas were, how they were taught, and how can those same ideas be applied to the practical questions of education confronting them in the persons of their own children.

But it would be a very great mistake to suppose that the question was raised out of nothingness, or out of the brilliancy of his own mind, by Francisco Ferrer. If it were, if he were the creator of the question instead of the response to it, his martyr's death could have given it but an ephemeral prominence which would speedily have subsided.

On the contrary, the inquiry stimulated by that tragic death was but the first loud articulation of what has been asked in thousands of school-rooms, millions of homes, all over the civilized world. It has been put, by each of the three classes concerned, each in its own peculiar way, from its own peculiar viewpoint,—by the Educator, by the Parent, and by the Child itself.

There is a fourth personage who has had a great deal to say, and still has; but to my mind he is a pseudo-factor, to be eliminated as speedily as possible. I mean the "Statesman." He considers himself profoundly important, as representing the interests of society in general. He is anxious for the formation of good citizens to support the State, and directs education in such channels as he thinks will produce these.

I prefer to leave the discussion of his peculiar functions for a later part of this address, here observing only that if he is a legitimate factor, if by chance he is a genuine educator strayed into statesmanship, *as* a statesman he is interested only from a secondary motive; i. e., he is not interested in the actual work of schools, in the children as persons, but in the producing of a certain type of character to serve certain subsequent ends.

The criticism offered by the child itself upon the prevailing system of instruction, is the most simple,—direct; and at the same time, the critic is utterly unconscious of its force. Who has not heard a child say, in that fretted whine characteristic of a creature who knows its protest will be ineffective: "But what do I have to learn that for?"—"Oh, I don't see what I have to know that for; I can't remember it anyway." "I hate to go to school; I'd just as lief take a whipping!" "My teacher's a mean old thing; she expects you to sit quiet the whole morning, and if you just make the least little noise, she keeps you in at recess. Why do we have to keep still so long? What good does it do?"

I remember well the remark made to me once by one of my teachers—and a very good teacher, too, who nevertheless did not see what her own observation ought to have suggested. "School-children," she said, "regard teachers as their natural enemies." The thought which it would have been logical to suppose would have followed this observation is, that if children in general are possessed of that notion, it is because there is a great deal in the teacher's treatment of them which runs counter to the child's nature: that possibly this is so, not because of natural cussedness on the part of the child, but because of inapplicability of the knowledge taught, or the manner of teaching it, or both, to the mental and physical needs of the child. I am quite sure no such thought entered my teacher's mind,—at least regarding the system of knowledge to be imposed; being a sensible woman, she perhaps occasionally admitted to herself that she might make mistakes in applying the rules, but that the body of knowledge to be taught was indispensable, and must somehow be injected into children's heads, under threat of punishment, if necessary, I am sure she never questioned. It did not occur to her any more than to most teachers, that the first business of an educator should be to find out what are the needs, aptitudes, and tendencies of children, before he or she attempts to outline a body of knowledge to be taught, or rules for teaching it. It does not occur to them that the child's question, "What do I have to learn that for?" is a perfectly legitimate question; and if the teacher cannot answer it to the child's satisfaction, something is wrong either with the thing taught, or with the teaching; either the thing taught is out of rapport with the child's age, or his natural tendencies, or his condition of development; or the method by which it is taught repels him, disgusts him, or at best fails to interest him.

When a child says, "I don't see why I have to know that; I can't remember it anyway," he is voicing a very reasonable protest. Of course, there are plenty of instances of wilful shirking, where a little effort can overcome the slackness of memory; but every teacher who is honest enough to reckon with himself knows he cannot give a sensible reason why things are to be taught which have so little to do with the child's life that to-morrow, or the day after examination, they will be forgotten; things which he himself could not remember were he not repeating them year in and year out, as a matter of his trade. And every teacher who has thought at all for himself about the essential nature of the young humanity he is dealing with, knows that six hours of daily herding and in-penning of young, active bodies and limbs, accompanied by the additional injunction that no feet are to be shuffled, no whispers exchanged, and no paper wads thrown, is a frightful violation of all the laws of young life. Any gardener who should attempt to raise healthy, beautiful, and fruitful plants by outraging all those plants' instinctive wants and searchings, would meet as his reward—sickly plants, ugly plants, sterile plants, dead plants. He will not do it; he will watch very carefully to see whether they like much sunlight, or considerable shade, whether they thrive on much water or get drowned in it, whether they like sandy soil, or fat mucky soil; the plant itself will indicate to him when he is doing the right thing. And every gardener will watch for indications with great anxiety. If he finds the plant revolts against his experiments, he will desist at once, and try something else; if he finds it thrives, he will emphasize the particular treatment so long as it seems beneficial. But what he will surely not do, will be to prepare a certain area of ground all just alike, with equal chances of sun and amount of moisture in every part, and then plant everything together without discrimination,—mighty close together!—saying beforehand, "If plants don't want to thrive on this, they ought to want to; and if they are stubborn about it, they must be made to."

Or if a raiser of animals were to start in feeding them on a regimen adapted not to their tastes but to his; if he were to insist on stuffing the young ones with food only fitted for the older ones; if he were to shut them up and compel them somehow to be silent, stiff, and motionless for hours together,—he would—well, he would very likely be arrested for cruelty to animals.

Of course there is this difference between the grower of plants or animals and the grower of children; the former is dealing with his subject as a superior power with a force which will always remain subject to his, while the latter is dealing with a force which is bound to become his equal, and taking it in the long and large sense, bound ultimately to supersede him. The fear of "the footfalls of the young generation" is in his ears, whether he is aware of it or not, and he instinctively does what every living thing seeks to do; viz., to preserve his power. Since he cannot remain forever the superior, the dictator, he endeavors to put a definite mould upon that power which he must share—to have the child learn what he has learned, *as* he has learned it, and to the same end that he has learned it.

The grower of flowers, or fruits, or vegetables, or the raiser of animals, secure in his forever indisputable superiority, has nothing to fear when he inquires into the ways of his subjects; he will never think: "But if I heed such and such manifestation of the flower's or the animal's desire or repulsion, it will develop certain tendencies as a result, which will eventually overturn me and mine, and all that I believe in and labor to preserve." The grower of children is perpetually beset by this fear. He must not listen to a child's complaint against the school: it breaks down the mutual relation of authority and obedience; it destroys the faith of the child that his olders know better than he; it sets up little centers of future rebellion in the brain of every child affected by the example. No: complaint as to the wisdom of the system must be discouraged, ignored, frowned down, crushed by superior dignity; if necessary, punished. The very best answer a child ever gets to its legitimate inquiry, "Why do I have to learn such and such a thing?" is, "Wait till you get older, and you will understand it all. Just now you are a little too young to understand the reasons."—(In ninety-nine cases out of a hundred the answerer got the same reply to his own question twenty years before; and he has never found out since, either). "Do as we tell you to, now," say the teachers, "and be sure that we are instructing you for your good. The explanations will become clear to you some time." And the child smothers his complaint, cramps his poor little body to the best of his ability, and continues to repeat definitions which mean nothing to him but strings of long words, and rules which to him are simply torture— apparatus invented by his "natural enemies" to plague

children.—I recall quite distinctly the bitter resentment I
felt toward the inverted divisor. The formula was easy
enough to remember: "Invert the terms of the divisor
and proceed as in multiplication of fractions." I memorized it in less than a minute, and followed the prescrip-
tion, and got my examples, correct. But Oh, how, how
was the miracle accomplished? Why should a fraction be
made to stand on its head? and how did that change a
division suddenly into a multiplication?"—And I never
found out till I undertook to teach some one else, years
afterward. Yet the thing could have been made plain
then; perhaps would have been, but for the fact that as
a respectful pupil I was so trained to think that my
teachers' methods must not be questioned or their explanations reflected upon, that I sat mute, mystified, puz-
zled, and silently indignant. In the end I swallowed it as
I did a lot of other "pre-digested" knowledge (?) and
consented to use its miraculous nature, very much as my
Christian friends use the body and blood of Christ to
"wash their sins away" without very well understanding
the modus operandi.

Another advantage which the botanical or zoölogical
cultivator has over the child-grower, by which incidentally the plants and animals profit, is that since he is not
seeking to produce a universal type, but rather to develop
as many new and interesting types as he can, he is very
studious to notice the inclinations of his subjects, observing possible beginnings of differentiation, and adapting
his treatment to the development of such beginnings.
Of course he also does what no child-cultivator could possibly do,—he ruthlessly destroys weaklings; and as the
superior intermeddling divinity, he fosters those special
types which are more serviceable to himself, irrespective
of whether they are more serviceable to plant or animal
life apart from man.

But is the fact that children are of the same race as ourselves, the fact that their development should be regarded from the point of how best shall they serve themselves, their own race and generation, not that of a discriminating overlord, assuming the power of life and death over them,—a reason for us to disregard their tendencies, aptitudes, likes and dislikes, altogether?—a reason for us to treat their natural manifestations of non-adaptation to our methods of treatment with less consideration than we give to a fern or a hare? I should, on the contrary, suppose it was a reason to consider them all the more.

I think the difficulty lies in the immeasurable vanity of the human adult, particularly the pedagogical adult, (I presume I may say it with less offense since I am a teacher myself), which does not permit him to recognize as good any tendency in children to fly in the face of his conceptions of a correct human being; to recognize that may be here is something highly desirable, to be encouraged, rather than destroyed as pernicious. A flower-gardener doesn't expect to make another voter or householder out of his fern, so he lets it show what it wants to be, without being at all horrified at anything it does; but your teacher has usually well-defined conceptions of what men and women have to be. And if a boy is too lively, too noisy, too restless, too curious, to suit the concept, he must be trimmed and subdued. And if he is lazy, he has to be spurred with all sorts of whips, which are offensive both to the handler and the handled. The weapons of shaming and arousing the spirit of rivalry are two which are much used,—the former with sometimes fatal results, as in the case of the nine year old boy who recently committed suicide because his teacher drew attention to his torn coat, or young girls who have worried themselves into fevers from a scornful word respecting their failures in scholarship, and arousing rivalry brings an evil train behind it of spites and jealousies. I do not say, as some enthusiasts do, "there are no bad children," or "there are no lazy children"; but I am quite sure that both badness and laziness often result from lack of understanding and lack of adaptation; and that these can only be attained by teachers comprehending that they must seek to understand as well as to be understood. Badness is sometimes only dammed up energy, which can no more help flooding over than dammed up water. Laziness is often the result of forcing a child to a task for which it has no natural liking, while it would be energetic enough, given the thing it liked to do.

At any rate, it is worth while to try to find out what is the matter, in the spirit of a searcher after truth. Which is the first point I want to establish: That the general complaints of children are true criticisms of the school system; and Superintendents of Public Instruction, Boards of Education, and Teachers have as their first duty to heed and consider these complaints.

Let us now consider the complaints of parents. It must be admitted that the parents of young children, particularly their mothers, and especially these latter when they are the wives of workingmen with good-sized families, regard the school rather as a convenience for getting rid of the children during a certain period of the day than anything else. They are not to be blamed for this. They have obeyed the imperative mandate of nature in having families, with no very adequate conception of what they were doing; they find themselves burdened with responsibilities often greatly beyond their capacity. They have all they can do, sometimes more than they can do, to manage the financial end of things, to see to their children's material wants and to get through the work of a house; very often they are themselves deficient in even the elementary knowledge of the schools; they feel that their children need to know a great deal that they have never known, but they are utterly without the ability to say whether what they learn is useful and important or not. With the helplessness of ignorance towards wisdom, they receive the system provided by the State on trust, presuming it is good; and with the pardonable relief of busy and overburdened people, they look at the clock as school hour approaches, and breathe a sigh of relief when the last child is out of the house. They would be shocked at the idea that they regard their children as nuisances; they would vigorously defend themselves by saying that they feel that the children are in better hands than their own, safe and well treated. But before long even these ignorant ones observe that their children have learned a number of things which are not good. They have mixed with a crowd of others, and somewhere among them they have learned bad language, bad ideas, and bad habits. These are complaints which may be heard from intelligent, educated, and conservative parents also,—parents who may be presumed to be satisfied with the spirit and general purpose of the knowledge imparted in the class-room. Also the children suffer in health through their schools; and later on, when the cramming and crowding of their brains goes on in earnest, as it does in the higher grades, and particularly the High Schools, Oh then springs up a terrible crop of headache, nervous prostration, hysterics, over-delicacy, anaemia, heart-palpitation (especially among the girls), and a harvest of other physical disorders which were very probably planted back in the primary departments, and fostered in the higher rooms. The students are so overtrained that they often "become good for nothing in the house," the parents say, and too late the mothers discover that they themselves become servants to the whimsical little ladies and gentlemen they have raised up, who are more interested in text-books than in practical household matters.

Such are the ordinary complaints heard on every side, uttered by those who really have no fault to find with the substance of the instruction itself,—some because they do not know, and some because it fairly represents their own ideas.

The complaint becomes much more vital and definite when it proceeds from a parent who is an informed person, with a conception of life at variance with that commonly accepted. I will instance that of a Philadelphia physician, who recently said to me: "In my opinion many of the most horrid effects of malformations which I have to deal with, are the results of the long hours of sitting imposed on children in the schools. It is impossible for a healthy active creature to sit stiffly straight so many hours; no one can do it. They will inevitably twist and squirm themselves down into one position or another which throws the internal organs out of position, and which by iteration and reiteration results in a continuously accentuating deformity. Motherhood often becomes extremely painful and dangerous through the narrowing of the pelvis produced in early years of so much uncomfortable sitting. I believe that the sort of schooling which necessitates it should not begin till a child is fourteen years of age."

He added also that the substance of our education should be such as would fit the person for the conditions and responsibilities he or she may reasonably be expected to encounter in life. Since the majority of boys and girls will most likely become fathers and mothers in the future, why does not our system of education take account of it, and instruct the children not in the Latin names of bones and muscles so much, as in the practical functioning and hygiene of the body? Every teacher knows, and most of our parents know, that no subject is more carefully ignored by our text-books on physiology than the reproductive system.

A like book on zoölogy has far more to say about the reproduction of animals than is thought fit to be said by human beings to human beings about themselves. And yet upon such ignorance often depends the ruin of lives. Such is the criticism of an intelligent physician, himself the father of five children. It is a typical complaint of those who have to deal with the physical results of our school system.

A still more forcible complaint is rising up from a class of parents who object not only negatively, but positively, to the instruction of the schools. These are saying: I do not want to have my children taught things which are positively untrue, nor truths which have been distorted to fit some one's political or religious conception. I do not want any sort of religion or politics to be put into his head. I want the accepted facts of natural science and discovery to be taught him, in so far as they are within the grasp of his intellect. I do not want them colored with the prejudice of any system. I want a school system which will be suited to his physical well-being. I want what he learns to become his, by virtue of its appealing to his taste, his aptitude for experiment and proof; I do not want it to be a foreign stream pouring over his lips like a brook over its bed, leaving nothing behind. I do not want him to be tortured with formal examinations, nor worried by credit marks with averages and per cents and tenths of per cents, which haunt him waking and sleeping, as if they were the object of his efforts. And more than that, and above all, I do not want him made an automaton. I do not want him to become abjectly obedient. I do not want his free initiative destroyed. I want him, by virtue of his education, to be well-equipped bodily and mentally to face life and its problems.

This is my second point: That parents, conservatives and radicals, criticise the school

1st, As the producer of unhealthy bodies;

2d, As teaching matter inappropriate to life; or rather, perhaps, as not teaching what is appropriate to life;

3d, As perverting truth to serve a political and religious system; and as putting an iron mould upon the will of youth, destroying all spontaneity and freedom of expression.

The third critic is the teacher. Owing to his peculiarly dependent position, it is very, very seldom that any really vital criticism comes out of the mouth of an ordinary employé in the public school service: first, if he has any subversive ideas, he dares not voice them for fear of his job; second, it is extremely unlikely that any one with subversive ideas either will apply for the job, or having applied, will get it; and third, if through some fortuitous combination of circumstances, a rebellious personage has smuggled himself into the camp, with the naive notion that he is going to work reforms in the system, he finds before long that the system is rather remoulding him; he falls into the routine prescribed, and before long ceases to struggle against it.

Still, however conservative and system-logged teachers may be, they will all agree upon one criticism; viz., that they have too much to do; that it is utterly impossible for them to do justice to every pupil; that with from thirty to fifty pupils all depending upon one teacher for instruc-

tion, it is out of the question to give any single one sufficient attention, to say nothing of any special attention
which his peculiar backwardness might require. He could
do so only at the expense of injustice to the rest.

And, indeed, the best teacher in the world could not
attend properly to the mental needs of fifty children, nor
even of thirty. Furthermore, this overcrowding makes
necessary the stiff regulation, the formal discipline, in
the maintenance of which so much of the teacher's energy
is wasted. The everlasting roll-call, the record of tardi-
ness and absence, the eye forever on the watch to see who
is whispering, the ear forever on the alert to catch the
scraper of feet, the mischievous disturber, the irrepressi-
ble noisemaker; with such a divided and subdivided attention, how is it possible to teach?

Here and there we find a teacher with original ideas,
not of subjects to be taught, but of the means of teaching. Sometimes there is one who inwardly revolts at
what he has to teach, and takes such means as he can to
counteract the glorifications of political aggrandizement,
with which our geographies and histories are redolent.

In general, however, public school teachers, like government clerks, believe very much in the system whereby
they live.

What they do find fault with, and what they have very
much reason to find fault with, is not the school system,
but the counteracting influences of bad homes. Teachers
are often heard to say that they think they could
do far better with the children, if they had entire control
of them, or, as they more commonly express themselves,
"if only their parents had some common sense!" Lessons
of order, neatness, cleanliness, and hygiene, are often entirely thrown away, because the children regard them as
statements to be memorized, not things to be practised.

Those children whose mothers know nothing of ventilation, the necessity for exercise, the chemistry of food, and the functioning of the organs of the body, will forget instructions because they are never made part of their lives. (Which criticism is a sort of confirmation of that sage observation: "If you want to reform a man, begin with his grandmother.")

So much for criticism.

What, now, can we offer in the way of suggestions for reform? Speaking abstractly, I should say that the purpose of education should be to furnish a child with such fundamental knowledge and habits as will preserve and strengthen his body, and make him a self-reliant social being, having an all-around acquaintance with the life which is to surround him and an adaptability to circumstances which will render him able to meet varying conditions.

But we are immediately confronted by certain practical queries, when we attempt to conceive such a school system.

The fact is that the training of the body should be begun in very early childhood; and can never be rightly done in a city. No other animal than man ever conceived such a frightful apparatus for depriving its young of the primary rights of physical existence as the human city. The mass of our city children know very little of nature. What they have learned of it through occasional picnics, excursions, visits in the country, etc., they have learned as a foreign thing, having little relation to themselves; their "natural" habitat is one of lifeless brick and mortar, wire and iron, poles, pavements, and noise. Yet all this ought to be utterly foreign to children. *This* ought to be the thing visited once in a while, not lived in.

There is no pure air in a city; it is *all* poisoned. Yet

the first necessity of lunged animals—especially little ones —is pure air. Moreover, every child ought to know the names and ways of life of the things it eats; how to grow them, etc. How are gardens possible in a city? Every child should know trees, not as things he has read about, but as familiar presences in his life, which he recognizes as quickly as his eyes greet them. He should know his oneness with nature, not through the medium of a theory, but through feeling it daily and hourly. He should know the birds by their songs, and by the quick glimpse of them among the foliage; the insect in its home, the wild flower on its stalk, the fruit where it hangs. Can this be done in a city?

It is the city that is wrong, and its creations can never be right; they may be improved; they can never be what they should.

Let me quote Luther Burbank here: he expressed so well, and just in the tumultuous disorder and un-co-ordination dear to a child's soul, the early rights of children. "Every child should have mud-pies, grasshoppers, water-bugs, tadpoles, frogs, mud-turtles, elderberries, wild strawberries, acorns, chestnuts, trees to climb, brooks to wade in, water-lilies, woodchucks, bats, bees, butterflies, various animals to pet, hay-fields, pine-cones, rocks to roll, sand, snakes, huckleberries, and hornets; and any child who has been deprived of these has been deprived of the best part of his education." He is of opinion that until ten years of age, these things should be the real educators of children,—not books. I agree with him. But neither city homes nor city schools can give children these things. Furthermore, I believe that education should be integral; that the true school must combine physical and intellectual education from the beginning to the end. But I am confronted by the fact that this is impossible to the mass of the people, because of the economic condition in which we are all floundering.

What is possible can be only a compromise. Physical education will go on in the home principally, and intellectual education in the school. Something might be done to organize the teaching of parents; lectures and demonstrations at the public schools might be given weekly, in the evenings, for parents, by competent nurses or hygienists. But they would remain largely ineffective. Until the whole atrocious system of herding working people in close-built cities, by way of making them serviceable cogwheels in the capitalistic machine for grinding out rent and profit, comes to an end, the physical education of children will remain at best a pathetic compromise.

We have left to consider what may be done in the way of improving intellectual education. What is really necessary for a child to know which he is not taught now? and what is taught that is unnecessary?

As to reading and writing there is no dispute, though there is much dispute about the way of doing it. But beyond that children should know—*things;* from their earlier school days they should know the geography of their own locality, not rehearsing it from a book, but by going over the ground, having the relations of places explained to them, and by being shown how to model relief maps themselves. They should know the indications of the weather, being taught the use of instruments for measuring air-pressures, temperatures, amount of sunshine, etc.; they should know the special geology of their own locality, the nature of the soil and its products, through practical exhibition; they should be allowed to construct, from clay, stone, or brick, such little buildings as they usually like to make, and from them the simple principles of geometry taught. You see, every school needs a big yard, and play-rooms with tools in them,— the use of which tools they should be taught.

Arithmetic, to be sure, they need to know—but arithmetic connected with things. Let them learn fractions by cutting up things and putting them together, and not be bothered by abstractions running into the hundreds of thousands, the millions, which never in time will they use. And drop all that tiresome years' work in interest and per cent; if decimals are understood, every one who has need will be amply able to work out systems of interest when necessary.

Children should know the industrial life through which they live, into which they are probably going. They should see how cloth is woven, thread is spun, shoes are made, iron forged and wrought; again not alone by written description, but by eye-witness. They should, as they grow older, learn the history of the arts of peace.

What they do not need to know, is so much of the details of the history of destruction; the general facts and results of wars are sufficient. They do not need to be impressed with the details of killings, which they sensibly forget, and inevitably also.

Moreover, the revolting patriotism which is being inculcated, whereby children learn to be proud of their country, not for its contributions to the general enlightenment of humanity, but for its crimes against humanity; whereby they are taught to consider themselves, their country, their flag, their institutions, as things to be upheld and maintained, right or wrong; whereby the stupid and criminal life of the soldier is exalted as honorable, should be wholly omitted from the educational system.

However, it is utterly impossible to expect that it will be, by anything short of general public sentiment against it; and at present such sentiment is for it. I have alluded before to the function of the statesman in directing education. So long as schools are maintained by governments, the Statesman, not the true educator, will determine what sort of history is to be taught; and it will be what it is now, only continually growing worse. Political institutions must justify themselves to the young generation. They begin by training childish minds to believe that what they do is to be accepted, not criticised. A history becomes little better than a catechism of patriotic formulas in glorification of the State.

Now there is no way of escaping this, for those who disapprove it, short of eliminating the statesman, establishing voluntarily supported schools, wherein wholly different notions shall be taught; in which the spirit of teaching history shall be one of honest statement and fearless criticism; wherein the true image of war and the army and all that it means shall be honestly given.

The really Ideal School, which would not be a compromise, would be a boarding school built in the country, having a farm attached, and workshops where useful crafts might be learned, in daily connection with intellectual training. It presupposes teachers able to train little children to habits of health, order, and neatness, in the utmost detail, and yet not tyrants or rigid disciplinarians. In free contact with nature, the children would learn to use their limbs as nature meant, feel their intimate relationship with the growing life of other sorts, form a profound respect for work and an estimate of the value of it; wish to become real doers in the world, and not mere gatherers in of other men's products; and with the respect for work, the appreciation of work, the desire to work, will come the pride of the true workman who will know how to maintain his dignity and the dignity of what he does.

At present the major portion of our working people are sorry they are working people (as they have good reason to be). They take little joy or pride in what they do; they consider themselves as less gifted and less valuable persons in society than those who have amassed wealth and, by virtue of that amassment, live upon their employees; or those who by attaining book knowledge have gotten out of the field of manual production, and lead an easier life. They educate their children in the hope that these, at least, may attain that easier existence, without work, which has been beyond them. Even when such parents themselves have dreams of a reorganization of society, wherein all shall labor and all have leisure due, they impress upon the children that no one should be a common workingman if he can help it. Workingmen are slaves, and it is not well to be a slave.

Our radicals fail to realize that to accomplish the re-organization of work, it is necessary to have *workers*,— and workers with the free spirit, the rebellious spirit, which will consider its own worth and refuse to accept the slavish conditions of capitalism. These must be bred in schools where work is done, and done proudly, and in full consciousness of its value; where the dubious services of the capitalist will likewise be rated at their true worth; and no man reckoned as above another, unless he has done a greater social service. Where political institutions and the politicians who oper-ate them—judges, lawmakers, or executives— will be candidly criticised, and repudiated when justice dictates so, whether in the teaching of their past history, or their present actions in current events.

Whether the workers, upon whom so many drains are

already made, will be able to establish and maintain such schools, is a question to be solved upon trial through their organizations.

The question is, Will you breed men for the service of the Cannon, to be aimed at you in the hour of Strikes and Revolts, men to uphold the machine which is crushing you, or will you train them in the knowledge of the true worth of Labor and a determination to reorganize it as it should be?

Sex Slavery

NIGHT in a prison cell! A chair, a bed, a small washstand, four blank walls, ghastly in the dim light from the corridor without, a narrow window, barred and sunken in the stone, a grated door! Beyond its hideous iron latticework, within the ghastly walls,—a man! An old man, gray-haired and wrinkled, lame and suffering. There he sits, in his great loneliness, shut in from all the earth. There he walks, to and fro, within his measured space, apart from all he loves! There, for every night in five long years to come, he will walk alone, while the white age-flakes drop upon his head, while the last years of the winter of life gather and pass, and his body draws near the ashes. Every night, for five long years to come, he will sit alone, this chattel slave, whose hard toil is taken by the State,—and without recompense save that the Southern planter gave his negroes,—every night he will sit there so within those four white walls. Every night, for five long years to come, a suffering woman will lie upon her bed, longing, longing for the end of those three thousand days; longing for the kind face, the patient hand, that in so many years had never failed her. Every night, for five long years to come, the proud spirit must rebel, the loving heart must bleed, the broken home must lie desecrated. As I am speaking now, as you are listening, there within the cell of that accursed penitentiary whose stones have soaked up the sufferings of so many victims, murdered, as truly as any outside their walls, by that slow rot which eats away existence inch-meal,—as I am speaking now, as you are listening, *there sits Moses Harman!*

Why? Why, when murder now is stalking in your streets, when dens of infamy are so thick within your city that competition has forced down the price of prostitution to the level of the wages of your starving shirt-makers; when robbers sit in State and national Senate and House, when the boasted "bulwark of our liberties," the elective franchise, has become a U. S. dice-box, where-with great gamblers play away your liberties; when de-bauchees of the worst type hold all your public offices and dine off the food of fools who support them, why, then, sits Moses Harman there within his prison cell? If he is so *great* a criminal, why is he not with the rest of the spawn of crime, dining at Delmonico's or enjoying a trip to Europe? If he is so bad a man, why in the name of wonder did he ever get in the penitentiary?

Ah, no; it is not because he has done any evil thing; but because he, a pure enthusiast, searching, searching always for the cause of misery of the kind which he loved with that broad love of which only the pure soul is capa-ble, searched for the data of evil. And searching so he found the vestibule of life to be a prison cell; the holiest and purest part of the temple of the body, if indeed one part can be holier or purer than another, the altar where the most devotional love in truth should be laid, he found this altar ravished, despoiled, trampled upon. He found little babies, helpless, voiceless little things, generated in lust, cursed with impure moral natures, cursed, prenatally, with the germs of disease, forced into the world to struggle and to suffer, to hate themselves, to hate their mothers for bearing them, to hate society and to be hated by it in return,—a bane upon self and race, draining the lees of crime.   And he said, this felon with the stripes upon his body, "Let the mothers of the race go free! Let the little children be pure love children, born of the mutual desire for parentage.   Let the manacles be broken from the shackled slave, that no more slaves be born, no more tyrants conceived."

He looked, this obscenist, looked with clear eyes into this ill-got thing you call morality, sealed with the seal of marriage, and saw in it the consummation of *im*-morality, impurity, and injustice.   He beheld every married woman what she is, a bonded slave, who takes her master's name, her master's bread, her master's commands, and serves her master's passion; who passes through the ordeal of pregnancy and the throes of travail at *his* dictation,—not at her desire; who can control no property, not even her own body, without his consent, and from whose straining arms the children she bears may be torn at his pleasure, or willed away while they are yet unborn.   It is said the English language has a sweeter word than any other,—*home*.   But Moses Harman looked beneath the word and saw the fact,—a prison more horrible than that where he is sitting now, whose corridors radiate over all the earth, and with so many cells, that none may count them.

Yes, our Masters!   The earth is a prison, the marriage-bed is a cell, women are the prisoners, and you are the keepers!

He saw, this corruptionist, how in those cells are perpetrated such outrages as are enough to make the cold sweat stand upon the forehead, and the nails clench, and the teeth set, and the lips grow white in agony and hatred. And he saw too how from those cells might none come forth to break her fetters, how no slave dare cry out, how all these murders are done quietly, beneath the shelter-shadow of home, and sanctified by the angelic benediction of a piece of paper, within the silence-shade of a marriage certificate, Adultery and Rape stalk freely and at ease.

Yes, for that is adultery where woman submits herself sexually to man, without desire on her part, for the sake of "keeping him virtuous," "keeping him at home," the women say. (Well, if a man did not love me and respect himself enough to be "virtuous" without prostituting me, he might go, and welcome. He has no virtue to keep.) And that is rape, where a man forces himself sexually upon a woman whether he is licensed by the marriage law to do it or not. And that is the vilest of all tyranny where a man compels the woman he says he loves, to endure the agony of bearing children that she does not want, and for whom, as is the rule rather than the exception, they cannot properly provide. It is worse than any other human oppression; it is fairly *God*-like! To the sexual tyrant there is no parallel upon earth; one must go to the skies to find a fiend who thrusts life upon his children only to starve and curse and outcast and damn them! And only through the marriage law is such tyranny possible. The man who deceives a woman outside of marriage (and mind you, such a amn will deceive *in* marriage too) may deny his own child, if he is mean enough. He cannot tear it from her arms—he cannot touch it! The girl he wronged, thanks to your very pure and tender morality-standard, may die in the street for want of food. *He* cannot force his hated presence upon her again. But his wife, gentlemen, his wife, the woman he respects so much that he consents to let her merge her individuality into his, lose her identity and become his chattel, his wife he may not only force unwelcome children upon, outrage at his own good pleasure, and keep as a general cheap and convenient piece of furniture, but if she does not get a divorce (and she cannot for such cause) he can follow her wherever she goes, come into her house, eat her food, force her into the cell, *kill* her by virtue of his sexual authority! And she has no redress unless he is indiscreet enough to abuse her in some less brutal but unlicensed manner. I know a case in your city where a woman was followed so for ten years by her husband. I believe he finally developed grace enough to die; please applaud him for the only decent thing he ever did.

Oh, is it not rare, all this talk about the preservation of morality by marriage law! O splendid carefulness to preserve that which you have not got! O height and depth of purity, which fears so much that the children will not know who their fathers are, because, forsooth, they must rely upon their mother's word instead of the hired certification of some priest of the Church, or the Law! I wonder if the children would be improved to know what their fathers have done. I would rather, much rather, not know who my father was than know he had been a tyrant to my mother. I would rather, much rather, be illegitimate according to the statutes of men, than illegitimate according to the unchanging law of Nature. For what is it to be legitimate, born "according to law"? It is to be, nine cases out of ten, the child of a man who acknowledges his fatherhood simply because he is forced to do so, and whose conception of virtue is realized by the statement that "a woman's duty is to keep her husband at home"; to be the child of a woman who

cares more for the benediction of Mrs. Grundy than the
simple honor of her lover's word, and conceives prostitution to be purity and duty when exacted of her by her
husband. It is to have Tyranny as your progenitor, and
slavery as your prenatal cradle. It is to run the risk of
unwelcome birth, "legal" constitutional weakness, morals
corrupted before birth, possibly a murder instinct, the
inheritance of excessive sexuality or no sexuality, either
of which is disease. It is to have the value of a piece
of paper, a rag from the tattered garments of the "Social
Contract," set above health, beauty, talent or goodness;
for I never yet had difficulty in obtaining the admission
that illegitimate children are nearly always prettier and
brighter than others, even from conservative women.
And how supremely disgusting it is to see them look from
their own puny, sickly, lust-born children, upon whom
lie the chain-traces of their own terrible servitude, look
from these to some healthy, beautiful "natural" child,
and say, "What a pity its *mother* wasn't virtuous!"
Never a word about *their* children's fathers' virtue, they
know too much! Virtue! Disease, stupidity, criminality! What an *obscene* thing "virtue" is!

What is it to be illegitimate? To be despised, or
pitied, by those whose spite or whose pity isn't worth the
breath it takes to return it. To be, possibly, the child
of some man contemptible enough to deceive a woman;
the child of some woman whose chief crime was belief
in the man she loved. To be free from the prenatal
curse of a slave mother, to come into the world without
the permission of any law-making set of tyrants who
assume to corner the earth, and say what terms the unborn must make for the privilege of coming into existence. This is legitimacy and illegitimacy! Choose.

The man who walks to and fro in his cell in Lansing

penitentiary to-night, this vicious man, said: "The mothers of the race are lifting their dumb eyes to me, their sealed lips to me, their agonizing hearts to me. They are seeking, seeking for a voice! The unborn in their helplessness, are pleading from their prisons, pleading for a voice! The criminals, with the unseen ban upon their souls, that has pushed them, pushed them to the vortex, out of their whirling hells, are looking, waiting for a voice! *I will be their voice*. I will unmask the outrages of the marriage-bed. I will make known how criminals are born. I will make one outcry that shall be heard, and let what will be, *be!*" He cried out through the letter of Dr. Markland, that a young mother lacerated by unskilful surgery in the birth of her babe, but recovering from a subsequent successful operation, had been stabbed, remorselessly, cruelly, brutally stabbed, not with a knife, but with the procreative organ of her husband, stabbed to the doors of death, and yet there was no redress!

And because he called a spade a spade, because he named that organ by its own name, so given in Webster's dictionary and in every medical journal in the country, because of this Moses Harman walks to and fro in his cell to-night. He gave a concrete example of the effect of sex slavery, and for it he is imprisoned. It remains for us now to carry on the battle, and lift the standard where they struck him down, to scatter broadcast the knowledge of this crime of society against a man and the reason for it; to inquire into this vast system of licensed crime, its cause and its effect, broadly upon the race. The Cause! Let woman ask herself, "Why am I the slave of Man? Why is my brain said not to be the equal of his brain? Why is my work not paid equally with his? Why must my body be controlled by my husband? Why may he take my labor in the household, giving me in exchange what he deems fit? Why may he take my children from me? Will them away while yet unborn?" Let every woman ask.

There are two reasons why, and these ultimately reducible to a single principle—the authoritarian, supreme-power, *God*-idea, and its two instruments, the Church—that is, the priests—and the State—that is, the legislators.

From the birth of the Church, out of the womb of Fear and the fatherhood of Ignorance, it has taught the inferiority of woman. In one form or another through the various mythical legends of the various mythical creeds, runs the undercurrent of the belief in the fall of man through the persuasion of woman, her subjective condition as punishment, her natural vileness, total depravity, etc.; and from the days of Adam until now the Christian Church, with which we have specially to deal, has made *woman* the excuse, the scapegoat for the evil deeds of *man*. So thoroughly has this idea permeated Society that numbers of those who have utterly repudiated the Church, are nevertheless soaked in this stupefying narcotic to true morality. So pickled is the male creation with the vinegar of Authoritarianism, that even those who have gone further and repudiated the State still cling to the god, Society as it is, still hug the old theological idea that they are to be "heads of the family" —to that wonderful formula "of simple proportion" that "Man is the head of the Woman even as Christ is the head of the Church." No longer than a week since an Anarchist (?) said to me, "I will be boss in my own house" —a "Communist-Anarchist," if you please, who doesn't believe in *"my* house." About a year ago a noted libertarian speaker said, in my presence, that his sister, who possessed a fine voice and had joined a concert troupe, should "stay at home with her children; that is *her place*." The old Church idea! This man was a Socialist, and since an Anarchist; yet his highest idea for woman was serfhood to husband and children, in the present mockery called "home." Stay at home, ye malcontents! Be patient, obedient, submissive! Darn our socks, mend our shirts, wash our dishes, get our meals, wait on us and *mind the children!* Your fine voices are not to delight the public nor yourselves; your inventive genius is not to work, your fine art taste is not to be cultivated, your business faculties are not to be developed; you made the great mistake of being born with them, suffer for your folly! You are *women!* therefore housekeepers, servants, waiters, and child's nurses!

At Macon, in the sixth century, says August Bebel, the fathers of the Church met and proposed the decision of the question, "Has woman a soul?" Having ascertained that the permission to own a nonentity wasn't going to injure any of their parsnips, a small majority vote decided the momentous question in our favor. Now, holy fathers, it was a tolerably good scheme on your part to offer the reward of your pitiable "salvation or damnation" (odds in favor of the latter) as a bait for the hook of earthly submission; it wasn't a bad sop in those days of Faith and Ignorance. But fortunately fourteen hundred years have made it stale. You, tyrant radicals (?), have no heaven to offer,—you have no delightful chimeras in the form of "merit cards"; you have (save the mark) the respect, the good offices, the smiles —of a slave-holder! This in return for our chains! Thanks!

The question of souls is old—we demand our bodies, now. We are tired of promises, God is deaf, and his

church is our worst enemy. Against it we bring the
charge of being the moral (or immoral) force which lies
behind the tyranny of the State. And the State has
divided the loaves and fishes with the Church, the magistrates, like the priests take marriage fees; the two fetters
of Authority have gone into partnership in the business
of granting patent-rights to parents for the privilege of
reproducing themselves, and the State cries as the
Church cried of old, and cries now: "See how we protect
women!" The State has done more. It has often been
said to me, by women with decent masters, who had no
idea of the outrages practiced on their less fortunate
sisters, "Why don't the wives leave?"

Why don't you run, when your feet are chained together? Why don't you cry out when a gag is on your
lips? Why don't you raise your hands above your head
when they are pinned fast to your sides? Why don't you
spend thousands of dollars when you haven't a cent in
your pocket? Why don't you go to the seashore or the
mountains, you fools scorching with city heat? If there
is one thing more than another in this whole accursed
tissue of false society, which makes me angry, it is the
asinine stupidity which with the true phlegm of impenetrable dullness says, "Why don't the women leave!"
Will you tell me where they will go and what they shall
do? When the State, the legislators, has given to itself,
the politicians, the utter and absolute control of the opportunity to live; when, through this precious monopoly,
already the market of labor is so overstocked that workmen and workwomen are cutting each others' throats
for the dear privilege of serving their lords; when girls
are shipped from Boston to the south and north, shipped
in carloads, like cattle, to fill the dives of New Orleans
or the lumber-camp hells of my own state (Michigan),
when seeing and hearing these things reported every day,

the proper prudes exclaim, "Why don't the women leave," they simply beggar the language of contempt.

When America passed the fugitive slave law compelling men to catch their fellows more brutally than runaway dogs, Canada, aristocratic, unrepublican Canada, still stretched her arms to those who might reach her. But there is no refuge upon earth for the enslaved sex. Right where we are, there we must dig our trenches, and win or die.

This, then, is the tyranny of the State; it denies, to both woman and man, the right to earn a living, and grants it as a privilege to a favored few who for that favor must pay ninety per cent. toll to the granters of it. These two things, the mind domination of the Church, and the body domination of the State are the causes of Sex Slavery.

First of all, it has introduced into the world the constructed crime of obscenity: it has set up such a peculiar standard of morals that to speak the names of the sexual organs is to commit the most brutal outrage. It reminds me that in your city you have a street called "Callowhill." Once it was called Gallows' Hill, for the elevation to which it leads, now known as "Cherry Hill," has been the last touching place on earth for the feet of many a victim murdered by the Law. But the sound of the word became too harsh; so they softened it, though the murders are still done, and the black shadow of the Gallows still hangs on the City of Brotherly Love. Obscenity has done the same; it has placed virtue in the shell of an idea, and labelled all "good" which dwells within the sanction of Law and respectable (?) custom; and all bad which contravenes the usage of the shell. It has lowered the dignity of the human body, below the level of all other animals. Who thinks a dog is impure or obscene because its body is not covered with suffocating and annoying clothes? What would you think of the meanness of a man who would put a skirt upon his horse and compel it to walk or run with such a thing impeding its limbs? Why, the "Society for the Prevention of Cruelty to Animals" would arrest him, take the beast from him, and he would be sent to a lunatic asylum for treatment on the score of an *impure* mind. And yet, gentlemen, you expect your wives, the creatures you say you respect and love, to wear the longest skirts and the highest necked clothing, in order to conceal the *obscene human body*. There is no society for the prevention of cruelty to women. And you, yourselves, though a little better, look at the heat you wear in this roasting weather! How you curse your poor body with the wool you steal from the sheep! How you punish yourselves to sit in a crowded house with coats and vests on, because dead Mme. Grundy is shocked at the "vulgarity" of shirt sleeves, or the naked arm!

Look how the ideal of beauty has been marred by this obscenity notion. Divest yourselves of prejudice for once. Look at some fashion-slaved woman, her waist surrounded by a high-board fence called a corset, her shoulders and hips angular from the pressure above and below, her feet narrowest where they should be widest, the body fettered by her everlasting prison skirt, her hair fastened tight enough to make her head ache and surmounted by a thing of neither sense nor beauty, called a hat, ten to one a hump upon her back like a dromedary,—look at her, and then imagine such a thing as that carved in marble! Fancy a statue in Fairmount Park with a corset and bustle on. Picture to yourselves the image of the equestrienne. We are permitted to ride, providing we sit in a position ruinous to the horse; providing we wear a riding-habit long enough to hide

the obscene human foot, weighed down by ten pounds
of gravel to cheat the Wind in its free blowing, so running the risk of disabling ourselves completely should
accident throw us from the saddle. Think how we swim!
We must even wear clothing in the water, and run the
gauntlet of derision, if we dare battle in the surf minus
stockings! Imagine a fish trying to make headway with
a water-soaked flannel garment upon it. Nor are you
yet content. The vile standard of obscenity even kills
the little babies with clothes. The human race is murdered, horribly, "in the name of" Dress.

And in the name of Purity what lies are told! What
queer morality it has engendered. For fear of it you
dare not tell your own children the truth about their
birth; the most sacred of all functions, the creation of a
human being, is a subject for the most miserable false-
hood. When they come to you with a simple, straight-
forward question, which they have a right to ask, you
say, "Don't ask such questions," or tell some silly hollow-
log story; or you explain the incomprehensibility by
another—God! You say "God made you." You know
you are lying when you say it. You know, or you ought
to know, that the source of inquiry will not be dammed
up so. You know that what you could explain purely,
reverently, rightly (if you have any purity in you), will
be learned through many blind gropings, and that around
it will be cast the shadow-thought of wrong, embryo'd
by your denial and nurtured by this social opinion everywhere prevalent. If you do not know this, then you are
blind to facts and deaf to Experience.

Think of the double social standard the enslavement
of our sex has evolved. Women considering themselves
very pure and very moral, will sneer at the street-walker,
yet admit to their homes the very men who victimized
the street-walker. Men, at their best, will pity the pros-

titute, while they themselves are the worst kind of prostitutes. Pity yourselves, gentlemen—you need it!

How many times do you see where a man or woman has shot another through jealousy! The standard of purity has decided that it is right, "it shows spirit," "it is justifiable" to—murder a human being for doing exactly what you did yourself,—love the same woman or same man! Morality! Honor! Virtue!! Passing from the moral to the physical phase; take the statistics of any insane asylum, and you will find that, out of the different classes, unmarried women furnish the largest cne. To preserve your cruel, vicious, indecent standard of purity (?) you drive your daughters insane, while your wives are killed with excess. Such is marriage. Don't take my word for it; go through the report of any asylum or the annals of any graveyard.

Look how your children grow up. Taught from their earliest infancy to curb their love natures—restrained at every turn! Your blasting lies would even blacken a child's kiss. Little girls must not be tomboyish, must not go barefoot, must not climb trees, must not learn to swim, must not do anything they desire to do which Madame Grundy has decreed "improper." Little boys are laughed at as effeminate, silly girl-boys if they want to make patchwork or play with a doll. Then when they grow up, "Oh! Men don't care for home or children as women do!" Why should they, when the deliberate effort of your life has been to crush that nature out of them. "Women can't rough it like men." Train any animal, or any plant, as you train your girls, and it won't be able to rough it either. Now *will* somebody tell me why either sex should hold a corner on athletic sports? Why any child should not have free use of its limbs?

These are the effects of your purity standard, your marriage law. This is your work—look at it! Half your children dying under five years of age, your girls insane, your married women walking corpses, your men so bad that they themselves often admit *Prostitution holds against* PURITY *a bond of indebtedness.* This is the beautiful effect of your god, Marriage, before which Natural Desire must abase and belie itself. Be proud of it!

Now for the remedy. It is in one word, the only word that ever brought equity anywhere—LIBERTY! Centuries upon centuries of liberty is the only thing that will cause the disintegration and decay of these pestiferous ideas. Liberty was all that calmed the bloodwaves of religious persecution! You cannot cure serfhood by any other substitution. Not for you to say "in this way shall the race love." Let the race *alone*.

Will there not be atrocious crimes? Certainly. He is a fool who says there will not be. But you can't stop them by committing the arch-crime and setting a block between the spokes of Progress-wheels. You will never get right until you start right.

As for the final outcome, it matters not one iota. I have my ideal, and it is very pure, and very sacred to me. But yours, equally sacred, may be different and we may both be wrong. But certain am I that with free contract, that form of sexual association will survive which is best adapted to time and place, thus producing the highest evolution of the type. Whether that shall be monogamy, variety, or promiscuity matters naught to us; it is the business of the future, to which we dare not dictate.

For freedom spoke Moses Harman, and for this he received the felon's brand. For this he sits in his cell to-night. Whether it is possible that his sentence be shortened, we do not know. We can only try. Those who would help us try, let me ask to put your signatures to this simple request for pardon addressed to Benj. amin Harrison. To those who desire more fully to inform themselves before signing; I say: Your conscientiousness is praiseworthy—come to me at the close of the meeting and I will quote the exact language of the Markland letter. To those extreme Anarchists who cannot bend their dignity to ask pardon for an offense not committed, and of an authority they cannot recognize, let me say: Moses Harman's back is bent, low bent, by the brute force of the Law, and though I would never ask anyone to bow for himself, I can ask it, and easily ask it, for him who fights the slave's battle. Your dignity is criminal; every hour behind the bars is a seal to your partnership with Comstock. No one can hate petitions worse than I; no one has less faith in them than I. But for *my* champion I am willing to try any means that invades no other's right, even though I have little hope in it.

If, beyond these, there are those here to-night who have ever forced sexual servitude from a wife, those who have prostituted themselves in the name of Virtue, those who have brought diseased, immoral or unwelcome children to the light, without the means of provision for them, and yet will go from this hall and say, "Moses Harman is an unclean man—a man rewarded by just punishment," then to *you* I say, and may the words ring deep within your ears UNTIL YOU DIE: Go on! Drive your sheep to the shambles! Crush that old, sick, crippled man beneath your Juggernaut! In the name of Virtue, Purity and Morality, do it! In the name of God, Home, and Heaven, do it! In the name of the Nazarene who preached the golden rule, do it! In the name of Justice, Principle, and Honor, do it! In the name of Bravery and Magnanimity put yourself on the side of the robber in the government halls, the murderer in the political convention, the libertine in public places, the whole brute force of the police, the constabulary, the court, and the penitentiary, to persecute one poor old man who stood alone against your licensed crime! Do it. And if Moses Harman dies within your "Kansas Hell," be satisfied *when you have murdered him!* Kill him! And you hasten the day when the Future shall bury you ten thousand fathoms deep beneath its curses. Kill him! And the stripes upon his prison clothes shall lash you like the knout! Kill him! And the insane shall glitter hate at you with their wild eyes, the unborn babes shall cry their blood upon you, and the graves that you have filled in the name of Marriage, shall yield food for a race that will pillory you, until the memory of your atrocity has become a nameless ghost, flitting with the shades of Torquemada, Calvin and Jehovah over the horizon of the World!

Would you smile to see him dead? Would you say, "We are rid of this obscenist"? Fools! The corpse would laugh at you from its cold eyelids! The motionless lips would mock, and the solemn hands, the pulseless, folded hands, in their quietness would write the last indictment, which neither Time nor you can efface. Kill him! And you write his glory and your shame! Moses Harman in his felon stripes stands far above you now, and Moses Harman *dead* will live on, immortal in the race he died to free! Kill him!

Literature the Mirror of Man

P ERHAPS I had better say the Mirror-reflection,—
the reflection of all that he has been and is, the
hinting fore-flashing of something of what he
may become. In so considering it, let it be understood
that I speak of no particular form of literature, but the
entire body of a people's expressed thought, preserved
either traditionally, in writing, or in print.

The majority of lightly thinking, fairly read people,
who make use of the word "literature" rather easily, do
so with a very indistinct idea of its content. To them it
usually means a certain limited form of human expression, chiefly works of the imagination—poetry, drama, the
various forms of the novel. History, philosophy, science
are rather frowning names,—stern second cousins, as it
were, to the beguiling companions of their pleasant leisure
hours,—not legitimately "literature." Biography,—well,
it depends on who writes it! If it can be made so much
like a work of fiction that the subject sketched serves the
purposes of a fictive hero, why then—maybe.

To such talkers about literature, evidence of familiarity
with it, and title to have one's opinions thereon asked and
respected, are witnessed by the ability to run glibly off
the names of the personages in the dramas of Ibsen,
Björnson, Maeterlinck, Hauptmann or Shaw; or in the

novels of Gorki, Andreyev, Tolstoy, Zola, Maupassant, Hardy, and the dozen or so of lesser lights who revolve with these through the cycle of the magazine issues.

Not only do these same people thus limit the field of literature, (at least in their ordinary conversation,—if you press them they will dubiously admit that the field may be extended) but they are also possessed of the notion that only one particular mode even of fiction, is in fact the genuine thing. That this mode has not always been in vogue they are aware; and they allow other modes to have been literature in the past, as a sort of kindly concession to the past—a blanket-indulgence to its unevolved state. At present, however, no indulgences are allowed; whatever is not the mode, is anathema; it is not literature at all. When confronted by the *very* great names of the Past, which they can neither consign to oblivion, nor patronize by toleration for their undeveloped condition, names which are names for all ages, which they need to use as conjuration words in their comparisons and criticisms, names such as Shakespeare or Hugo, they complacently close their eyes to contradictions and swear that fundamentally these men's works *are in the modern mode, the accepted mode, the one and only enduring mode,* the mode that they approve.

"Which is?"—I hear you ask. *Which is* what they are pleased to call "Realism."

If you wish to know how far they are obsessed by this notion, go pick yourself a quiet corner in some café where light literature readers meet to make comparisons, and listen to the comments. Before very long, voices will be getting loud about some character at present stalking across the pages of the magazines, or bestirring itself among the latest ton of novel; and the dispute will be, "Does such a type exist?"—"Of course he exists,"—"He

does not exist,"—"He must exist,"—"He cannot exist,"—
"Under such conditions,"—"There are no such conditions,"—"But be reasonable: you have not been in all
places, and you cannot say there may not be such conditions; supposing—" "All right: I will give you the conditions; all the same, no man would act so under any conditions." "I swear L have seen such men—" "Impossible—" "What is there impossible about it?—"

And the voices get louder and louder, as the disputants
proceed to pick the character to pieces, speech by speech,
and action by action, till, nothing being left, each finally
subsides somehow, each confirmed in his own opinion,
each convinced that the main purpose of literature—
Realism—has either been served, or not served, by the
author under discussion.   To such disputants "Literature
the Mirror of Man," means that only such literature as
gives so-called absolutely faithful representations of life
as it is demonstrably lived, is a genuine Mirror.   No
author is to be considered worthy of a place, unless his
works can be at least twisted to fit this conception.   With
some slight refinement of idea, in so far as it recognizes
the obscurer recesses of the mind as entitled to represen-
tation as well as the externals, it corresponds to the one-
time development of portrait painting, which esteemed it
necessary to paint the exact number of hairs in the wart
on Oliver Cromwell's nose, in order to have a true likeness of him.

As before suggested, I do not, when I speak of Literature as the Mirror of Man, have any such 12x18 mirror
in view; nor the limitation of literature to any one
form of it, to any one age of it, to any set of standard names; nor the limitation of Man to any pre-
conceived notion of just what he may logically be
allowed to be.   The composite image we are seeking
to find is an image wrought as much of his dreams

of what he would like to be, as of his actual being; that is no true picture of Man, which does not include his cravings for the impossible, as well as his daily performance of the possible. Indeed, the logical, calculable man, the man who under certain circumstances may be figured out to turn murderer and under others saint, is hardly so interesting as the illogical being who upsets the calculation by becoming neither, but something not at all predictable.

The objects of my lecture then are these:

1. To insist on a wider view of literature itself than that generally accepted.

2. To suggest to readers a more satisfactory way of considering what they read than that usually received.

3. To point to certain phases of the human appearance reflected in the mirror which are not generally noticed, but which I find interesting and suggestive.

You would think it very unreasonable, would you not, for any one to insist that because your highly polished glass backed by quicksilver, gives back so clear and excellent an image, *therefore* the watery vision you catch of yourself in the shifting, glancing ripples of a clear stream is not an image at all! With all the curious elongating and drifting and shortening back and breaking up into wavering circles, done by that unresting image, you know very certainly that is you; and if you look into the still waters of some summer pool, or mountain rain-cup, the image there is almost as sharp-lined as that in your polished glass, except for the vague tremor that seems to move under the water rather than on its surface, and suggest an ethereal something missing in your drawing-room shadow. Yet that vision conjured in the water-depth is you—surely you. Nay, even more,—that *first* image of you, you perceived when as a child you danced in the firelight and saw a misshapen darkness rising and falling along the wall in teasing mockery,—that too was surely an image of you—an image of interception, not of reflection; a blur, a vacancy, a horror, from which you fled shrieking to your mother's arms;—and yet it was the distorted outline of you.

You grew familiar with it later, amused yourself with it, twisted your hands into strange positions to see what curious shapes they would form upon the wall, and made whole stories with the shadows. Long afterward you went back to them with deliberate and careful curiosity, to see how the figures stumbled on by accident could be definitely produced, at will, according to the laws of interception.

Even so the first *Man-Images*, cast back from the blank wall of Language, are uncouth, ungraspable, vague, vacant, menacing—to the men who saw them, frightful. Mankind produced this paradox: the early *lights* of literature were *darkness!*

Later these darknesses grew less fearsome; the child-man began to jest with them; to multiply figures and send them chasing past each other up and down the wall, with fresh glee at each newly created shadow-sport. The wall at last became luminous, the shadows shining. And out of the old monosyllabic horror of the primitive legend, out of Man's fright at the projection of his own soul, out of his wide stare at those terrific giants on the wall who suddenly with shadow-like shifting became grotesque dwarfs, and mocking little beasts that danced and floated, ever most fearful because of their elusive emptiness; out of this, bit by bit, grew the steady contemplation, the gradual effacement of fright, the feeling of power and amusement, and the sense of Creative Mastery, which, understanding the shadows, began to command them, till there arose all the beauty of fairy tales and shining myths and singing legends.

Now any one who desires to see in Literature the most that there is in it; who desires to read not merely for the absorption of the moment but for the sake of permanent impression; who wishes to have an idea of Man not only as he is now, but through the whole articulate record of his existence; who would know the thoughts of his infancy and the connected course of his development,—and no one has any adequate conception of the glory of literature, unless he includes this much in it—any such a reader, I say, must find among its most attractive pages, the stories of early superstitions, the fictions of Fear, the struggles of the Race-Child's intelligence with overlooming problems. Think of the Ages and Ages that men saw the Demon Electricity riding the air; think that even now they do not know what he is; and yet he played mightily with their daily lives for all those ages. Think how this staring savage was put face to face with world-games which were spun and tossed around him, and compelled by the nature of his own activity to try to find an explanation to them; think that most of us, if we were not the heritors of the ages that have passed since then, should be staggered and outbreathed even now by all these lights and forms through which we move; and then turn to the record of those pathetic strivings of the frightened child with some little tenderness and sympathy, some solemn curiosity to know *what* men were able to think and feel when they led their lives as in a threatening Wonder-house, where everything was an Unknown, invested with crouching hostility. And never be too sure you know just how men will act, or try to act, under any conditions, if you have not read the record of what they have thought and fancied and done; and after you have read it, Oh, then you will never be sure you know! For then you will realize that every man is a burial-house, full of dead men's ghosts,—and the ghosts of very, very ancient days are there, forever whispering in an ancient, ancient tongue of ancient passions and desires, and prompting many actions which the doer thereof can give himself no accounting for.

There are two ways of reading these old stories; and as one who has gotten pleasure and profit, too, from both, I would recommend them both to be used. The first way is to read yourself backward into it as much as possible. Do not be a critic, on first reading; put the critic asleep. Let yourself *seem to believe it,* as did he who wrote it. Read it aloud, if you are where you will not annoy anybody; let the words sing themselves over your lips, as they sung themselves over the lips of the people who were dead so long ago,—in their strange far-away homes with their vanished surroundings; sung themselves, just as the wind sung through the echoing forests, and murmured back from the rocks; just as the songs slipped out of the birds' throats. You will find that half the beauty and the farce of old-time legend lies in the bare sound of it. Far, far more is it dependent on the voice, than any modern writings are. And surely, the reason is simple enough: for *it* was not *writing* in its creation; ancient literature addressed itself to the ear, always, while modern literature speaks to the eye.

If once you can get your ears washing with the sounds of the old language, as with the washing of the seas when you sit on the beach, or the lapping of the rivers when the bank-grass caresses you some idle summer afternoon, it will be much easier for you to forget that you are the child of another age and thought. You will begin to luxuriate in fancies and prefigure impossibilities; then you will know how it feels to be fancy free, loosed from the chain of the possible; and once having felt, you will also understand better, when you re-read with other intent.

When you are ready for such re-reading, then be as critical as you please,—which does not necessarily mean be condemnatory. It means rather take notice of all generals and particulars, and question them.

You will naturally pose yourself the question, Why is it that the bare sounds of these old stories are so much more vibrating, drum-like, shrilling, at times, than any modern song or poem? You will find that the mitigating influence of civilization,—knowledge, moderation,—creeping into expression, produces flat, neutral, diluted sounds,—watery words, so to speak, long-drawn out and glidingly inoffensive. In any modern writing remarkable for strength, will be found a preponderance of "barbaric yawp"—as Whitman called it.

Fear creates sharp cries; the rebound of Fear, which is Bravado, produces drum-tones, roars, and growls; unrestrained Passions howl in wind-notes, irregular, breaking short off. God carries a hammer, and Love a spear. The hymn clangs, and the love-song clashes. Through those fierce sounds one feels again hot hearts.

Those who perceive colors accompanying sounds, sense clean cut lights streaking the night-ground of these early word-pictures; sharp, hard, reds and yellows. It is our later world which has produced green tintings not to be told fom gray, nor gray from blue, nor anything from anything. In our fondness for smoothness and gradation we have attained practical colorlessness.

If it appears to you that I am talking nonsense, permit me to tell you it is because you have dulled your own powers of perception; in seeking to become too intellectually appreciative, you have lost the power to feel primitive things. Try to recover it.

Another source of interesting observation, especially in English literature of early writing: this time the eye.

It is admitted by everybody that as a serviceable instrument for expressing definite sounds in an expeditious and comprehensible manner, English written language is a woeful failure. If any inventor of a theory of symbols should, would, or could have devised such a ridiculous conception of spelling, such a hodge-podge of contradictory jumbles, he would properly have been adjudged to an insane asylum; and that, every man who ever contrived an English spelling-book, and every teacher who is obliged to worry this incongruous mess through the steadily revolting reason-and-memory process of children, is ably convinced. But Man, English-speaking Man, has actually—*executed* such conception; (he probably executed it first and conceived it afterward, as most of our poor victims do when they start on that terrible blind road through the spelling-book). Whether or no, the thing is here, and we've all to accept it, and deal with it as best we may, sadly hoping that possibly the tenth generation from now may at least be rid of a few unnecessary "e's."

And since the thing is here, and is a mighty creation, and very indicative of how the human brain in large sections works; since we've got to put up with it anyway, we may as well, in revenge for its many inconveniences, get what little satisfaction we can out of it. And I find it one of the most delightful little side amusements of wandering through the field of old literature, while in the critical vein, to stray around among the old stumps and crooked cowpaths of English spelling. Much pleasure is to be derived from seeing what old words grew together and made new ones; what syllables or letters got lopped off or twisted, how silent letters

became silent and why; from what older language
planted, and what its relatives are.   It is much the same
pleasure that one gets from trailing around through the
narrow crooked steets and senseless meanderings of
London City.   Everybody knows it's a foolish way to
build a city; that all streets should be straight and wide
and well-distributed.   But since they are not, and London is too big for one's individual exertion to reform, one
consents to take interest in explaining the crookedness—
in mentally dissolving the great city into the hundred
little villages which coalesced to make it; in marking this
point as the place where St. Somebody-or-Other knelt
and prayed once and therefore there had to be a cross-
street here; and this other point as the place where the
road swept round because martyrs were wont to be burnt
there, etc., etc.   The trouble is that after a while one
gets to love all that quaint illogical tangle, seeing always
the thousand years of history in it; and so one's senses
actually become vitiated enough to permit him to love
the outrages of English spelling, because of the features
of men's souls that are imaged therein.   When I look at
the word "laugh," I fancy I hear the joyous deep gut-
tural "gha-gha-gha" of the old Saxon who died long before the foreign graft on the English stock softened the
"gh" to an "f"!

Really one must become more patient with the "un-
system," knowing how it grew, and feeling that this is
the way of Man,—the way he always grows,—not as he
ought, but as he can.

I have spoken of forms: word-sounds, word-symbols;
as to the spirit of those early writings, full of inarticulate
religious sentiment, emotions so strong they burst from
the utterer's throat one might almost say in barks;
gloomy and foreboding; these gradually changing to

more lightsome fancies,—beauty, delicacy, airiness taking their place, as in the fairy tales and folk-songs of the
people, wherein the deeds of supernaturals are sported
with, and it becomes evident that love and winsomeness
are usurping the kingdom of Power and Fear,—through
all we are compelled to observe one constant tendency
of the human mind,—the desire to free itself from its
own conditions, to be what it is not, to represent itself
as something beyond its powers of accomplishment. In
their minds, men had wings, and breathed in water, and
swam on land, and ate air, and thrived in deserts, and
walked through seas, and gathered roses off ice-bergs,
and collected frozen dew off the tails of sunbeams, dispersed mountains with mustard seeds of faith, and
climbed into solid caves under the rainbow; did everything which it was impossible for them to do.

It is in fact this imaginative faculty which has fore-
run the accomplishments of science and while, under the
influence of practical experiment and the extension of
knowledge such dreams have passed away, this much remains and will long, long remain in humankind, covered
over and shamefacedly concealed as much as may be—
that men perpetually conceive themselves as chrysalid
heroes and wonder workers; and, under strain of occasion, this element crops out in their actions, making
them do all manner of curious things which the standard-
setters of realism will declare utterly illogical and impossible.   Often it is the commonest men who do them.

I have a fondness for realism myself; at least I have
a very wicked feeling towards what is called "symbolism," and various other things which I don't understand;
but as the "Unrealists," the "Exaggeratists," the what-
ever-you-call-them express what I believe to be a very
permanent characteristic of humankind, as evidenced in

all the traces of its work, I think they probably give quite as true reflections of Man's Soul as the present favorites.

These early literatures, most of which have of course been lost, were the embryos of our more imposing creations; and it is a pleasant and an instructive thing to follow the unfolding of Monster Tales into Great Religious Literatures; to compare them and see how the same few simple figures, either transplanted or spontaneously produced at different points, evolved into all manner of Creators, Redeemers and miracles in their various altered habitats. No one can so thoroughly appreciate what is in the face of a man turned upward in prayer, as he who has followed the evolution of the black Monster up to that impersonal conception of God prettily called by Quakers "the Inner Light."

Fairy Tales on the other hand have evolved into allegories and Dramas,—first the dramas of the sky, now the dramas of earth.

Tales of Sexual exploits have become novels, novelettes, short stories, sketches,—a many-expressioned countenance of Man. But the old Heroic Legend,—and the Hero is always the next born after the Monster in the far-back dawn-days, is the lineal progenitor of History,—History which was first the glorification of a warrior and his aids; then the story of Kings, courts, and intrigues; now mostly the report of the deeds of nations in their ugly moods; and *to become* the record of what people have done in their more amiable moments,—the record of the conquests of peace; how men have lived and labored; dug and built, hewn and cleared, gardened and reforested, organized and coöperated, manufactured and used, educated and amused themselves. Those of us who aspire to be more or less suggesters of social change, are greatly at a loss, if we do not know the face of Man as reflected in history; and I mean as much the reflection of the minds of historians as seen in their histories as the reflection of the minds of others they sought to give; not so much in the direct expression of their opinions either, as in the choice of what they thought it worth while to try to stamp perpetuity upon.

When we read in the Anglo-Saxon Chronicle these items which are characteristic of the whole:

"A. D. 611. This year Cynegils succeeded to the government in Wessex, and held it 31 winters. Cynegils was the son of Ceol, Ceol of Cutha, Cutha of Cymric."

And then,

"614. This year Cynegils and Cuiehelm fought at Bampton and slew 2046 of the Welsh."

And then

"678. This year appeared the comet star in August, and shone every morning during three months like a sunbeam. Bishop Wilfred being driven from his bishopric by King Everth, two bishops were consecrated in his stead."

—when we read these we have not any very adequate conception of what the Anglo-Saxon people were doing; but we have a very striking and lasting impression of what the only men who tried to write history at all in that period of English existence, thought it was worth while to record.

"Cynegils was the son of Ceol, and he of Cutha, and Cutha of Cymric." It reads considerably like a stock-raiser's pedigree book. The trouble is, we have no particular notion of Cymric. Probably if we went back we should find he was the son of Somebody. But at any rate, he had a grandson, and the grandson was a king, and the chronicler therefore recorded him. Nothing happened for three years; and then the chronicle records that two kings fought and slew 2046 men. Then comes the momentous year 678 when a comet appeared and a bishop lost his job. No doubt the comet foretold the loss. There are no records of when shoemakers lost their jobs that I know of, nor how many shoemakers were put in their places; and I imagine it would have been at least as interesting for us to know as the little matter of Bishop Wilfred. But the chronicler did not think so; he preserved the Bishop's troubles—no doubt he did just what the shoemakers of the time would also have done, providing they had been also chroniclers. It is a fair sample of what was in men's minds as important.—If any one fancies that this disposition has quite vanished, let him pick up any ordinary history, and see how many pages, relatively, are devoted to the doings of persons intent on slaying, and those intent on peaceful occupation; and how many times we are told that certain politicians lost their jobs, and how we are not told anything about the ordinary people losing their jobs; and then reflect whether the old face of Man-the-Historian is quite another face yet.

Biography, as a sort of second offspring of the Hero legend, is another revelation, when we read it, not only to know its subject, but to know its writer,—the standpoint from which he values another man's life. Ordinarily there is a great deal of "Cynegils the son of Cutha the son of Cymric" in it; and a great deal of emphasis upon the man as an individual phenomenon; when really he would be more interesting and more comprehensible left in connection with the series of phenomena of which he was part. As an example of what to me is a perfect biography, I instance Conway's Life of Thomas Paine, itself a valuable history. But it is not so correct a mirror of the general attitude of biographers and readers of biography as Bosworth's Life of Johnson, except in so far as it indicates that the great face in the glass is changing. It is rather the type of what biography is *becoming*, than what it has been, or is.

There are two divisions of literature which are generally named in one breath, and are certainly closely connected; and yet the one came to highly perfected forms long, long ago, while the other is properly speaking very young; and for all that, the older is the handmaid of the younger. I mean the literatures of philosophy and science.

Philosophy is simply the coördination of the sciences; the formulation of the general, and related principles deduced from the collection and orderly arrangement of the facts of existence. Yet Man had rich literatures of philosophy, while his knowledge of facts was yet so extremely limited as hardly to be worth while writing books about. None of the appearances of Man's Soul is more interesting than that reflected in the continuous succession of philosophies he has poured out. Let him who reads them, read them always twice; first, simply to know and grasp what is said, to become familiar with the idea as it formed itself in the minds of those who conceived it; second, for the sake of figuring the restless activity of brain, the positive need of the mind under all conditions to formulate what knowledge it has, or thinks it has, into some sort of connected whole. This is one of the most pronounced and permanent features seen in the mirror: the positive refusal of the mind to accept the isolation of existences; no matter how far apart they lie, Man proceeds to spin connecting threads somehow. The woven texture is often comical enough, but the weaver is just as positively revealed in the cobwebs of ancient philosophy as in the reasoning of Herbert Spencer.

Concerning the literature of Science itself, in strict terms, I should be very presumptuous to speak of it, because I know extremely little about it; but of those general popularizations of it, which we have in some of the works of Haeckel, Darwin, and their similars, I should say that beyond the important information they contain in themselves (which surely no one can afford to be in ignorance of) they present the most transformed reflection of Man which any literature gives. Their words are cold, colorless, burdened with the labor of exactness, machine like, sustained, uncompromising, careless of effect. The spirit they embody is like unto them. They offer the image of Man's Soul in the time while imagination is in abeyance, reason ascendent.

This coldness and quietness sound the doom of poetry. A people which shall be fully permeated with the spirit and word of Science will never conceive great poems. They will never be overcome long enough at a time by their wonder and admiration, by their primitive impulses, by their power of simple impression, to think or to speak poetically. They will never see trees as impaled giants any more; they will see them as evolved descendants of phytoplasm. Dewdrops are no more the jewels of the fairies; they are the produce of condensation under given atmospheric conditions. Singing stones are not the prisons of punished spirits, but problems in acoustics. The basins of fjords are not the track of the anger of Thor, but the pathways of glaciation. The roar and blaze and vomit of Etna, are not the rebellion of the Titan, but the explosion of so and so many million cubic feet of gas. The comet shall no more be the herald of the wrath of heaven, it is a nebulous body revolving in an elliptical orbit of great elongation. Love—love will not be the wound of Cupid, but the manifestation of universal reproductive instincts.

No, the great poems of the world *have been* produced; they have sung their song and gone their way. Imagination remains to us, but weakened, mixed, tamed, calmed. Verses we shall have,—and *many* fragments,—fragments of beauty and power; but never again the thunder-roll of the mighty early song. We have the benefits of science; we must have its derogations also. The powerful fragments will be such as deal with the still unexplored regions of Man's own internity—if I may coin the word. Science is still balking here. But not far long. We shall soon have madmen turned inside out, and their madness painstakingly reduced to so-and-so many excessive or deficient nerve-vibrations per second. Then no more of Poe's "Raven" and Ibsen's "Brand."

I have said that I intended to indicate a wider concept of literature than that generally allowed. So far I have not done it; at least all that I have dealt with is usually mentioned in works on literature. But I wish now to maintain that some very lowly forms of written expression must be included in literature,—always remembering that I am seeking the complete composite of Man's Soul.

Here then: I include in literature, beside what I have spoken on, not only standard novels, stories, sketches, travels, and magazine essays of all sorts, but the poorest, paltriest dime novel, detective story, daily newspaper report, baseball game account, and splash advertisement.

Oh, what a charming picture of ourselves we see therein! And a faithful one, mind you! Think what a speaking likeness of ourselves was the report of national, international, racial importance — the Jeffries-Johnson fight! Nay, I am not laughing. The people of the future are going to look back at the record a thousand years from now; and say, "This is what interested men in the year 1910." I wonder which will appear most ludicrous then, Bishop Wilfred in juxtaposition with the

comet star, or the destiny of the white race put in
jeopardy by a pugilistic contest between one white and
one black man! O the bated breath, the expectant eyes,
the inbitten lip, the taut muscles, the riveted attention,
of hundreds of thousands of people watching the great
"scientific" combat. I wonder whether the year 3000
will admire it more or less than the Song of Beowulf
and the Battle of Brunanburh.

Consider the soul reflected on the sporting page. Oh,
how mercilessly correct it is! Consider the soul reflected on the advertising page. Oh, the consummate liar
that strides across it! Oh, the gull, the simpleton, the
would-be getter of something for nothing whose existence
it argues! Yea, commercial man has set his image therein; let him regard himself when he gets time.

And the body of our reform literature, which really
reflects the very best social aspirations of men, how
prodigal in words it is,—how indefinite in ideas! How
generous of brotherhood—and sisterhood—in the large;
how chary in the practice! Do we not appear therein as
curious little dwarfs who have somehow gotten "big
heads"? Mites gesticulating at the stars and imagining
they are afraid because they twinkle. I would not discourage any comrade of mine in the social struggle, but
sometimes it is a wholesome thing to reconsider our size.

A word in defense of the silly story. Let us not forget that lowly minds have lowly needs; and the mass of
minds are lowly, and have a right to such gratification
as is not beyond their comprehension. So long as I do
not *have to read* those stories, I feel quite glad for the
sake of those who are not able to want better that such
gratification is not denied them. I would not wish to
frown the silly story out of existence so long as it is a
veritable expression of many people's need. There are
those who have only learned the art of reading at all be-

cause of the foolish story. And quite in a side way I learned the other day through the grave assertion of a physician that the ability to read even these, whereby some little refinement of conception is introduced into the idea of love, is one of the restraining influences upon sexual degradation common among poor and ignorant young women. The face of man revealed in them is therefore not altogether without charm, though it may look foolish to us. I said there were some appearances in the Mirror not generally remarked, but which to me are suggestive. One of these is the evident delight of the human soul in *smut*. In the older literature these things are either badly set down, as law and cursing, as occasionally in the Bible; or they are clothed and mixed with sprightly imaginations as in the tales of Boccaccio and Chaucer; or they are thinly veiled with a possible modest meaning as in the puns of the Shakespearian period; but in our day, they compose a subterranean literature of themselves, like segregated harlots among books. Should I say that I blush for this face of Man? I ought to, perhaps, but I do not: all I say is, the thing is there, a very real, a very persistent image in the glass; no one who looks straight into it can avoid seeing it. Mixed with the humorous, as it often—rather usually—is, it seems to be one of the normal expressions of normal men. We deceive ourselves greatly if we fancy that Man has become purified of such imaginations because they are not used openly in modern dramas and stories, as they were in the older ones.

It may be dangerous to say it, but I believe from the evidence of literature as a whole, that a moderate amount of amusement in smut is a saving balance in the psychology of nearly every man and woman,—a sign of anchorage in a robust sanity, which takes things as they are—and laughs at them. I believe it is a much more wholesome appearance, than that betrayed in our fever-bred stories and sketches which deal with the abnormalities of men, and which are growing more and more in vogue, in spite of our cry about realism.

Personally, I am more interested in the abnormalities, which I find very fascinating. And I am very eager to know whether they will prove to be the result of the abnormal conditions of life which Modern Man has created for himself in his tampering with the forces of nature,—his strenuous industrial existence, his turning of night into day, his whirling himself over the world at a pace not at all in conformity with his native powers of locomotion, and other matters in accordance. Or will they prove to be the revenge of the dammed up, cribbed, cabined, and confined imagination, which can no longer exert itself upon externals,—since the Investigating Man has explained and mastered these or is doing so—and now turns in to wreak frightful wreck upon the mind itself?

At any rate, the fact is that we have some very curious appearances in the Mirror just now; madmen explaining their own madness, diseased men picking apart their own diseases, perverted men analyzing their own perversions, anything, everything but sane and normal men. Does it mean that in our day there is nothing interesting in good health, in well-ordered lives? Or does it mean that the rarest thing in all the world is the so-called normal man, whom tacit consent assumes to be the commonest? That everybody, while outwardly wearing a mask of reputable common sense, is within a raging conglomeration of psychic elements that hurl themselves on one another like hissing flames? Or does it mean simply that the most powerful writers are themselves diseased, and can only paint disease?

I put these questions and do not presume to answer

them. I point to the mirror,—the Ibsen Drama, the Andreyev Story, the Maeterlinck Poem, the Artzibashev
novel,—and I say the image is there. Explain it as you
can.

For the rest, let me recall to you what I told you was
my intent:

First: To insist on a more inclusive view of Literature;
you see I would have it extended both up and down,—
down even to the advertisement, the sporting page, and
the surreptitious anecdote,—*up* to the fullest and most
comprehensive statements of the works of reason.

Second: To suggest that readers acquire the habit
of reading twice, or at least with a double intent. When
serious literature is to be considered, I would insist on
actually reading twice; but of course it would be both
impractical and undesirable to apply such a method to
most of the print we look at.

Those who are confirmed in the habits of would-be
critics will have the greatest trouble in learning to read
a book from the simple man's standpoint,—and yet no
one can ever form a genuine appreciation of a work who
has not first forgotten that he is a critic, and allowed
himself to be carried away into the events and personalities depicted therein. In that first reading, also, one
should train himself to feel and hear the music of language,—this great instrument which Men have jointly
built, and out of which come great organ tones, and
trumpet calls, and thin flute notes, sweeping and wailing,
an articulate storm—a conjuring key whereby all the
passions of the dead, the millions of the dead, have given
to the living the power to call their ghosts out of the
grave and make them walk. Yea, every word is the
mystic embodiment of a thousand years of vanished
passion, hope, desire, thought—all that battled through

the living figures turned to dust and ashes long ago. Train your ears to hear the song of it; it helps to feel what the writer felt.

And after that read critically, with one eye on the page, so to speak, and the other on the reflection in the mirror, looking for the mind behind the work, the things which interested the author and those he wrote for.

Third: To suggest inquiry into the curious paradox of the people of the most highly evolved scientific and mechanical age taking especial delight in psychic abnormalities and morbidities,—whereby the most utterly unreasonable fictive creation becomes the greatest center of curiosity and attraction to the children of Reason.

A Mirror Maze is literature, wherein Man sees all faces of himself, lengthened here, widened there, distorted in another place, restored again to due proportion, with every possible expression on his face, from abjectness to heroic daring, from starting terror to icy courage, from love to hate and back again to worship, from the almost sublime down to the altogether grotesque,—now giant, now dwarf,—but always with one persistent character,—his *superb curiosity to see himself*.

The Drama of the Nineteenth Century

THE passions of men are actors, events are their motions, all history is their speech. In the long play of the ages a human being sometimes becomes an event; a nation's passion takes a *personnel*. Such beings are the expression of the gathered mind-force of millions.

He only who keeps himself aloof from all feeling can remain the spectator of the hour. All that humanity which is held within the beating, coiling, surging tides of passion, has no individuality; it sinks its personality to become a vein in the limb of this giant, a pulse in the heart of that Titan. Only when out of the spirit of the times the event is born, only when the act is complete, the curtain rung down, only then does the intellectuality of the vein, the pulse, rise to the level of the dispassionate. Only then can it survey a tragedy and say, "This was necessary"—a reaction, and say, "This was inevitable."

Yet as a drop of blood is a quivering, living, flashing ruby beside the dead, pale pearl of a stagnant pool, so is one drop of feeling a shining thing, a living thing, beside the deadness of the intellect which judges while the heart is stone; beside those quiet bayous of brain which reflect back the images before them very purely, very stilly, giving no heed to the great rushing river of heart that rolls on, hurries on so close beside them. Bye and bye, bye and bye, the river reaches the grand, great sea, and the waters spread out calm and deep, so deep that the stars of the upper sea, the lights of the higher life, shine far up from them as a babe smiles up into its mother's eyes, and up still to the distant source of the light within the eyes.

It is to men and women of feeling that I speak, men and women of the millions, men and women in the hurrying current! Not to the shallow egotist who holds himself apart and with the phariseeism of intellectuality exclaims, "I am more just than thou"; but to those whose every fiber of being is vibrating with emotion as aspen leaves quiver in the breath of Storm! To those whose hearts swell with a great pity at the pitiful toil of women, the weariness of young children, the handcuffed helplessness of strong men! To those whose blood runs quick along the veins like wild-fire on the dry grass of prairies when the wind whirls aside the smokings of the holocaust, and, courting the teeth of the flame, the black priestess, Injustice, beckons it on while her feet stamp on the cinders of the sacrifice! To those whose heart-strings thrill at the touch of Love like the sweet, low, musical laugh of childhood, or thrum with hate like the singing vibration of the bowstring speeding the arrow of Death! I speak to those whose eyes behold all things through a haze of gray, or rose, or gold, born of their surroundings, and which mist slips away only when the gaze is leveled on that dead Past whose passions and whose deeds are ended: to whom the present is always a morning with the dimness of morning around it—the past clear and still—no veil on its face, for the veil has been shredded asunder.

For he only who intensely perceives the nature of his surroundings, he, and he only, who has felt, and keenly felt, all the throbs and throes of life, can judge with any degree of truth of the action of that which is past. You, you who have loved, you who have joyed, you who have suffered, it belongs to you to people the silent streets of the silent cities with forms now vanished, to comprehend something of the passions which animated their action; it belongs to you to understand how the fury of a great energy, striking terrible aimless blows in the dark, may yet, across the chasm of awful mistake, touch the hand of a greater Justice.

If from a panoramic survey of the past some wisdom may be gathered, then let the dramas of old ages tell us what have been the mainsprings of their motions; so we shall understand what action ushered in the drama of the nineteenth century.

"Westward the Star of Empire holds its way." Following the course of those majestic spheres of fire which whirl each in its vast ellipse, trending away in a long, southwesterly path athwart the heavens, obedient to that superior attraction which through all the universe holds good, the attraction of greater for lesser things, the tide of life upon our world has risen and swelled and rolled away to the south and west. Away in the orient source of the sunlight, away where the glitter of ice shines up to meet the morning, nations have risen and plunged down impetuously over the sleeping regions of darkness and of heat, bearing with them the breeze-stirring life of the north and the on-trending light of the east. And out of this conquered earth have arisen the mixed passions of another life and another race. Still the governing stars wheel on, and the tide of life which paused only to gather strength rolls up again;

and once more a nation is born, and new passions dictate the action of the peoples. Down, down it sweeps over the Altaian hills, over the Himalayan ranges, over the land of the Euphrates and Tigris, over the deserts of Arabia the barren, the fields of Arabia the stony, and the grasses and waters of Arabia the happy, to those low shores, the home of dark mausoleums and darker pyramids, on to the now classic land of Greece, and golden Italy, and the home of the dark-eyed Moors. Sweeps till it touches the frothing sea, and brightly borne upon its upper crest shines the glory, the splendor, the magnificence of the warring powers which dictated the action of Greece and Rome. For centuries their hoisted spears send back the burnished glitter of the sun, and then—the light dies out; down rushing from the North-land again the tide of vigor pours, and the health and strength of barbarism conquers the weakness of a tottering civilization! Far away—away over the miles of sparkling sea, in the darkness and the silence a continent lies waiting; waiting for the coming of the light, waiting for the swelling of the tide. Slowly at last a ripple creeps up over the strange beach, and the flood rolls on, and again a continent becomes a cradle, and the Empire Star sends on its rays to kiss the forehead of the rising world. Over the breadth of all our continent that mighty wave is flowing still.

Standing to-day almost upon the threshold of another world, and looking back down this long-vista'd past, gradually there dawns upon Reflection's vision, gradually there grows out of the confusion of forms and the Babel of sounds, a clearer perception of the motor powers which have dictated the action of this past, a better idea of the grand plot which, driven by these motor powers, the passions are working out. For, above the long procession of scenes and events, above the monster massings of happiness and woe, above the War and Peace of centuries, above the nations that have risen and fallen, above the life and above the grave, the winged and shadowy embodiments of two great ideas float and rest. And those two principles are called Authority and Liberty; or, if it please you better, *God* and Liberty. The one is all clad in the purple and scarlet of pomp and of power, while the other stands a glorious shining center in the white radiance of Freedom.

Yet not always; far back in time Authority stood on thrones and altars, with the plumed sables of despotism waving on his brow, while in his hands he held two iron gyves, the one to fetter thought, the other to fetter action; and these two gyves were called *the Church and State*.

Liberty! Ah, Liberty was then a name scarcely to pass the lips; dreamed of only in solitude, spoken of only in dungeons! Yet out of the blackest mire the whitest lily blooms! Out of the dungeon, out of the sorrow, out of the sacrifice, out of the pain, grew this child of the heart; and pure and strong she grew until the sabled plumes have tottered on the despot's brow, and a great palsy shakes the hands that once so firmly held the gyves of Church and State. For, ever seeking to overthrow each other, the one for the aggrandizement of self, the other for the love of all mankind, these two powers have contended; and every energy, every passion, every desire, good or evil, has been ranged on this side or on that, blunderingly or wisely, and nations have swung to and fro in their breath as upon a hinge. And one by one the powers of Authority have been crippled, and step by step Liberty has advanced, until to-day mankind is beginning to measure the forces that, struggling blindly together, are yet evolving light, to drink in the sublime ideal of freedom. Yet, oh, how long the struggle with vested ignorance, with greed in power!

When upon the Drama of the Nineteenth Century the curtain rose, Liberty, triumphant on the younger shores, lay prone and hurled in Europe. Against fifteen centuries of crowned and throned and tithed curse and woe unutterable, she had risen with such a fearful convulsive strength that when she had mown down king, priest and throne, and gorged the guillotine with blood, she sank back, exhausted from the struggle, and the hated tyrant rose again. The wild desire to conquer, to possess, to control, to hold in subjection, seemed to dominate with an unconquerable strength, and the gathered mind-force of millions of people wrought itself into the single brain of Napoleon Bonaparte. This human being became an event—this nation's passion took a *personnel!* The spirit of the times produced this man, and Authority smiled as one after another the despots of Europe plotted and planned, only to be overthrown by this incarnation of Ambition, while the scenes were shifted from the Vine-land to the Rhine-land, from the sun-land to the snow-land, and through them all the great event glowed out, lit high by the rust-red light.

How well the plot was working! The Empire triumphant, nations subjected, the fetter of action closing its terrible teeth! Liberty manacled on the left! The armies of God massing their forces—advancing—preparing to close down the iron jaw of the iron gyve upon the right; to imprison thought, to re-establish the union of fetters, to link up the broken chains, to burden human hope and human will and human life once more with the awful oppression of Church and State!

But Liberty will not, cannot die! Wounded and bruised

and pinioned sore, condemned to the use of instruments
that were none of hers, she wrought with England's
jealousy, with Wellington's emulation, with fear, with
love, with hate! Impelled by one motive or another
the nations of the coalition moved in concert. Napoleon
had been Marengo—he had been Austerlitz! He became *Waterloo!* And when across that awful field rolled
the last long cannon boom, when the silence settled,
when the Quick and the Dead lay sleeping and the
Wounded died, Justice and Suffering touched hands
across the gulf of blood, and Liberty heard them whisper, *"Sic semper tyrannis."* In the tableau that followed,
she, the ideal of our dreams, still stood pale and fettered;
but a smile lit up her face and a light gleamed in her
eyes as she saw Authority reel and stagger from the blow
which, though it did not sever, yet shattered half the
strength of both its fetters.

For the strength of God lies in a vast unity, an ownership of ideas backed up by the brute force under the
command of the individual in whom that ownership of
ideas is vested; while the strength of Liberty lies in the
very essence of things themselves, the fact that no law
or force ever *can* destroy the individualities of existence;
and of necessity the natural tendency to break all bonds
which seek to control thought, and all force which locks
up those bonds entailing liberty of action as the outcome
of liberty of thought. And just in proportion as Churches
have been dismembered and States have been broken up,
no matter that each new Church and each new State
were but another form of despotism, just in that proportion has the principle of liberty been served; for
each new religious establishment has been an assertion
of the right to think differently from the fashionable
creed, each change has been a movement away from the
centralization of power.

So with Waterloo in the background, with Authority lashed to impotent rage before it, and Liberty pinioned, yet with the lit smile still upon her countenance, the tableau light flames up and dies, and the curtain falls upon the first great act. Those who think, those who feel, those who hope, know why that smile was there. For looking away over the long blue roll of water that swelled like an interlude between, she beheld the sublime opening scene of the act that followed.

Far up the wonderful stage the distant mountains lift their circling crests, at their feet the waters sweep like a march of music, vast acres of untrodden grass-land shower their emerald wealth, nearer the front the lower hills rise up, and then the short Atlantic slope, all rife with busy life, bends down to meet the sea. On the right the hoar-frost sheens and shines on the majestic northern forests, while the glittering earth, dipped in its bath of frozen crystal, spreads like a field of diamonds; on the left the white flakes of the orange bloom fall like a shimmering bridal veil, the wind floats up like a perfume, and the hazy, lazy languor of warmth creeps all about. Behind it all, behind the hills and the prairies and the lifted summits, the mystical golden light of the west drops down, filling the dim-lit distance with the glory of promise. The silver light of the Empire Star glides over the Atlantic slope, and its rays, like guiding fingers, point onward to the gathering shadows.

Now the Passions of men begin to move upon this vast platform with an energy never before witnessed. Diverted from their old-time channels of struggle against the oppression of Gods and kings and the bitterness of birth-hatred, with a freedom of opportunity denied in the old world, and with such unstinted natural resources waiting for the magic transformer, the genius of human-

ity, Ambition of power, Avarice, Pride, Jealousy, all
those motors born out of the old *régime* of a State-
propped God, bred and multiplied through generations
till they have come to be looked upon as natural laws
of human existence, begin to work together to plant this
untrodden earth, to sow in its furrows the seed of a
newer race—and, paradoxical as it may sound, to work
for their own destruction, their final elimination from
the human brain.   Or perhaps it were more correct to
say, that, with the barriers of old institutions taken away,
they naturally begin their retransformation into those
beautiful sentiments from which they were originally
warped, distorted, misshapen by that warped, distorted,
misshapen idea called God.   So do they inaugurate the
grand era of development; so do they answer the oft-
repeated question, "What incentive would there be for
labor or genius if the institutions that compel them to
struggle were broken down?"   Look at the stage of the
past and see!   Never before had thought been so free,
never before had ability been less cramped, less starved
or less compelled!   And never before did genius dare
so much for purposes so great; never before did the
engines which drive the tide of life along a continent
send forth a stream of so much vigor.   A new light
breaks along the pathway of the stars, and swells and
rolls and floods the great scene with a dawn-burst so
magnificent that the very hills blush in its rising splendor.
It is the dawn which the night of God so long held
shrouded; it is that which is born when Superstition dies;
it is that Phœnix which rises from the ashes of religion;
it is that clear blent flame of all the great forces of nature,
brought to the knowledge of mankind by delving Reason, and shot like northern streamers from the heart
of her the Church of God so long held throttled—Science!

It is that which shone reflected in the eyes of Liberty when pale and manacled she stood before the field of Waterloo! The ray of the under earth came up to join the ray of the clouds shot down, the energies of sky and mine and sea were clasped to bring down the wealth of the mountains to the shore, and to transport the life of the now populous strip of slope to the unclaimed regions of the west.

In the broad blaze of light the scene is shifted, the golden effulgence melts and flows round that sea-girdled kingdom, where quietly but surely the two great engines of Authority are being shriven apart. The dynasties of kings are growing dusty—much of their power is but a legend; the Church is shrinking in her garments. The desires of this people are slow to move, but deeply rooted and strong; and so far as they have moved forward, they have never moved back. There have been no gigantic strides, no reactions. Little by little the idea of divinely-delegated power has been crippled till the English bishop and the English lord have become mere titled mockeries in comparison with their ancient feudal meaning. But stop! Close lying there, almost beneath her stretching shadows, another island flashes like a green star in its sea-blue setting. And from that island there rises up the cry of a great devotion, clinging blindly to its greatest curse, its priest-hedged God, while persecuted even unto death by the fanaticism of another faith; and the pleading of Hunger while day long and night long the shuttle flies in the flax loom, and the earth yields her golden fruition, only to lade the ships that bear it away from the famine-white lips and the toil-hardened hands that produced it. Blindly Devotion prays to its God, that God whom it calls all-wise, all-powerful and all-just, and the English ord, who cannot thus subdue his own countrymen, reaches out the long arm of the law across the channel for his rent—and, with God looking on, it is given; and still while the hollow-eyed women kneel at the altar for help, the scene widens out, and away in the distance the seven-hilled city lifts up from the sea, and from the dome of the Vatican, from that great mortared hill of God, the Vicar of Christ calls out, "My tribute, my Peter pence!" And with God looking on, it is given! And then from the foot of that tear-stained altar, where so many lips of Woe have pressed, where so many helpless hands have clasped, where so many hearts have broken, comes the ironical promise of Jehovah, "Ask and thou shalt receive."

Oh, God is a very promising personage indeed—very promising, but, like some of his disciples, very poor pay.

Liberty! Shadowed, invisible! Yet a muffled voice is repeating the words which not so long ago rang from the lips of one who stood almost beneath the shadow of the scaffold, who walks to-day in prison gloom:

"Ye see me only in your cells, ye see me only in the grave,
Ye see me only wand'ring lone beside the exile's sullen wave!
Ye fools! Do I not also live where you have sought to pierce in vain?
Rests not a nook for me to dwell in every heart, in every brain?
Not every brow that boldly thinks erect with manhood's honest pride?
Does not each bosom shelter me that beats with honor's generous tide?
Not every workshop brooding woe, not every hut that harbors grief?
Ha! Am I not the breath of life that pants and struggles for relief?"

Ah, poor, panting, struggling, misery-laden Ireland!
How God laughs with glee to see his shackles weight
your misery!

The scene is shifting, the stage is dark'ning—a strange
eclipse obscures the shafted light! Darker, darker! Now
a low, red fire gleams like a winking eye along the fore-
ground; it runs, it hisses like a snake; there another leaps
up, there another; France, Germany, Italy—the continent
blazes with the fires of the Commune! That spirit which,
drunken with blood, reeled from the guillotine at '93, to
be crushed beneath the upbuilding of the Empire, has
once more arisen. And out of the hot hells of Fury, and
Jealousy, and Hate, out of the pitiless struggle between
"vested rights" and wrongs with high ancestral lineage,
and the great outcrying of a piteous ignorance against
an oppression whose injustice it feels but cannot analyze,
grows the sublime idea which priests have anathematized
and States have outlawed—"the sacred dogma of
EQUALITY."

In so far as that ideal was made possible of conception,
in so far as the masses began to understand something
of the causes of their ills, in so far the purpose of Liberty was served: no matter that the arms of Oppression
were triumphant, the dawn of the thought of equal liberty upon the mass of the unthinking was a far greater
victory than any triumph of arms.

So when the fires died down, and the low reflection
gleamed for an instant over those quiescent Indian valleys
and Altaian ranges, where the main plot of old centuries
had been laid, and then paled out before the white flare
lighting the tableau of the second act, Liberty stood with
chained hands lifted toward her enemy, while a proud
look, playing like an iridescent flame in her eyes, said,
plain as lips could speak it, "I have unbound their
thoughts; they will one day unbind my hands."

Slowly the curtain falls on the fair prisoner and the glowering God.

The solemn ocean interlude rolls in again; again the rising curtain shows the curving slope, the rock-romance of hills, the wide, green valley with its threading silver, the sweeping mountains with the mirage of the blue Pacific lifted high in the sky behind them, the frosted pines, the orange groves. Moving upon the nearer stage two great masses of humanity are seen facing each other; the fires of ambition, of stubborn pride, of determination for the mastery flash like flint-sparks in the eyes of both. Rage is gathering as the stage-light darkens!

Yet these two opposing forces are not all. From under the groves of bridal bloom comes a mournful, chant-like requiem; under the bloom four million voices cry in pain; upon the darkened faces, upturned to that darkening day, fall the white petals helplessly, as Hope falls on the faces of the dead—to die beside them. In the beautiful land of the sun four million human beings clank the chains of the chattel slave! Ah! what music!

Liberty! Liberty was a wraith, fleeting ghost-like through the lonely rice-swamps, terrible *ignis fatuus* of the quagmire, strange, mystical, vanishing moon-shimmer on the darkly ominous waters lying so silent, so level, beneath the droop of Spanish moss and cypress! There it was they drove thee, *there*—THERE—where the quaking earth shivered with its branded burden, where the fever and the miasm were thy breathing, and thy sacred eyes were dimmed with winding-sheets of mist that floated, O so dankly, O so coldly, a steam of tears that rose as fast as their dews might fall: there wast thou exiled, Thou, the God-hunted, Thou, the Law-driven, THOU, THE IMMORTAL! Yet, Oh, so dear men love thee,

Liberty, that even here in thy last terrible citadel of woe, Humanity linked arms with Death, and wooed thee still! Wooed thee, with the ringing bay of bloodhounds in its ears; wooed thee, with the wolf of hunger gnawing at its throat; wooed thee with the clinging miasm winding its anacondine folds around its fever-thin body; wooed thee with the dark pathos of a dying eye, while the diseased and hungered limbs lay stiffening in their agony. And thou wast true, O Liberty! Out of thy bitter exile thou didst call to them, and point them on to hope; and thou didst call, too, to those strange-eyed dreamers, whose faces shone amidst the rank and file of those dominated by local Hate alone, as shines a clear star among driving clouds. Against them Authority has hurled his curses. Spit upon by the godly, despised by the law abiding, they yet have dared to say to Church and Law, "Think what you please of me, but free the slave." Aye, the Church persecuted, and the Law hunted down, and for the love of God, men set traps to catch their fellow-men: even the "wise men," the wise men at Washington, against whose mandates it is treason to speak, aye, a matter for the scaffold in these days, even the wise men built a trap to uphold the divine institution and sent it forth to the people labelled, "The Fugitive Slave Law", and as in other days, human beings died for their opinions—*but the opinions did not die.* Has not one of our latter-day martyrs said, "Men die, but principles live"?

See! The light which has been slowly fading from the right and left shines with a frightful brilliancy upon one point: North and South lie darkened, but Harper's Ferry glows! There is a wild, mad charge, a shifting of the light, a scaffold, a doomed old man bending his grand, white head, to mount the fatal steps with a child-slave's kiss yet warm upon his lips, and then—only a dull, life-

less pendulum in human form, swinging to and fro. And
the Church and the Law were satisfied, when those dumb
lips were cold, and the dead limbs were stiff, and God
and Harper's Ferry had no more to fear from old John
Brown.

But the Church and the Law have not always been
wise; they have not always understood that the martyrs
to Creed and Code have done as much by their death for
the propagation of their principles as the martyrs *of*
creed and code; and God and the State sowed a wind
whose reaping was a terrible whirlwind, when they hung
John Brown.

Across the dim platform the Passions of hate and
pride move toward each other; it is the old combat of
the forces of Authority, each contending not for the
vindication of right, but for the maintenance of power
over the other. It is a terrific struggle of brute strength
and strategy and cunning and ferocity, and well might
those who conceived the ideal beautiful of freedom,
shrink horror-struck from the blood-soaked path their
feet must tread to reach it. Not strange if some should
pause and shudder and cry out, "Is it worth the sacrifice?" But up from the dust where Hope lay trodden,
and out of the trenches where the sacrificed lay hid, and
over the plains all scarred with bullets and plowed with
shells, breathed the whisper, "It is not vain." It was
not in vain; for as at Waterloo the struggle of ambition
against ambition defeated the first purpose of Authority,
the centralization of power, and gave a partial victory to
her whom both hated, so Antietam, Fredericksburg,
Vicksburg, Gettysburg, while in themselves representing
only the brutish struggle of opposition, based on the desire to domineer, really wrought out the victory of that
ideal which dwelt in the minds of those anathematized

by God and outlawed by the State. For when the hot lips
of the iron mouths grew cold, Liberty forsook her lonely
fastness, came forth upon the desolated plain, and mount-
ing still to the summits of the blue-hazed hills looked
away over the ruined homes, the depopulated cities, the
gloom-clouded faces, and though her tears fell fast, an
ineffable tenderness shone upon her features as the torrent of pale light flowed round her form, defining its
snow-whiteness in relief against the sable of four million
freedmen smiling o'er their stricken chains.

Swiftly following the tableau fire comes the eastern
scene, where, in the very center of its power the Church
is shaken by an invader, and Garibaldi becomes the *personnel* of the event. Then follows the Conclave of the
Vatican, where by that singular logic known to the
Roman Church, the vote of fallible beings renders the
pope infallible; upon the heels of this, the breaking of
that strong tooth of the Church in the expulsion of the
Order of the Society of Jesus by the German Reichstag,
and the overthrow of kingcraft in France.

The curtain falls. Behind, the scene is being prepared
for the last great act!

And now, in the interval of waiting, let us think. So
far we have been surveying the completed. While we
can understand something of the passions which animated
this past, can feel something of the pulsations which
throbbed in its arteries, flowed in its veins, we yet can
speak of it without over-riding emotion either upon one
side or the other. The river of heart has reached the
sea—the troubled waters have spread out deep, and up
from their depths shine the still reflections of those great
lights which gilt the stages of the past. Calmly now we
can look at the reaction from the French Revolution to
the Empire, and say, "This was inevitable,"—of Na-

poleon's fall, "this was necessary"; of the awakening of
Science, "this was a natural result"; of the uprising of
'48, "this was the premature birth of an idea forced upon
the people by the oppression of Authority"; we can forget the choking agony of John Brown, and declare his
death a victory. We can look upon the awful waste of
blood in the Civil War and say, "It was pitiful, but the
goblet of woe must needs have been spilled full of red
life wine, ere the hoarse and hollow throat of tyranny
were satisfied." We can see where each of the contending principles has lost and gained, and measuring the
sum totals against each other, *must* decide that the old
despotism is losing ground; that instead of the supreme
authority of God, the supreme sovereignty of the Individual is the growing idea.

But now we have come to a stage where we can no
longer be cool spectators. In what happens now we
too must be part and parcel of the action; we too must
hope, and toil, and struggle and suffer. We are no longer
looking through the clear still atmosphere of the dead:
around our forms the wheeling mists are circled, and
before our eyes the haze lies thick—the haze of gold or
the haze of gray. The dimness of the "yet to be" befogs
our sight, and the rush of hope and fear blinds all our
faculties. You who stand well upon the heights of love,
of comfort, of happiness, heeding not the darkness and
the sorrow beneath you, behold, with up-cast eyes, the
great figures of God and Freedom wound about, showered
with light. To you there is no menace in their darting
eyes, there is no purpose in their full-drawn statures,
there is no jarring in their clarion voices. No! for your
senses are stupid in your luxury, your brains are dulled,
too dulled to think, your ears are glutted with the ring
of gold. In your vain and foolish hearts you dream that

what you see there is a shadowy bridal; that there, at last, Religion and Science, Statecraft and Freedom, are meeting to embrace each other.

Ah, go on, book-makers, press-writers, doctors and lawyers and preachers and teachers! Go on talking your incompatibilities; go on teaching your absurdities! Dream out your short-lived dream! At your feet, beneath the shadow of your capitols and domes, under the tuition of your few-facted, much-fictioned literature, from out your chaos of truth-flavored lies, from before your pulpits, your rostrums and your seats of learning, something is growing. Something that is looking *you* in the eyes, that is analyzing your statements, that is revolving your institutions in its brain, that is crushing your sophistries in its merciless machinery as fine as grain is ground between the whitened mill-rollers. Freethought is looking at you, gentlemen!—more than that, it questions you, it puts you on the witness-stand, it cross-examines you. It says, "Do you believe in God?" and you answer, "Yes." "Do you believe him to be omnipotent, omniscient, and all-just?" "Certainly; less than this would not be God." "Then you believe he has the power to order all things as he wills, and being all-just he wills all things according to justice?" "Yes." "Then you believe him to be the impartially-loving father of all his created children?" "Yes." "And each one of those children has an equal right to life and liberty?" "Yes." Then look upon this earth beneath you, this earth of beings whose lives are of so poor account to you, and tell us, where *is* God and *what* is he doing?

Everyone has a right to life! What mockery! When the control of the necessaries of life is given to the few by the State, and above the seal of the law the priest has set the seal of the Church! Verily,

"You do take my life
When you take that whereby I live."

Is this your Divine Justice?

What irony to tell me I am free if at that same time you have it in your power to withhold the means of my existence! Free! Will you look down here at these whose sight is shadowed with the ebon shadow of despair, these, the homeless, the disinherited, the product of whose toil you take and leave them barely enough to live upon—live to toil on and keep you in your luxury! You, the monied idlers, you, the book-makers and the journalists, who do more to cry down truth, to laud our social lies, our economic despots and our pious frauds, than any other propaganda can! You, the doctors, whose drugs have cursed the world with poison-eaten bodies, corroded the health of unborn generations with your medicated slime, and when the sources of life have yielded to the hungry body so poor a stream that for lack of air, and earth, and sun, and food, and clothing, and recreation, it drooped and sickened, have bottled up some nauseating stuff, and with oracular wisdom have taught them to imagine it could undo what years of misery had done! You, the law-makers, who have twisted Nature's code till to be natural is to be a criminal; you, who have lawed away the earth that was not yours to give; you, who even seek to charter the sea and make the commandment "across the middle of this river thou shalt not go unless thou render tribute unto Cæsar!" you, who never inquire "what is *justice*," but "what is law!" And you, the teachers, you who prate of the glory of knowledge as the remedy for the evils of the world, and boast your compulsory law of education, while a stronger law than all the wordy sentences ever graven upon statute books, is driving the children out of the schoolground into the factory, into the saw-mill, into the shaft, into the furrow, into the myriad camps of toil, to the dust of the wheel, to the heat of the furnace, till their pallid cheeks and blood-less lips are bleached like bones beneath the desert sun, and their clogged lungs rattle in their breathing pain! Will you look at these, the under-stratum of your social earth, and tell them they are free? Will you tell them ignorance is their greatest curse and education their only remedy? Will you say to these children, "We have pro-vided free schools for you, and now we compel you to attend them whether you have anything to eat and wear or not"? Will you tell these people there is a good, kind, merciful God who loves them, meting out justice to them from the skies?

No, you *will* not, you *cannot*. The words will die upon your lips ere you utter them.

Do you know what it is they see up there above you, they whose eyes look through the mist of gray and the shroud of darkness? They see your God of justice a pitiless slave-driver, his Church more brutal than the lash, his State more merciless than the bloodhound; they see themselves a thousand million serfs more hopelessly enthralled, more helplessly chained down than e'en the lashed and tortured body of the chattel slave. For them there is no refuge, no escape; in every land the Master rules; no fugitive slave law need now be passed—there is no place to flee—the whole horizon is iron-bound. White and black alike are yoked together, and the master yields no distinction, shows no mercy. The bare pittance of existence is the meed for him who toils, and for him who *cannot*—starvation! with a preacher to help him die! That is the justice that they see there, in the shadow lines above your golden haze. And they see, too, a conflict preparing between those two antagonistic forces such as

never before the world has witnessed. They see your
God concentrating his strength to fight so bitter a battle
with Liberty as shall crush the spirit of individuality forever from the race. They see him ranging his forces.
those forces blood-imbrued through all the anguished
past, the blacklist, the club, the sword, the rifle, the prison,
aye, the scaffold; they see them all, and know that ere your
God will yield his vested rights, the noblest of the race
will have been stricken, the most unselfish will have been
tortured in his dungeons, the white robes of innocence
will have been reddened in her own martyr's blood, and
Death will have shadowed many and many a home, unless
you shall hearken to the voice of Liberty and save yourselves while there is yet time. They see the wide stage
spreading out, they see the passions moving over it; they
see there, in the center, beneath the rolling brilliance of
the Empire State, the tragic inauguration of the act!
They see a grim and blackened thing, a silent thing, the
demoniac effigy of Torquemada's spirit, the frozen laugh
of the Dark Ages at our boasted civilization; they see
twelve stolid fools before this Nineteenth Century gallows; they see the hiding place of that thing masquerading
under the sacred name of Justice, which shrinks even
from the gaze of the lauding press and the imbecile jury-
men, and does unknown its deed of murder; they see
four shrouded forms, they hear four muffled voices, a
broken sentence, and—an awful hush! And then, O
crowning irony of all, they see advancing to speak to
them over the bodies of the murdered (and mouthed
back from a hundred pulpits comes the echo), Jehovah
masked as Jesus. Ah, the divine cowardice of it! Mild
is the light in the Nazarene eyes, tender the tone of the
Nazarene voice!

"Ah, people whom I love! For whom my life was
given long ago on Calvary! What rashness is it that

you meditate? Is it that you are weary of the yoke of love I lay on you? Is this your faith? Have I not promised you a sweet release when your dark pilgrimage on earth is o'er? Exiles ye are upon this world of pain and if oppression comes to weigh you down, if hunger shows his long fangs at your hearth, if your chilled limbs are cramped with bitter cold the while your neighbor hoards his fuel up, if you are driven out upon the street with crying children clinging piteously and begging you for shelter from the storm, if your hard toil is taken by the law to satisfy a corporation's greed, if fever and distress gnaw at your heart and still you tread the weary wine-press out, knowing no rest until the death-hour comes; if all these things discourage and perplex, know 'tis for love of you I order it. For thus would I point you to paradise, win you from all the pleasure of the world, and fix your hopes on Heaven's eternity. 'Whom the Lord loveth, him he chasteneth'; so then it is for love that these things are. For love of you I press your life-blood out; for love of you I load you down with pain; for love of you I take your rights away; for love of you I institute the law that slaves you to the grasping millionaire; for love of you I pile the glutted hoards of Vanderbilt and Gould and Rothschild and the rest; for love of you I rent the right to breathe in a poor tenement of dingy dirt; for love of you I make machines a curse; for love of you I make you toil long hours, and those who cannot toil, I turn adrift to wander as they may —sons into dens where thievery is learned as a fine art, daughters to barter their virginity till competition forces down the price of lust and death is left them as a last resort. Ah, what a golden crown, and sweet-toned harp, what a resplendent whit robe, await the soul whom so God loves while on the earth it dwells. Aye, for the love of you these men were murdered, and for my glory; and through my holy love they roast in hell: for they would take away the instruments whereby I lure you to my blest abode. They would have taught you what your freedom meant; they would have told you to regain your rights; they would have contradicted my commands and lost you heaven, perchance—and if not heaven, *hell*. Keep to your faith, my people, trust in God! Break not the altars where your fathers knelt; trust to your teachers, keep within the law; bow to the Church and kiss the State's great toe! So shall good order be observed, obeyed, and as 'Peace reigned in Warsaw,' so anon shall 'Peace, good-will to men reign on the earth.'"

These are the words that fall from the lips of him you call "the merciful," "the just." These are the sounds that sink into the ears of those upon whose toil *you* are dependent for your existence; judge you how they will be received. And now, you, the dwellers on the lifted heights, listen to the voice that follows him, for these are words that concern *you*, and if you listen to their warning you may yet save yourselves the desolation and the ruin that otherwise must come. This deep, bell-pealing voice that echoes through the corridors of thought till almost Death's chill sleepers might arise again, is the voice which called for centuries to the Empire, "Cease your oppressions or the people rise"; and to the Kingdom, "Curse not the new world with your tyrannies, it will rebel"; and to the Master, "Put not the lash upon your bonded slave, for the time will come when every stroke will rise like a warrior armed, to burn and waste and kill." The Empire laughed, the Kingdom ignored, the Planter sneered; but the time came when laugh and sneer died to white ashes. The time came when "France got drunk with blood, to vomit crime," when England "lost the brightest jewel in her coronal," when the South waded in blood and tears and knelt her pride before a conqueror. And now, she, the liberator, the destined conqueror of God, calls out to you, "Yield up your scepters ere they be torn from you; give back the stolen earth, the mine, the sea! Give back the source of life, give back the light! For a black, bitter hour is waiting you, an awful gulf unfathomed in its depth, if now you do not pause and render *justice."*

Ah, thou, whatever be thy awful name, which like a serpent's trail hath marked the earth, whether Jehovah, Buddha, Joss, or Christ! Thou who hast done for *love* what others do for most envenomed *hate,* how hast thou hated these the happy ones! Is this impartial justice then to these, to pour the golden treasures of the earth into their laps, that these may feast and toast and so forget thee and thy promised heaven? Truly thou hast been most unkind to them, since kindness means with thee a tearing out of e'en the heart and entrails of existence. Bah! how thou liest! To what most pitiable trick of speech hast thou been forced! Think'st thou the dwellers in the darkness longer take thy creed of crystalline deception! No! They laugh at thee, they spew thee out, they spit at thee.

Love! Say! Look—this long procession coming here! Here are the murderers, with their red-hued eyes; here the adulterers, with their lecherous glance; here are the prostitutes, with their mark of shame; here are the gamblers, with their itching hands; here are the thieves, with furtive lips and eyes; here are the liars with their dastard tongues; here all the train that Crime can muster up reviews before thee! And after them, a ghastly, fearful sight, follow the victims of their blackened hearts, slain, ruined, desolated by thy love! And now, behold, another train comes on—a train whose name is legion! Here the dark, bruted faces from the mines, here the hard, sun-browned cheeks from out the furrow, here the dull visage from the lumber-camp, here the wan eyes from whirling factory, here the gaunt giants from the furnace fire, here the tarred hands from off the stream and sea, here all the aching limbs that stand behind the fashionable counter, here, O pitiful sight of all, those whose home is in the street, whose table is the garbage pile, the vast, helpless body of the unemployed. And, ever as they march, they drop, and drop, into the earth that swallows them, and over their graves the march goes on. These are thy victims, God! These are the creatures of thy Church and Law! Speak no more of the breaking of altars, thou who hast broken every altar that the human heart holds dear! Take thy position at the head of the murderers' column! And when thou hast marched away into the past, thou and thy preachers and thy praters of justice, then will the world *return* to justice and the great law of Nature reign upon the earth. Then will her broad, green acres yield their wealth to him who toils, and him alone; then will the store-houses of Nature yield her fuel and her light, not to the corporation whose high-priced lobbying can buy it, for in that time no wealth nor intrigue can purchase the heritage of all, but to all the sons and daughters of Labor. And then upon *this* earth there shall be no hungry mouths, no freezing limbs; no children spending the hours of youth in gaining a miserable livelihood, no women crying,

> "It's Oh, to be a slave
> Along with the barbarous Turk,
> Where woman has never a soul to save
> If this is *Christian* work!"

no men wandering aimlessly in search of a master for their slavery.

But O, careless dwellers upon the heights, awaken now!—do not wait till reason, persuasion, judgment, coolness are swept down before the rising whirlwind. Bend your energies *now* to the eradication of the Authority idea, to righting the wrongs of your fellow-men. Do it for your own interest, for if you slumber on—ah me! ye will awaken one day when an ominous rumble prefaces the waking of a terrific underground thunder, when the earth shakes in a frightful ague fit, when from out the parched throats of the people a burning cry will come like lava from a crater, " 'Bread, bread, bread!' No more preachers, no more politicians, no more lawyers, no more gods, no more heavens, no more promises! Bread!" And then, when you hear a terrible leaden groan, know that at last, here in your free America, beneath the floating banner of the stars and stripes, more than fifty million human hearts have burst! A dynamite bomb that will shock the continent to its foundations and knock the sea back from its shores!

> "It is no boast, it is no threat,
>   Thus History's iron law decrees;
> The day grows hot! O Babylon,
>   'Tis cool beneath thy willow trees!"

SKETCHES

AND

STORIES

A Rocket of Iron

IT was one of those misty October nightfalls of the
north, when the white fog creeps up from the
river, and winds itself like a corpse-sheet around
the black, ant-like mass of human insignificance, a
cold menace from Nature to Man, till the foreboding
of that irresistible fatality which will one day lay us
all beneath the ice-death sits upon your breast, and
stifles you, till you start up desperately crying, "Let
me out, let me out!"

For an hour I had been staring through the window
at that chill steam, thickening and blurring out the
lines that zig-zagged through it indefinitely, pale
drunken images of facts, staggering against the invul-
nerable vapor that walled me in—a sublimated grave
marble. Were they all ghosts, those figures wandering across the white night, hardly distinguishable
from the posts and pickets that wove in and out, like
half-dismembered bodies writhing in pain? My own
fingers were curiously numb and inert; had I, too,
become a shadow?

It grew unbearable at last, the pressure of the foreboding at my heart, the sense of that on-creeping of
Universal Death. I ran out of doors, impelled by the
vague impulse to assert my own being, to seek relief
in struggle, even though foredoomed futile—to seek
warmth, fellowship, somewhere, though but with those

ineffective pallors in the mist, that dissolved even
while I looked at them. Once in the street, I ran
on indifferently, glad to be jostled, glad of the snarl-
ing of dogs and the curses of laborers calling to one
another. The penumbra of the mist, that menacing
dim foreshadow, had not chilled these, then! On, on,
through the alleys where human flesh was close, and
when one listened one could hear breathings and many
feet, drifting at last into the current that swept
through the main channel of the city, and presently,
whirled round in an eddy, I found myself staring
through the open door of the great Iron Works. Perhaps it was the sensation of warmth that held me
there first, some feeling of exhilaration and wakening
defiance in the flash and swirl of the yellow flames—
this, mixed with an indistinct desire to clutch at something, anything, that seemed stationary in the midst
of all this that slipped and wavered and fell away . . .
No, I remember now: there was something before
that; there was a sound—a sound that had stopped
my feet in their going, and smote me with a long
shudder—a sound of hammers, beating, beating, beating a terrific hail, momentarily faster and louder, and
in between a panting as of some great monster catch-
ing breath beneath the driving of that iron rain.
Faster, faster — CLANG! A long reverberant shriek!
The giant had rolled and shivered in his pain. Invol-
untarily I was drawn down into the Valley of the
Sound, words muttering themselves through my lips
as I passed: "Forging, forging—what are they forging there? Frankenstein makes his Monster. How
the iron screams!" But I heard it no more now; I
only saw!—saw the curling yellow flames, and the

red, red iron that panted, and the Masters of the Hammers. How they moved there, like demons in the abyss, their bodies swinging, their eyes tense and a-glitter, their faces covered with the gloom of the torture-chamber!

Only *one* face I saw, young and fair — young and very fair—whereon the gloom seemed not to settle. The skin of it was white and shining there in the midst of that black haze; over the wide forehead fell tumbling waves of thick brown hair, and two great dark eyes looked steadily into the red iron, as if they saw therein something I did not see; only now and then they were lifted, and looked away upward, as if beyond the smoke-pall they beheld a vision. Once he turned so that the rose-light cast forth his profile as a silhouette; and I shivered, it was so fine and hard! Hard with the hardness of beaten iron, and fine with the fineness of a keen chisel. Had the hammers been beating on that fair young face?

A comrade called, a sudden terrified cry. There was a wild rush, a mad stampede of feet, a horrible screech of hissing metal, and a rocket of iron shot upward toward the black roof, bursting and falling in a burning shower. Three figures lay writhing along the floor, among the leaping, demoniac sparks.

The first to lift them was the Man with the white face. He had stood still in the storm, and ran forward when the others shrank back. Now he passed by me, bearing his dying burden, and I saw no quiver upon brow or chin; only, when he laid it in the ambulance, I fancied I saw upon the delicate curved lips a line of purpose deepen, and the reflection of the iron-fire glow in the strange eyes, as if for an instant the door of a hidden furnace had been opened and smouldering coals had breathed the air. And even then he looked up!

It was all over in half an hour. There would be weeping in three little homes; and one was dead, and one would die, and one would crawl, a seared human stump, to the end of his weary days. The crowd that had gathered was gone; they would not know the Stump when it begged from them with its maimed hands, six months after, on some street corner. "Fakir" they would say, and laugh. There would be an entry on the company's books, and a brief line in the newspapers next day. But the welding of the iron would go on, and the man who gave his easy money for it would fancy he had paid for it, not seeing the stiff figures in their graves, nor the crippled beggar, nor the broken homes.

The rocket of iron is already cold; dull, inert, fireless, the black fragments lie upon the floor whereon they lately rained their red revenge. Do with them what you will, you cannot undo their work. The men are clearing way. Only he with the white face does not go back to his place. Still set and silent he takes his coat, "presses his soft hat down upon his thick, damp locks," and goes out into the fog and night. So close he passed me, I might have touched him; but he never saw me. Perhaps he was still carrying the burden of the dying man upon his heart; perhaps some mightier burden. For one instant the shapely, boyish figure was in full light, then it vanished away in the engulfing mist—the mist which the vision of him had made me forget. For I knew I had seen a Man of Iron, into whose soul the iron had driven, whose nerves were tempered as cold steel, but behind whose still, impassive features slumbered a white-hot heart. And others should see a rocket and a ruin, and feel the Vengeance of Beaten Iron, before the mist comes and swallows all.

   *   *   *   *   *   *   *

I had forgotten! Upon that face, that young, fair face, so smooth and fine that even the black smoke would not rest upon it, there bloomed the roses of Early Death. Hot-house flowers!

The Chain Gang

IT is far, far down in the southland, and I am back again, thanks be, in the land of wind and snow, where life lives. But that was in the days when I was a wretched thing, that crept and crawled, and shrunk when the wind blew, and feared the snow. So they sent me away down there to the world of the sun, where the wind and the snow are afraid. And the sun was kind to me, and the soft air that does not move lay around me like folds of down, and the poor creeping life in me winked in the light and stared out at the wide caressing air; stared away to the north, to the land of wind and rain, where my heart was,—my heart that would be at home.

Yes, there, in the tender south, my heart was bitter and bowed, for the love of the singing wind and the frost whose edge was death,—bitter and bowed for the strength to bear that was gone, and the strength to love that abode. Day after day I climbed the hills with my face to the north and home. And there, on those southern heights, where the air was resin and balm, there smote on my ears the sound that all the wind of the north can never sing down again, the sound I shall hear till I stand at the door of the last silence.

Cling—clang—cling—From the Georgian hills it sounds; and the snow and the storm cannot drown it,—the far-off, terrible music of the Chain Gang.

I met it there on the road, face to face, with all the light of the sun upon it. Do you know what it is? Do you know that every day men run in long procession, upon the road they build for others' safe and easy going, bound to a chain? And that other men, with guns upon their shoulders, ride beside them—with orders to kill if the living links break? There it stretched before me, a serpent of human bodies, bound to the iron and wrapped in the merciless folds of justified cruelty.

Clank—clink—clank— There was an order given. The living chain divided; groups fell to work upon the road; and then I saw and heard a miracle.

Have you ever, out of a drowsy, lazy conviction that all knowledges, all arts, all dreams, are only patient sums of many toils of many millions dead and living, suddenly started into an uncanny consciousness that knowledges and arts and dreams are things more real than any living being ever was, which suddenly reveal themselves, unasked and unawaited, in the most obscure corners of soul-life, flashing out in prismatic glory to dazzle and shock all your security of thought, toppling it with vague questions of what *is* reality, that you cannot silence? When you hear that an untaught child is able, he knows not how, to do the works of the magicians of mathematics, has it never seemed to you that suddenly all books were swept away, and there before you stood a superb, sphinx-like creation, Mathematics itself, posing problems to men whose eyes are cast down, and all at once, out of whim, incorporating itself in that wide-eyed, mysterious child? Have you ever felt that all the works of the masters were swept aside in the burst of a singing voice, unconscious that it sings, and that Music itself, a master-presence, has entered the throat and sung?

No, you have never felt it? But you have never heard the Chain Gang sing!

Their faces were black and brutal and hopeless; their brows were low, their jaws were heavy, their eyes were hard; three hundred years of the scorn that brands had burned its scar upon the face and form of Ignorance,— Ignorance that had sought dully, stupidly, blindly, and been answered with that pitiless brand. But wide beyond the limits of high man and his little scorn, the great, sweet old Music-Soul, the chords of the World, smote through the black man's fibre in the days of the making of men; and it sings, it sings, with its ever-thrumming strings, through all the voices of the Chain Gang. And never one so low that it does not fill with the humming vibrancy that quivers and bursts out singing things always new and new and new.

I heard it that day.

The leader struck his pick into the earth, and for a moment whistled like some wild, free, living flute in the forest. Then his voice floated out, like a low booming wind, crying an instant, and fell; there was the measure of a grave in the fall of it. Another voice rose up, and lifted the dead note aloft, like a mourner raising his beloved with a kiss. It drifted away to the hills and the sun. Then many voices rolled forward, like a great plunging wave, in a chorus never heard before, perhaps never again; for each man sung his own song as it came, yet all blent. The words were few, simple, filled with a great plaint; the wail of the sea was in it; and no man knew what his brother would sing, yet added his own without thought, as the rhythm swept on, and no voice knew what note its fellow voice would sing, yet they fell in one another as the billow falls in the trough or rolls to the crest, one upon the other, one within the other, over, under, all in the great wave; and now one led and others followed, then it dropped back and another swelled upward, and every voice was soloist and chorister, and never one seemed conscious of itself, but only to sing out the great song.

And always, as the voices rose and sank, the axes swung and fell. And the lean white face of the man with the gun looked on with a stolid, paralyzed smile.

Oh, that wild, sombre melody, that long, appealing plaint, with its hope laid beyond death,—that melody that was made only there, just now, before me, and passing away before me! If I could only seize it, hold it, stop it from passing! that all the world might hear the song of the Chain Gang! might know that here, in these red Georgian hills, convicts, black, brutal convicts, are making the music that is of no man's compelling, that floods like the tide and ebbs away like the tide, and will not be held—and is gone, far away and forever, out into the abyss where the voices of the centuries have drifted and are lost!

Something about Jesus, and a Lamp in the darkness —a gulfing darkness. Oh, in the mass of sunshine must they still cry for light? All around the sweep and the glory of shimmering ether, sun, sun, a world of sun, and these still calling for light! Sun for the road, sun for the stones, sun for the red clay—and no light for this dark living clay? Only heat that burns and blaze that blinds, but does not lift the darkness!

"And lead me to that Lamp——"

The pathetic prayer for light went trembling away out into the luminous gulf of day, and the axes swung and fell; and the grim dry face of the man with the gun looked on with its frozen smile. "So long as they sing, they work," said the smile, still and ironical.

"A friend to them that's got no friend"—Man of Sorrows, lifted up upon Golgotha, in the day when the forces of the Law and the might of Social Order set you there, in the moment of your pain and desperate accusation against Heaven, when that piercing "Eloi, Eloi, lama sabachthani?" went up to a deaf sky, did you presage this desolate appeal coming to you out of the unlived depths of nineteen hundred years?

Hopeless hope, that cries to the dead! Futile pleading that the cup may pass, while still the lips drink! For, as of old, Order and the Law, in shining helmets and gleaming spears, ringed round the felon of Golgotha, so stand they still in that lean, merciless figure, with its shouldered gun and passive smile. And the moan that died within the Place of Skulls is born again in this great dark cry rising up against the sun.

If but the living might hear it, not the dead! For these are dead who walk about with vengeance and despite within their hearts, and scorn for things dark and lowly, in the odor of self-righteousness, with self-vaunting wisdom in their souls, and pride of race, and iron-shod order, and the preservation of Things that Are; walking stones are these, that cannot hear. But the living are those who seek to know, who wot not of things lowly or things high, but only of things wonderful; and who turn sorrowfully from Things that Are, hoping for Things that May Be. If these should hear the Chain Gang chorus, seize it, make all the living hear it, see it!

If, from among themselves, one man might find "the Lamp," lift it up! Paint for all the world these Georgian hills, these red, sunburned roads, these toiling figures with their rhythmic axes, these brutal, unillumined faces, dull, groping, depth-covered,—and then unloose that song upon their ears, till they feel the smitten, quivering hearts of the Sons of Music beating against their own; and under and over and around it, the chain that the dead have forged clinking between the heart-beats!

Clang—cling—clang—ng— It is sundown. They are running over the red road now. The voices are silent; only the chain clinks.

The Heart of Angiolillo

SOME women are born to love stories as the sparks
fly upward. You see it every time they glance
at you, and you feel it every time they lay a finger
on your sleeve. There was a party the other night, and
a four-year old baby who couldn't sleep for the noise
crept down into the parlor half frightened to death and
transfixed with wonderment at the crude performances
of an obtuse visitor who was shouting out the woes of
Othello. One kindly little woman took the baby in her
arms and said: "What would they do to you, if you
made all that noise."—"Whip me," whispered the child,
her round black eyes half admiration and half terror,
and altogether coquettish, as she hid and peered round
the woman's neck. And every man in the room forthwith fell in love with her, and wanted to smother his
face in the bewitching rings of dark hair that crowned
the dainty head, and carry her about on his shoulders, or
get down on his hands and knees to play horse for her,
or let her walk on his neck, or obliterate his dignity in
any other way she might prefer. The boys tolerated
their fathers with a superior "huh!" Fourteen or fifteen
years from now they will be playing the humble cousin
of the horse before the same little ringed-haired lady,
and having sported Nick Bottom's ears to no purpose,
half a dozen or so will go off and hang themselves, or
turn monk, or become "bold, bad men," and revenge

themselves on the sex. But her conquests will go on, and when those gracious rings are white as snow the children of those boys will follow in their grandfathers' and fathers' steps and dangle after her, and make drawings on their fly leaves of that sweet kiss-cup of a mouth of hers, and call her their elder sister, and other devotional names. And the other girls of her generation, who were not born with that marvelous entangling grace in every line and look, will dread her and spite her, and feel mean satisfaction when some poor fool does swallow laudanum on her account. Smiles of glacial virtue will creep over their faces like slippery sunshine, when one by one her devotees come trailing off to them to say that such a woman could never fill a man's heart nor become the ornament of his hearthstone; the quiet virtues that wear, are all their desire; of course they have just been studying her character and that of the foolish men who dance her attendance, but even those are not doing it with any serious motives. And the neglected girls will serve him with home-made cake and wine which he will presently convert into agony in that pearl shell ear of hers. And all the while the baby will have done nothing but be what she was born to be through none of her own choosing, which is her lot and portion; and that is another thing the gods will have to explain when the day comes that they go on trial before men; which is the real day of judgment.

But this isn't the baby's story, which has yet to be made, but the story of one who somehow received a wrong portion. Some inadvertent little angel in the destiny shop took down her name when the heroine of a romance was called for, and put her where she shouldn't have been, and then ran off to play no doubt, not stopping to look twice. For even the most insouciant angel that looked twice would have seen that Effie was no woman to play the game of hearts, and there's only one thing more undiscerning than an angel, and that is a social reformer. Effie ran up against both.

They say she had blood in her girlhood, that it shone red and steady through that thin, pure skin of hers; but when I saw her, with her nursing baby in her arms, down in the smutching grime of London, there was only a fluctuant blush, a sort of pink ghost of blood, hovering back and forth on her face. And that was for shame of the poverty of her neat bare room. Not that she had ever known riches. She was the daughter of Scotch peasants, and had gone out to service when she was still a child; her chest was hollowed in and her back bowed with that unnatural labor. There was no gloss on the pale sandy hair, no wilding tendrils clinging round the straight smooth forehead, no light of coquetry or grace in the glimmering blue eyes, no beauty in her at all, unless it lay in the fine, hard sculptured line of her nose and mouth and chin when she turned her head sideways. You could read in that line that having spoken a word to her heart, she would not forget it nor unsay it; and if it took her down into Gethsemane, she would never cry out though by all forsaken.

And that was where it had taken her then. Some ready condemner of all that has been tried for less than a thousand years, will say it was because she had the just reward of those who, holding that love is its own sanction and that it cannot be anything but degraded by seeking permissions from social authorities, live their love lives without the consent of Church and State. But you and I know that the same dark garden has awaited the woman whose love has been blessed by both, and that many such a life lamp has flickered out in a night as

profound as poverty and utter loneliness could make it.
So if it was justice to Effie, what is it to that other woman? In truth, justice had nothing to do with it; she
loved the wrong man, that was all; and married or unmarried, it would have been the same, for a formula
doesn't make a man, nor the lack of it unmake him.
The fellow was superior in intellect. It is honesty only
which can wring so much from those who knew them
both, for as to any other thing she sat as high over him
as the stars are. Not that he was an actively bad man;
just one of those weak, uncertain, tumbling about characters, having sense enough to know it is a fine thing
to stand alone, and vanity enough to want the name
without the game, and cowardice enough to creep around
anything stronger than itself, and hang there, and spread
itself about, and say, "Lo, how straight am I!" And
if the stronger thing happens to be a father or a brother
or some such tolerant piece of friendly, self-sufficient
energy, he amuses himself awhile, and finally gives the
creeper a shake and says, "Here, now, go hang on somebody else if you can't stand alone", and the world says
he should have done it before. But if it happens to be
a mother or a sister or a wife or a sweetheart, she en-
courages him to think he is a wonderful person, that all
she does is really his own merit, and she is proud and
glad to serve him. If after a while she doesn't exactly
believe it any more, she says and does the same; and
the world says she is a fool,—which she is. But if, in
some sudden spurt of masculine self-assertiveness, she
decides to fling him off, the world says she is an un-
womanly woman,—which again she is; so much the
better.

Effie's creeper dabbled in literature. He wanted to be
a translator and several other things. His appearance

was mild and gentlemanly, even super-modest. He always spoke respectfully of Effie, and as if momentously impressed with a sense of duty towards her. They had started out to realize the free life together, and the glory of the new ideal had beckoned them forward. So no doubt he believed, for a pretender always deceives himself worse than anybody else. But still, at that particular period, he used to droop his head wearily and admit that he had made a great mistake. It was nobody's fault but his own, but of course—Effie and he were hardly fitted for each other. She could not well enter into his hopes and ambitions, never having had the opportunity to develop when she was younger. He had hoped to stimulate her in that direction, but he feared it was too late. So he said in a delicate and gentlemanly way, as he went from one house to the other, and was invited to dinner and supper and made himself believe he was looking for work. Effie, meanwhile, was taking home boys' caps to make, and worrying along incredibly on bread and tea, and walking the streets with the baby in her arms when she had no caps to make.

Of course when a man drinks other people's teas a great many times, and sits in their houses, and borrows odd shillings now and then, and assumes the gentleman, he is ultimately brought to the necessity of asking some one to tea with him; so one spring night the creeper approached Effie rather dubiously with the statement that he had asked two or three acquaintances to come in the next evening, and he supposed she would need to prepare tea. The girl was just fainting from starvation then, and she asked him wearily where he thought she was to get it. He cast about a while in his pusillanimous way for things that *she* might do, and finally proposed that she pawn the baby's dress,—the white dress she had made from one of her own girlhood dresses, and the only thing it had to wear when she took it out for air. That was the limit, even for Effie. She said she would take anything of her own if she had it, but not the baby's; and she turned her face to the wall and clung to the child.

When the tea-time came next day she went out with the baby and walked up and down the surging London streets looking in the windows and crushing back tears. What the creeper did with his guests she never knew, for she did not return till long after dusk, when she was too weary to wander any more, and she found no one there but himself and a dark stranger, who spoke little and with an Italian accent, but who measured her with serious, intense eyes. He listened to the creeper, but he looked at her; she was quite fagged out and more blood-less than ever as she sat motionless on the edge of the bed. When he went away he lifted his hat to her with the grace of an old time courtier, and begged her pardon if he had intruded. Some days after that he came in again, and brought a toy for the baby, and asked her if he might carry the child out a little for her; it looked sickly shut up there, but he knew it must be heavy for her to carry. The creeper suddenly discovered that he could carry the baby.

All this happened in the days when a pious queen sat on the throne of Spain. With eyes turned upward in much holiness, she failed to see the things done in her prisons, or hear the groans that rose up from the "zero" chamber in the fortress of Montjuich, though all Europe heard, and even in America the echo rang. While she told her beads her minister gave the order to "torture the An-archists"; and scarred with red-hot irons, maimed and deformed and maddened with the nameless horrors that the good devise to correct the bad, even unto this day the evidences of that infamous order live. But two men do not live,—the one who gave the order, and the one who revenged it.

It happened one night, in April, that Effie and the creeper and their sometime visitor met all three in one of those long low smothering London halls where many movements have originated, which in their developed proportions have taken possession of the House of Commons, and even stirred the dust in the House of Lords. There was a crowd of excited people talking all degrees of sense and nonsense in every language of the continent. Letters smuggled from the prison had been received; new tales of torture were passing from mouth to mouth; fresh propositions to arouse a general protest from civilization were bubbling up with the anger of every indignant man and woman. Drifting to the buzzing knots Effie heard some one translating: it was the letter of the tortured Noguès, who a month later was shot beneath the fortress wall. The words smote her ears like something hot and stinging:

"You know I am one of the three accusers (the other two are Ascheri and Molas) who figure in the trial. I could not bear the atrocious tortures of so many days. On my arrest I spent eight days without food or drink, obliged to walk continually to and fro or be flogged; and as if that did not suffice, I was made to trot as though I were a horse trained at the riding school, until worn with fatigue I fell to the ground. Then the hangmen burnt my lips with red-hot irons, and when I declared myself the author of the attempt they replied, 'You do not tell the truth. We know that the author is another one, but we want to know your accomplices. Besides you still retain six bombs, and along with little

Oller you deposited two bombs in the Rue Fivaller.
Who are your accomplices?'

"In spite of my desire to make an end of it I could
not answer anything. Whom should I accuse since all
are innocent? Finally six comrades were placed before
me, whom I had to accuse, and of whom I beg pardon.
Thus the declarations and the accusations that I made.
. . . I cannot finish; the hangmen are coming.

Noguès."

Sick with horror Effie would have gone away, but her
feet were like lead. She heard the next letter, the
pathetic prayer of Sebastian Sunyer, indistinctly; the
tortures had already seared her ears, but the crying for
help seemed to go up over her head like great sobs; she
felt herself washed round, sinking, in the desperate pain
of it. The piteous reiteration, "Listen you with your
honest hearts," "you with your pure souls," "good and
right-minded people," "good and right-feeling people,"
wailed through her like the wild pleading of a child who,
shrieking under the whip "Dear papa, good, sweet papa,
please don't whip me, please, please," seeks terror-wrung
flattery to escape the lash. The last cry, "Aid us in our
helplessness; think of our misery," made her quiver like
a reed. She walked away and sat down in a corner
alone; what could she do, what could any one do? Miserable creature that she was herself, her own misery
seemed so worthless beside that prison cry. And she
thought on, "Why does he want to live at all, why does
any one want to live, why do I want to live myself?"

After a while the creeper and his friend came to her,
and the latter sat down beside her, undemonstrative as
usual. At the next buzz in the room they two were left
alone. She looked at him once as she said, "What do
you think the people will do about it?"

He glanced at the crowd with a thin smile: "Do? Talk."

In a little time he said quietly: "It does you no good here. I will take you home and come back for David afterward." She had no idea of contradicting him; so they went out together. At the threshold of her room he said firmly, "I will come in for a few minutes; I have to speak to you."

She struck a light, put the baby on the bed, and looked at him questioningly. He had sat down with his back against the wall, and with rigidly folded arms stared straight ahead of him. Seeing that he did not speak, she said softly, falling into her native dialect, as all Scotch women do when they feel most: "I canna get thae poor creetyer's cries oot o' ma head. It's no human."

"No," he said shortly, and then with a sudden look at her, "Effie, what do you think love is?"

She answered him with surprised eyes and said nothing. He went on: "You love the child, don't you? You do for it, you serve it. That shows you love it. But do you think it's love that makes David act as he does to you? If he loved you, would he let you work as you work? Would he live off you? Wouldn't he wear the flesh off his fingers instead of yours? He doesn't love you. He isn't worth you. He isn't a bad man, but he isn't worth you. And you make him less worth. You ruin him, you ruin yourself, you kill the child. I can't see it any more. I come here, and I see you weaker every time, whiter, thinner. And I know if you keep on you'll die. I can't see it. I want you to leave him; let me work for you. I don't make much, but enough to let you rest. At least till you are well. I would wait till you left him of yourself, but I can't wait when I see you dying like this. I don't want anything of you, ex-

cept to serve you, to serve the child because it's yours.
Come away, to-night. You can have my room; I'll go
somewhere else. To-morrow I'll find you a better
place. You needn't see him any more. I'll tell him
myself. He won't do anything, don't be afraid. Come."
And he stood up.

Effie had sat astonished and dumb. Now she looked
up at the dark tense eyes above her, and said quietly,
"I dinna understand."

A sharp contraction went across the strong bent face:
"No? You don't understand what you are doing with
yourself? You don't understand that I love you, and
I can't see it? I don't ask you to love me; I ask you to
let me serve you. Only a little, only so much as to give
you health again; is that too much? You don't know
what you are to me. Others love beauty, but I—I see in
you the eternal sacrifice; your thin fingers that always
work, your face—when I look at it, it's just a white
shadow; you are the child of the people, that dies without crying. Oh, let me give myself for you. And leave
this man, who doesn't care for you, doesn't know you,
thinks you beneath him, uses you. I don't want you to
be his slave any more."

Effie clasped her hands and looked at them; then she
looked at the sleeping baby, smoothed the quilt, and said
quietly: "I didna take him the day to leave him the
morra. It's no my fault if ye're daft aboot me."

The dark face sharpened as one sees the agony in a
dying man, but his voice was very gentle, speaking always in his blurred English: "No, there is no fault in
you at all. Did I accuse you?"

The girl walked to the window and looked out. Some
way it was a relief from the burning eyes which seemed
to fill the room, no matter that she did not look at them.
And staring off into the twinkling London night, she

heard again the terrible sobs of Sebastian Sunyer's letter
rising up and drowning her with its misery. Without
turning around she said, low and hard, "I wonder ye
can thenk aboot thae things, an' yon deils burnin' men
alive."

The man drew his hand across his forehead. "Would
you like to hear that they,—one,—the worst of them,
was dead?"

"I thenk the worl' wadna be muckle the waur o't," she
answered, still looking away from him. He came up and
laid his hand on her shoulder. "Will you kiss me once?
I'll never ask again." She shook him off: "I dinna feel
for't." "Good-bye then. I'll go back for David." And
he returned to the hall and got the creeper and told him
very honestly what had taken place; and the creeper, to
his credit be it said, respected him for it, and talked a
great deal about being better in future to the girl. The
two men parted at the foot of the stairs, and the last
words that echoed through the hallway were: "No, I
am going away. But you will hear of me some day."

Now, what went on in his heart that night no one
knows; nor what indecision still kept him lingering fit-
fully about Effie's street a few days more; nor when the
indecision finally ceased; for no one spoke to him after
that, except as casual acquaintances meet, and in a week
he was gone. But what he did the whole world knows;
for even the Queen of Spain came out of her prayers to
hear how her torturing prime minister had been shot at
Santa Agueda, by a stern-faced man, who, when the
widow, grief-mad, spit in his face, quietly wiped his
cheek, saying, "Madam, I have no quarrel with women."
A few weeks later they garrotted him, and he said one
word before he died,—one only, "Germinal."

Over there in the long low London hall the gabbling
was hushed, and some one murmured how he had sat

silent in the corner that night when all were talking. The creeper passed round a book containing the history of the tortures, watching it jealously all the while, for said he, "Angiolillo gave it to me himself; he had it in his own hands."

Effie lay beside the baby in her room, and hid her face in the pillow to keep out the stare of the burning eyes that were dead; and over and over again she repeated, "Was it my fault, was it my fault?" The hot summer air lay still and smothering, and the immense murmur of the city came muffled like thunder below the horizon. Her heart seemed beating against the walls of a padded room. And gradually, without losing consciousness, she slipped into the world of illusion; around her grew the stifling atmosphere of the torture-chamber of Montjuich, and the choked cries of men in agony. She was sure that if she looked up she should see the demoniac face of Portas, the torturer. She tried to cry, "Mercy, mercy," but her dry lips clave. She had a whirling sensation, and the illusion changed; now there was the clank of soldiers' arms, a moment of insufferable stillness as the garrotte shaped itself out of the shadows in her eyes, then loud and clear, breaking the sullen quiet like the sharp ringing of a storm-bringing wind, "Germinal." She sprang up: the long vibration of the bell of St. Pancras was waving through the room; but to her it was the prolongation of the word, "Germ-inal-l-l—germinal-l-l——" Then suddenly she threw out her arms in the darkness, and whispered hoarsely, "Ay, I'll kiss ye the noo."

An hour later she was back at the old question, "Was it my fault?"

Poor girl, it is all over now, and all the same to the grass that roots in her bone, whether it was her fault or not. For the end that the man who had loved her foresaw, came, though it was slow in the coming. Let the creeper get credit for all that he did. He stiffened up in a year or so, and went to Paris and got some work; and there the worn little creature went to him, and wrote to her old friends that she was better off at last. But it was too late for that thin shell of a body that had starved so much; at the first trial she broke and died. And so she sleeps and is forgotten. And the careless boy-angel who mixed all these destinies up so unobservantly has never yet whispered her name in the ear of the widowed Lady Canovas del Castillo.

Nor will the birds that fly thither carry it now; for *it was not "Effie."*

The Reward of an Apostate

I HAVE sinned: and I am rewarded according to my sin, which was great. There is no forgiveness for me; let no man think there is forgiveness for sin: the gods cannot forgive.

This was my sin, and this is my punishment, that I forsook my god to follow a stranger—only a while, a very brief, brief while—and when I would have returned there was no more returning. I cannot worship any more,—that is my punishment; I cannot worship any more.

Oh, that my god will none of me? That is an old sorrow! My god was Beauty, and I am all unbeautiful, and ever was. There is no grace in these harsh limbs of mine, nor was at any time. I, to whom the glory of a lit eye was as the shining of stars in a deep well, have only dull and faded eyes, and always had; the chiseled lip and chin whereover runs the radiance of life in bubbling gleams, the cup of living wine was never mine to taste or kiss. I am earth-colored, and for my own ugliness sit in the shadow, that the sunlight may not see me, nor the beloved of my god. But, once, in my hidden corner, behind the curtain of shadows, I blinked at the glory of the world, and had such joy of it as only the ugly know, sitting silent and worshiping, forgetting themselves and forgotten. Here in my brain it glowed, the shimmering of the dying sun upon the shore, the long gold line between the sand and sea, where the sliding foam caught fire and burned to death. Here in my brain it shone, the white moon on the wrinkling river, running away, a dancing ghost line in the illimitable night. Here in my brain rose the mountain curves, the great still world of stone, summit upon summit sweeping skyward, lonely and conquering. Here in my brain, my little brain, behind this tiny ugly wall of bone stretched over with its dirty yellow skin, glittered the far high blue desert with its sand of stars, as I have watched it, nights and nights, alone, hid in the shadows of the prairie grass. Here rolled and swelled the seas of corn, and blossoming fields of nodding bloom; and flower-flies on their hovering wings went flickering up and down. And the quick spring of lithe-limbed things went scattering dew across the sun; and singing streams went shining down the rocks, spreading bright veils upon the crags.

Here in my brain, my silent unrevealing brain, were the eyes I loved, the lips I dared not kiss, the sculptured heads and tendriled hair. They were here always in my wonder-house, my house of Beauty, the temple of my god. I shut the door on common life and worshiped here. And no bright, living, flying thing, in whose body Beauty dwells as guest, can guess the ecstatic joy of a brown, silent creature, a toad-thing, squatting on the shadowed ground, self-blotted, motionless, thrilling with the presence of All-Beauty, though it has no part therein.

But the gods are many. And once a strange god came to me. Sharp upon the shadowy ground he stood, and beckoned me with knotted fingers. There was no beauty in his lean figure and sunken cheeks; but up and down the muscles ran like snakes beneath his skin, and his dark eyes had somber fires in them. And as I looked at him, I felt the leap of prisoned forces in myself, in the earth, in the air, in the sun; all throbbed with the pulse of the wild god's heart. Beauty vanished from my wonder-house; and where his images had been I heard the clang and roar of machinery, the forging of links that stretched to the sun, chains for the tides, chains for the winds; and curious lights went shining through thick walls as through air, and down through the shell of the world itself, to the great furnaces within. Into those seething depths, the god's eyes peered, smiling and triumphing; then with an up-glance at the sky and a waste-glance at me, he strode off.

This is my great sin, for which there is no pardon: I followed him, the rude god Energy; followed him, and in that abandoned moment swore to be quit of Beauty, which had given me nothing, and to be worshiper of him to whom I was akin, ugly but sinuous, resolute, daring, defiant, maker and breaker of things, remoulder of the world. I followed him, I would have run abreast with him; I loved him, not with that still ecstasy of flooding joy wherewith my own god filled me of old, but with impetuous, eager fires, that burned and beat through all the blood-threads of me. "I love you, love me back," I cried, and would have flung myself upon his neck. Then he turned on me with a ruthless blow, and fled away over the world, leaving me crippled, stricken, powerless, a fierce pain driving through my veins—gusts of pain!—And I crept back into my old cavern, stumbling, blind and deaf, only for the haunting vision of my shame and the rushing sound of fevered blood.

The pain is gone. I see again; I care no more for the taunt and blow of that fierce god who was never mine. But in my wonder-house it is all still and bare; no image lingers on the blank mirrors any more. No singing bell floats in the echoless dome. Forms rise and pass; but neither mountain curve nor sand nor sea, nor shivering river, nor the faces of the flowers, nor flowering faces of my god's beloved, touch aught within me now. Not one poor thrill of vague delight for me, who felt the glory of the stars within my finger tips. It slips past me like water. Brown without and clay within! No wonder now behind the ugly wall; an empty temple! I cannot worship, I cannot love, I cannot care. All my life-service is unweighed against that faithless hour of my forswearing.

It is just; it is the Law; I am forsworn, and the gods have given me the Reward of An Apostate.

At the End of the Alley

IT is a long narrow pocket opening on a little street which runs like a tortuous seam up and down the city, over there. It was at the end of the summer; and in summer, in the evening, the mouth of the pocket is hard to find, because of the people, in it and about, who sit across the passage, gasping at the dirty winds that come loafing down the street like crafty beggars seeking a hole to sleep in—like mean beggars, bereft of the spirit of free windhood. Down in the pocket itself the air is quite dead; one feels oneself enveloped in a scum-covered pool of it, and at every breath long filaments of invisible roots, swamp-roots, tear and tangle in your floundering lungs.

I had to go to the very end, to the bottom of the pocket. There, in the deepest of these alley-holes, lives the woman to whom I am indebted for the whiteness of this waist I wear. How she does it, I don't know; poverty works miracles like that, just as the black marsh mud gives out lilies.

At the very last door I knocked, and presently a man's voice, weak and suffocated, called from a window above. I explained.—"There's a chair there; sit down. She'll be home soon." And the voice was caught in a cough.

This, then, was the consumptive husband she had told

me of! I looked up at the square hole dimly outlined in
the darkness, whence the cough issued, and suddenly felt
a horrible pressure at my heart and a curious sense of
entanglement, as if all the invisible webs of disease had
momentarily acquired a conscious sense of prey within
their clutch, and tightened on it like an octopus. The
haunting terror of the unknown, the dim horror of an
inimic Presence, recoil before the merciless creeping and
floating of an enemy one cannot grasp or fight, repulsive
turning from a Thing that has reached behind while you
have been seeking to face it, that is there awaiting you
with the frightful ironic laughter of the Silence—all this
swept round and through me as I stared up through the
night.

Up there on the bed he was lying, he who had been
meshed in the fatal web for three long years—and was
struggling still! In the darkness I felt his breath draw.

The sharp barking of a dog came as a relief. I turned
to the broken chair, and sat down to wait. The alley was
hemmed in by a high wall, and from the farther side of
it there towered up four magnificent old trees, whose
great crowns sent down a whispering legend of vanished
forests and the limitless sweep of clean air that had
washed through them, long ago, and that would never
come again. How long, how long since those far days
of purity, before the plague spot of Man had crept upon
them! How strong those proud old giants were that had
not yet been strangled! How beautiful they were! How
mean and ugly were the misshapen things that sat in the
doorways of the foul dens that they had made, chattering,
chattering, as ages ago the apes had chattered in the forest! What curious beasts they were, with their paws and
heads sticking out of the coverings they had twisted
round their bodies—chattering, chattering always, and

always moving about, unable to understand the still strong growths of silence.

So a half hour passed.

At last I saw a parting in the group of bodies across the entrance of the pocket, and a familiar weary figure carrying a basket, coming down the brickway. She stopped half way where a widening of the alley furnished the common drying place, and a number of clothes lines crossed and recrossed each other, casting a net of shadows on the pavement; after a glance at the sky, which had clouded over, she sighed heavily and again advanced. In the sickly light of the alley lamp the rounded shoulders seemed to droop like an old crone's. Yet the woman was still young. That she might not be startled, I called "Good evening."

The answer was spoken in that tone of forced cheerfulness which the wretched always give to their employers; but she sank upon the step with the habitual "My, but I'm glad to sit down," of one who seldom sits.

"Tired out, I suppose. The day has been so hot."

"Yes, and I've got to go to work and iron again till eleven o'clock, and it's awful hot in that kitchen. I don't mind the washing so much in summer; I wash out here. But it's hot ironing. Are you in a hurry?"

I said no, and sat on. "How much rent do you pay?" I asked.

"Seven dollars."

"Three rooms?"

"Yes."

"One over the other?"

"Yes. It's an awful rent, and he won't fix anything. The door is half off its hinges, and the paper is a sight."

"Have you lived here long?"

"Over three years. We moved here before he got sick.

I don't keep nothing right now, but it used to be nice.
It's so quiet back here away from the street; you don't
hear no noise. That fence ought to be whitewashed. I
used to keep it white, and everything clean. And it was
so nice to sit out here in summer under them trees. You
could just think you were in the park."

A curious wonder went through me. Somewhere back
in me a voice was saying, "To him that hath shall be
given, and from him that hath not, it shall be taken away
even that which he hath." This horrible pool had been
"nice" to her! Again I felt the abyss seizing me with
its tentacles, and high overhead in the tree-crowns I
seemed to hear a spectral mockery of laughter.

"Yes," I forced myself to say, "they are splendid trees.
I wonder they have lived so long."

"'Tis funny, aint it? That's a great big yard in there;
the man that used to own it was a gardener, and there's
a lot of the curiousest flowers there yet. But he's dead
now, and the folks that's got it don't keep up nothing.
They're waiting to sell it, I suppose."

Above, over our heads, the racking cough sounded
again. "Aint it terrible?" she murmured. "Day and
night, day and night; he don't get no rest, and neither do
I. It's no wonder some people commits suicide."

"Does he ever speak of it?" I asked. Her voice
dropped to a semi-whisper. "Not now so much, since
the church people's got hold of him. He used to; I
think he'd a done it if it hadn't been for them. But
they've been kind o' talkin' to him lately, and tellin' him
it wouldn't be right,—on account of the insurance, you
know."

My heart gave a wild bound of revolt, and I shut
my teeth fast. O man, man, what have you made of yourself! More stupid than all the beasts of the earth, for a

dole of the things you make to be robbed of, living,—to be robbed of and poisoned with—you consent to the death that eats with a million mouths, eats inexorably. You submit to unnamable torture in the holy name of— Insurance! And in the name of Insurance this miserable woman keeps alive the bones of a man!

I took my bundle and went. And all the way I felt myself tearing through the tendrils of death that hung and swayed from the noisome wall, and caught at things as they passed. And all the way there pressed upon me pictures of the skeleton and the woman, clothed in firm flesh, young and joyous, and thrilling with the love of the well and strong. Ah, if some one had said to her then, "Some day you will slave to keep him alive through fruitless agonies, that for your last reward you may take the price of his pain"!

II.—ALONE

I WAS wrong. I thought she wanted the insurance money, but I misunderstood her. I found it out one wild October day more than a year later, when for the second time I sought the end of the alley.

The sufferer had "suffered out"; the gaunt and wasted shell of the man lay no more by the window in the upper story. The woman was free. "Rest at last," I thought, "for both of them."

But it was not as I thought.

I expected ease to come into the woman's drawn face, and relaxation to her stooping figure. But something else came upon both, something quite unwonted and inexplicable; a wandering look in the eyes, a stupid drop to the mouth, an uncertainty in her walk, as of one who is half minded to go back and look for something. There was, too, an irritating irregularity in the performance of her work, which began to be annoying.

At last, on that October day, this new unreliability reached the limit of provocation. I was leaving the city; I needed my laundry, needed it at once; and here it was four o'clock in the afternoon, the train due at night, and packing impossible till the wash came. It was five days overdue.

The wind was howling furiously, the rain driving in sheets, but there was no alternative; I must get to the "End of the Alley" and back, somehow.

The gray, rain-drenched atmosphere was still grayer in the alley,—still, still grayer at the end. And what with the gray of it and the rain of it, I could scarcely see the thing that sat facing me when I opened the door,— a sort of human blur, hunched in a rocking-chair, its head sunken on its breast.

In response to my startled exclamation, the face was lifted vacantly for a second, and then dropped again. But I had seen: drunk, dead drunk!

And this woman had never drunk.

I looked around the wretched room. By the window, where the gray light trailed in, stood a table covered with unwashed dishes; some late flies were crawling in the gutters of slop, besotted derelicts of insects, stupidly staggering up and down the cracked china. On the stove stood a number of flat-irons, but there was no fire. A mass of unironed clothes lay on an old couch and over the backs of two unoccupied chairs. On the wall above the couch, hung the portrait of the dead man.

I walked to the slumping figure in the rocker, and with ill-contained brutality demanded: "So this is why you did not bring my clothes! Where are they?"

I heard my own voice cutting like the edge of a knife, and felt half-ashamed when that weak, shaking thing lifted up its foolish face, and stared at me with watery, uncomprehending eyes.

"My clothes," I reiterated; "are they here or upstairs?"

"Guess-s-so," stammered the uncertain voice, "g-guess so."

"Nothing for it but to find them myself," I muttered, beginning the search through the pile on the couch. Nothing of mine there, so I needs must climb to the Golgotha on the second floor, from which the Cross had disappeared, but which still bore traces of its victim's long crucifixion,—a pair of old bed-slippers still by the window, a sleeping-cap on the wall. Some cannot but leave so the things that have touched their dead.

One by one I found the "rough-dry" garments, here, there, in the hall-way, in the garret, hanging or crumpled up among dozens of others. And all the while I hunted, the rain beat and the wind blew, and a low third sound kept mingling with them, rising from the lower floor. My heart smote me when I heard it, for I knew it was the woman sobbing. The self-righteous Pharisee within me gave an impatient sneer: "Alcohol tears!" But something else clutched at my throat, and I found myself glancing at the dead man's shoes.

When I went downstairs, I avoided the rocking-chair, tied up my bundle, counted out the money, laid it on the table, and then turning round said, deliberately and harshly: "There is your money; don't buy whisky with it, Mrs. Bossert."

Crying had a little sobered her. She looked up, still with less light in her face than in an intelligent dog's, but with some dim self-consciousness. It was as a face that had appeared behind deforming bubbles of water. She half lifted her hand, let it fall, and stammered, "No, I won't, I won't. It don't do nobody no good."

The senseless desire to preach seized hold of me. "Mrs. Bossert," I cried out, "aren't you ashamed of yourself? A woman like you, who went through so much, and so long, and so bravely! And now, when you could get along all right, to act like this!"

The soggy mouth dropped open, the glazy eyes stared at me, fixedly and foolishly, then shifted to the portrait on the wall; and with a mawkish simper, as of some old drab playing sixteen, she slobbered out, nodding to the portrait: "All—for the love—o' him."

It was so utterly ludicrous that I laughed. Then a cold rage took me: "Look here," I said (and again I heard my own voice, grim and quiet, cutting the air like a whip), "if you believe, as I have heard you say, that your husband can look down on you from anywhere, remember you couldn't do a thing to hurt him worse than you're doing now. 'Love' indeed!"

The lash went home. The stricken figure huddled closer; the voice came out like a dumb thing's moan: "Oh—I'm all alone."

Then suddenly I understood. I had taken it for mockery, and profanation, that leering look at the shadow on the wall, that driveling stammer, "All—for the love—o' him." And it had been a solemn thing! No lover's word spoken in the morning of youth with the untried day before it, under the seductive witchery of answering breath and kisses, rushing blood and throbbing bodies; but the word of a woman bent with service, seamed with labor, haggard with watching; the word of a woman who, at the washtub, had kept her sufferer by the work of her hands, and watched him between the snatches of her sleep. The immemorial passion of a common heart, that *is* not much, that *had* not much, and has lost all. Years were in it. For years she had had her burden to carry; and she had carried it to the edge of the grave. There it had fallen from her, and her arms were empty. Nothing to do any more. Alone.

She sat up suddenly with a momentary flare of light in her face.—"As long as I had him," she said, "I could do. I thought I'd be glad when he was gone, a many and many a time. But I'd rather he was up there yet. . . . I did everything. I didn't put him away mean. There was a hundred and twenty-five dollars insurance. I spent it all on him. He was covered with flowers."

The flare died down, and she fell together like a collapsing bag. I saw the gray vacancy moving inward toward the last spark of intelligence in her eyes, as an ashing coal whitens inward toward the last dull red point of fire. Then this heap of rags shuddered with an inhuman whine, "A-l-o-n-e."

In the crowding shadows I felt the desolation pressing me like a vise. Behind that sunken heap in the chair gathered a midnight specter; for a moment I caught a flash from its royal, malignant eyes, the Monarch of human ruins, the murderous Bridegroom of widowed souls, King Alcohol.

"After all, as well that way as another," I muttered: and aloud (but the whip-cord had gone out of my voice), "The money is on the table."

She did not hear me; the Bridegroom "had given His Beloved Sleep."

I went out softly into the wild rain, and overhead, among the lashing arms of the leafless trees, and around the alley pocket, the wind was whining: "A-l-o-n-e."

To Strive and Fail

THERE was a lonely wind crying around the house, and wailing away through the twilight, like a child that has been refused and gone off crying. Every now and then the trees shivered with it, and dropped a few leaves that splashed against the windows like big, soft tears, and then fell down on the dark, dying grass, and lay there till the next wind rose and whirled them away. Rain was gathering. Close by the gray patch of light within the room a white face bent over a small table, and dust-dim fingers swept across the strings of a zither. The low, pathetic opening chords of Albert's "Herbst-Klage" wailed for a moment like the wind; then a false note sounded, and the player threw her arms across the table and rested her face upon them. What was the use? She knew how it ought to be, but she could never do it,—never make the strings strike true to the song that was sounding within, sounding as the wind and the rain and the falling leaves sounded it, as long ago the wizard Albert had heard and conjured it out of the sound-sea, before the little black notes that carried the message over the world were written. The weary brain wandered away over the mystery of the notes, and she whispered dully, "A sign to the eye, and a sound to the ear—and that is his gift to the world—his will—and he is dead, dead, dead;—he was so great, and

they are so silly, those little black foolish dots—and yet
they are there—and by them his soul sings—"

The numb pain at her heart forced some sharp tears
from the closed eyes. She bent and unbent her fingers
hopelessly, two or three times, and then let them lie out
flat and still. It was not their fault, not the fingers'
fault; they could learn to do it, if they only had the
chance; but they could never, never have the chance.
They must always do something else, always a hundred
other things first, always save and spare and patch and
contrive; there was never time to do the thing she
longed for most. Only the odd moments, the unexpected freedoms, the stolen half-hours, in which to live
one's highest dream, only the castaway time for one's
soul! And every year the fleeting glory waned, wavered.
sunk away more and more sorrowfully into the gray,
soundless shadows of an unlived life. Once she had
heard it so clearly,—long ago, on the far-off sun-spaced,
wind-singing fields of home,—the wild sweet choruses,
the songs no man had ever sung. Still she heard them
sometimes in the twilight, in the night, when she sat
alone and work was over; high and thin and fading,
only sound-ghosts, but still with the incomparable
glory of a first revelation, a song no one else has ever
heard, a marvel to be seized and bodied; only,—they
faded away into the nodding sleep that would conquer,
and in the light and rush of day were mournfully silent.
And she never captured them, never would; life was
half over now.

With the thought she started up, struck the chords
again, a world of plaint throbbing through the strings;
surely the wizard himself would have been satisfied. But
ah, once more the fatal uncertainty of the fingers. . . .
She bit the left hand savagely, then touched it, softly
and remorsefully, with the other, murmuring: "Poor

fingers! Not your fault." At last she rose and stood at the window, looking out into the night, and thinking of the ruined gift, the noblest gift, that had been hers and would die dumb; thinking of the messages that had come to her up out of the silent dark and sunk back into it, unsounded; of the voices she would have given to the messages of the masters, and never would give now; and with a bitter compression of the lips she said: "Well, I was born to strive and fail."

And suddenly a rush of feeling swept her own life out of sight, and away out in the deepening night she saw the face of an old, sharp-chinned, white-haired, dead man; he had been her father once, strong and young, with chestnut hair and gleaming eyes, and with his own dream of what he had to do in life. Perhaps he, too, had heard sounds singing in the air, a new message waiting for deliverance. It was all over now; he had grown old and thin-faced and white, and had never done anything in the world; at least nothing for himself, his very own; he had sewn clothes,—thousands, millions of stitches in his work-weary life—no doubt there were still in existence scraps and fragments of his work,—in some old ragbag perhaps—beautiful, fine stitches, into which the keen eyesight and the deft hand had passed, still showing the artist-craftsman. But *that* was not his work; that was the service society had asked of him and he had rendered; himself, his own soul, that wherein he was different from other men, the unbought thing that the soul does for its own outpouring,—that was no-where. And over there, among the low mounds of the soldiers' graves, his bed was made, and he was lying in it, straight and still, with the rain crying softly above him. He had been so full of the lust of life, so alert, so active! and nothing of it all!—"Poor father, you failed too," she muttered softly.

And then behind the wraith of the dead man there rose an older picture, a face she had never seen, dead fifty years before; but it shone through the other face, and outshone it, luminous with great suffering, much overcoming, and complete and final failure. It was the face of a woman not yet middle-aged, smitten with death, with the horror of utter strangeness in the dying eyes; the face of a woman lost in a strange city of a strange land, and with her little crying, helpless children about her, facing the inexorable agony there on the pavement, where she was sinking down, and only foreign words falling in the dying ears!—She, too, had striven; how she had striven! Against the abyss of poverty there in the old world; against the load laid on her by Nature, Law, Society, the triune God of Terror; against the inertia of another will. She had bought coppers with blood, and spared and saved and endured and waited; she had bent the gods to her will; she had sent her husband to America, the land of freedom and promise; she had followed him at last, over the great blue bitter water with its lapping mouths that had devoured one of her little ones upon the way; she had been driven like a cow in the shambles at the landing stage; she had been robbed of all but her ticket, and with her little children had hungered for three days on the overland journey; she had lived it through, and set foot in the promised land; but somehow the waiting face was not there, had missed her or she, him,—and lost and alone with Death and the starving babes, she sank at the foot of the soldiers' monument, and the black mist came down on the courageous eyes, and the light was flickering out forever. With a bitter cry the living figure in the room stretched its hands toward the vision in the night. There was nothing there, she knew it; nothing in the heavens above nor the earth beneath to hear the cry,—not so much as a crumbling bone any more,—but she called brokenly, "Oh, why must she die so, with nothing, nothing, not one little reward after all that struggle? To fall on the pavement and die in the hospital at last!"

And shuddering, with covered eyes and heavy breath, she added wearily, "No wonder that I fail; I come of those who failed; my father, his mother,—and before her?"

Behind the fading picture, stretched dim, long shadows of silent generations, with rounded shoulders and bent backs and sullen, conquered faces. And they had all, most likely, dreamed of some wonderful thing they had to do in the world, and all had died and left it undone. And their work had been washed away, as if writ in water, and no one knew their dreams. And of the fruit of their toil other men had eaten, for that was the will of the triune god; but of themselves was left no trace, no sound, no word, in the world's glory; no carving upon stone, no indomitable ghost shining from a written sign, no song singing out of black foolish spots on paper,— nothing. They were as though they had not been. And as they all had died, she too would die, slave of the triple Terror, sacrificing the highest to the meanest, that somewhere in some lighted ball-room or gas-bright theater, some piece of vacant flesh might wear one more jewel in her painted hair.

"My soul," she said bitterly, "my soul for their diamonds!" It was time to sleep, for to-morrow—WORK.

The Sorrows of the Body

I HAVE never wanted anything more than the wild creatures have,—a broad waft of clean air, a day to lie on the grass at times, with nothing to do but slip the blades through my fingers, and look as long as I pleased at the whole blue arch, and the screens of green and white between; leave for a month to float and float along the salt crests and among the foam, or roll with my naked skin over a clean long stretch of sunshiny sand; food that I liked, straight from the cool ground, and time to taste its sweetness, and time to rest after tasting; sleep when it came, and stillness, that the sleep might leave me when it would, not sooner— Air, room, light, rest, nakedness when I would not be clothed, and when I would be clothed, garments that did not fetter; freedom to touch my mother earth, to be with her in storm and shine, as the wild things are,—this is what I wanted, —this, and free contact with my fellows;—not to love, and lie and be ashamed, but to love and say I love, and be glad of it; to feel the currents of ten thousand years of passion flooding me, body to body, as the wild things meet. I have asked no more.

But I have not received. Over me there sits that pitiless tyrant, the Soul; and I am nothing. It has driven me to the city, where the air is fever and fire, and said, "Breathe this;—I would learn; I cannot learn in the empty fields; temples are here,—stay." And when my poor, stifled lungs have panted till it seemed my chest must burst, the Soul has said, "I will allow you, then, an hour or two; we will ride, and I will take my book and read meanwhile."

And when my eyes have cried out with tears of pain for the brief vision of freedom drifting by, only for leave to look at the great green and blue an hour, after the long, dull-red horror of walls, the Soul has said, "I cannot waste the time altogether; I must know! Read." And when my ears have plead for the singing of the crickets and the music of the night, the Soul has answered, "No: gongs and whistles and shrieks are unpleasant if you listen; but school yourself to hearken to the spiritual voice, and it will not matter."

When I have beat against my narrow confines of brick and mortar, brick and mortar, the Soul has said, "Miserable slave! Why are you not as I, who in one moment fly to the utterest universe? It matters not where you are, *I* am free."

When I would have slept, so that the lids fell heavily and I could not lift them, the Soul has struck me with a lash, crying, "Awake! Drink some stimulant for those shrinking nerves of yours! There is no time to sleep till the work is done." And the cursed poison worked upon me, till *Its* will was done.

When I would have dallied over my food, the Soul has ordered, "Hurry, hurry! Do I have time to waste on this disgusting scene? Fill yourself and be gone!"

When I have envied the very dog, rubbing its bare back along the ground in the sunlight, the Soul has exclaimed, "Would you degrade me so far as to put yourself on a level with beasts?" And my bands were drawn tighter.

When I have looked upon my kind, and longed to embrace them, hungered wildly for the press of arms and

lips, the Soul has commanded sternly, "Cease, vile creature of fleshly lusts! Eternal reproach! Will you forever shame me with your beastliness?"

And I have always yielded: mute, joyless, fettered, I
have trod the world of the Soul's choosing, and served
and been unrewarded. Now I am broken before my
time; bloodless, sleepless, breathless,—half-blind, racked
at every joint, trembling with every leaf. "Perhaps I
have been too hard," said the Soul; "you shall have a
rest." The boon has come too late. The roses are beneath my feet now, but the perfume does not reach me;
the willows trail across my cheek and the great arch is
overhead, but my eyes are too weary to lift to it; the
wind is upon my face, but I cannot bare my throat to its
caress; vaguely I hear the singing of the Night through
the long watches when sleep does not come, but the answering vibration thrills no more. Hands touch mine—
I longed for them so once—but I am as a corpse. I remember that I wanted all these things, but now the
power to want is crushed from me, and only the memory
of my denial throbs on, with its never-dying pain. And
still I think, if I were left alone long enough—but already
I hear the Tyrant up there plotting to slay me.—"Yes,"
it keeps saying, "it is about time! I will not be chained
to a rotting carcass. If my days are to pass in perpetual idleness I may as well be annihilated. I will make
the wretch do me one more service.—You have clamored
to be naked in the water. Go now, and lie in it forever."

Yes: that is what It is saying, and I—the sea stretches
down there——

The Triumph of Youth

THE afternoon blazed and glittered along the motionless tree-tops and down into the yellow dust of
the road. Under the shadows of the trees, among
the powdered grass and bushes, sat a woman and a man.
The man was young and handsome in a way, with a
lean eager face and burning eyes, a forehead in the old
poetic mould crowned by loose dark waves of hair; his
chin was long, his lips parted devouringly and his glances
seemed to eat his companion's face. It was not a pretty
face, not even ordinarily good looking,—sallow, not
young, only youngish; but there was a peculiar mobility
about it, that made one notice it. She waved her hand
slowly from East to West, indicating the horizon, and
said dreamingly: "How wide it is, how far it is! One
can get one's breath. In the city I always feel that the
walls are squeezing my chest." After a little silence she
asked without looking at him: "What are you thinking
of, Bernard?"

"You," he murmured.

She glanced at him under her lids musingly, stretched
out her hand and touched his eyelids with her finger-tips,
and turned aside with a curious fleeting smile. He
caught at her hand, but failing to touch it as she drew it
away, bit his lip and forcedly looked off at the sky and
the landscape: "Yes," he said in a strained voice, "it is

beautiful, after the city. I wish we could stay in it."

The woman sighed: "That's what I have been wishing for the last fifteen years."

He bent towards her eagerly: "Do you think—" he stopped and stammered, "You know we have been planning, a few of us, to club together and get a little farm somewhere near—would you—do you think—would you be one of us?"

She laughed, a little low, sad laugh: "I wouldn't be any good, you know. I couldn't do the work that ought to be done. I would come fast enough and I would try. But I'm a little too old, Bernard. The rest are young enough to make mistakes and live to make them good; but when I would have my lesson learned, my strength would be gone. It's half gone now."

"No, it isn't," burst out the youth. "You're worth half a dozen of those young ones. Old, old—one would think you were seventy. And you're not old; you will never be old."

She looked up where a crow was wheeling in the air. "If," she said slowly, following its motions with her eyes, "you once plant your feet on my face, and you will, you impish bird—my Bernard will sing a different song."

"No, Bernard won't," retorted the youth. "Bernard knows his own mind, even if he is 'only a boy.' I don't love you for your face, you—"

She interrupted him with a shrug and a bitter sneer. "Evidently! Who would?"

A look of mingled pain and annoyance overspread his features. "How you twist my words. You are beautiful to me; and you know what I meant."

"Well," she said, throwing herself backward against a tree-trunk and stretching out her feet on the grass, ripples of amusement wavering through the cloudy expression, "tell me what do you love in me."

He was silent, biting his lower lip.

"I'll tell you then," she said. "It's my energy, the life in me. That is youth, and my youth has overlived its time. I've had a long lease, but it's going to expire soon. So long as you don't see it, so long as my life seems fuller than yours—well—; but when the failure of life becomes visible, while your own is still in its growth, you will turn away. When my feet won't spring any more, yours will still be dancing. And you will want dancing feet with you."

"I will not," he answered shortly. "I've seen plenty of other women; I saw all the crowd coming up this morning and there wasn't a woman there to compare with you. I don't say I'll never love others, but now I don't; if I see another woman like you— But I never could love one of those young girls."

"Sh—sh," she said glancing down the road where a whirl of dust was making towards them, in the center of which moved a band of bright young figures, "there they come now. Don't they look beautiful?" There were four young girls in front, their faces radiant with sun and air, and daisy wreaths in their gleaming hair; they had their arms around each other's waists and sang as they walked, with neither more accord nor discord than the birds about them. The voices were delicious in their youth and joy; one heard that they were singing not to produce a musical effect, but from the mere wish to sing. Behind them came a troop of young fellows, coats off, heads bare, racing all over the roadside, jostling each other and purposely provoking scrambles. The tallest one had a nimbus of bright curls crowning a glowing face, dimpled and sparkling as a child's. The girls glanced shyly at him under their lashes as he danced about now in front and now behind them, occasionally tossing them a flower, but mostly hustling his comrades about. Behind these came older people with three or four very little children riding on their backs.

As the group came abreast of our couple they stopped to exchange a few words, then went on. When they had passed out of hearing the woman sat with a sphinx-like stare in her eyes, looking steadily at the spot where the bright head had nodded to her as it passed.

"Like a wildflower on a stalk," she murmured softly, narrowing her eyes as if to fix the vision, "like a tall tiger-lily."

Her companion's face darkened perceptibly. "What do you mean? What do you see?" he asked.

"The vision of Youth and Beauty," she answered in the tone of a sleep-walker, "and the glory and triumph of it, —the immortality of it—its splendid indifference to its ruined temples, and all its humble worshipers. Do you know," turning suddenly to him with a sharp change in face and voice, "what I would be wicked enough to do, if I could?"

He smiled tolerantly: "You, wicked? Dear one, you couldn't be wicked."

"Oh, but I could! If there were any way to fix Davy's head forever, just as he passed us now,—forever, so that all the world might keep it and see it for all time, I would cut it off with this hand! Yes, I would." Her eyes glittered mercilessly.

He shook his head smiling: "You wouldn't kill a bug, let alone Davy."

"I tell you I would. Do you remember when Nathaniel died? I felt bad enough, but do you know the week before when he was so very sick, I went out one day to a beautiful glen we used to visit together. They had been improving it! they had improved it so much that the water is all dying out of the creek; the little boats that used to float like pond lilies lie all helpless in the mud, and hardly a ribbon of water goes over the fall, and the old giant trees are withering. Oh, it hurt me so to think the glory of a thousand years was vanishing before my eyes and I couldn't hold it. And suddenly the question came into my head: 'If you had the power would you save Nathaniel's life or bring back the water to the glen?' And I didn't hesitate a minute. I said, 'Let Nathaniel die and all my best loved ones and I myself, but bring back the glory of the glen!"

"When I think," she went on turning away and becoming dreamy again, "of all the beauty that is gone that I can never see, that is lost forever—the beauty that had to alter and die,—it stifles me with the pain of it. Why must it all die?"

He looked at her wonderingly. "It seems to me," he said slowly, "that beauty worship is almost a disease with you. I wouldn't like to care so much for mere outsides."

"We never long for the thing we are rich in," she answered in a dry, changed voice. Nevertheless his face lighted, it was pleasant to be rich in the thing she worshiped. He had gradually drawn near her feet and now suddenly bent forward and kissed them passionately. "Don't," she cried sharply, "it's too much like self-abasement   And besides—"

His face was white and quivering, his voice choked. "Well—what besides—"

"The time will come when you will wish you had reserved that kiss for some other foot. Some one to whom it will all be new, who will shudder with the joy of it,

who will meet you half way, who will believe all that
you say, and say like things in fullness of heart. And I
perhaps will see you, and know that in your heart you are
sorry you gave something to me that you would have
ungiven if you could."

He buried his face in his hands. "You do not love me
at all," he said. "You do not believe me."

A curious softness came into the answer: "Oh, yes,
dear, I believe you. Years ago I believed myself when
I said the same sort of thing. But I told you I am getting old. I can not unmake what the years have made,
nor bring back what they have stolen. I love you *for
your face*", the words had a sting in them, "and for your
soul too. And I am glad to be loved by you. But, do
you know what I am thinking?"

He did not answer.

"I am thinking that as I sit here, beloved by you and
others who are young and beautiful—it is no lie—in a—
well, in a triumph I have not sought, but which I am
human enough to be glad of, envied no doubt by those
young girls,—I am thinking how the remorseless feet of
Youth will tramp on me soon, and carry you away. And"
—very slowly—"in my day of pain, you will not be near,
nor the others. I shall be alone; age and pain are un-
lovely."

"You won't let me come near you," he said wildly. "I
would do anything for you. I always want to do things
for you to spare you, and you never let me. When you
are in pain you will push me away."

A fairly exultant glitter flashed in her face. "Yes,"
she said, "I know my secret. That is how I have stayed
young so long. See," she said, stretching out her arms,
"other women at my age are past the love of men. Their
affections have gone to children. And I have broken the

law of nature and prolonged the love of youth because—
I have been strong and stood alone. But there is an end.
Things change, seasons change, you, I, all change; what's
the use of saying 'Never—forever, forever—never,' like
the old clock on the stairs? It's a big lie."

"I won't talk any more," he said, "but when the time
comes you will see."

She nodded: "Yes, I will see."

"Do you think all people alike?"

"As like as ants. People are vessels which life fills
and breaks, as it does trees and bees and other sorts of
vessels. They play when they are little, and then they
love and then they have children and then they die. Ants
do the same."

"To be sure. But I don't deceive myself as to the
scope of it."

The crowd were returning now, and by tacit consent
they arose and joined the group. Down the road they
jumped a fence into a field and had to cross a little
stream. "Where is our bridge?" called the boys. "We
made a bridge. Some one has stolen our bridge."

"Oh, come on," cried Davy, "let's jump it." Three ran
and sprang; they landed laughing and taunting the rest.
Bernard sought out his beloved. "Shall I help you
over?" he asked.

"No," she said shortly, "help the girls," and brushing
past him she jumped, falling a little short and muddying
a foot, but scrambling up unaided. The rest debated
seeking an advantageous point. At last they found a big
stone in the middle, and pulling off his shoes, Bernard
waded in the creek, helping the girls across. The small-
est one, large-eyed and timid, clung to his arm and let
him almost carry her over.

"He does it real natural," observed Davy, who was

whisking about in the daisy field like some flashing butterfly.

They gathered daisies and laughed and sang and chattered till the sun went low. Then they gathered under a big tree and spread their lunch on the ground. And after they had eaten, the conversation lay between the sallow-faced woman and one of the older men, a clever conversation filled with quaint observations and curious sidelights. The boys sat all about the woman questioning her eagerly, but behind in the shadow of the drooping branches sat the girls, silent, unobtrusive, holding each other's hands. Now and then the talker cast a furtive glance from Bernard's rather withdrawn face to the faces in the shadow, and the enigmatic smile hovered and flitted over her lips.

*   *   *

Three years later on the anniversary of that summer day the woman sat at an upstairs window in the house on the little farm that was a reality now, the little co-operative farm where ten free men and women labored and loved. She had come with the others and done her best, but the cost of it, hard labor and merciless pain, was stamped on the face that looked from the window. She was watching Bernard's figure as it came swinging through the orchard. Presently he came in and up the stairs. His feet went past her door, then turned back irresolutely, and a low knock followed. Her eyebrows bent together almost sternly as she answered, "Come in."

He entered with a smile: "Can I do anything for you, this morning?"

"No," she said quietly, "you know I like my own cranky ways. I—I'd rather do things myself." He nodded: "I know. I always get the same answer. Shall you go to the picnic? You surely will keep our foundation-day picnic?"

"Perhaps—later. And perhaps not." There was a curious tone of repression in the words.

"Well," he answered good-naturedly, "if you won't let me do anything for you, I'll have to find some one who will. Is Bella ready to go?"

"This half hour. Bella. Here is Bernard." And Bella came in. Bella, the timid girl with the brilliant complexion and gazelle soft eyes, Bella radiant in her youth and feminine daintiness, more lovely than she had been three years before.

She gave Bernard a lunch basket to carry and a shawl and a workbag and a sun umbrella, and when they went out she clung to his arm besides. She stopped near one of their own rose bushes and told him to choose a bud for her, and she put it coquettishly in her dark hair. The woman watched them till they disappeared down the lane; he had never once looked back. Then her mouth settled in a quiet sneer and she murmured: "How long is 'forever'? Three years." After a while she rose and crossed to an old mirror that hung on the opposite wall. Staring at the reflection it gave back, she whispered drearily: "You are ugly, you are eaten with pain! Do you still expect the due of youth and beauty? Did you not know it all long ago?" Then something flashed in the image, something as if the features had caught fire and burned. "I will not," she said hoarsely, her fingers clenching. "I will not surrender. Was it he I loved? It was his youth, his beauty, his life. And younger youth shall love me still, stronger life. I will not, I will not die alive." She turned away and ran down into the yard and out into the fields. She would not go on the common highway where all went, she would find a hard way through woods and over hills, and she would come there before them and sit and wait for them where the ways met. Bareheaded, ill-dressed and careless she ran along, finding a fierce pleasure in trampling and breaking the brush that impeded her. There was the road at last, and right ahead of her an old, old man hobbling along with bent back and eyes upon the ground. Just before him was a bad hole in the road; he stopped, irresolute, and looked around like a crippled insect stretching its antennæ to find a way for its mangled feet. She called cheerily, "Let me help you." He looked up with dim blue eyes helplessly seeking. She led him slowly around the dangerous place, and then they sat down together on the little covered wooden bridge beyond.

"Ah!" murmured the old man, shaking his head, "it is good to be young." And there was the ghost of admiration in his watery eyes, as he looked at her tall straight figure.

"Yes," she answered sadly, looking away down the road where she saw Bella's white dress fluttering, "it is good to be young."

The lovers passed without noticing them, absorbed in each other. Presently the old man hobbled away. "It will come to that too," she muttered looking after him. "The husks of life!"

The Old Shoemaker

HE had lived a long time there, in the house at the end of the alley, and no one had ever known that he was a great man. He was lean and palsied, and had a crooked back; his beard was grey and ragged, and his eyebrows came too far forward; there were seams and flaps in the empty, yellow old skin, and he gasped horribly when he breathed, taking hold of the lintel of the door to steady himself when he stepped out on the broken bricks of the alley. He lived with a frightful old woman who scrubbed the floors of the rag-shop, and drank beer, and growled at the children who poked fun at her. He had lived with her eighteen years, she said, stroking the furry little kitten that curled up in her neck as if she had been beautiful.

Eighteen years they had been drinking and quarreling together—and suffering. She had seen the flesh sucking away from the bones, and the skin falling in upon them, and the long, lean fingers growing more lean and trembling, as they crooked round his shoemaking tools.

It was very strange she had not grown thin; the beer had bloated her, and rolls of weak, shaking flesh lapped over the ridges of her uncouth figure. Her pale, lacklustre blue eyes wandered aimlessly about as she talked: No—he had never told her, not even in their quarrels, not even when they were drunken together, of the great Visitor who had come up the little alley, yesterday,

walking so stately over the sun-beaten bricks, taking
no note of the others, and coming in at the door without
asking. She had not expected such an one; how could
she? But the Old Shoemaker had shown no surprise
at the Mighty One. He smiled and set down the tea-
cup he was holding, and entered into communion with
the Stranger. He noticed no others, but continued to
smile; and the infinite dignity of the Unknown fell upon
him, and covered the wasted old limbs and the hard,
wizened face, so that all we who entered, bowed, and went
out, and did not speak.

But we understood, for the Mighty One gave understanding without words. We had been in the presence
of Freedom! We had stood at the foot of Tabor, and
seen this worn, old, world-soiled soul lose all its dross
and commonplace, and pass upward smiling, to the Trans-
figuration. In the hands of the Mighty One the crust
had crumbled, and dropped away in impalpable powder.
Souls should be mixed of it no more. Only that which
passed upward, the fine white playing flame, the heart
of the long, life-long watches of patience, should re-
kindle there in the perennial ascension of the great Soul
of Man.

Where the White Rose Died

IT was late at night, a raw, rough-shouldering night, that shoved men in corners as having no business in the street, and the few people in the northbound car drew themselves into themselves, radiating hedgehog quills of feeling at their neighbors. Presently there came in a curious figure, clothed in the drapery of its country's honor, the blue flannel flapping very much about its legs. I looked at its feet first, because they were so very small and girlish, and because the owner of them adjusted the flapping pants with the coquetry of a maiden switching her skirts. Then I glanced at the hands: they also were small and womanish, and constantly in motion. At last, the face, expecting a fresh young boy's, not long away from some country village. It was the sunk, seamed face of a man of forty-five, seared, and with iron-gray eyebrows, but lit by twinkling young eyes, that gleamed at everything good-humoredly. The sailor's pancake with its official lettering was pushed rakishly down and forward, and looking at hat and wearer, one instinctively turned milliner and decorated the "shape" with aigrette and bows,—they would nod so accordant with the flirting head. Presently the restless hands went up and gave the hat another tilt, went down and straightened the "divided skirt," folded themselves an instant while the little feet began tattooing the car floor, and the scintillant eyes looked general invitation all round the car. No perceptible shrinkage of quills, however, so the eyes wandered over to their image in the plate glass, and directly the hat got another coquettish dip, and the skirts another flirt and settle.

The conductor came in: some one to talk to at last! "Will you let me off at Ninth and Race?"

The dim chill of a smile shivered over the other faces in the car. Ninth and Race! Who ever heard a defender of his country's glory ask a conductor on a street car in Philadelphia for any other point than Ninth and Race!

The conductor nodded appreciatively. "Just come to the city, I suppose," he said interlocutively.

The sailor plucked off his hat, exhibiting his label with child-like vanity: "S. S. Alabama. Here for three days just. Been over in New York."

"Like it?" remarked the conductor, prolonging his stay inside the car.

The hat went on again, proudly. "Sixteen years in the service. Yes, sir. *Six*-teen years. The service is all right. The service is good enough for me. Live there. Expect to die there. Sixteen years. You won't forget to let me off at Ninth and Race."

"No. Going to see Chinatown?"

"Sure. Chinatown's all right. Seen it in Hong Kong. Want to see it in Philadelphia."

O cradle of my country's freedom! These are your defenders, — these to whom your chief delight is your stews and your brothels, your fantans and your opium dens, your sinks of filth and your cesspools of slime! Let them only be as they were "at Hong Kong"—or worse—and "the service" asks no more. He will live in it and die in it, and it's good enough for him. Oh, not your old-time patriotic legends, nor the halls of the great Rebel Birth, nor the solemn, silent Bell that once proclaimed liberty throughout the land, nor the piteous relics of your dead wise men, nor any dream of your bright, pure young days when yet you were "a fair greene country towne," swims up in the vision of "the service" when he sets his foot within your borders, filling him with devotion to Our Lady Liberty, and drawing him to New World pilgrim shrines. Not these, oh no, not these. But your leper spot, your Old World plague-house, your breeding-ground of pest-begotten human vermin! So there is Chinatown, and electric glare enough upon it, and rat-holes enough within it, "the service" is good enough for him,—he will shoot to order in your defense till he dies!

Rat-tat-tat went the little feet upon the floor, and the pancake got another rakish pull. Presently the active figure squared sharply about and faced the door. The car had stopped, and a drunken man was staggering in. The sailor caught him good-humoredly in his arms, swung him about, and seated him beside himself with a comforting "Now you're all right, sir; sit right here, my friend."

The drunkard had a sodden, stupid face and bleary eyes from which the alcohol was oozing. In his shaking hand he held a bunch of delicate half-opened roses, hot-house roses, cream and pink; the odor of them drifted faintly through the car like a whiff of summer. Something like a sigh of relaxation exhaled from the hedge-hogs, and a dozen commiserating eyes were fastened on the ill-fated flowers,—so fragile, so sweet, so inoffensive, so wantonly sacrificed. The hot, unsteady, clutching hand had already burned the stems, and the pale, help-less faces of the roses drooped heavily.

The drunkard, full of beery effervescence, cast a bubbling look over the car, and spying a young lady opposite, suddenly stood up and offered the bouquet to her. She stared resolutely through him, seeing and hearing nothing, not even the piteous child-blossoms, with their pleading, downbent heads, and with a confused muttering of "No offense, no offense, you know," the man sank back again. As he did so the uncertain fingers released one stem, and a cream-white bloom went fluttering down, like a butterfly with broken wings. There it lay, jolting back and forth on the dirty floor, and no one dared to pick it up.

Presently the drunkard sopped over comfortably on the sailor's shoulder, who, with a generally directed wink of bonhomie, settled him easily, bestowing a sympathetic pat upon the bloated cheek. The conductor disturbed the situation by asking for his fare. The drunkard stupidly rubbed his eyes and offered his flowers in place of the nickel. Again they were refused; and after a fluctuant search in his pockets between intervals of nodding, the dirty, over-fingered bit of metal was produced, accepted—and still the dying blossoms shivered in the torturer's hands.

He was drowsing off again, when, by some sudden turn of the obstructed machinery in his skull, his lids opened and he struggled up; the image of myself must have swum suddenly across the momentarily acting eye-nerve, and with gurgling deference, at the immanent risk of losing his equilibrium once more, he proffered the bouquet to me, grabbing the heads and presenting them stem-end towards. A smothered snuffle went round the car.

I wanted them, Oh, how I wanted them! My heart beat suffocatingly with the sense of baffled pity and rage and cowardice. Who was he, that drunken sot, with his smirching, wabbling hand, that I should fear to take the roses from him? Why must I grind my teeth and sit there helpless, while those beautiful things were crushed and blasted and torn in living fragments? I could take them home, I could give them drink, they would lift up their heads, they would open wide, for days they would make the room sweet, and the pale, soft glory of their inimitable petals would shine like a luminous promise across the winter. Nobody wanted them, nobody cared; this sodden beast in the flare-up of his consciousness wished to be quit of them. *Why* might I not take them? Something sharp bit and burned my eyelids as I glanced at the one on the floor. The conductor had stepped on it and crushed it open; and there lay the marvelous creamy leaves, curled at their edges like kiss-seeking lips, each with its glory greater than Solomon's, all fouled and ruined in the human reek.

And I dared not save the others! Miserable coward!

I forced my hands tighter in my pockets and turned my head away towards the outside night and the backward slipping street. Between me and it, a dim reflection wavered, the image of the thing that stood there before me; and somewhere, like a far-off, dulled bell, I heard the words, "And God created man in his own image, in the image of God created He him." The sailor, no doubt with the kindly intention of relieving me from annoyance, and not averse to play with anything, made pretence of seizing the roses. Then the drunkard, in an abandon of generosity, began tearing off the blossoms by the heads, scrutinizing, and casting each away as unfit for the exalted service of his "friend," till the latter reaching out managed to get hold of a white one with a stem. He trimmed its sheltering green carefully, brought out a long black pin, stuck it through the stalk, and fastened the pale shining head against his dark blue blouse. All hedgehoggery smiled. We had thrust the roses through with our forbidding quills,—what matter

that a barbarian nail crucified this last one? The drunkard slept again, limply holding his scattering bunch of
headless stems and torn foliage. Pink and cream the
petals strewed the floor. Where was the loving hand
that had nursed them to bloom in this hard, unwonted
weather; loved and nursed and—*sold* them?

"Ninth and Race," sang out the conductor. The sailor
sprang up with a merry grin, bowed gaily to everyone,
twinkled his fingers in the air with a blithe "Ta ta; I'm
off for Chinatown," as he slid through the door, and was
away in a trice, tripping down to the pestiferous sink
that was awaiting him somewhere. And on his breast he
wore the pallid flower that had offered its stainless beauty
to me, that I had loved,—and had not loved enough to
save. The rest were dead; but that one—somewhere
down there in a den where even the gas-choked lights
were leering like prostitutes' eyes, down there in that
trough of swill and swine, that pure, still thing had yet
to die.

AK Press is small, in terms of staff and resources, but we also manage to be one of the world's most productive anarchist publishing houses. We publish close to twenty books every year, and distribute thousands of other titles published by like-minded independent presses and projects from around the globe. We're entirely worker-run and democratically managed. We operate without a corporate structure—no boss, no managers, no bullshit.

The Friends of AK program is a way you can directly contribute to the continued existence of AK Press, and ensure that we're able to keep publishing books like this one! Friends pay $25 a month directly into our publishing account ($30 for Canada, $35 for international), and receive a copy of every book AK Press publishes for the duration of their membership! Friends also receive a discount on anything they order from our website or buy at a table: 50% on AK titles, and 20% on everything else. We have a Friends of AK ebook program as well: $15 a month gets you an electronic copy of every book we publish for the duration of your membership. You can even sponsor a very discounted membership for someone in prison.

Email friendsofak@akpress.org for more info, or visit the Friends of AK Press website: https://www.akpress.org/friends.html

There are always great book projects in the works—so sign up now to become a Friend of AK Press, and let the presses roll!